MW00633451

The Personal Strategy Institute
Presents for Review

Title: Only 1 Shot: Aligning the Inner Soul with Action
Author: Randall Scott Rogers
Category: Self-Help / Personal Growth
Edition: First
ISBN: 978-0984125104
LCCN: 2009932521
Pages: 730 pages Perfect Bound
Cover: www.personalstrategy.org/pressroom.php
Price: $34.95
Season: Summer 2010
Publication date: June 2010
Contact: Randall Rogers, Publisher
        P.O. Box 169
        Itasca, IL 60143
        Tel: (630) 290-9673
        Fax: (630) 296-8550
        rrogers@personalstrategy.org

<< Please send 2 copies of review to above address >>

We Take Our Clues from Nature

SOURCE: GRANITE ROCK, GLACIER NATIONAL PARK

ONLY
1
SHOT

ALIGNING THE INNER SOUL WITH ACTION

HOW TO REENGINEER YOUR EXISTENCE, DESIGN A LIFELONG PERSONAL STRATEGY, AND REDISCOVER THE JOY OF LIVING

RANDALL SCOTT ROGERS

FOUNDER, PERSONAL STRATEGY INSTITUTE

Only 1 Shot
Aligning the Inner Soul with Action

Images by Randall Scott Rogers

ISBN 10: 0-9841251-0-8
ISBN 13: 978-0-9841251-0-4

Library of Congress Control Number: 2009932521

Printed in the United States of America

Published by: Personal Strategy Institute
                P.O. Box 169
                Itasca, IL 60143-0169
                (630) 290-9673
                orders@personalstrategy.org
                www.personalstrategy.org

Interior Photos/Website: Dan Loftus (LoftusPhoto.com)
Editing/Proofreading: FirstEditing.com
Cover Design: Brion Sausser (BookCreatives.com)
Book Design/Typesetting: Sue Balcer (JustYourType.biz)
Printing: Thomson-Shore, Inc.

First Edition 2010

Please visit:
www.Only1Shot.com

Dedication

To Renee, my Love; my Life

To Ethan, my Inspiration

To All, my Hope

The vast majority of humans wander along the pathway of years without any destination or goal or even a road map
— Og Mandino

Contents

PART V

Setting a Course for Personal Excellence

PART VI

Let Soul Sing

Acknowledgments

I would first like to thank those who assisted with perfecting, assembling, and printing this book: FirstEditing.com for providing timely, exceptional editing, Brion Sausser (Book Creatives.com) for a wonderful cover design, Sue Balcer (JustYourType.biz) for exceptional interior book design and typesetting, Thomson-Shore for professional printing and packaging, and Dan Loftus (LoftusPhoto.com) for expert photography and website design. Without each of you, this book would not be the polished gem that it is.

I would like to offer special thanks to Drs Robert S. Kaplan and David P. Norton for writing their books, The Balanced Scorecard and Strategy Maps, from which I adapted certain content to develop the Personal Strategy Map and Personal Strategic Theme frameworks contained herein.

I would also like to offer special thanks to Dr. C. Otto Scharmer for writing his books, Presence and Theory U. Both books had a profound and marked effect on me and, consequently, this book.

Lastly, I would like to thank all those with whom I have worked and met over the years who encouraged me, pushed me, and helped me realize that we do have Only One Shot at life and, therefore, should pursue passion, should live passionately, should live fragrantly. I must also thank my wife Renee for enduring four years of early morning, late night, and weekend sacrifice while I wrote, edited, and packaged this book.

Thank you all.

Introduction

"We do not ask for life, but having arrived,
our innate desire is to live while alive"
— Randall Scott Rogers

The year is 1990. I am a recent college graduate but already into my second career, selling insurance. I am sitting in my local library, depressed, confused, feeling anything but 'alive'. I am depressed, confused over the direction of my life, of what I should do, how to operate on the surface of life. I sit, with self-help book in hand. I turn the pages; some words resonate, most do not. I leave the library hours later still depressed, still confused, still wondering what to do with my life. The years roll by; now it is August, 2005. I am driving to work, different career, same condition. Then, out of nowhere, I am struck with almighty wisdom; of what to finally do with my life. Fifteen years have passed, but I do not dwell on such fact, as wisdom-awareness now consumes me. I see clearly my intended purpose on earth. I see clearly who to be and how to operate on the surface of life. I am giddy with excitement, inspiration, and hope. What you hold in your hands is the result of that flash of genius I had years ago.

I share this story with you to make a few points. Few people are born with innate wisdom, a special 'knowing' of what to do with their life. Fewer still are born with immense innate talent (e.g. in music, dance, art, athletics, mathematics, etc.) that might suggest, indicate, influence what to do. As such, each of us must find our way; find our purpose, our passion in life. Trouble is at no point in our schooling do we learn how to find purpose; discover passion. Consequently, and at varying points, many turn to self-help books to learn such things, to fill such void. Sadly, most self-help books offer only 'what' advice, lacking vital 'how to' instruction resulting in reading that makes you feel good, inspires for a time (due to right words, colorful stories), but at book's end, you are no better off than had you not read it at all. This book ends such practice. In this book, you will find more how-to instruction, less story telling. While stories are nice, and I do include much of my own story throughout, this book correctly assumes that you desire the 'what' AND 'how' of transforming self and life and, therefore, scores low on the SOS (same old stuff) index. My last point relates to time. Before I woke up, found my way, discovered my purpose, fifteen years got behind me; time lost. I do not want <u>you</u> to lose any more time, especially considering that you have Only One Shot to live. What this last point suggests, advises, requires us do is to live as soul would live.

To Live as Soul Would Live

To live as soul would live – this is the goal! Sadly, few people operate this way. That is, few people reflect authentic being, who they really are and were meant to be on the surface of life. Reflecting instead, imposter self, imposter living. So many of us act as if we have nine lives to 'get it right', but, alas, we have Only One Shot. For example, we continue working in a profession/role long past the point of caring. We perpetuate relations with others, where although love exists, life interests diverged long ago. And we extend our stay in locations that discourage soul rather than inspire it. Why do we do such things? Why do we continue, perpetuate, extend *'more of the same'* when we long to *'go the other way'*? Why do we settle for lesser living; a life diminished? It is because most people do not live as soul would live, do not operate from soul, that they are in the condition they are in and as a result are suffering; the suffering the result of being disconnected, misaligned with who they are and want to be. We know this to be true as the signs are everywhere.

According to the World Health Organization, Centers for Disease Control, and other leading sources, annually, within the United States:

- 33,000+ people commit **suicide**
- 400,000+ people **attempt suicide**
- 17 million suffer **depression**
- 27 million suffer **alcohol and drug addiction**
- 60 million suffer some form of **mental illness**
- $11 billion is spent on **self-improvement** books, CDs, seminars, coaching and stress-management programs

What these statistics ('signs') collectively indicate is that we are not happy, not aligned, not living free. For if we were, we would not see such high numbers of the despondent, depressed, and numb. Moreover, what does it say about humanity when, for many, the better option to live or to die is the latter? What does it say about humanity when many suffer mental illness; suffer depression? What does it say about humanity when millions ingest alcohol, take drugs to cope with the stresses of reality? Lastly, what does it say about humanity when increasing numbers turn to self-help books/seminars to quell, end the suffering?

The world operates under false pretense that to follow the standard life design will bring happiness, riches, and success. Nothing could be further from the truth. History has proved that personal happiness, greater riches, and eminent success only come when pursuing <u>own</u> design, that is, when pursuing desires of soul. It is because we blindly follow the standard life design, because we do not pursue desires of soul, that we get stuck in a hole. For some, the moment brief; for others, the moment lasting years, decades; and still for others, the moment never ends; never resolves; *lasts a lifetime*. In what ways do we get stuck? We get stuck in the wrong profession/role. We get stuck with the wrong life partner. And we get stuck living in drab surroundings, among other things. What is the result? You already know

– a life diminished. Consequently, this book is about reclaiming one's life, about living as soul would live, but it is also about many other things, such as:

- Increasing personal happiness
- Finding one's truth
- Unleashing spirit within
- Meeting imperative
- Seizing opportunity
- Establishing alignment
- Maximizing the life experience
- Living free

Perhaps the best way to know what a book is about is to examine the questions it addresses.

Key Questions

There are ten questions which underlie this book and to which this book addresses. They are:

- How does one reengineer oneself; one's life?
- What are the factors that drive personal happiness?
- How does one develop a personal strategy for living?
- How does one manage personal strategy to reflect changes occurring within and without?
- How does one become self-aligned; stay aligned?
- How does one find soul, bring it forward, into the present, onto the surface of life, for self to live as soul would live?
- How should one see, will, think, act, and feel to improve the quality of one's life?
- How does one maximize the personal, professional, and financial potential that life offers?
- How does one rediscover the joy of living?
- How does one find the path which leads home?

Why do we ask *these* questions? It is because the answers illuminate next steps. That is, they reveal <u>how</u> to restore alignment, increase personal happiness, and maximize the quality of one's life. More than this, asking such questions helps us find soul, to converse with soul, to know soul, to operate from soul.

Soul to Soul

Why do we cheer when...

- The orphan child rises above poverty, lack of resources, and lack of opportunity to achieve the American dream?
- The addicted shake addiction; remake themselves in inspiring ways?
- The retired man/woman decides to pursue a passion late in life?

Why do we cry when...

- Witnessing the triumph of the human spirit?
- Seeing the downtrodden of life provided food, shelter, and healthcare?
- Hearing of the terminal boy who desires to help feed, clothe the homeless as his final act on earth?

Why do we chill when...

- Someone speaks from the heart; reveals true empathy?
- An event connects us with something larger than ourselves?
- A song, movie, or book transports us to a deeper, higher place?

The reason we cheer, cry, chill is because we are witness to soul, to an *expression of soul,* and it is beautiful. Each of us is connected at soul level, soul-to-soul. As such, we innately share common goal, share One voice, share a common bond. Consequently, we cheer the rise of soul as in some alien way, we rise. Similarly, we cry when soul suffers, soul triumphs as in some alien way, we too suffer; triumph. And we chill when in the presence of soul as in some alien way, we too feel empathy, feel connected, sense higher placement.

All living things possess soul. Most people recognize soul as 'the voice within', the place from which authentic being resides. Although most people <u>recognize</u> soul, few people <u>know</u> soul. Therein lies the problem.

It requires no effort for lion, tiger, or bear to act naturally, to live authentically. The same is true for fish, tree, and flower. In fact, it can be said that all of nature authentically adheres to innate design. The same cannot be said of the human species. *For each person who attends, surrenders to his own nature, countless others do not.* This is the problem, hence the need to write this book. Most people today are not living authentically, not acting in one's own nature, not acting in the service of soul. Consequently, this book's aim is to find one's soul and pull it forward, into the present, onto the surface of life. We do this, as to find one's soul, <u>to operate from soul</u>, is to restore happiness, joy to one's life, thus revealing this book's purpose.

On Purpose

This book sets out to do three things. It is intended to help you:

- Reengineer your existence
- Design a lifelong personal strategy
- Rediscover the joy of living

To reengineer something means to create anew. Thus, to reengineer your existence means to create your life anew, to create a new reality for self and life. Our primary tool to achieve this goal is a personal strategy. Although it is possible to reengineer one's existence without a personal strategy, your success improves dramatically with one. As such, in this book we discuss how to design, implement, and manage a personal strategy for living. Utilizing a personal strategy is how we reengineer our existence, but we use personal strategy to achieve an even nobler, more immediate, more private, goal: *to rediscover the joy of living*. Forty years of living have taught me an important fact. When we are not happy, life lacks joy. And a joyless life is no life at all. As such, there is no more important human endeavor than to pursue and sustain one's happiness. Consequently, if life lacks joy, as it does for so many people today, there is need to intervene; quickly, decidedly.

Intervention

To seek, consider this book is to indicate some amount of dissatisfaction with life, with living. As such, I know why you have come (*a quest for freedom, a desire to live, a search for the truth*), as I have walked in your shoes, felt your pain, operated on your plane. Although perhaps unaware, your reading this book represents an intervention of your-self on behalf of your soul.

Today, few people deliberately 'stop their life' long enough to improve their life; that is, few people intervene. We are so busy 'living life' that we never pause to 'work on' our life. Part of the reason for this is that we were never educated in such matters. At no point, did we learn the need for, or how to, stop one's life to assess and improve one's life. As such, few do. What is more tragic is that even with such education, contemporary living offers few 'breaks', little reprieve, *to* stop one's life as the pressures, stresses, workload of life continue to escalate; each of us reduced to rat-in-cage. This is not your story, however, as you did pause, did intervene on behalf of soul, and you are not alone. Increasingly, people around the globe, regardless of age, gender, ethnicity, wealth, education level, or citizenship, are intervening on behalf of soul. Why is this happening? Why do we intervene? We intervene because we must. Our innate desire is to live while alive; consequently, when we do not feel that we are living, when we do not feel alive, we intervene. What this tells us is that self-intervention knows no bounds; as the desire to live exists within One, as the suffering afflicts One, so it is with All.

As with One, So with All

To write a book requires considering one's audience. When thinking about the audience for this book, the answer came quickly: all of humanity. As such, this book is as much for the successful as it is for the suffering. It is as much for the inspired as it is for the tired. It is as much for the young as it is for the old. In short, just as self-intervention knows no bounds, is open to all, so, too, does this book know no bounds, is open to all. Regardless of your station in life, this book can help you. Whether looking to reengineer your existence, design a rigorous personal strategy, and/or rediscover the joy of living, this book represents alpha and omega; *it is the only book you need.*

Now, in thinking about audience, I made some assumptions about you, the reader:

- You are not getting what you want <u>in</u> life or <u>from</u> life at this point in your life
- You are looking for a way forward, a way through, to transform self and life
- You desire meaningful, purposeful, fragrant living
- Your goal is to maximize the personal, professional, and financial potential that life offers and you are willing to pay-the-price for success
- You seek more the 'how' (of transforming self and life) than the 'what'

While such assumptions guided, shaped this book from the onset, what was not known initially was the complete story.

In Search of the Truth

I began this book writing exclusively about developing a personal strategy for living. The thought being that with a personal strategy, one could live a happier, more fragrant life experience. Then, over time, like an archeologist uncovering old ruins, the full shape of this book revealed itself. I realized that personal strategy is just a means to a more important end: personal alignment. Thus, I explored the notion of personal alignment. As I dug deeper, I learned that one must first align self with soul to align self with other aspects of one's life (e.g. work, family, nature). Consequently, I explored soul, and in so doing, I came to discover that the *truth* of Only One Shot is not so much about developing a personal strategy or establishing personal alignment as it is about finding one's soul and bringing it forward onto the surface of life through willful action. It is my hope that in finding the truth of this book, in uncovering the essence that is Only One Shot, you are so enabled to find the truth of who you are, uncover your essence; *soul*.

One Act, Six Parts

The story of Only One Shot represents one act in six parts:

Part I – The Case for Action

In Part I, we discuss the case for action. That is, we discuss our reasons, need to, reengineer self, design a personal strategy, and rediscover the joy of living. We approach by asking not only 'Where is the world?' knowing world affects self, but also 'Where are you?' We do this, as to change one's condition first requires assessing, acknowledging condition. Then, so informed, we discuss the opportunity and imperative before you. That is, we discuss the opportunity each of us is afforded and the imperative each of us must meet. Lastly, we discuss how meeting (life's) imperative enables seizing opportunity.

Part II – Aligning the Inner Soul with Action

In Part II, we discuss aligning the inner soul with action. That is, we discuss the process and tools to bring soul to the surface of life via a personal strategy that reflects soul. We focus first on learning how to define inner soul goals (Personal Strategy Map). Then, we learn how to design a personal strategy (Personal Strategic Themes) to achieve each goal. Next, we build your personal strategy based on such learnings. Lastly, we discuss how to keep score. That is, we discuss how to monitor personal strategy to improve personal strategy.

Part III – On Personal Alignment

In Part III, we learn that personal strategy represents but means to achieve a more desired end: personal alignment. We discuss what personal alignment is, the dimensions of personal align-ment, and the process to achieve personal alignment. We discuss the tools of personal alignment and what it means to align self with soul, work, family, and nature. Lastly, we discuss how to stay aligned once achieved.

Part IV – Adaptation and Responding to Change

In Part IV, we discuss how to adapt and respond to changes oc-curring within and without, that is, within oneself and within one's environment. We discuss the stumbling blocks of personal strategy and how to eliminate, or minimally reduce, stumbling blocks from impeding personal strategy. We also discuss the process and tools to manage personal strategy, knowing that personal strategy is not static; as we change, as our environment changes, so, too, must our personal strategy change.

Part V – Setting a Course for Personal Excellence

In Part V, we set a course for personal excellence. We do this in part by discussing new ways to see, think, act, and feel about self and life. Then, we discuss a matter of will and how will is *the* determining factor to transform one's life. We learn what will is, its relation to soul, mind, and body, the determinants of will strength, and most importantly, how to grow will. Lastly, we bring together all topics, tools, and discussions summarizing our journey from a 'systems' point of view.

Part VI – Let Soul Sing

Finally, in Part VI, we discuss the spiritual side of things. We discuss first the process of finding soul, of bringing soul forward, into the present. We discuss the differences between operating from self versus operating from soul and how the source from which we operate affects all that follows. Then, we discuss bringing soul to the surface of life. We discuss the notion of a life design, comparing and contrasting the standard life design, which results in a life diminished, with intentional design, which results in a life lived. Finally, we discuss living as soul would live. That is, we discuss the path which leads home. We conclude with some final words – on accomplishment, to inspire, and on this book.

At bottom, the story of Only One Shot is about finding soul and pulling it forward, into the present, onto the surface of life, for self to live as soul would live. It is a true story, the whole story, *the only story that matters*.

Back to the Start

In the span of one's life, this book represents but one event among many. It represents a moment in time, a mere blip of one's existence. When viewed this way, this book hardly seems significant. Having said this, experience shows that not all life events are created equal. That is, some leave greater marks on our life than others like the death of a loved one, the birth of a child, earning a degree, and yes, even reading a book. Few events in life are capable of penetrating our internal chamber, of touching soul, awakening soul, arousing soul. This book represents such an event. I hope that with the last page turned, you find that this book touched, awakened, aroused that which lies within: *almighty soul*. That is, I hope that at book's end, no longer do you respond as self, you respond as soul. No longer do you identify with self, you identify with soul. No longer do you operate from self, **<u>you operate from soul</u>**.

<u>(your name here)</u> **your name has been called.** I invite you now to join me in quiet conversation, on a *heart-felt* journey back to the start to determine who you are and were meant to be before living changed you.

PART I
The Case for Action

Where is the World?

"All truths are easy to understand once they are discovered; the point is to discover them."

- Galileo

A PROFOUND SADNESS EXISTS TODAY; it lies deep, below the surface of things, within our planetary heart. "What kind of sadness?" you ask. It is the kind that comes when a species has lost its way; forgotten how to operate, what to stand for, on the surface of life. This is the state of the human species. We have lost our way, forgotten how to operate, what to stand for on the surface of life, and we are suffering. The standard life design has failed us, or, more precisely, mankind has failed us. Mankind has broken the covenant; all that is sacred. No longer is it a priority that all are healthy, all are fed, and all are free. No longer is it a priority that all are loved, all are educated, and all prosper. Instead, we live in a world of haves and have not's, a world more interested in attending to economic goals, advancing the economic story, than attending to humanitarian goals, advancing the human story. This is tragic, if not reckless. No longer is humanity a model of that which inspires, but that which debilitates. We have indeed lost our way, and we are suffering. In this first chapter, we ask, "Where is the world?" as this will provide context to, help resolve, a more personal, more private inquiry: "Where are you?"

So, where is the world? What is the state of humanity today? How do we answer such questions; so broad, so much to comment on? For purposes herein, we focus on that which is problematic, that which is debilitating, that which is causing much suffering in the world today. When I step back to reflect, to view our planet from above, there seems to be much sadness in the world today. The world's aura seems ominous as if our planetary heart feels trepidation, danger, loss. Our planetary heart feels these things because, I believe, most of humanity feels these things. In recent years, I have become sensitized to the undercurrent of emotion (and discontent) that is sweeping the globe, as I, too, feel that the world is disconnected, deceptive, replete with mistruths. I, too, feel the suffering that many others feel. I, too, feel that the world has advanced in a way that few benefit from; few enjoy. In short, I, too, feel that humanity's story needs rewriting. Thus, in this chapter, we unfold from a premise that *the world is disconnected, which has led to much suffering.* We discuss the disconnectedness that exists today, from self, to community, to nation, to planet. After which, we discuss "The Suffering" and how it has led to "The Great Escape". We conclude by answering the question: "Are We Living?" along with presenting the central challenge of our time. It is with this storyline that, we begin.

At many points throughout this book, we ask important questions, define words, central to our discussion. Our first word is "disconnected"; our first question: "What does it mean to be disconnected?"

To disconnect means to:

- Sever
- Separate
- Fragment

As the above indicates, disconnectedness is something more to avoid than embrace. In fact, for most things to which the word applies, to be "disconnected" is a bad thing. For example, to disconnect a hose while the water is running is bad, as water sprays everywhere. To disconnect a household appliance from its electrical source is bad, as the appliance stops working. And when the two parties of Congress disconnect on vision and priorities, it's bad, as the government is less efficient at legislating law. Although these examples illustrate the bad that comes with disconnectedness, they pale in comparison to the bad that comes when self and environment (work, family, community, nation, planet) are disconnected. What results when self and environment are disconnected? We answer this question next, beginning with understanding the disconnectedness that exists within each of us. We then examine the disconnectedness that exists within larger systems of which we are but a part (see Figure 1.1).

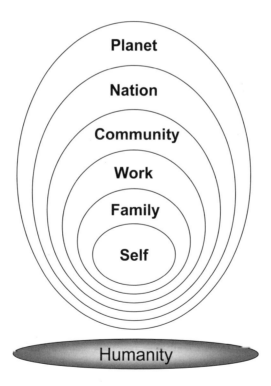

Fig. 1.1

Self

For many people, life resembles more "something to get through" than "a journey to enjoy". This is sad, but true. What is the cause of this sad state? It is the result of *self being disconnected from soul*. In the course of my own life journey, I have learned that most people exist or operate in one of two states. In one state, we operate from self, pursuing desires of self, living a life of "default". In the other state, we operate from soul, pursuing desires of soul, living as soul would live. What is the difference between these two states? When we operate from soul we are doing what we want **in** life and getting what we want **from** life. We pursue goals inspired from soul and we achieve them. We are happy, alive, and free. When we operate from self, life's "default", we are not doing what we want in life and, therefore, not getting what we want from life. We set goals but rarely achieve them. And for these reasons, we are not happy, do not feel alive, do not live free. Sadly, most people live not as soul would live, but live a life of default. In other words, they operate not as one entity, soul, but as disconnected parts, self and soul.

    Unfortunately, to exist as parts is highly debilitating as it results in thinking, acting, and feeling in ways that diminish the life experience rather than lift it up. Not long ago, this is how I operated. Because I was disconnected, not operating as one entity but as two, I felt great inner turmoil that diminished not only my experiences in life but also my view of life. One day, I am pursuing desires of soul, feeling good about my life, the direction I am heading, the next I am abandoning my goals succumbing to desires of self; living a life of default. Like many people, I was working at cross-purposes with my-self; never advancing, never achieving. Instead of operating from higher ground, I operated from self, living an alternate, lesser reality. Perhaps, this is how you operate; experience life today. If so, not to worry, as by book's end, no longer will you operate as parts, but as One. No longer will imposter self dominate emerging self; *soul*. No longer will you question the truth of your existence or ask: "What is this life for?" Having said this, it is important you acknowledge that *unless you deliberately pursue desires of soul, you will, by default, pursue desires of self,* and pursuing desires of self has but one outcome: a life diminished.

There are <u>three primary ways</u> that self can be disconnected from soul:

- What one is doing (one's 'work')
- Who one is living with (one's 'spouse or partner')
- Where one lives (one's 'surroundings')

Many people today work in a profession/role in which they have little interest, and one that does not represent passion. To have a passion and not pursue it, not live it, represents disconnectedness between self and soul. Others live with a spouse/partner where, although love exists, life interests diverged long ago, leaving both questioning the relevance of the relationship. To be with someone for the sake of being also represents disconnectedness between self and soul. Finally, others live in surroundings that fail to inspire, fail to stir the soul, living in the city, for example, when one desires to walk into the wild. To be out of your element, to live in an environment that does not inspire soul also represents disconnectedness between self and soul. For such people, each passing day perpetuates heartache, prolongs the suffering, diminishes all that is good in life. Because personal disconnectedness afflicts so many people today, in Chapter 14, we discuss what it means to operate from soul rather than from self, as only when parts become whole, *only when one operates from soul,* is life meaningful, joyful, full of color.

Self-disconnectedness, however, is not the only form of disconnectedness that exists in the world today. Other, equally debilitating, forms afflict our work, our family, our community, our nation, and our planet. We continue by discussing the disconnectedness that exists at work.

Work

It is bad enough that most people live disconnected lives, not doing what they love and loving what they do, but when you combine this with the fact that most companies are also disconnected, operating as parts rather than as whole, it diminishes the life experience that much more. The rampant disconnectedness that exists in companies today did not exist long ago, but that is certainly the case today. Most companies today are disconnected, fragmented, misaligned – from strategy, to operations, to people. The problem with operating this way is that it results in people working at cross-purposes with one another, which destroys company unity, company value, and makes for very unpleasant work experiences. Although companies suffer from such debilitations, its people suffer more. To spend forty percent of one's day and sixty percent of one's life working in environments where infighting, stress, and rampant misalignment rule the day, is devastating. It is devastating because such things diminish our view of work and, therefore, our desire to work. In such environments, our work lacks meaning, purpose, and joy, as we spend more time arguing than collaborating, more time performing non-value-added work than value-added work, more time perpetuating old rather than advancing new. Making matters worse is that most companies seem more interested in *playing politics* than *playing to win,* further diminishing the work experience. Such environments do not inspire us, lift us up; they wear us out, tear us down. Not surprisingly, few people enjoy working in such companies leaving most asking, at some point in their career: "What have I done with my life?" Because people can deal with rampant disconnectedness, high workplace stress, and petty politicking for only so long, people quickly lose interest in working for such companies and they quit. Unfortunately, disconnectedness afflicts more than self and work; it afflicts family as well.

Family

What has happened to family today? More than ever, it seems that family is becoming increasingly disconnected, divided and it is causing much suffering. We spend less time with one another. We communicate less. We seek isolation. As with self and work, family operates not as a whole, but as disconnected parts. Part of the reason for this is that we live in a world where it costs too much to live; from food and transportation to education and housing to healthcare. Each of us is forced to work (parents and children alike) just to make ends meet preventing us from being together, sharing together, bonding together. Another reason is that we simply have forgotten the value family offers. We have forgotten the support, love, and instruction family provides. In short, we have forgotten the ties that bind. And as our knowing of one another lessens, so, too, does our ability to help one another lessen. When combined with the disconnectedness of self and work, the added disconnectedness of family becomes, for many, more than one can bear, resulting in a host of serious debilitations, ranging from depression to drug/alcohol dependency to suicide. For many, disconnectedness of self, work, and family represents the perfect storm, diminishing all that is good in life; reducing the life experience to something to get through rather than a journey to enjoy. But the debilitations, disconnectedness that exists with family does not end there; it extends to community as well.

Community

We live in communities, yet we are strangers. We wave from a distance, yet avoid conversation. We lock our doors, rather than open them. This is the state of community today. The days of small town charm have evaporated. "Help thy neighbor" has become an afterthought as the days of giving ourselves to each other have passed. Not long ago, we acted as community. We interacted, we conversed, we opened our doors, and we gave ourselves to each other. Contemporary living seems to have destroyed community rather than built it up. Increasingly, it seems that only tragedy can bring us together. We come together in the wake of natural disaster. We come together when the innocent are shot. And we come together when terrorism strikes. Are we not capable of coming together in idle times? Our sense of community is eroding and we are suffering. Gone are the days when community meant something: common goals, a shared voice, a feeling of 'One'. As with family, we have forgotten the value, purpose, and support that community provides. Like self, work, and family, our communities exist not as a whole but as disconnected parts. This is troubling, to be sure, but what is more troubling is that as communities erode, so, too, does nation.

Nation

I am an American citizen, born and raised in the USA. I am proud and grateful of this fact as my nation stands for opportunity, freedom, and hope. The United States was founded on such principles, but today, such ideals are withering away. The gap between the haves and have not's continues to widen with fewer and fewer people experiencing opportunity, maintaining freedom, or possessing hope. Our nation has lost its way, has forgotten what to stand for, has forgotten the words of our founding fathers that each person realizes life, liberty, and happiness. Consider that, today, instead of making secondary education accessible and affordable to all, we escalate tuition, diminishing our potential as a nation and a people for all to prosper and become productive members of society. Today, instead of providing affordable shelter, food, and healthcare to all, we drive up prices to maximize profit; to please the cancerous ill that is Wall Street. Today, instead of pursuing shared vision, common goals that represent all, benefit all, not just the privileged few, we march blindly, recklessly into a future few people want. As a nation, we are disconnected from where we are and should aspire to be. Should not all of a nation's people be richly educated, well fed, provided healthcare, and given shelter? Must we advance the economic story to the exclusion of humanity's story? Is not humanity's growth more important than company growth? I need not answer these questions, as soul knows the truth. Unfortunately, as systems get bigger (self → family → work → community → nation) so, too, do the debilitations, consequences when disconnectedness exists. When one considers the debilitating effects of disconnectedness on a nation-level, the effects only worsen on a global level.

Planet

As with the systems just discussed, the world operates as parts, not as a whole. This is evidenced by widespread disease, famine, and poverty across the globe when ample resources exist to eradicate disease, eliminate famine, and end poverty. Further, serious disconnects exist between expectations of mother earth and humanity. For example, we continue to pollute land, water, and air for the sake of commerce. We continue to dismiss our relationship and linkage with nature as if it does not matter. And we continue to pay little attention to nature's signs that all is not right. These examples, and others like it, represent disconnects on the grandest scale, and when combined with disconnects ranging from self to nation, it makes for a highly disconnected planet (see Figure 1.2).

The covenant has indeed been broken, and we are suffering. The rampant disconnectedness that exists today has created a world of deception and mistruths leaving many asking: "What is the truth?" More than this, it has diminished the life experience for many people, perhaps even you. Many people are confused about where the world is today. Many people are wondering if their current existence is as good as it gets. Many people are wondering how we became so fragmented. The good news is that, with proper instruction, we can quell confusion, we can improve condition, we can eliminate fragmentation. As such, this book is a book of truths; a book providing you space,

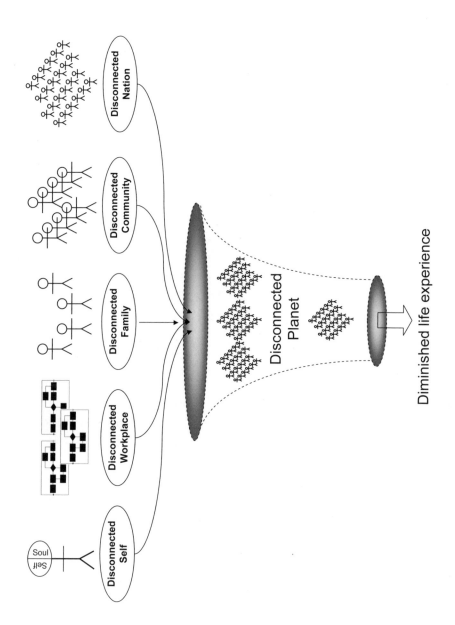

Fig. 1.2

opportunity, and occasion to improve condition; to answer your most pressing personal inquiries; to learn how to remove disconnectedness that exists within and how to respond to disconnectedness that exists without. And in learning this, you will position your self to increase not only personal happiness, but also to maximize the personal, professional, and financial potential that life offers.

Disconnectedness is a disease that knows no boundaries. Having said this, it is a disease unique to our kind: *the human species*. Disconnectedness severs us. It separates us. It fragments us. Despite the disconnectedness, despite the debilitations, however, hope remains, as we still have time to restore that which is broken. Hope remains because we can rewrite the world story; realize new beginnings. Hope remains because each of us is connected by heart; *by soul*. Being connected, as we are, at soul level, we have the collective power of seven billion souls to change condition; to rewrite the human story. Because our connection is deep, represents core, essence, we **innately** share a single voice, speak a single language, seek a shared vision. Consequently, we know, soul-to-soul, the injustice that exists when humanity degrades to the point of haves and have not's. We know the injustice that exists when education, housing, food, and healthcare is not provided to all. We know that regardless of race, gender, citizenship, education level, or economic level, each of us is equal. We know all this as *when you peel away the layers of self, what remains is soul,* and soul knows not race, gender, citizenship, education, nor economics. Soul precedes such things; it is above such things. We know these things to be true; yet, we continue, 'more of the same'; turn a blind eye. We can continue to turn a blind eye, we can continue to dismiss reality, but a universal truth remains: the longer humanity operates as it does today, the more pervasive the disconnectedness from self to planet becomes, the greater will be...*the suffering*.

The Suffering

Humanity is suffering. We have not always existed this way, but this is where we find ourselves today. The suffering is with us; it is all around us. It is something you can see, hear, feel, and be affected by. We learned in the prior section that there is much disconnectedness in the world today. To be disconnected is unnatural. All things yearn to be whole. A tree yearns to be whole. A flower yearns to be whole. And we yearn to be whole as well. Consequently, when disconnectedness exists, we suffer. The question is, "How do we suffer?" It is important to know, at the onset of this book, that self-disconnectedness, self-suffering contribute separately, but significantly, to disconnectedness and suffering that exists in all other systems of which we are but a part. Therefore, to answer the question "How do we suffer?" we apply the systems framework shown in Figure 1.1, highlighting how self-disconnectedness, self-suffering causes disconnects, suffering in all other systems. Now, because all suffering begins with self, we continue by first discussing the suffering that results when self is disconnected from soul.

Each of us has an innate desire to exist as One, to operate as One, to be whole: self with soul. Thus, when self and soul do not exist as One, self suffers. Just to refresh, disconnectedness between self and soul exists along three dimensions: work, spouse/partner, and surroundings. To highlight how deep, pervasive, debilitating this type of suffering is, I will share with you my suffering. That is, I will make visible, share with you, the effects that self-disconnectedness has had on my life.

For many years prior to writing this book, I felt lost, confused about what to do in life and what I wanted from life. Although successful in my work, I felt unaccomplished. I felt that my life had not amounted to anything significant. I felt disconnected, and I was suffering. Because I was not working in a profession/role representing passion, it affected my-self, my work, my family, my relationship with nature, and my soul (see Figure 1.3).

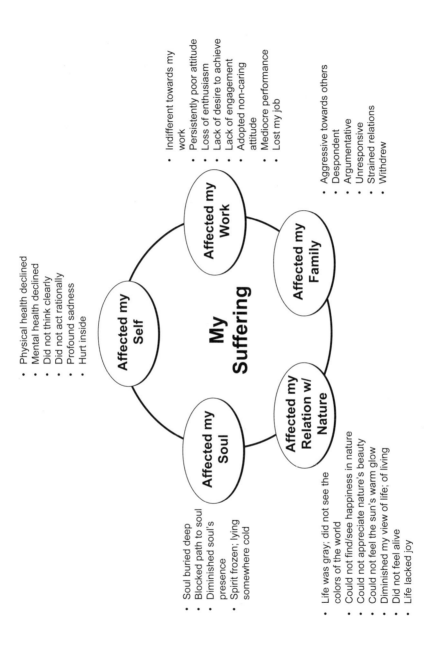

Fig. 1.3

My suffering initially affected my-self. Saddened I was not doing what I wanted in life or getting what I wanted from life, my physical health declined. I gained much weight, my cholesterol level spiked, and my blood pressure was dangerously high. My mental health declined as well. I became increasingly depressed about my situation; anxiety overcame me. I could not think clearly nor act rationally. The profound sadness I felt inside about how my life had unfolded affected me deeply; I hurt inside. My suffering also affected my work. I became indifferent towards my work. I lost all enthusiasm to achieve, to succeed. My lack of desire buried the 'A' player within. As a result of this suffering, my performance deteriorated and I lost my job. For self to be disconnected from soul regarding one's work is highly debilitating. It is debilitating because we spend so much of our day and life at work, and to do something that does not inspire soul, which characterized my situation, leads to much suffering. Only when we live our passions are we truly happy. All other pursuits lack authenticity leaving us unfulfilled, wanting more. Consequently, when our work represents little more than a pay stub, we suffer. Now, while my work was suffering, so, too, was my family. Because of the suffering, I became irritable, hostile, and aggressive towards others. I became despondent towards my wife. I argued with my wife, something I rarely did prior to my suffering. I withdrew, not wanting to socialize or participate in family events. In time, my suffering led to my family suffering. My pain became their pain. But the effects did not end with family. They extended further to my relationship with nature.

During my suffering, I did not see the colors of the world; a world gone gray. I could not find happiness in nature. Whether walking in a park, hiking a trail, or strolling through a zoo, I did not feel the sun's warm glow; could not appreciate nature's beauty. This saddened me, as I had always appreciated nature, always felt a connection with nature. Consequently, my view of life diminished that much more, as I did not feel alive. Ultimately, the suffering descended to the core of me, to soul, where, sitting in a McDonalds parking lot one day, I cried; my tears, coming not from self, but from soul, as I realized that my life-spirit was buried deep, frozen, lying somewhere cold. I was suffering. I was helpless. I was alone.

Perhaps this is where you are today, or once were. So many people today live disconnected lives; are suffering. From working in the wrong profession, to partnering with the wrong person, to living in the wrong location disconnectedness is with us, debilitating us. My debilitation was working in the wrong profession/role, not doing what I love and loving what I do, and you know the story. What is your story? How are you suffering?

Now, because all things are connected, the suffering that begins with self inevitably affects work and the workplace suffers (see Figure 1.4).

Fig. 1.4

Although difficult to measure, it is nonetheless true that
the greater the number of disconnected employees a company
has, the more it suffers. How does it suffer? It suffers from a
less committed workforce. It suffers from a more dysfunctional,
disinterested workforce. And it suffers from a more apathetic
workforce. Because of my self-disconnectedness, because I was
working in a profession/role at odds with soul, I was less committed, I was dysfunctional, I was disinterested. Because I was
not doing what I love and loving what I do, I was depressed, had
a bad attitude and it affected my performance. I was less effective and efficient. I was less interested in helping the company
succeed. I was less tolerant of change, and as my stress levels
grew, I withdrew.

Not only did I pay the price in losing my job, my company paid the price by employing an underperforming asset:
me! Because of self-disconnectedness, self-suffering, companies
pay the price in that they become less productive and, therefore,
more expensive to operate. This negatively affects revenue, profitability, and market value. They become less competitive, unable to grow, as capacity/productivity leakage escalates. Over
time, such debilitations diminish the workplace; make it a less
inspiring place to work, which further undermines a company's
ability to compete effectively. Unfortunately, the suffering that
begins with self and extends to work does not end there, as it
extends to family as well.

Earlier, I stated that my suffering affected my family. This
is an unfortunate consequence of self being disconnected from
soul – family suffers (see Figure 1.5).

Tragically, family pays the price when parts of family are
disconnected; that is, when you and I are disconnected. As our
suffering escalates, as we become more depressed, despondent,
and numb, we become less attentive to others; with spouse, siblings, children, and friends. We become angry, hostile and take
out such hostility on family, as they are nearest to us. We withdraw from family, not wanting to converse with anyone, and as

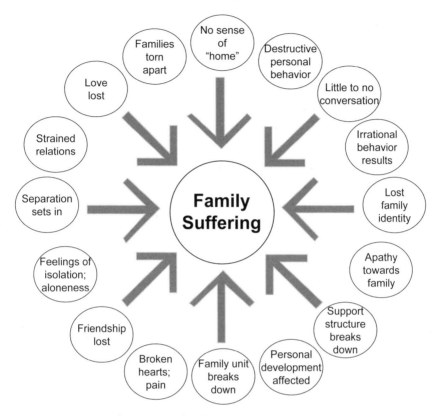

Fig. 1.5

separation sets in, friendship and love squeeze out. Over time, as these unwanted behaviors ramp up, the family unit breaks down. The support structure breaks down, leading to ever more debilitations: apathy towards family, broken hearts, no sense of 'home'. For most people, family represents, offers strength, stability, love, and support. Consequently, when the family unit disintegrates, because of spending less time together, communicating less, or self-disconnectedness, so do we. And, as family disintegrates, as love fades from all that we are (brother, sister, father, mother, husband, wife) so, too, does community.

Communities, like families, are made up of parts; individual households. Earlier, we established that when parts of a whole are disconnected, the whole suffers. This is what happens when families become disconnected – community suffers (see Figure 1.6).

Fig. 1.6

One way that communities suffer is through community apathy. Unfortunately, when communities separate, apathy sets in, and as apathy sets in, as people care less and less about community, community breaks down. We see this all the time. A community thrives, apathy sets in, and community dies. In between the bookends of community thriving and community dying, much suffering occurs: increased crime, increased violence, rampant distrust, and wasted resources. And these debilitations result in further debilitations, deeper suffering, as community cannot attract new residents, cannot attract new businesses, cannot achieve its goals. In time, as with family, community erodes. It loses its voice, its spirit, and its identity. What is distressing about this 'loss' is that as communities' breakdown, so, too, does nation.

As with other systems, nations are comprised of parts; each part a community. Consequently, when the parts of a nation become disconnected, nation suffers (see Figure 1.7).

Fig. 1.7

As debilitations manifest locally, their effects only worsen nationally. For example, the lack of pride, spirit, and trust towards community escalates to a lack of pride, spirit, and trust towards nation. As crime, violence, fear, and apathy debilitate one community, soon, it debilitates all communities. Lastly, wasted resources, declining growth, and decay at a community level only worsen on a nation level as nation works at cross-purposes with one another; is unable to advance, is denied reaching its full potential. Collectively, these debilitations diminish a nation's reputation; diminish global respect, global support. The fact that so many in the US today are homeless, hungry, and hurting is indictment enough; already condemns nation, diminishes nation. And as a nation's importance diminishes globally, so begins its slow, steady decline. Nation suffers economically, spiritually, morally. What remains is a nation bruised; a nation torn apart. Tragically, when this occurs, when civil unrest grows (and we may be in the middle of it right now), like an unstoppable cancerous growth, it soon envelops host; planet.

What we have established thus far is that the suffering that begins with self, in time, affects family, and family suffers. And when families suffer, in time, it affects community, and community suffers. Lastly, when communities suffer, in time, it affects nation, and nation suffers. Until eventually, we arrive at where we are today, a planet, suffering (see Figure 1.8).

How did we get to this point, a planet suffering? If one acknowledges that all things are connected, then it is inevitable that if disconnectedness, suffering exists in the lowest system (self), in time, disconnectedness, suffering would consume the largest system (planet). It might be surprising to learn that self-disconnectedness leads to so much suffering, but, alas, *all things are connected*. Consequently, the disconnectedness/suffering that begins with self inevitably cascades to all (see Figure 1.9).

I opened this chapter asking: "Where is the world?" We can now answer this question. ***The world is disconnected and we are suffering.*** We know this to be true as we continue to wage

Fig. 1.8

war, continue to toxify our host, continue to waste resources, and continue to advance a reality few people want. As a species, we are disconnected, and it has diminished our (innate) spirit; bruised our (collective) soul. Today, where we demand truth, we have mis-truth. Where the goal is re-ception, we have de-ception. Where 'One' is the vision, we have di-vision. This, I am sad to say, is where the world is today. Disconnectedness, suffering not only debilitates us, it defines us. And it is the reason why millions around the globe have opted to 'go the other way'; that is, to escape.

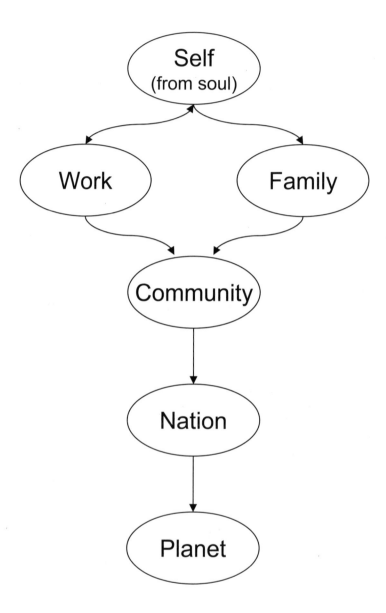

Fig. 1.9

The Great Escape

Increasingly our world does not prompt engagement, but, rather, escape. From what are we escaping? We are escaping from a life without meaning. We are escaping from a life of confinement. We are escaping from a life of unpleasantness, unhappiness, and unwanted outcomes. For many, the life experience lacks purpose, lacks freedom, results in outcomes few people want. As such, we escape. We escape as we seek more than 'default'. We seek an alternate reality, a more authentic reality, a more inspired reality. In short, we escape to feel alive, to be happy, to be free. People 'escape' on their own terms, in their own way, but all forms fall into one of three buckets: 'the good', 'the bad', and 'the ugly'. We begin by looking at good ways people escape a life they do not want.

The Good

Not all forms of escape end with an empty bottle or an attempt at life. Many forms represent positive, soulful attempts to join the living, to reclaim one's life. The following examples represent 'good' attempts at finding happiness, establishing meaning, and restoring joy to one's life:

- Pursue a passion
- Start a business
- Advance a hobby
- Change careers
- Perform volunteer work
- Practice meditation/yoga/exercise
- Travel
- Read self-help books
- Attend wellness seminars/resorts
- Change life partner
- Change surroundings
- Seek professional help

Like you, I seek more from life. But I do more than seek, I demand. I demand happiness. I demand purposeful living. I demand freedom. I am not alone with such requests, as many people demand as I demand. As such, more and more people are starting their own business; pursuing their passion. More and more people are leaving the highly paid, overly stressful corporate job for a more satisfying, but lesser paying one. Finally, more than ever it seems that people are practicing meditation, reading self-help books, and seeking professional help. Why is humanity acting this way? It is simple: *we want to live while we are alive*. Unfortunately, not all attempts at finding happiness, establishing meaning, and restoring joy are good. Many are bad.

The Bad

To be given life and feel that you are not living is crushing. Not long ago this is how I felt about my life. Sadly, because of genetic disposition, life situation, or other factors unseen, many people resort/fall victim to one or more debilitating actions to escape a life they do not want:

- Withdraw from society; seek isolation
- Depression
- Mental illness
- Prescription drugs
- Increased alcohol use
- Medical treatment

When what we think is real in life amounts to mistruths and deception, it hurts. A different kind of pain consumes us; debilitates us. We withdraw. We isolate. We depress. I understand these actions and feelings, as I, too, withdrew, isolated self, felt depressed but such debilitations pale in comparison to those afflicted with deeper suffering, prolonged depression, greater loss from living an imposter existence. For such tormented souls, the escape turns ugly.

The Ugly

It is tragic that the world loses so many souls because of not knowing how to find happiness, not knowing how to find purpose, not knowing how to resolve the suffering. For many people, the life experience is more struggle than successful, more painful than joyful, more debilitating than inspiring leaving many to opt out of life; some methods slow, others more deliberate, all ugly:

- Drug abuse
- Alcoholism
- Violence
- Crime
- Suicide

Although my suffering never deepened to the point where I felt that my only escape was drugs, alcohol, or death, I, nonetheless, understand the behavior, I understand those who operate on such plane. I understand because when we suffer, we seek escape. Earlier, I mentioned that we escape to avoid unpleasant reality, to avoid unwanted outcomes. We do escape for these reasons but the question becomes, "What do we seek?" We answer this question next.

Things We Seek

We seek much from life including one thing already mentioned: freedom. Each of us innately desires to be free; to live free, to do what we want **in life** so that we get what we want **from life**. Freedom, however, represents but the tip of the iceberg, as we innately seek many other things from life, such as:

- Purpose
- Love
- Happiness
- Spirituality
- Inspiration
- Opportunity

- Balance
- Simplicity
- Authenticity
- Alignment

We seek these things, and when the default of life does not offer them, we escape. Perhaps you seek escape. It is ok to admit this fact. The standard life design does not offer such things by default. Today, it requires explicit, deliberate action to escape default, that is, to be free. Having said this, to escape in a manner characterized as bad or ugly represents not escape but defeat. At bottom, 'The Great Escape' is a cry for help. _**It is a desire to live; to die alive.**_ The fact that so many people today seek escape is symptom enough that a very troubling, pervasive problem exists. 'The Great Escape' is not a new phenomenon. It has been with us, among us, defining us, for quite some time. Only now, the problem has escalated to epidemic proportions, as more and more people are dissatisfied with life, with living. We grow up with an optimistic, albeit naive, view of how our life is going to unfold, only to discover that the world is not how we imagined it. We discover that what we thought was real (about life) is disconnected, deceptive, full of mistruths. With so many finding the life experience unpleasant, unfulfilling, it begs the question: "Are we living?"

Are we Living?

Given all the suffering, all the disconnectedness that exists in the world today, one wonders whether we are living. One wonders whether our current existence is as good as it gets. One wonders whether our current reality is the highest form humanity can achieve; ascend. Today, the life experience offers a reality few people want. We live in a world too expensive to live, where the social divide continues to escalate, where many feel disconnected, deceived, are searching for the truth. The indicators are clear. We are not living, for if we were, we would not see, hear, or feel the suffering that now afflicts us, debilitates us, diminishes all that is good in life.

What is needed is to rewrite humanity's story with different themes; different outcomes. To rewrite this story is not difficult, as it simply requires us 'go the other way'. The world story today is not relevant, engaging, or memorable as it reads not of that which inspires, but of that which debilitates (see Figure 1.10).

Having said this, a new movement is among us. The tide is turning. I can <u>feel</u> it, and perhaps you do too. An undercurrent of emotion, discontent, is sweeping the globe, as humanity will no longer tolerate its current story; current condition. We have tired of the suffering; tired of the stress, famine, homelessness, poverty, disease, and inequality. The soul of humanity wants more, demands more. It is desperate for a new movement to believe in. We demand that a new story be written for what is possible for humanity; what the 'life experience' means, represents. We demand that disconnectedness leave us along with its troublesome cousins: deception and mistruth. We demand an end to the suffering. Everywhere I look today, I see signs that humanity demands new priorities, seeks a different existence, a better reality for all. On the radio, I hear songs about living purposefully, of seeking a better life. In the theatre, I see movies illuminating our desire to live happily, simply, freely. On bookstore shelves, I see books about finding one's purpose, about increasing happiness, about living an inspired existence. Finally, in casual conversation, I hear people joke about not having a life but desperately wanting one. When you 'tune in', expand your periphery to the undercurrent of emotion, to the discontent that exists today, you will see the signs and they are everywhere. From what we believe, to what we see and think, to how we act and feel, the signs of humanity wanting more, demanding more abound.

Collectively, the signs indicate we are in the middle of an epochal shift. A new world order is emerging; the world's story is being rewritten and we are its authors. An epochal shift is a

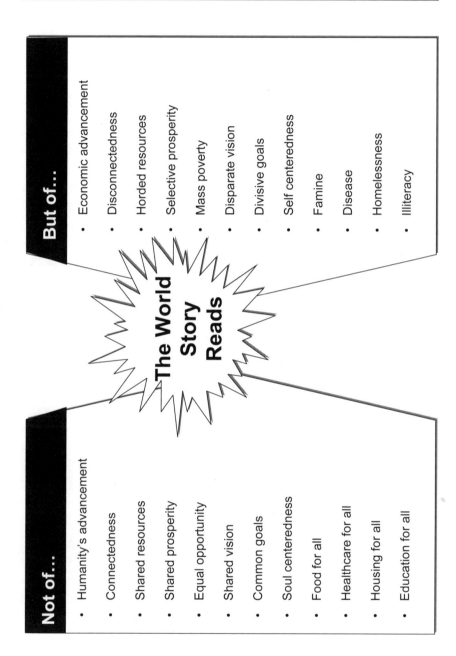

Fig. 1.10

particular period of time marked by distinctive features, events, and state of affairs. For example, capitalism and globalism represent epochal shifts, as such movements changed the world. So of what epochal shift are we in the midst? We are in the midst of a profound shift where humanity, human consciousness, is reaching, striving for 'higher ground', as 'more of the same' will not do. Humanity is dictating new priorities, new details for the world to focus on and what tops the list is to advance the human story, to attend to humanistic concerns, *to give rather than receive*. When economics drives the world agenda, some win, but most lose. Thus, it is no surprise that humanity has had enough. It has rejected this reality and declared, with a single voice, that **all must win**, not just the privileged few. Figure 1.11 highlights the conditions responsible for the epochal shift, in addition to describing the features and texture, of a future that wants to emerge.

When one considers our affairs today, it is not too surprising that many people have responded in desperate and destructive ways. Increasingly, we see people kill others and then themselves as their final acts on earth. On a grander scale, we see groups of people who are intolerant with where the world is and who desire to make a stronger statement: 9/11? Fortunately, humanity has responded in another way as well. Today, millions around the globe are 'tuned in' to the undercurrent of change and in fact are responsible for the change. Each of these change agents seeks to live while they are alive. Each seeks to live an inspired life, to see the colors of the world again. Each seeks to live authentically, to live as soul would live. These actions, desires define the features, texture, of a new era, a new age that is starting to emerge: the *Age of Happiness*. Despite entering a new era, a new age, many people are still suffering; living in quiet desperation. One reason for this is that they do not know the way through. They, do not know how to supplant heartache with happiness. This is where this book gains relevance as it is a means to end the suffering, to become whole, self with soul; to find a new place to start. Achieving these goals may not be the

State of Affairs

- Deep unhappiness
- To expensive to live
- Increasing suicides
- People questioning more and more the 'purpose of life'
- Wage war
- Waste resources
- Rampant discontentment
- People living in quiet desperation
- Misalignment
- Depression
- A world of haves and have not's
- Famine
- Disease
- Profound loss
- More focus on attending to economic goals than humanitarian goals
- Homelessness
- People living imposter lives; living a lie

Events

- Mass killings in schools, shopping centers, workplaces
- Movies/ books/ articles/ conversation about needing change, about living a more purposeful, free existence
- Music events aimed at raising awareness of the ills in the world and demanding humanity lend a helping hand (e.g. Farm Aid, Live Aid, 'Idol gives back')
- 9/11 (other terrorist attacks)

Features

- Greater focus on quality of life; a desire to 'live while alive'
- People doing what they want in life to get what they want from life
- More people starting their own businesses to be free; to live free
- Humanity becoming more spiritual
- Desire to get back with nature; to reconnect with nature
- Desire to live as soul would live
- Desire to resolve the missing that exists between self and soul
- Rise in meditation, Buddhism, journal writing, and 'looking within'
- Desire to live authentically
- Personal awakening; rise of soul
- Desire to return to one's youth; to happier times; back to the start

Fig. 1.11

primary reason(s) you purchased this book, as it might be to create a personal strategy for living. This is fine. Regardless, before we start your journey, before we set off to reengineer your-self to maximize the personal, professional, and financial potential that life offers, we must first discuss one more topic: *the challenge of our time*.

The Challenge of our Time

To be happy, *to live while alive*, is the goal. Sadly, few people live this way. Personal happiness, it seems, is in short supply today. Thus, the challenge of our time is to find happiness, to live again, to love life again. We are challenged, to do all of this in a world designed to deliver the opposite and determined to knock it out of you when it does exist. What this tells us is that happiness does not arrive by default; we must deliberately pursue happiness. We must make it happen. As this is a book of truths, know this: *those who deliberately pursue happiness, find it, and those who do not, rarely do.* And, although we do not ask for life, but having arrived, we do have choices. For example, we choose what profession to work in, we choose who to share our life with, and we choose where to live. It is the choices we make in life that determine our quality of life; that determine our mode of living. Generally speaking, there are three modes of living:

- Thriving
- Surviving
- Dying

To "thrive" means to live joyfully, meaningfully, happily. It means that you are doing what you want in life and getting what you want from life throughout life. Few people live this way. To "survive" means just the opposite. It means that one is living in quiet desperation, a life lacking joy, meaning, or happiness. The majority of people live this way. Lastly, to "die" means that one is alive on the outside but dead on the inside; soul buried deep, spirit sleeping somewhere cold. Tragically, many people live this way as well.

I wrote this book as a 'wake up call' to those who are merely surviving or worse yet, dying. Because we have Only One Shot at the life experience and because the years pass so quickly, it is imperative that one elevate the self from a state of dying, or surviving, to thriving. Having said this, there is a catch.

A famous adage states that the best way to predict your future is to create your future, *to manufacture it.* What this means is that if you are serious about reengineering your life, about restoring joy to your life, about maximizing the personal, professional, and financial potential that life offers it will require work; significant effort. It will require reading this book and using the tools, techniques, and instruction provided herein. Through deliberate action, and with faith, courage, and enthusiasm, you will realize a new life and increase personal happiness. How can I be certain? Because I once stood where you now stand, and today, I am happy, alive, and free. Our stories are the same. As I ascended and escaped a life that I did not want, so, too, will you ascend and escape. As such, I look forward to seeing you on the other side, where all are happy because all are free.

In this chapter, we asked, 'Where is the world?' We learned that the world is disconnected and as a result, many are suffering. We also learned that all things are connected, from self, to community, to planet, and that the disconnectedness and suffering that begins with self, in time, cascades to all other systems of which we are a part. Lastly, we learned that humanity has had enough; rejected its current story. It desires something new. It is probably true that if you care enough about self to read this book, you also care about planet. This is admirable, as I, too, share this concern. One bit of advice: before you put forth significant energies to save the planet, you may want to heed the subtle, but important message from our recent learnings, and that is *to rewrite the world story, it first requires rewriting your story.* In other words, before we pick up the broken pieces of others' lives, we must first pick up the broken pieces of our life. The good news is that there still is time to do both. Therefore, in the spirit of improving planet by first improving self, we continue by assessing *where are you.*

Where are You?

*"Let the world know you as you are, not as you
think you should be, because sooner or later, if
you are posing, you will forget the pose, and then
where are you?"*

- Fanny Brice

IN CHAPTER 1, WE DISCUSSED MACRO, considered the world story, asking 'Where is the world?' Now, we discuss micro, consider your story, ask: 'Where are you?' We assessed the world story first to provide context, offer insights, clues, when assessing your story. To assess your-self, to consider your story, requires examining external and internal. That is, it requires examining that which is visible, on the surface of life, and that which is invisible, your world within, knowing that both realms represent the whole you. To do this, we ask questions of self and then listen for the answer. By assessing self, we can understand self, to transform self – this is the process and this is our goal – and if we are successful, that is, if we transform self, rewrite our story, we will, together, transform world, rewrite humanity's story. We begin, as we did in Chapter 1, with a premise. In this case, that *you are not getting what you want in life or from life at this point in your life.* For if you were, you would not be reading this book.

It is important to acknowledge that something brought you to this book. Whether prompts from self, soul, or some other source, divine or otherwise, something brought you and I together. From my perspective, this is no coincidence, as I believe that your story and my story are the same. That is, I believe the force that inspired me to write this book is the same force that inspired you to seek this book. We may be of different genders, ethnicity, or citizenship, but we are connected, you and I. As such, your journey, your field walk, is my journey, my field walk. The good news is that you can benefit from my past learnings. You can leverage the wisdom of someone who suffered as you might suffer, who desired more from life as you desire, and who found a better way to live as you now seek. Having said this, there are multiple 'on ramps' or motivations to seek this book. For example, some seek this book because they are disconnected, suffering, desire to live as soul would live, and desperately seek escape of the 'good' kind. Others are living a good life, but know that there is a better way to live, desire a more purposeful existence, seek a different life story, and believe having a personal strategy will help realize new story. Finally, there are those who seek both. Now, regardless of 'on ramp', motivation in reading this book, the process we must follow to end disconnectedness, end the suffering, and/or to maximize the life experience via a personal strategy is the same. We must first assess our-self. That is, we must first find out *where we are.*

Because this is a book of truths, let me share an important truth with you. Through observing self and others, I have learned that when <u>soul</u> cannot wait any longer, that is, when the desire of soul to operate on the surface of life becomes too strong, and when <u>self</u> will no longer tolerate current condition, we intervene. To be precise, self intervenes on behalf of soul. We intervene because we must. Not satisfied to operate in darkness, soul rises. Not wanting to live a diminished life, to live in quiet desperation, self acts (see Figure 2.1). Now, because so

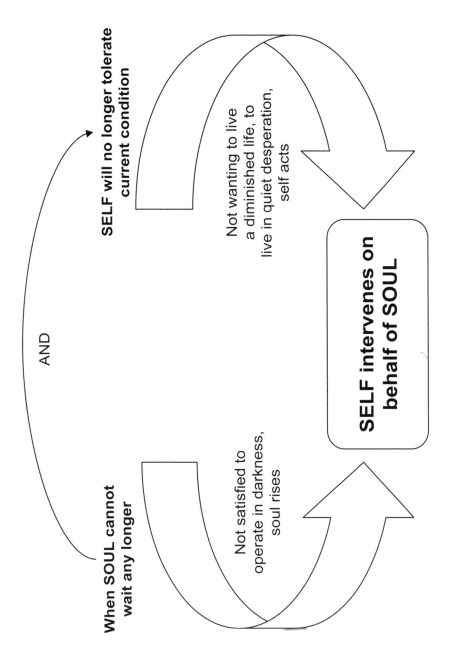

Fig. 2.1

few people stop their life to assess their life, because the act of descending within to alter without is so rare, we discuss such intervention.

The Intervention

Today, few people deliberately 'stop their life' long enough to assess their life; to improve their life. We are so busy 'living life' that we never pause to 'work on' our life. Part of the reason for this is that we were never educated in such matters. At no point did we learn the need for, or how to, stop one's life to assess one's life, as such, few do. What is more tragic is that even with such education, contemporary living offers few 'breaks', little reprieve, *to* stop one's life as the pressures, stresses, workload of life continue to escalate; each of us reduced to rat-in-cage. This is not your story, however, as you did pause; you did intervene on behalf of soul. Thus, we continue this intervention by first asking these questions of self:

- How often do you stop your life to assess your life?
- How much time do you spend weekly, monthly, annually asking questions of self, to understand self, to transform self?
- Can you articulate the source of your frustrations with self, life?

How did you score? If you are like most people, not very well. Most people do not allocate time weekly, monthly, annually to review their life with the intention of improving their life. That is where this book gains relevance. This book represents 'pause' in your life, to assess your life, *to hear what soul has to say*. It is an opportunity for you to step back, view your life from above, and ask: "Am I getting what I want in life and from life at this point in my life?" As the reader, what you make of the 'pause' is up to you. You have the opportunity to reengineer self, develop a rigorous personal strategy, and rediscover the joy of living OR you can continue 'more of the same' – perpetuate current story. Something brought you to this book. The question is whether you have resolve enough to rise up, dig in, and realize the emerging you. Do not be mistaken: what brought you to this book, to this point, is **loss**; feelings of wanting more, desiring more, living more. You have intervened on behalf of soul. Do not deny the emerging you from seeing light of day. Do not dismiss the opportunity before you. A new life awaits you. A new story is about to be written and you are the author. Thus, if committed to the effort, let us continue by assessing your-self.

Assessing Self

So, what does it mean to assess something? To assess means to evaluate, to know direction, or to estimate the quality of something. Therefore, to assess self, means to evaluate where one is at; to know direction of one's life. It also means to estimate or measure the quality of one's life. To 'know' such things is a prerequisite to reengineer one's life. Only by knowing 'where we are' can we know 'what to do' to get 'where we want to go'. In Chapter 1, we learned that each of us is a system, operating in much larger systems. As such, to assess one-self is to assess the [self-system]. This entails assessing not only self, but also self's interactions with soul, work, family, and nature. By doing this, we gain deeper awareness of *where we are*. At first, we gain a 1st order awareness when evaluating the interactions between self and soul and this provides context, gives rise, to a 2nd order awareness from evaluating the interactions between self and work, self and family, and self and nature. From evaluating our interactions, we learn about our interactions. That is, we become aware of those areas of our life that are problematic, misaligned, demand greatest attention (see Figure 2.2).

It is because few people take time to know self, to discover soul and the universe about them, that they are in the condition

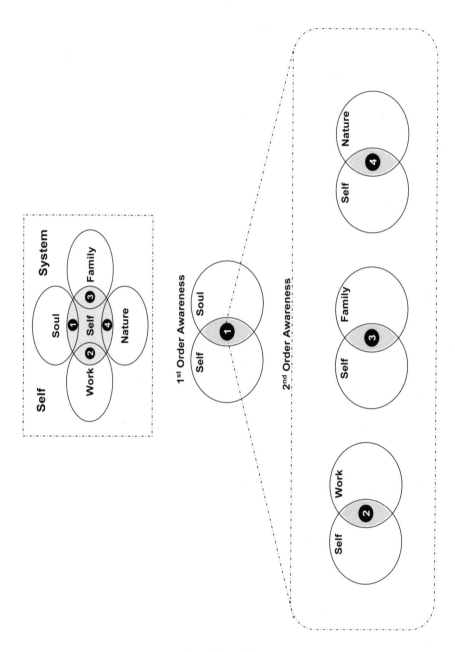

Fig. 2.2

they are in; suffer ill condition. Consequently, our goal is to overcome poverty of soul, to rise above ill condition by knowing one-self, by discovering things about one-self; from knowing soul. With this as a backdrop, we begin.

Using questioning as our tool, we explore where you are within (that which is invisible) and where you are without (that which is visible). We ask questions ranging from soul, to career, to health, to your relationship with nature, as such questions, collectively, represent the whole you (see Figure 2.3).

Now, as this chapter is about self-exploration, self-discovery, self-assessment, it is vital that you answer all questions honestly. You gain nothing from embellishing your answers, skirting reality, *as soul knows the truth*. Therefore, be truthful with your inquiries and, as the saying goes, the truth will set you free.

We begin by assessing that which lies within; soul. To know soul means to know desires of soul but it also means to know condition of soul. In Chapter 4, we explore desires of soul as knowing one's inner soul goals represent the foundation of personal strategy, so for now, we assess condition of soul. To determine inner condition, we ask these questions of self:

Note: Allow 30 minutes to consider these questions. <u>Listen</u> for the answers.

Questions of Soul:

- What is the state of your soul?
- When alone, what does soul say?
- Are you doing what you want <u>in</u> life?
- Are you getting what you want <u>from</u> life?
- Is life meaningful, purposeful?
- Are you living an imposter life?
- Do you desire a new life story?
- Are you living as soul would live?

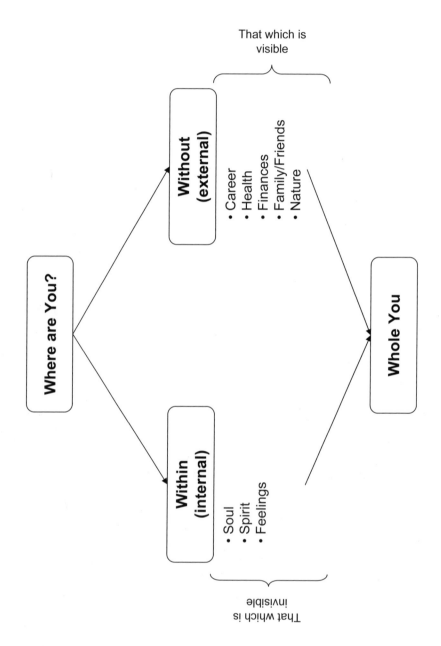

Fig. 2.3

Questions of Spirit:

- What is the condition of your spirit?
- Is spirit alive or sleeping somewhere cold?
- Are you living an inspired existence?
- Is life fragrant, vibrant, full of color?

Questions of Feeling:

- What do you feel inside?
- How do you feel about life, living?
- Do you feel alive?
- Do you feel the sun's warm glow?
- Are you happy with where you are personally, professionally, financially?
- Are you happy with your current life story?
- Do you feel inner conflict between *where* you are and *where* you want to be?
- Do you feel inner conflict between *who* you are and *who* you want to be?
- Are you free?

<Pause>

What did you hear? What did soul have to say? Depending on how you answered these questions indicates where are you. In Chapter 1, I shared with you my suffering, *where I was*. Not long ago, had I been asked the questions above, I would have responded, "Soul is gray, spirit is frozen, I hurt inside". As such, I understand those who hurt inside as I, too, hurt inside. I understand the heartache, desperation, and pain that comes with frozen spirit; soul gone gray. To live this way is to not live at all. The questions asked of you thus far reveal inner condition. Now we assess outer condition, where you are on the surface of life (e.g. career, family, finances, health, relationship with nature).

To determine outer condition, we ask these questions of self:

Note: Allow 30 minutes to consider these questions. <u>Listen</u> for the answers.

- Are you working in the right profession/role?
- Are you with the right person?
- Are you living in the right location?

< Pause >

What did you hear? What did soul have to say? If you answered no to any of the questions above, disconnectedness is with you, debilitating you, diminishing all that is good in life. When misalignment exists between what we are doing relative to what we want to do, we suffer. Similarly, when misalignment exists between who we are relative to whom we are with, we suffer. Lastly, when misalignment exists between where we are relative to where we long to be, we suffer. Perhaps, in considering the questions above, you were not sure how to answer such questions. If so, consider the 'signs of suffering' in Figure 2.4 as indication of where are you.

The message is clear: personal disconnectedness, in any form, is devastating, as it debilitates us, diminishes us; causes much suffering. The stress, pain, and heartache that results from personal misalignment affects our health, finances, and relations with others.

Ask these questions of self:

- How is disconnectedness affecting your health?
- How is disconnectedness affecting your finances?
- How is disconnectedness affecting your relations with family?
- How is disconnectedness affecting your view of life; your relation with nature?

How you answer these questions also reveals where are you. When assessing oneself, it is important to ask questions about that which lies within and that which lies without, as

Signs of Suffering

Signs of Working in the Wrong Profession/Role

- Looking at job boards
- Clock watching
- Maximizing one's PTO time
- Feelings of being trapped
- Feelings of personal crisis
- Arguments with spouse/partner
- Distracted all the time
- Unremarkable job performance
- Job hopping
- Paralyzed with inaction
- Escaping work during lunch
- Resistant to change
- Seeking professional guidance
- Negative speak
- Stinking thinking
- Irritable with partner, kids, etc.
- Depressed/despondent/numb
- Destructive behavior (drinking)
- No desire to achieve
- Uncaring attitude
- No willingness to go the extra mile
- Irrational behavior

Signs of Partnering with the Wrong Person

- Endless arguments
- Different life priorities
- Different interests/hobbies
- Live together, but apart
- Focusing on partner's flaws
- Little interaction
- Separate vacations
- Increased separation
- Constant irritability
- Lack of intimacy
- Not 'knowing' one another
- Disengagement
- Desire to be with someone else
- Diminished social activity
- Little conversation
- Depressed/despondent/numb

Signs of Living in the Wrong Location

- Thoughts of living elsewhere
- No desire to explore local environment
- Anxious to escape surroundings; to travel elsewhere
- No spiritual connection with surroundings
- Surroundings do not stir the soul
- Surroundings does not inspire soul
- Surroundings do not excite the senses
- Irritated by current surroundings
- Surroundings do not energize
- Depressed/despondent/numb

Fig. 2.4

external affects internal and vice versa. Said differently, where
we are on the outside of life (self) affects where we are on the
inside of life (soul); cycle repeating. Figure 2.5 illustrates this
linkage, dependency between self and soul, between outer and
inner.

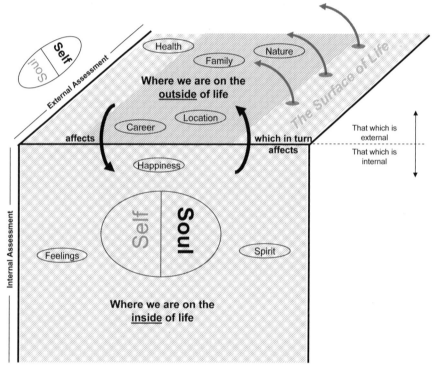

Fig. 2.5

Because outer condition affects inner condition, if soul is
suffering, the only way to change condition is to change how we
operate on the surface of life. I hope that by asking/answering
the questions in this chapter, you were able to determine 'where
you are' relative to 'where you want to be'. Asking questions
of self helps reveal self; helps indicate 'where we are' spiritually, emotionally, mentally, physically. Questions help us measure
self, reveal self, find self. Although the questions asked of you
in this chapter are important, of value, in assessing self, what is

more important, of greater value, is the questions **you** ask self. When gazing at the starry sky, when lying in bed, when alone, what questions do you ask self? What does soul tell you then? How you answer these questions also reveals where are you. Know this: *our current life story is the way it is not so much because of what we know (about self and soul), but what we do not know.* Because so few people stop their life, to know where they *are* in life, few people can articulate their source of discontent. And when one cannot articulate discontent, one cannot eliminate discontent. By understanding one's internal and external structure, one can transform life in meaningful and effective ways. The insights we gain from interrogating self, from engaging in quiet conversation with soul, illuminate our path; indicate 'where to go'. More than this, such insights enable us to restore balance to our life.

Balance

Earlier, we learned that each of us innately desires to be whole; self with soul, but this is not the only thing we desire, as we also seek balance. We know this to be true, as when we are imbalanced, we feel it, we know it, and it hurts. When I was not doing what I love and loving what I do, I felt imbalance, and it hurt. I suspect that this is your story as well. When the parts of our life are imbalanced (work, partner, location), we seek balance. It is an innate reflex to make that which is wrong, right. But what does it mean to be balanced? To be 'balanced' means:

- To be in a state of equilibrium
- The degree to which attributes of a whole are in harmony
- To be whole

Based on your self-assessment, would you say that your inner/outer life is in a state of equilibrium? Are the parts of you (self and soul) in harmony with one another? Are you whole? How you answer these questions also reveals where are you.

When discussing balance, it is important to acknowledge that what we want in life and from life evolves. For example, what we want today may not be what we want one year from now, five years from now, or 10 years from now. Each of us is continually growing, unfolding throughout life. As the world changes, so, too, do we change. What this tells us is that establishing equilibrium, maintaining harmony, staying whole is a balancing act (see Figure 2.6).

Life's Balancing Loop

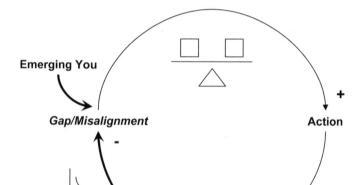

Fig. 2.6

You and I, we are constantly emerging, from what we believe, to what we see, to how we think, act, and feel. While this behavior is completely normal, this dynamic, unfortunately, is also the cause of much suffering, as most people react slowly, if at all, to changes occurring within. For example, we continue working in a profession/role long past the point of caring. We perpetuate relations with others, where although love exists, life interests diverged long ago. And we extend our stay in locations that discourage soul rather than inspire it. Why do we do this? Why do we continue, perpetuate, extend 'more of the same' when we long to 'go the other way'? Know this: the longer you deny that which is emerging relative to that which exists, the greater the gap/misalignment within self and your life. Figure 2.6 illustrates this truth. It also illustrates that if we wish to close the gap between where we are versus where we want to be, it requires deliberate action and time. The good news is that you possess both: time and the ability to act. Most people live with 'the gap', never taking action to maintain equilibrium, establish harmony, stay whole. Do not let this be your life story. Achieving balance, staying balanced, this is our challenge; today, everyday.

Now, perhaps without recognizing it, you have already taken action. Reading this book is an attempt to establish balance; to close the gap. More than this, it represents your awakening.

Awakening

I have walked the earth for forty years, and in this time, I have seen much disconnectedness, much suffering. So many people today live diminished lives; *are living a lie*. This is tragic. Nay one soul should live a diminished life, but many do. Nay one soul should be denied life, but many are. Not long ago, I lived a diminished life, was living a lie, as I was not doing what I wanted in life nor getting what I wanted from life. Perhaps this is your story. Only recently did I awake from my slumber, only recently did I become aware that there is a better way to live, only recently did I reclaim my life; *act*. Because of the quick pace of life today, few people stop their life to reclaim their life, that is, to act; to craft a better way to live. Our nine-to-five life traps us, as do the routines and habits that support and perpetuate such life. As such, our life is not our own, as the world dictates to us, manhandles us, robs us of our freedoms. Feeling dictated to, feeling manhandled, and desiring freedom, I awoke one day; it was a Tuesday. I was determined not to remain captive to a life I did not want, and so, I escaped.

How did I escape?

>   1. I stopped my life
>   2. I assessed my life
>   3. I found a better way to live

Now it is your time to escape. The good news is that this book can help you accomplish all three tasks stated above. Consider that every time you read this book, you stop your life. Every page turned helps you assess your life. Each paragraph read reveals a better way to live. Since my awakening, I have emerged from *world dictating my life* to *me dictating my life*. Whereas before I was discouraged, dependent, captive, today, I am inspired, independent, and free. Are you inspired, independent, free? How you answer this question also reveals where are you. Most people today are not living an inspired, independent, free existence and, as a result, are suffering. This is not your fate, however, as utilizing the tools, techniques, and instruction herein will ensure different results; different outcomes. Just as I opened my eyes, awoke from my slumber, so, too, will you open your eyes, awake from your slumber. You may be asking, "What enabled my awakening, facilitated my freedom?" One thing: I discovered soul.

Although each of us *has* soul, few *know* soul. At an abstract level, each of us recognizes soul as our 'voice within', the inner part of us that periodically speaks to us; occasionally comes into view; penetrates our consciousness. Unfortunately, most people dismiss soul. That is, they hear soul, but quickly dismiss tones heard; do not listen to what soul has to say. Why is this? It is partly the result of not knowing how to respond to tones heard or how to converse with soul, but it is also the result of living at the speed of sound. Like you, my schooling never addressed how to converse with soul. Consequently, I rarely did. Further, because I was busy living life, I never took time to work on my life. As a result, I did not know soul. Then, I stopped my life; descended within. I listened to what soul had to say, and in hearing soul, I discovered soul; *finally acknowledged soul.* And upon acknowledging soul, in listening to what soul had to say, I became aware of two *life-changing* insights:

1. What to do with my life
2. What I wanted from life

In short, I found home. This is now your challenge, your goal. You, too, must find home. In the chapters that follow, certain exercises, your efforts, will help you to illuminate, discover *the path which leads home*. How can I be certain? It is because your story and my story are the same and just as I found my way, found my home, so, too, will you find your way, find your home. Although too early for you to realize, **this book is a homeward-bound journey**; to find soul; to learn from soul; to live as soul would live. As your journey and my journey are connected, each of us plays complementary roles.

Your role:

1. To stop your life
2. To read
3. To reflect
4. To use the tools, techniques, and instruction herein

My role:

1. To help you find soul, and pull it forward, into the present, onto the surface of life
2. To wake you up inside
3. To save you from a life diminished; from living a lie
4. To lead you back home

As much as I believe that the world is in-between stories, I suspect that you are also in-between stories; *in-between who you are (self) and who you want to be (soul)*. The purpose of this chapter was for you to discover <u>where</u> you are; to determine current condition to change condition. In questioning self, we enable self to transform self. More than this, we enable personal awakening. I hope that you are awake with eyes wide open. I wrote this book as a wakeup call for the sleeping and the sleepy, as life is too short to navigate with eyes wide shut.

This chapter addressed the question: '*Where are you?*' As important as answering this question is, there is a more important question, more immediate inquiry now to resolve, '*Where you want to be?*' Before we address this question, resolve this inquiry, however, we must first understand two things: opportunity and imperative.

Opportunity and Imperative

*"You have a great world of opportunity awaiting
your determination to possess it."*
- Frank Channing Haddock

*"This is our purpose: to make as meaningful as
possible this life that has been bestowed upon us."*
- Eleanor Roosevelt

WHAT INSPIRES A MAN OR WOMAN to start a business, pursue Olympic gold, or disappear, happily, into nature? What directs a corporate executive to relinquish (or forego) wealth, power, and prestige to pursue a lesser role? What compels the orphan child not to give up, to rise above poverty and the pressures of reality? What motivates the terminally ill to continue pursuing passion till final days? Lastly, what prevents the suffering from seeking escape of the ugly kind when the colors of life have turned gray? It is two things: 1) opportunity and 2) imperative. What opportunity? What imperative, you ask? The opportunity is life itself, the life experience, and specifically, *a desire to maximize the personal, professional, and financial potential that life offers.*

The imperative is *a desire to live while alive*, to live purposeful-ly, meaningfully, fragrantly. Those described above, and others like them, seek both: **to seize opportunity and meet imperative.** Such people are rare. You are among such company.

Let us recap our learnings. We learned where the world is: disconnected and suffering. We also learned where you are: not getting what you want in life or from life. With all the discon-nectedness and suffering that exists today, one thing is clear: we are not individually or collectively seizing opportunity, meeting imperative. This sad state must change, beginning with indi-vidual, with <u>you</u>. The good news is that regardless of your age, there is still time to reengineer your life (opportunity), to join the living (imperative). But as the years pass quickly, there is no time to waste. Therefore, let us discuss the opportunity before you.

Opportunity

It is a fact; you will pass this earth but once. As such, you have Only One Shot at the life experience, at living. To acknowledge this fact, and assuming you value life, is to realize that you have no time to lose. You have no time to lose working in the wrong profession/role. You have no time to lose living with the wrong partner. You have no time to lose living in drab surroundings. This directive becomes significant when you consider that the average life expectancy for man living in the US is 78 years, for woman: 83 years. And when you factor out the first 15 years of life and the last 10 years of life what remains is 53 productive years for man and 58 productive years for woman. Not much time to seize opportunity; meet imperative. I am age forty as I write this chapter, and only recently have I begun to live; twenty-five years have got behind me. How many years have got behind you? Regardless of 'lost years', you and I still have time, only now, urgency exists to maximize remaining time on earth. We need to seize the opportunity before us. This is our time, our moment; the present is our servant. But what does it mean to seize opportunity? Before we answer this question, let us first define what opportunity is.

Opportunity is:

- A state of affairs; an occasion
- A possibility
- A chance to do something
- A time for executing purpose

It has been said that, occasion makes opportunity. The occasion each of us has been blessed with is life, the life experience. And this opportunity spawns endless other opportunities in life. For example, life offers us opportunity to love, to be loved, to learn, to teach others what we have learned, to see, to be seen, to inspire, to be inspired, to do something meaningful/purposeful in life, and to contribute to the world. As each of us is gifted life, so must we create a life; to vision possibility, to accomplish things, to realize our purpose on earth. Of all the opportunities before us, however, the opportunity that is life is clearly the one opportunity we must seize.

Therefore, for purposes herein, 'seizing opportunity' means:

- To live with urgency as you will pass this earth but once
- To not waste time
- To maximize the personal, professional, and financial potential that life offers

The ability to seize opportunity lies within us all, but to seize opportunity first requires acknowledging opportunity. Do you acknowledge the opportunity before you? Do you see, think, act, and feel in ways that reflect the urgency of passing this earth but once? Most people do not act with urgency, do not see the opportunity before them, and, therefore, do not seize opportunity. They merely exist. For many years, this is how I operated. I did not approach life with urgency; I merely existed, my actions reflecting not an attitude of wanting to maximize the life experience, but something lesser. I have changed my ways; I am now living with urgency, as I know that there will not be a second opportunity to get it right. With the time I have remaining, I am looking to achieve, to accomplish, to live authentically, to realize the highest form of me. I seek these things as I know that living authentically, for example, brings freedom, and to be free is to seize opportunity; to live happily.

Each of us was gifted an opportunity <u>at life</u> and therefore an opportunity <u>to live</u>. Do not be mistaken: an opportunity at life is not the same as an opportunity to live. The former was determined for you; the latter is determined by you. 'To exist' requires little effort, but 'to live' requires much effort. This is why so few people really 'live' while alive. Partly the result of not wanting to pay the price and partly the result of a flawed education, few people live vibrant, fragrant lives. Thus, the question is: "Will you seize opportunity?" "Will you achieve, accomplish great things, live authentically, and realize the highest form of you?" "Will you act with urgency, not waste time, and maximize the life experience?" Tread slowly when answering these questions as your responses will determine the balance of your life; the quality of your life; *all that follows*. But, know this: the highest earners, the great achievers, the 'happy' in life are the way they are not because of possessing ancient secrets or due to dumb luck, but because they seized opportunity, which also implies meeting imperative.

Imperative

Because you will pass this earth but once, it is imperative that you live authentically, **as you are,** not as who you (or others) think you should be. It is imperative that you live your passions; live passionately. Finally, it is imperative that you find soul, learn from soul, live as soul would live. It is imperative that you do these things as you will not have another opportunity to do so. Just so we are clear, let us define what imperative means.

Imperative is:

- Something that demands attention or action
- An unavoidable obligation
- A compelling behavior
- Some duty that is essential and urgent

To exist and not live one's passion, not live passionately, is to not live at all. Perhaps this is what brought you to this book; a desire to live; to join the living. All people share this innate desire. Consequently, when we feel that we are not 'living', and most people are not, something within demands that we take action. Who initiates such demands? You already know. It is soul. Now, because our desire 'to live' is innate, it represents an unavoidable obligation. To the extent that we meet this obligation, we are happy, joyful, and free. To the extent that we do not, we are dissatisfied, irritable, and numb. Is this how you feel? Perhaps these feelings brought you to this book. It is because of ill feeling within our heart and an innate desire 'to live' that compels us to see, think, and act differently about the life experience. And when we get to this point, when soul cannot wait any longer and self has tired of its current story, we act with newfound purpose, energy, and urgency. We act differently to right that which is wrong, to mend that which is broken, to align that which is skewed. In short, we act to meet imperative.

Therefore, for purposes herein, 'meeting imperative' means:

- Doing what you want <u>in</u> life
- Getting what you want <u>from</u> life
- To live passionately; live one's passions
- To live as soul would live

Despite our discussion, one thing that may not be altogether intuitive is that *only by meeting imperative <u>can we</u> seize
opportunity*. What this suggests, implies is that we cannot seize
opportunity, for example, by working in a profession/role that
does not: 1) represent what we want to do in life, 2) allow us
to acquire what we want in life, 3) enable living passionately, 4)
reflect living as soul would live. This is where I went awry. For
many years, I worked in a profession/role that did not inspire
soul, thereby <u>denying me opportunity</u> to maximize the life experience; to live a fragrant life. When we are not inspired, when
we are not doing what we love and loving what we do, it is impossible to maximize the life experience, as we will never put
forth the effort, never pay the price, never sustain needed enthusiasm to become world class; to achieve. Only when we live our
passions can we seize opportunity; this life rule is undeniable.
Having said all this, what is your story? Are you meeting life's
imperative? Are you living passionately? If not, do not anguish
over current condition, as this is not your fault. The fact is, our
schooling never taught us how to seize opportunity and/or how
to meet imperative. Consequently, few do. Sadly, because of
our flawed education, the masses traverse life ignorant of *The
Missing Insight* (see Figure 3.1).

What this illustration tells us is that when we pursue passion, our interest and enthusiasm is strong. Our enthusiasm is
strong because our actions are aligned with soul and when this
type of alignment exists, it energizes us, inspires us; inspires excellence. And when were performing with excellence, when our
efforts are inspired by soul, it opens the doors of opportunity;
opportunities to maximize the personal, professional, and financial potential that life offers. Finally, what results from continued opportunity is professional recognition, high income, respect
from others, high achievement, and most importantly, lifelong
happiness. Now, while not all people seek such things, we do all
share a common goal; seek one thing: *happiness*.

The Missing Insight

If you do what you love

Desire/interest is strong;
passion and enthusiasm
inspire our best work;
inspires excellence

Excellence opens
the doors of opportunity
for you to walk through

Opportunity will result in:
Recognition * High income
* Respect * Achievement
* Happiness

Fig. 3.1

Opportunity/Imperative: A Summary

We did not ask for life, but having arrived, we must seize opportunity and meet imperative. We must seek these things because the alternative is a life diminished. What we learned in this chapter is that 1) meeting imperative enables seizing opportunity and 2) seizing opportunity indicates meeting imperative (see Figure 3.2).

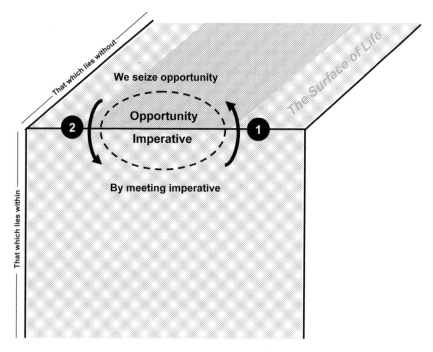

Fig. 3.2

Although the innate desire to maximize the life experience, to live purposefully, lies within us all, most people take life for granted. That is, most do not see the opportunity, imperative before them. This would not be problematic if we had nine lives to 'get it right' but, alas, we are not so fortunate, as we have Only One Shot at life. Consequently, if we desire to live purposefully, meaningfully, happily, it requires we approach life with urgency to maximize our time on earth; to realize the fragrant life we all desire and were meant to live. Moreover, it requires adopting a new attitude towards life, towards living. To be precise, it requires new ways of seeing, thinking, and acting (see Figure 3.3).

We opened this chapter with two quotes, the first by Frank Haddock, who told us that opportunity is waiting for us; we just have to be determined enough to want it, to possess it. The question is, how determined are you to realize opportunity; seize opportunity? How committed are you to realize a better life; to live a fragrant life? The second quote was from Eleanor Roosevelt, who told us that having arrived, we must live purposefully, as it represents our core imperative in life. Are you living purposefully, meaningfully? Are you pursuing, living your passions? I am confident that, like those profiled at the beginning of this chapter, you seek both to seize opportunity and meet imperative, as you would not be reading this book otherwise. Having said this, to meet life's imperative, to seize opportunity, requires clarity of, knowing one's inner soul goals. In Chapter 2, we learned where you are; now, we must learn where you want to be. In Part II of this book, we explore this space, consider this inquiry. We discuss personal vision and how to realize vision by developing and implementing a personal strategy for living. We discuss such things, as knowing where you want to go (vision) and having a plan to get there (personal strategy) are the means, the key prerequisites, to meet imperative, seize opportunity (see Figure 3.4).

You have reached the end of Part I of this book. I hope that learning where the world is and where you are, in addition to learning of the opportunity and imperative before you has altered your perspective of life; provided certain contrast of where you are relative to where you want to be. I hope that our discussion established _The Case for Action_ for you to transform self, if not the world. Lastly, I hope that the dialogue we shared influenced all that is to come – your experiences not only with this book but also with those within your life. We continue this journey, this field walk, by learning how to **align the inner soul with action.**

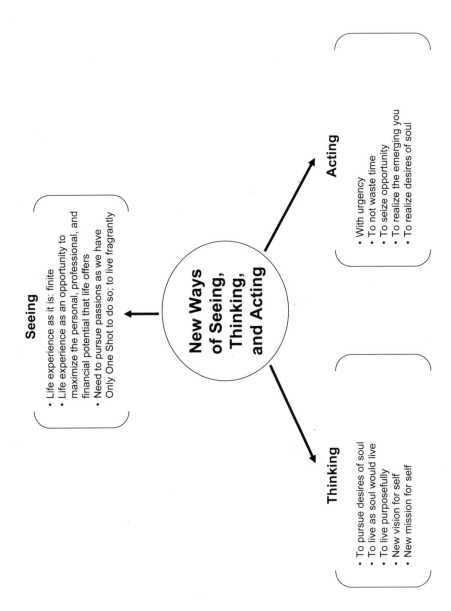

Fig. 3.3

OPPORTUNITY

We have Only One Shot at life, at living. Consequently, we must not waste time. We must live with urgency to seize the opportunity before us; to maximize the personal, professional, and financial potential that life offers.

IMPERATIVE

We must live our passions, live passionately, as we will not have a second opportunity to do so. To do what we want in life and get what we want from life, is the goal. This is our purpose.
This is our imperative.

When we meet imperative, we seize opportunity.

Fig. 3.4

PART II
Aligning the Inner Soul with Action

Introduction to Personal Strategy Maps

"Vision - It reaches beyond the thing that is, into the conception of what can be. Imagination gives you the picture. Vision gives you the impulse to make the picture your own."

- Robert Collier

IN PART I, WE ESTABLISHED 'The Case for Action'. That is, we discussed the reasons, need to transform self, if not the world. We sought to understand self and world, and the opportunity and imperative that befalls us all. We sought such things to learn *where you are* if not to reveal *where you want to be*. Now, in Part II, we build upon such insights. We turn down and in, up and in, to learn more of self in order to transform self. In short, we learn how to change condition now that we are aware of condition. But, to do this efficiently and effectively, knowing that we have no time to waste, requires a plan, an approach. What we need is a *personal strategy*.

What is Strategy?

Before we discuss personal strategy, let us first define what strategy is. Strategy is, quite simply, a long-term plan or policy. Although brief, this definition is useful as it describes the result of a typical strategy planning exercise - *a plan.* Now, to create effective strategy, to develop a precise, actionable plan, first requires understanding the purpose or essence of strategy:

- Strategy represents movement from a 'present position' to a desirable, but uncertain, 'future position'
- Strategy requires doing many things well, not just a few, and integrating them
- Strategy is about overcoming obstacles, achieving goals, and delivering results

We may be most familiar with a company developing a strategy to improve its market share, increase revenue, or better serve its customer base. However, nations, communities, sports teams, and individuals find reason to develop strategy as well. The focus of this book is on the latter entity, the individual. More than ever, there is need for individuals to create a personal strategy for living.

What is Personal Strategy?

Developing strategy applies to individuals as it does for businesses, nations, and sports teams. For example, just as a sports team may develop a strategy to move from its present position of 'last place' to a more desirable future position of 'first place' or a nation may develop a strategy to move from a present position of 'few tourists visiting the country' to a future position of 'many tourists visiting the country' so, too, might an individual develop a strategy to move from a present position of 'unhappiness' to a future position of 'happiness' or from a present position of 'average professional success' to a future position of 'extraordinary professional success'. Table 4.1 highlights the differences between personal strategy versus strategy developed for a business, nation, or team.

Table 4.1

Personal Strategy	Business/Nation/Team Strategy
Authored by an individual	Authored by a group of individuals
Focus is on individual	Focus is on group
Benefits an individual	Benefits a group
Takes days and weeks to define and implement	Takes months and years to define and implement
Reflects individual goals; personal vision	Reflects group goals; group vision
Essence is to improve one's life	Essence is to improve a business, nation, or team

Using the distinctions above, we could say the essence of personal strategy is:

- To move from our 'present position' in life, to a desirable, but uncertain, 'future position' in life
- To do many things well in life, not just a few, and integrate them
- To overcome obstacles, achieve goals, and realize a fragrant life

Developing personal strategy is foreign to most people. To illustrate my point, ask yourself how many people you know who have developed and implemented a personal strategy for living. Few, I would imagine. Strategy development has largely been the concern of business, but that is now changing. Today, people acknowledge the complex and ever changing times in which we live, and responding with a personal strategy to navigate life is both smart and relevant. The question is how does one create personal strategy? What content does one include in a personal strategy? What does personal strategy look like? We address these questions next in the section on Personal Strategy Maps.

Personal Strategy Maps

Okay. Let us reflect on what we have learned. We learned that to have a strategy is to have a plan. We also learned the essence of personal strategy is to help us realize a new existence, a better life. Lastly, we learned that while the majority of people do not have a personal strategy, it is becoming increasingly relevant to have one. Which brings us current, to discuss how to define personal strategy using a Personal Strategy Map (PSM). As you have some familiarity with the phrase 'personal strategy', you might be asking what the word 'map' signifies. As will be shown, the way we document personal strategy is in map or illustration form. In the same way a road map shows us visually how to reach some <u>geographic destination</u>, a Personal Strategy Map shows us visually how to reach some <u>personal destination</u>. The reasons for documenting personal strategy in map form will become evident soon enough. We begin our discussion of Personal Strategy Maps by characterizing their essence.

A Personal Strategy Map is...

- A framework for defining, organizing, and documenting your personal strategy for living
- A graphical representation of your current life strategy
- A way to communicate what you want in life and from life at any point in your life
- A roadmap to achieve your goals and maximize the quality of your life
- The 'what' of personal strategy

Four components comprise a Personal Strategy Map. They are: 1) The Life Experience, 2) The Inner Soul, 3) Life Pathways, and 4) Commitments. The Life Experience component represents the quality of your life; the totality that is *your life*. The Inner Soul component reflects soul; specifically, it reflects the desires of soul – what you want in life and from life at this point in your life (a.k.a. inner soul goals). Life Pathways represent the activities you must perform to achieve your inner soul goals. They are 'personal processes' that characterize everyday living. Finally, commitments represent the personal commitments you must make and keep to sustain life's work (i.e., life's pathways). It is through linkages, cause and effect relations between the components of the Personal Strategy Map, which enables it to serve as a roadmap to achieve your dreams (see Figure 4.1).

Personal Strategy Map
A Roadmap to Achieve your Dreams

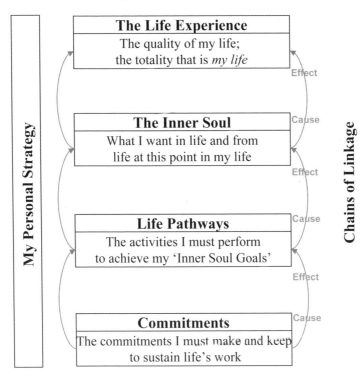

Fig. 4.1

When viewed together, the four components of a Personal Strategy Map provide us a framework from which we can define, organize, and document our personal strategy. To understand the power, usefulness of this framework, we define each component individually then look at how the Personal Strategy Map Framework brings it all together to form personal strategy.

Components of a Personal Strategy Map

A Personal Strategy Map consists of four components that work together as a system to achieve our goals.

The components are:

- The Life Experience
- The Inner Soul
- Life Pathways
- Commitments

The Life Experience

The Life Experience component represents the quality of your life; the totality that is *your life*. As I make this statement, questions may arise, such as: "How does one evaluate the life experience, the totality of one's life?" "How does one assess the quality of one's life?" "By what measure does one gauge whether life has been fragrant, fulfilling, and characteristic of high achievement?" These are important questions, to be sure. To evaluate, assess, measure our life experience, we use four generic categories, each representing a different aspect of our life. They are: 1) financial independence, 2) family stability, 3) personal wellness, and 4) professional success. Collectively, the 'state' of these four categories reflects the *quality of your life* and how you will look back upon your life in totality (see Figure 4.2).

Fig. 4.2

The life experience component represents life outcomes. As such, the life experience reflects, is determined by, choices made or not made, paths taken or not taken, and goals pursued or not pursued, among other things. And what drives the life experience is *the inner soul.*

The Inner Soul

The Inner Soul component reflects soul; specifically, it reflects the desires of soul – what you want in life and from life at this point in your life (a.k.a. inner soul goals). And what we <u>want</u> in life really depends on where we <u>are</u> in life. For example, what we want as a teenager is likely to be much different from what we want in our mid-20's which is again likely to be different from what we want in our 30's, 40's, 50's, and at retirement. The significance of 'wants' is that they represent the foundation of personal strategy. To determine wants, to reveal one's inner soul goals, we use the following personal strategy building blocks (see Figure 4.3):

- Family
- Profession
- Wellness
- Financial
- Leisure

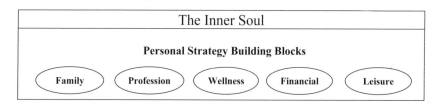

Fig. 4.3

   Most of our inner soul goals align with one of these categories and, therefore, using such categories is helpful in determining what we want in life and from life. However, to get what
we want requires knowing, performing certain key activities; life
pathways.

Life Pathways

Life Pathways represent the activities you must perform to
achieve your inner soul goals. They are 'personal processes' that
characterize everyday living. What is a process? A process is
an organized group of related activities that, together, accom-
plishes a goal. For example, getting ready for work or school in
the morning represents a 'personal process'. There is an organized group of related activities we perform (e.g. wake up, take
a shower, brush our teeth, comb our hair, get dressed, eat break-
fast, leave the house) to accomplish our goal: 'face the world
another day'. In the course of a day, week, month, and year,
each of us initiates and participates in many personal processes
such as:

- The process of [getting ready in the morning]
- The process of [preparing dinner]
- The process of [planning a birthday party]
- The process of [getting to work or school]
- The process of [obtaining employment]
- The process of [planning a vacation]
- The process of [investing]
- The process of [doing homework]

- The process of [maintaining the lawn]
- The process of [completing a tax return]
- The process of [hosting a dinner party]

Some life pathways are common from person to person (e.g. 'shop for groceries') and some are unique (e.g. 'give back to the community'). It is through performing life pathways that we achieve our inner soul goals. As such, inner soul goals provide context for *what* activities (life pathways) to perform; what activities are most important; have a higher priority on the surface of life. Because life pathways derive from inner soul goals, they, by default, align with the personal strategy building blocks mentioned earlier (see Figure 4.4).

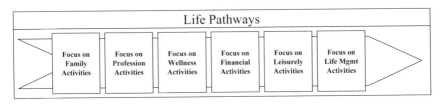

Fig. 4.4

Knowing one's inner soul goals and the life pathways to achieve such goals, however, does not make for complete personal strategy. We need the final link in the causal chain. What we need is commitment.

Commitment

The commitments component of a PSM represents the personal commitments you must make and keep to sustain life's work. There are three forms of personal commitment (see Figure 4.5):

- Mental commitment
- Physical commitment
- Resource commitment

Mental commitment reflects belief that the goal pursued (e.g. lose weight, pursue a college degree, start a business) is

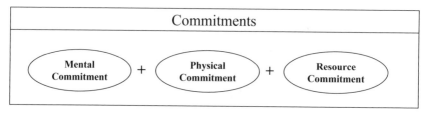

Fig. 4.5

worth paying the price. It reflects keeping our goal top-of-mind
and in our face. Now, while mental commitment is necessary
to achieve a goal, it is not sufficient. It requires deeper commitment; physical commitment. Physical commitment differs in intensity and form in that it represents a movement from belief to
action. For example, you may have a belief of wanting to lose
weight, but if you do not exercise, eat the right foods, and acquire knowledge of healthy living practices, belief alone will not
accomplish your goal. That said, belief and action are still not
sufficient to achieve a goal. It requires yet another form of commitment; resource commitment. To commit resources means to
commit both your time and your money. Continuing with our
example goal of losing weight, if you do not allocate <u>time</u> to exercise and <u>funds</u> to obtain a gym membership or purchase home
exercise equipment, it is unlikely that you will accomplish said
goal. What this example tells us is that all three commitments
(mental, physical, resource) are necessary to achieve a goal; that
each needs the other. We know this to be true, as belief, alone,
is not nearly enough to achieve a goal, and physical commitment
usually requires the follow-on commitment of resources.

To summarize, committing to a goal means that you believe in your goal, act on your goal, and allocate the necessary
resources of time and money to realize your goal. Discussing
the three forms of commitment reveals a chain of linkages that
extends from mental to physical to resource commitment. As
our commitment (to a goal) deepens over time, it increases our
momentum and the probability of achieving our goal (see Figure
4.6). Commitment is the foundation of achievement and achievement requires <u>surrender</u> into commitment.

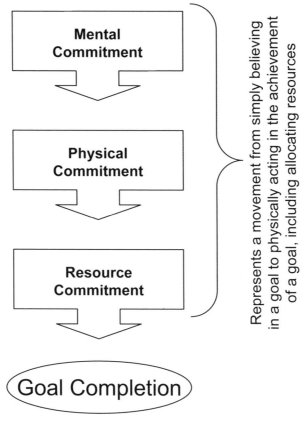

Fig. 4.6

There you have it, the key components to: define personal strategy, establish a roadmap to achieve your goals, and realize a fragrant and fulfilling life experience. The Personal Strategy Map components (see Figure 4.7) define the chain of logic by which one's life experience is driven by one's inner soul goals, the life pathways required to achieve one's goals, and the commitments necessary to sustain life's work.

The power in applying this framework comes from knowing that hidden cause and effect linkages exist from component to component, and it is only through coordinated thinking and acting between each component that we achieve our goals.

Personal Strategy Map Components - Summary Level

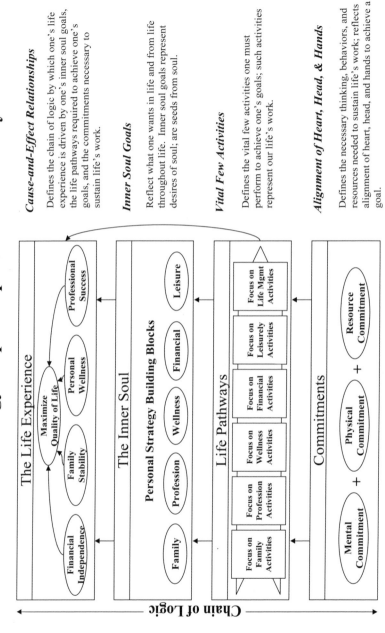

Fig. 4.7

Cause-and-Effect Relationships

Defines the chain of logic by which one's life experience is driven by one's inner soul goals, the life pathways required to achieve one's goals, and the commitments necessary to sustain life's work.

Inner Soul Goals

Reflect what one wants in life and from life throughout life. Inner soul goals represent desires of soul; are seeds from soul.

Vital Few Activities

Defines the vital few activities one must perform to achieve one's goals; such activities represent our life's work.

Alignment of Heart, Head, & Hands

Defines the necessary thinking, behaviors, and resources needed to sustain life's work; reflects alignment of heart, head, and hands to achieve a goal.

The Life Experience

Maximize Quality of Life

Professional Success

Personal Wellness

Family Stability

Financial Independence

The Inner Soul

Personal Strategy Building Blocks

Family | Profession | Wellness | Financial | Leisure

Life Pathways

Focus on Family Activities | Focus on Profession Activities | Focus on Wellness Activities | Focus on Financial Activities | Focus on Leisurely Activities | Focus on Life Mgmt Activities

Commitments

Mental Commitment + Physical Commitment + Resource Commitment

Chain of Logic

Consequently, if I exert necessary mental, physical, and resource commitments, it will result in successfully performing key activities, which will lead to achieving my inner soul goal(s), which will increase my personal happiness and, therefore, the quality of my life.

The time invested in defining and documenting personal strategy is time well spent. However, defining personal strategy requires more than just knowing component parts. It requires knowing form. That is, it requires knowing how to document personal strategy. The tool we use to document personal strategy, to bring it all together, is a Personal Strategy Map Framework.

PSM Framework – Bringing It All Together

Okay. So we know what comprises personal strategy, but how do we document it? To help define personal strategy, to ensure that it is complete, accurate, and effective, we utilize a set of personal strategy frameworks. What is a framework? A framework is a template or container for supporting or enclosing something else (e.g. data, information). As it relates to personal strategy, frameworks help us:

- Organize personal strategy
- Document personal strategy
- Communicate personal strategy
- Adjust and sharpen personal strategy

Because personal strategy is comprised of parts, and because it is only when we bring parts together that we have complete personal strategy, we utilize the PSM Framework (see Figure 4.8).

The PSM Framework represents the first of many frameworks we use to define personal strategy. With the framework serving as our guide, let us review the structure of a Personal Strategy Map. At first glance, we see that the PSM Framework is organized around the four components of personal strategy:

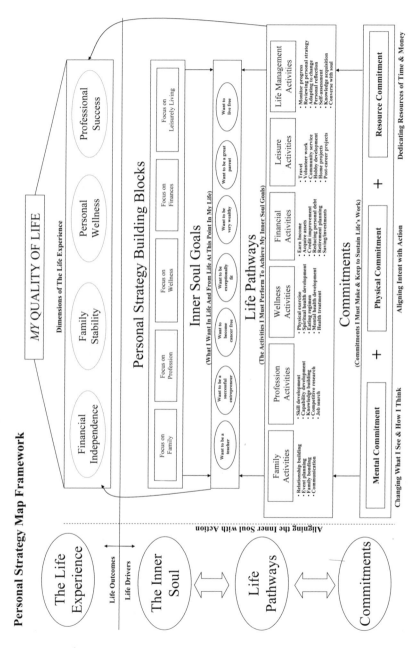

Fig. 4.8

- The Life Experience
- The Inner Soul
- Life Pathways
- Commitments

The life experience component sits atop the PSM Framework. This is deliberate. The life experience component not only highlights the dimensions used to assess our life experience, but also symbolically represents the totality that is *our life* – the outcome from having walked the earth. Our life experience is the culmination of all outcomes experienced over time whether of a financial, family, wellness, or professional nature. And how we perceive such outcomes determines how we perceive our life; the quality of our life. Now, as each of us has different needs, desires, and wants in life, it follows that each of us makes for a different life experience. Despite our differences, however, most people want to live a fragrant life, a life characterized by financial independence, family stability, personal wellness, and professional success. We aspire for financial independence. We aspire for family stability. We aspire for personal wellness. And we aspire for professional success. Each of the dimensions of the life experience represents a shared, innate human desire.

Having said this, the 'what' of life (inner soul goals) and the 'how' of life (life pathways, commitments) largely determine our life. We know this to be true, as to achieve financial independence, have strong family bonds, live a long life, and achieve professional success is largely the result of what we think, what we do, and the personal commitments we keep over time. Therefore, to change the quality of our life, to live a more fragrant life, requires focusing on the 'drivers' of life, beginning with defining our inner soul goals.

The top component of the 'life drivers' section is 'The Inner Soul'. The placement of this component just below the life experience component is also deliberate. Designing personal strategy begins with defining one's inner soul goals; with determining what we want in life and from life. Without knowing such things, we have no context to create meaningful personal strategy; to know what to focus on in life, to improve the quality of our life. The arrow drawn from the inner soul component to the life experience component signifies the relation between inner soul goals and the quality of one's life. Now, to help derive our inner soul goals, we use the personal strategy building blocks. The placement of these building blocks above the inner soul goal component illustrates the support role they play to help define our goals. We document inner soul goals as singular goal statements, as illustrated in the middle of Figure 4.8. Once we define our inner soul goals, we can identify the life pathways to achieve such goals.

Life pathways are personal processes, specific activities, we must perform to achieve our inner soul goals. They represent the 'action' part of the phrase: *'aligning the inner soul with action'*. As such, inner soul goals provide context for which processes to perform; which activities have higher priority on the surface of life. Now, because life pathways derive from inner soul goals, we document life pathways beneath the inner soul goal component on the PSM Framework. To identify which life pathways to perform, we use the same building block categories used to derive our inner soul goals with the addition of one new category*:

- Wellness activities
- Profession activities
- Family activities
- Financial activities
- Leisure activities
- Life-management activities*

These activity categories (see Table 4.2) help us identify, organize, and classify the types of activities we must perform to achieve our goals. With knowing what activities to perform to achieve a goal, the final step to complete a Personal Strategy Map is to identify commitments to sustain life's work.

Table 4.2

Activity Category	Description of Category	Example Activities
Wellness Activities	Wellness is a generic category that encompasses our physical, mental, and spiritual health. Goals of this type require wellness-based activities to achieve such goals.	• Perform exercise • Eat healthy foods • Practice meditation
Profession Activities	Profession is a generic category that represents all professions (e.g. athlete, executive, office worker, homemaker, plumber, musician, educator, etc.) Goals of this type require profession-based activities to achieve such goals.	• Acquire knowledge • Develop skills • Improve capabilities • Search for jobs • Manage career
Family Activities	Family is a generic category that encompasses all aspects of family living (e.g. communication, event planning, family bonding, relationship building, etc.) Goals of this type require family-based activities to achieve such goals.	• Strengthen relationships • Plan family events • Improve communications • Plan family bonding exercises
Financial Activities	Financial is a generic category that encompasses all aspects of personal finance (e.g. maximizing earning power, credit improvement, asset development, debt reduction, retirement planning, etc.) Goals of this type require financial-based activities to achieve such goals.	• Improve credit • Build assets • Maximize earning power • Manage investment portfolio
Leisure Activities	Leisure is a generic category that encompasses all aspects of leisurely living (e.g. traveling, community service, volunteer work, post-career projects, writing a book, etc.) Goals of this type require leisure-based activities to achieve such goals.	• Perform community service • Plan travel • Develop hobbies • Volunteer time and money
Life Management Activities	Life management activities are support activities we perform to assess condition/change condition, to course correct personal strategy, and to keep goals top-of-mind and in our face.	• Personal reflection • Assess personal strategy • Adapt to change • Monitor results • Acquire knowledge

We document commitments at the bottom of the PSM Framework. This, too, is deliberate. Commitments are the foundation of achievement. As such, its placement at the bottom of the PSM framework symbolically represents its importance in achieving personal strategy. Without mental, physical, and resource commitment, it is impossible to achieve any goal. You can know <u>what</u> you want in life and <u>how</u> to get what you want, but without commitment, your goals will die on the vine. This is certain.

So, to summarize, the PSM framework is a container we use to define, organize, and document personal strategy. The PSM Framework provides needed structure to create our Personal Strategy Map, which, when complete, represents our high-level strategy for living. It communicates: 1) what we want in life and from life at any point in life, 2) how we are going to get what we want, and 3) the commitment needed to sustain life's work. To cement our learnings of the PSM components and the PSM Framework, an example Personal Strategy Map follows.

Understanding a Personal Strategy Map: An Illustrated Example

Up to this point, our discussion has focused on the components and structure of a Personal Strategy Map. We conclude our introduction to Personal Strategy Maps by reviewing a sample PSM. Now, because Personal Strategy Maps derive from the PSM Framework, we would expect to see the usual suspects: The Life Experience component, Inner Soul component, Life Pathways component, and Commitments component (see Figure 4.9).

The only notable differences between our sample PSM and the PSM Framework are the removal of the personal strategy building blocks and a rearrangement of the life management section in the life pathways component. Personal strategy building blocks represent more a tool of personal strategy than an element

Personal Strategy Map

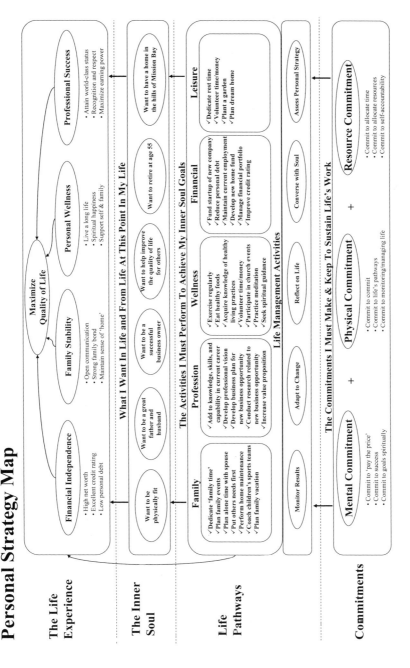

Fig. 4.9

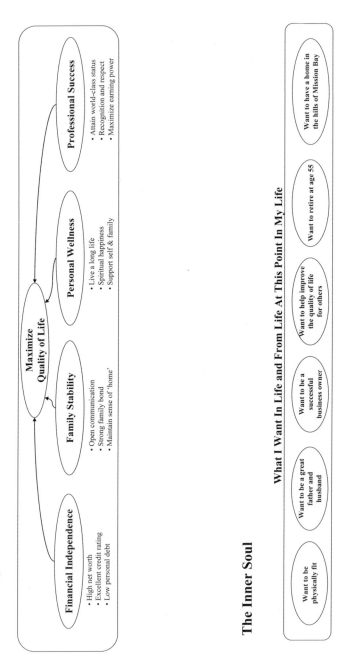

The Life Experience

Fig. 4.10

The Inner Soul

Fig. 4.11

of personal strategy. As such, we do not show personal strategy building blocks on our Personal Strategy Map. In addition, positioning the life management activities beneath the other life pathway activities illustrates the support role life management activities play to achieve our goals. We begin by discussing the life experience component (see Figure 4.10).

Because the life experience component represents effect rather than cause, we document our <u>hoped-for</u> life outcomes in this area. The illustration shows us that this individual hopes for many things. Concerning finances, he hopes to achieve high net worth, an excellent credit rating, and to maintain low debt. Concerning family, he hopes for open communication, strong family bond, and maintaining a sense of 'home'. Concerning wellness, he hopes to live a long life, possess happy spirit, and support self and family. Lastly, concerning profession, he hopes to attain world-class status, receive recognition and respect, and earn a high income. By making explicit our hoped-for outcomes in life, we can subsequently design a strategy to realize such life.

As discussed, the inner soul goals component communicates desires of soul. They represent bold, significant goals that will maximize personal happiness. Collectively, such goals reflect our vision for self. Similar to how companies develop corporate vision (to realize corporate soul) by answering the question: 'Wouldn't it be great if in five years we...', so, too, do we, as individuals, develop personal vision (to realize individual soul) by answering the question: 'What do I want in life and from life at this point in my life?' Figure 4.11 reflects sample vision, sample goals.

What Figure 4.11 communicates is an individual's desire to:

- Be physically fit
- Be a great father and husband
- Be a successful business owner
- Help improve the quality of life for others
- Retire at age 55
- Have a house in the hills of Mission Bay

It is worth noting that such goals span all personal strategy building block categories (see Table 4.3). Although this practice is not mandatory, it is recommended, as defining goals that span all building block categories ensures balance in your life.

Table 4.3

Building Block Category	Inner Soul Goal
Focus on family	• Be a great father and husband
Focus on profession	• Be a successful business owner
Focus on personal wellness	• Be physically fit • Help improve the quality of life for others
Focus on finances	• Retire at age 55
Focus on leisurely living	• Live in the hills of Mission Bay

Only when we identify our inner soul goals do we have proper context to identify the activities to achieve such goals. Figure 4.12 highlights the activities to perform to achieve the inner soul goals stated above.

Because inner soul goals provide context for identifying life's pathways, it follows that if we define a wellness-based goal, we would also define wellness-based life pathways to achieve such goal. Similarly, if we define professional goals, it follows that we would define related activities within the profession life pathway category. For example, one of the goals stated above is 'be physically fit'. To achieve this goal requires performing the following activities as reflected under the wellness category:

- Exercise regularly
- Eat healthy foods
- Acquire knowledge of healthy living practices

In addition to performing these <u>primary</u> activities, to achieve this goal also requires performing the following <u>support</u> activities as reflected in the life management category:

- Monitor results
- Adapt to change

Life Pathways

The Activities I Must Perform To Achieve My Inner Soul Goals

Family	Profession	Wellness	Financial	Leisure
✓Dedicate 'family time' ✓Plan family events ✓Plan alone time with spouse ✓Put others needs first ✓Perform home maintenance ✓Coach children's sports teams ✓Plan family vacation	✓Add to knowledge, skills, and capability in current career ✓Develop professional vision ✓Develop business plan for new business opportunity ✓Conduct research related to new business opportunity ✓Increase value proposition	✓Exercise regularly ✓Eat healthy foods ✓Acquire knowledge of healthy living practices ✓Volunteer time/money ✓Participate in church events ✓Practice meditation ✓Seek spiritual guidance	✓Fund startup of new company ✓Reduce personal debt ✓Maintain current employment ✓Develop new home fund ✓Manage financial portfolio ✓Improve credit rating	✓Dedicate rest time ✓Volunteer time/money ✓Plant a garden ✓Plan dream home

Life Management Activities

(Monitor Results)   (Adapt to Change)   (Reflect on Life)   (Converse with Soul)   (Assess Personal Strategy)

Fig. 4.12

Commitments

The Commitments I Must Make & Keep To Sustain Life's Work

(**Mental Commitment**) + (**Physical Commitment**) + (**Resource Commitment**)

- Commit to 'pay the price'
- Commit to success
- Commit to goals spiritually

- Commit to commit
- Commit to life's pathways
- Commit to monitoring/managing life

- Commit to allocate time
- Commit to allocate resources
- Commit to self-accountability

Fig. 4.13

- Reflect on life
- Converse with soul
- Assess personal strategy

Lastly, it is only through personal commitment that we maintain energy, enthusiasm, and focus to sustain life's work (see Figure 4.13).

As we will discuss in Chapter 6, the commitment required to achieve one goal is often times the same commitment required to achieve other goals. For example, all inner soul goals require mental commitment to 'pay the price', physical commitment to monitor and manage one's progress, and resource commitment of time. Now, in addition to these more 'generic' commitments, certain goals require unique commitments. As such, when defining personal strategy, we need to make these 'other' commitments explicit as well.

There you have it, a complete Personal Strategy Map. What can we say about this personal strategy? Earlier, we discussed how the essence of personal strategy represents a movement from 'present position' in life to a desirable, but uncertain, 'future position' in life. If we apply this to our sample PSM, we could say this individual is moving from an undesirable present position in life to an uncertain, but desirable, future position in life (see Table 4.4):

Table 4.4

Undesirable Present Position	Desirable Future Position
Overweight	Physically fit
Perceived as a less attentive father and husband	Perceived as a great father and husband
Spend little time helping others	Dedicated to helping others improve the quality of their life
Work for others	Work for self
Unable to retire at age 55	Able to retire at age 55
Location does not inspire soul	Living in a location of inspiration

What else can we observe about this personal strategy?

- Represents a new life plan leading to a happier, more meaningful, and fragrant life experience
- Strategy is balanced across all personal strategy building blocks
- Strategy is focused on five to seven inner soul goals
- Inner soul section represents what one wants in life and from life at this point in life (i.e., desires of soul)
- Life pathways section highlights the vital few activities to achieve stated goals
- Commitments section highlights needed commitment to sustain life's work

The observations listed above represent best practices, guidelines, to define complete, accurate, and effective personal strategy. We will revisit such guidelines in Chapter 6.

Let us pause to review our learnings thus far:

- We understand the content of personal strategy
- We understand how to create personal strategy
- We know what personal strategy looks like

This is a good start. When building personal strategy, it is important to establish foundational knowledge first. Then, with theory, tools, and practical examples to work from, you too can define and execute your own personal strategy, and what great things will come from that! One question you may now be asking is, 'How does one use a Personal Strategy Map?' I know what comprises a PSM, I understand the structure of a PSM, I've seen a sample PSM, but how do I use it? This is an important question, which we address in the next chapter on Personal Strategic Themes. In the meantime, let us conclude our introduction to Personal Strategy Maps by answering a related question, "Why use a personal strategy?" After all, it's not like at any point during our schooling were we required to take a class on 'Developing Personal Strategy'. Furthermore, are there not people who are getting along just fine without having a personal strategy? Well, the short answer is life does not mandate using personal strategy. To have personal strategy is to exercise choice, a choice that proudly asserts, "I do not want to live an average life or simply get by. I want to live a remarkable life, and having a personal strategy will help me realize it". To exercise such choice reminds me of an insight obtained when selling insurance, and that is people do not plan to fail (in life) they fail to plan. The point is if you do not have an explicit plan for your life, then, by default, you have no plan, and not having a plan for your life has but one outcome: *a life diminished*.

Developing personal strategy is becoming increasingly relevant given the complex and ever changing times in which we live. We are not living in simple times! As a case in point, compare the complexities and pace of life today with that of life in the mid 1850's. Which time period was more complex and characteristic of change? Now fast forward. Compare today's complexities and pace of life with that of the 1950's. There is still no comparison. Today's complexities are far greater and pace of life faster than of any other period in human history and this will only accelerate. If we acknowledge the complex, fast-paced, competitive times in which we live, then having a method (i.e., personal strategy) to manage such complexity, manage such change would be of high value. Every January, millions of people declare to self and world their New Year's resolutions. This activity represents a good, albeit, beginner's approach to developing personal strategy. For some, the exercise is formal, with goals explicitly defined, complete with milestone dates, action plans, etc. For others, the process is less formal, involving simple declarations. Whatever the form, both approaches suffer limitations:

- Lack a holistic approach to define goals that span all dimensions of one's life (family, profession, wellness, financial, leisure)
- Ad-hoc approach results in gaps in one's personal strategy

- The drivers of personal strategy (inner soul goals, life pathways, and commitment) and the cause and effect relations between them are largely ignored
- Inconsistent approach to document and track goals over time
- Lack of supporting process to manage goals and adapt personal strategy as circumstances change (e.g. self and environment)
- Approach lacks rigor, precision, and structure thereby diminishing effectiveness of personal strategy

When one considers the limitations of using alternative approaches to defining personal strategy, injecting rigor, formality into the process should be a precondition for all such work. Unfortunately, because most people do not seek to understand the whole of personal strategy, their actions to enact personal change are often limited and, therefore, ineffective. Hence, the value of the PSM Framework is at last revealed.

We have reached chapter's end. As such, we can now answer the question, 'Why use a Personal Strategy Map'? We use a Personal Strategy Map because it:

- Provides structure for defining, organizing, and documenting personal strategy
- Injects rigor to the process of developing personal strategy
- Ensures balance; it results in a well-defined strategy reflective of one's inner soul goals
- Enables quick development of personal strategy to realize dreams and maximize the quality of life
- Approaches building personal strategy from a systems (holistic) point of view
- Considers the design of personal strategy from multiple perspectives (family, profession, wellness, financial, leisure)
- Considers the drivers of the life experience (inner soul goals, life pathways, and commitments) and their relations to one another to create effective personal strategy

Creating personal strategy is relevant for all groups of people. I use the phrase 'groups of people' versus individual because
personal strategy differs quite significantly, depending on <u>where</u>
one is in life. Having said this, Personal Strategy Maps are applicable to all segments of the population:

- Students
- Working professionals
- Retirees

Naturally, there are many shades of gray within each category. For example, 'Students' represent high school students,
undergraduate students, graduate students, or adult-learning
students. Working professionals represent those who have just
entered the workforce, mid-career professionals, or seasoned
professionals and encompasses all professions, whether artist,
athlete, executive, laborer, musician, river guide, or homemaker.
Retirees represent those who have exited the workforce. Figures
4.14, 4.15, and 4.16 illustrate sample Personal Strategy Maps
for the generic groupings stated above.

You will notice that the design and purpose of each
Personal Strategy Map is the same regardless of group. That
is, each map communicates personal vision, inner soul goals,
and high-level strategy based on stage in life. Goals, life pathways, and commitments may differ, but the underlying essence
is the same – to help people realize a better life; to maximize
the quality of life. Think of a Personal Strategy Map as your
roadmap for living. Consequently, as you change, so, too, does
your PSM change. What this implies is that personal strategy is not static. Just as you are a living, breathing entity, so,
too, is your PSM a living, breathing entity. In this way, your
personal strategy always reflects <u>what</u> you want in life based
on <u>where</u> you are in life (see Figure 4.17). Whether you are a
student, working professional, or retiree, having a personal strategy to navigate life is smart and relevant.

Consider your present day position in life. Now, imagine
you had a personal strategy long ago. Imagine you had a personal strategy before entering college or at the beginning of your

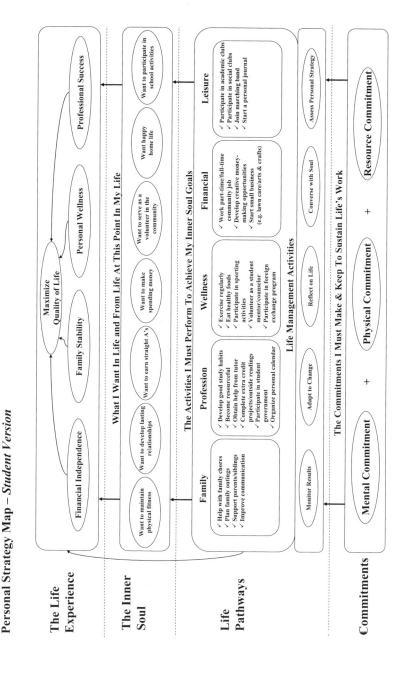

Fig. 4.14

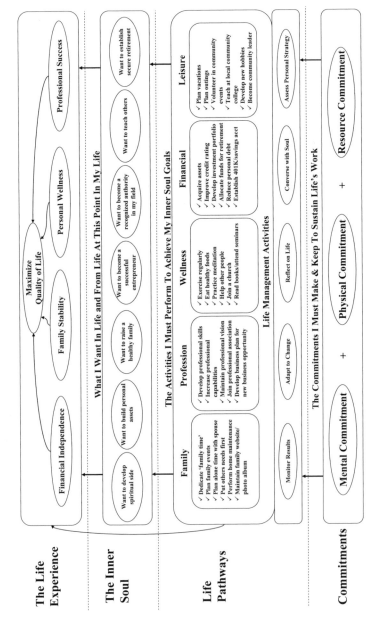

Fig. 4.15

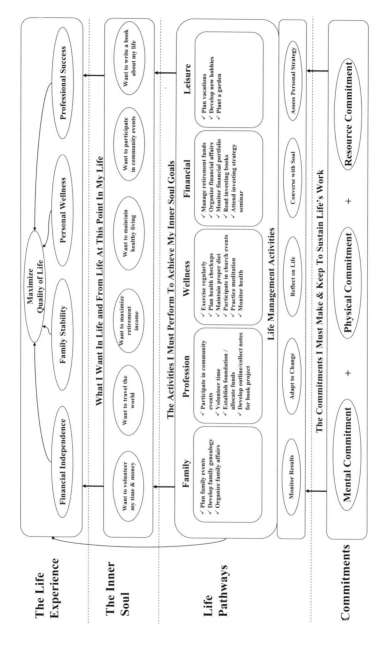

Fig. 4.16

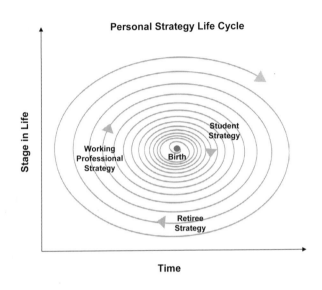

Fig. 4.17

professional career. I can envision a completely different trajectory for my life. I can imagine greater happiness, greater success,
and faster execution of goals and dreams. Not all is lost, however, as there is still time to align your inner soul with action. For
me, writing this book represents, in part, living a new trajectory.
I am pursuing an inner soul goal long dormant but now fiercely
front-and-center. Having a personal strategy (plan) reflecting
soul coupled with a methodology and set of frameworks to drive
soul's plan is a profoundly powerful state to live in. **The future
you wants to 'emerge'.** My goal is to help you make that happen. Stay with me, continue this journey, field walk, and with
courage, faith, and enthusiasm, you, too, will be free.

Personal Strategy Maps are powerful tools for implementing personal change. However, use of PSM's alone is not
enough, as they only communicate the 'what' of personal strategy. Consequently, we have more work to do, as we need to
define the 'how' of personal strategy, the nuts and bolts details.
To define the 'how' of personal strategy, we use a companion
framework to the PSM called a Personal Strategic Theme. We
discuss this next.

Introduction to Personal Strategic Themes

"He who every morning plans the transaction of the day and follows out that plan, carries a thread that will guide him through the maze of the most busy life. But where no plan is laid, where the disposal of time is surrendered merely to the chance of incidence, chaos will soon reign."

-Victor Hugo

IN THE PREVIOUS CHAPTER, we learned what personal strategy is, including how to define the 'what' of personal strategy using a Personal Strategy Map. However, defining personal strategy requires more than simply asserting *what* you want in life. It also requires defining *how* to get what you want in life. As such, our work is not yet done. To define the 'how' of personal strategy, we utilize another framework from the personal strategy toolbox: a Personal Strategic Theme. A Personal Strategic Theme (PST) is a companion framework to the PSM used to help define, organize, and document tactical level details to achieve a goal. In this way, Personal Strategic Themes are a natural extension of PSM's in that they capture, reflect lower level granularity when defining personal strategy. In this chapter, you will learn that PST's represent our 'theories of success'; of how vision becomes reality. They are our plans to which, and with which, we greet each day. They are our way out, our way through, our way to a better life.

Personal Strategic Themes

We began our discussion of Personal Strategy Maps by defining the terms 'personal strategy' and 'map'. We continue this approach by first defining the word 'theme', as in Personal Strategic Theme. The word 'theme' represents, equates to, a specific inner soul goal. For example, if we had an inner soul goal to 'be exceptionally fit', then the goal 'be exceptionally fit' would become the 'theme' of a PST, and the resulting PST would reflect content (i.e., strategy) related to achieving only this goal. Consequently, if we view a PSM as a tool to help define and communicate our entire personal strategy, we can view a PST as a tool to help define and communicate a piece of our personal strategy (see Figure 5.1).

What this tells us is that while each PST spans, reflects the four components of a PSM, each is focused on achieving only a single inner soul goal (e.g. 'start my own business'). Because the focus of PST's is to achieve a single inner soul goal, a PST is, in effect, a single-goal strategy. We segment personal strategy into multiple PST's because each inner soul goal requires its own activities, commitments, and action plans to achieve the goal. An alternative would be to create a single PST to represent all inner soul goals but the resulting document would prove too complex and too confusing to be useful. Segmenting personal strategy allows us to focus effort and manage complexity by planning the achievement of only one inner soul goal at a time. Similar to how problem solving is improved by dividing a complex problem into several smaller, but more manageable, sub-problems, so, too, is personal strategy development improved by dividing whole personal strategy (PSM) into several smaller, but more manageable, sub-strategies (PST's). What results from segmenting personal strategy into parts is a portfolio of PST's (see Figure 5.2).

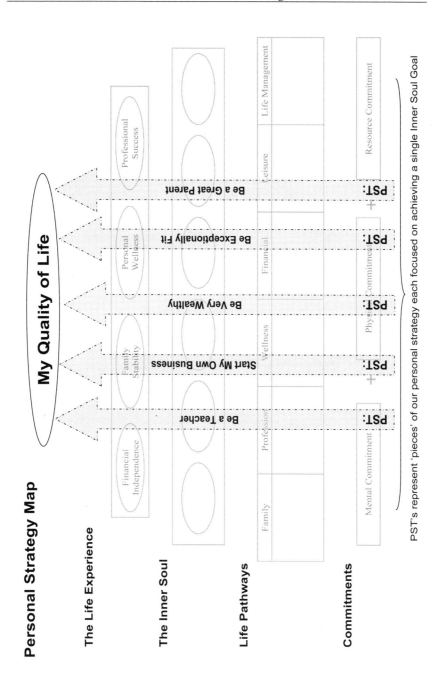

Fig. 5.1

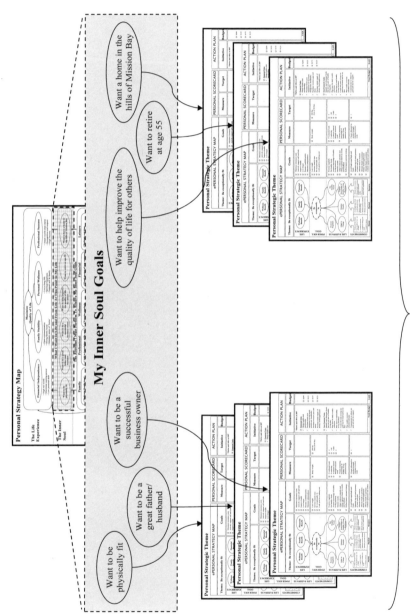

Fig. 5.2

Hence, the more inner soul goals we have, the more effort is required to define and manage personal strategy. For this reason, we limit the number of inner soul goals to <u>between five and seven,</u> as this will enable achievement of all your goals. To ensure clarity, Table 5.1 summarizes the differences between a PSM and a PST:

Table 5.1

Personal Strategy Map	Personal Strategic Theme
√ Communicates our <u>entire</u> personal strategy	√ Communicates a <u>piece of</u> our personal strategy
√ Reflects all inner soul goals	√ Reflects one inner soul goal
√ Reflects high-level activities to achieve all inner soul goals	√ Reflects activities to achieve a single inner soul goal
√ Reflects high-level commitments to achieve all inner soul goals	√ Reflects commitments to achieve a single inner soul goal
√ We create one PSM	√ We create many PST's
√ Represents whole	√ Represents part of a whole
√ Is the parent document	√ Is the child document

Knowing the purposes of and differences between a PSM and a PST is important, as we need both frameworks to define personal strategy. Since Personal Strategic Themes derive from Personal Strategy Maps, each PST is comprised of parts that, like a PSM, work together as a system to achieve our goals.

The components of a PST are:

- Embedded Personal Strategy Map (ePSM)
- Personal Scorecard
- Action Plan

The ePSM defines strategy to achieve a single inner soul goal. The Personal Scorecard defines performance measures to monitor our progress. Finally, the Action Plan details specific initiatives and tasks to execute strategy. It is through the interconnections, cause and effect relations between components of the Personal Strategic Theme that enable it to serve as a roadmap to achieve your goals (see Figure 5.3).

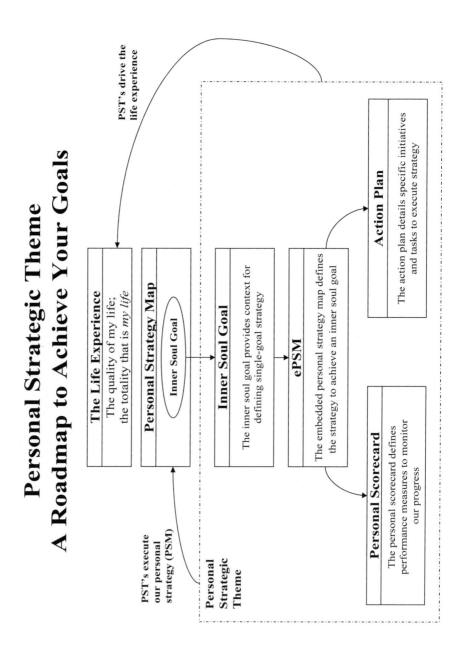

Fig. 5.3

Together, the components of a Personal Strategic Theme provide us a framework from which we can define, organize, document, and now implement personal strategy. To understand the power and usefulness of this framework, we define each component individually then look at how the Personal Strategic Theme Framework brings it all together to form single-goal strategy.

Components of a Personal Strategic Theme

As discussed, each PST consists of three components that work together as a system to achieve our goals. We discuss first the Embedded Personal Strategy Map.

Embedded Personal Strategy Map

When creating Embedded Personal Strategy Maps, our focus is to define strategy to achieve a <u>single</u> inner soul goal. We do this as each inner soul goal is unique and, thus, requires its own strategy to achieve the goal. For example, the activities and commitments required to achieve the goal 'be exceptionally fit' are not the same as those required to achieve the goal 'start my own business'. There may be some overlap, but for all intents and purposes, each goal requires its own strategy. Therefore, the ePSM serves as a container to define, organize, and document strategy to achieve a single goal. The components of an ePSM are the same as those that comprise our parent PSM with one additional component*:

- Inner Soul Goal
- Life Pathways
- Commitments
- Support Goals*

Collectively, the inner soul goal, life pathways, and commitments sections represent single-goal strategy. Such components communicate not only what we want, but also our plan to get what we want. Now, to this we add support goals. We add support goals to drive our inner soul goal. For example, suppose you had a goal 'start my own business'. To achieve this goal, it requires you achieve several smaller, but no less important, <u>support goals</u>:

- Develop business plan
- Incorporate business
- Develop product
- Develop marketing material
- Develop business website
- Establish corporate checking account
- Establish line-of-credit
- Develop press release

As the above indicates, support goals represent short-term goals, whereas our inner soul goal represents a long-term goal. The significance, relevance of support goals is that *if we achieve our support goals, we will, by default, achieve our inner soul goal.* Figure 5.4 illustrates the two components that comprise an ePSM.

To distinguish the two PSM types, Table 5.2 summarizes the differences between an embedded PSM and its parent PSM.

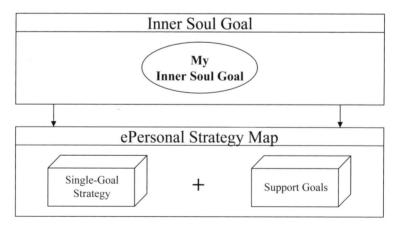

Fig. 5.4

Table 5.2

Embedded PSM	Parent PSM
Defines tactical-level strategy to achieve a single inner soul goal	Defines high-level strategy to achieve all inner soul goals
Life experience component highlights life outcomes from achieving a single inner soul goal	Life experience component highlights life outcomes from achieving all inner soul goals
Life pathways component highlights activities to achieve a single inner soul goal	Life pathways component highlights activities to achieve all inner soul goals
Commitments component highlights commitments to achieve a single inner soul goal	Commitments component highlights commitments to achieve all inner soul goals
Includes support goals	Does not include support goals

Personal Scorecard

Each Personal Strategic Theme also includes a 'personal scorecard' comprised of performance measures and target values (see Figure 5.5).

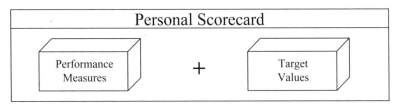

Fig. 5.5

We use performance measures to obtain feedback and indicate progress with achieving our inner soul goal and support goals. What is a measure? For our purposes, a measure is a quantitative data point that, when graphed, helps us determine degree and direction of progress made with achieving our goals.

For example, if your goal is 'be exceptionally fit', you might define the following performance measures to indicate progress with achieving this goal:

- # pounds weight lost/week
- # times exercised/week
- # hours exercised/week
- # carbohydrates consumed/daily
- # calories burned exercising/week
- # hours acquiring knowledge of healthy living practices/ week

By tracking the measures above, we can evaluate whether our strategy (ePSM) to become exceptionally fit is working. We may discover, for example, that carbohydrate intake has no bearing on our fitness. Similarly, we may discover that unless we exercise 10 hours/week, we do not lose weight. In addition to identifying performance measures, we also define target values for each measure. What is a target value? A target value represents our personal performance goal with respect to a measure. For example, we may specify a target value of [90] for the performance measure [# carbohydrates consumed/daily] or specify a target value of [5] for the performance measure [# times exercised/week]. Target values not only drive personal performance, but also establish a comparative against which to evaluate one's progress. Together, performance measures and target values help us achieve our inner soul goal.

Now, as tracking and reporting performance measures requires time and effort, we must define measures judiciously so as not to overburden ourselves with busy work. Because our parent PSM has between five and seven inner soul goals, we limit the number of performance measures to the same amount for each goal. Thus, if you have five inner soul goals, you might have upwards of 35 performance measures across all goals. This may seem like a lot of 'performance measuring', but I can assure you that the effort required to track even 35 measures will not prove burdensome. Ultimately, the number of measures you implement is your choice. It is important to remember that while tracking scorecard measures is useful, we do not want to lose sight of our real mission: *to achieve our inner soul goal*. In other words, do not let the tool (Personal Scorecard) get in the way of the work. Having said all this, support goals, measures, and targets, while necessary, are not sufficient to achieve an inner soul goal. What we also need is an action plan.

Action Plan

The 'action plan' section of a PST is comprised of two components: initiatives and budgets (see Figure 5.6).

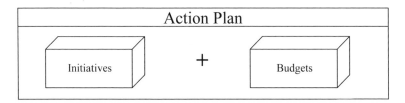

Fig. 5.6

Initiatives are the mechanism by which we execute personal strategy. And initiatives are comprised of tasks; specific actions we perform to achieve a goal. As such, action plans detail our 'opening moves'. For example, if I had an inner soul goal to 'be exceptionally fit' by reaching a target weight of 205 pounds, I might define an initiative, 'Thrive and Alive at 205'. Defining initiatives to achieve one's inner soul goal is similar to how a company might define an initiative to improve product quality (e.g. 'Quality is Job 1' at Ford Motor Company). The <u>tasks</u> associated with the initiative, 'Thrive and Alive at 205', might be:

- Obtain gym membership
- Hire personal trainer
- Purchase exercise gear
- Purchase dietary supplements

- Schedule time to exercise
- Begin healthy eating regimen
- Purchase health magazine subscription
- Enroll in nutrition education class
- Etc…

Some tasks require investing money. All tasks require investing time. This echoes back to our need to commit resources of time and money to accomplish a goal, as desire alone will not suffice. If a task requires investing money, establish a budget, as this will help with planning the timing and execution of initiative tasks.

There you have it, the key components to define precise strategy to achieve any goal. The Personal Strategic Theme Components (see Figure 5.7) define the chain of logic by which we achieve a goal through the coordinated action of an ePSM, Personal Scorecard, and Action Plan.

The power in applying this framework comes from knowing that hidden cause and effect linkages exist from component to component and that it is only through coordinated thinking and acting that we achieve our goals.

Defining tactical-level strategy to achieve a goal, however, requires more than just knowing component parts. It requires knowing form. That is, it requires knowing how to document single-goal strategy. We discuss documenting single-goal strategy, bring it all together, next, in the section on the Personal Strategic Theme Framework.

PST Framework – Bringing It All Together

Okay. So we know what comprises single-goal strategy. Now the question is, "How do we document it?" To document single-goal strategy, we use another framework from the personal strategy toolbox: the PST Framework (see Figure 5.8).

The PST Framework is another framework we use to define, organize, document, and, now, implement personal strategy. Using the framework as a guide, let us review the structure

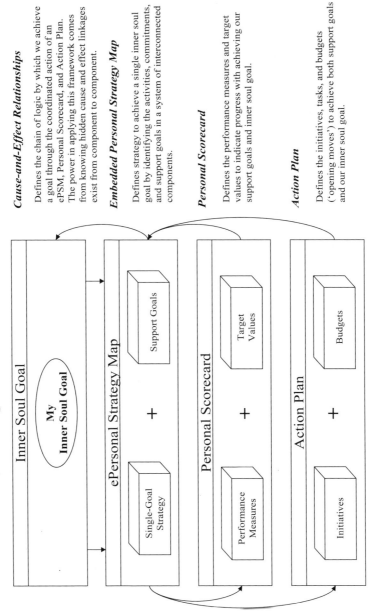

Personal Strategic Theme Components - Summary Level

Inner Soul Goal

My Inner Soul Goal

ePersonal Strategy Map

Single-Goal Strategy + Support Goals

Personal Scorecard

Performance Measures + Target Values

Action Plan

Initiatives + Budgets

Cause-and-Effect Relationships

Defines the chain of logic by which we achieve a goal through the coordinated action of an ePSM, Personal Scorecard, and Action Plan. The power in applying this framework comes from knowing hidden cause and effect linkages exist from component to component.

Embedded Personal Strategy Map

Defines strategy to achieve a single inner soul goal by identifying the activities, commitments, and support goals in a system of interconnected components.

Personal Scorecard

Defines the performance measures and target values to indicate progress with achieving our support goals and inner soul goal.

Action Plan

Defines the initiatives, tasks, and budgets ('opening moves') to achieve both support goals and our inner soul goal.

Fig. 5.7

Personal Strategic Theme Framework

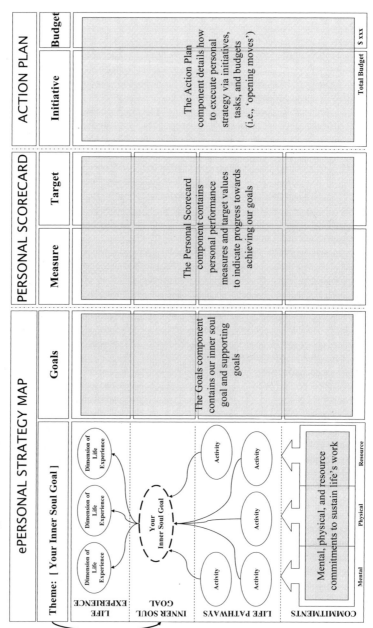

Fig. 5.8

of a Personal Strategic Theme. As described in the last section, the PST Framework is organized around three components:

- ePersonal Strategy Map
- Personal Scorecard
- Action Plan

When creating a PST, the ePersonal Strategy Map is the first component to define. You will notice in Figure 5.8 that there are placeholders to record the following:

- PST theme (i.e., inner soul goal)
- Dimensions of the life experience that benefit from achieving your inner soul goal
- Inner soul goal (restatement from PSM)
- Life pathways to achieve your inner soul goal
- Mental, physical, and resource commitments to sustain life's work
- Support goals

Upon developing your Personal Strategy Map, you should have nearly all the raw material needed to complete an ePSM. Consequently, completing the ePSM is largely a matter of filling in the blanks. Having said this, some refinement of past work may be required. For example, you may need to redefine your life pathways in more specific (granular) terms. Further, you may need to define more precise commitments to support life pathways. Also, the goals section of an ePSM is new and, therefore, will require additional effort to complete. The goals section contains placeholders to record support goals in addition to your inner soul goal. Once we define our ePSM, we can then develop our personal scorecard.

Within the PST Framework, the personal scorecard component lies just to the right of the ePSM. This is deliberate. Only upon developing strategy to achieve a goal can we define measures to monitor progress towards such achievement. The personal scorecard contains placeholders to define measures and targets for the Life Experience, Inner Soul Goal, Life Pathways, and Commitments sections. Defining performance measures to indicate progress, effectiveness with personal strategy, is a matter of trial and error. We will discuss the art and science that is defining performance measures in Chapter 6 on Building Personal Strategy.

The personal scorecard, as discussed, is comprised of two components: measures and targets. Whereas a goal statement communicates desired outcome, a measure tells us (directly/indirectly) how we are doing to realize outcome. For example, I may have a goal to 'lose 40 lbs'. The goal communicates desired outcome, but, on its own, does little to indicate progress towards achieving my goal. This is the role of performance measures. Consequently, to indicate weight loss, I would measure 'body weight' or '# pounds lost' or both. Because measures are specific and precise, they are good proxies for indicating progress. Targets, on the other hand, communicate a specific desired outcome relative to each measure. Establishing targets is necessary, as measures are only relevant within the context of a target value. Target values not only inspire us to achieve our goals, but also establish a comparative against which we can evaluate progress. Once we define our personal scorecard, we can then develop an action plan to implement strategy. Action plans represent our 'opening moves'. They detail the initiatives and tasks to achieve our goals. The PST Framework contains a placeholder to record specific actions to achieve our goals. Additionally, the Action Plan section contains a placeholder to record budget information for tasks requiring funding.

Now, to fully leverage the PST Framework requires understanding the dependencies, cause and effect relations, between the components of the PST framework, beginning with the ePSM component. For example, it requires understanding that the life experience is driven by inner soul goals and inner soul goals are driven by life pathways, which in turn are driven by personal commitments. Without understanding such interdependencies and others that underlie the framework, you lack the knowledge of how framework components work together as a system to achieve our goals, resulting in flawed personal strategy (see Figure 5.9).

PST Framework Interdependencies

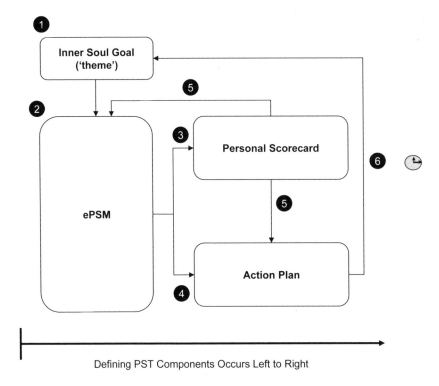

Defining PST Components Occurs Left to Right

Fig. 5.9

As illustrated, defining a Personal Strategic Theme occurs left to right, beginning with 1) stating the 'theme' of the PST (i.e., inner soul goal). With theme defined, we have context to 2) create the strategy (ePSM) to achieve our goal. With strategy defined, we can 3) develop a personal scorecard to monitor our progress and 4) draft an action plan that constitutes our 'opening moves'. Over time, 5) our personal scorecard reveals the effectiveness of our strategy and action plan initiatives and, therefore, the type of course corrections required to improve strategy, tweak initiatives. Lastly, 6) with willful action and time, we achieve our inner soul goal.

To summarize, Personal Strategic Themes:

- Are a companion framework to the PSM
- Serve as a container to define, organize, document, and implement tactical-level strategy to achieve a goal
- Represent single-goal strategy
- Are comprised of parts that work together as a system for a common goal

Whereas, before, we only knew the 'what' of personal strategy (PSM), now, we know the 'how' (PST). This is perhaps the single greatest benefit from using PST's. *We now know HOW to manufacture achievement with confidence, rigor, and precision.* No longer does life direct us; we direct life. To cement our learnings of the PST components and the PST Framework, an example Personal Strategic Theme follows.

Understanding a Personal Strategic Theme: An Illustrated Example

Up to this point, our discussion has focused on the components and structure of a Personal Strategic Theme. We conclude our introduction to Personal Strategic Themes by reviewing a sample PST (see Figure 5.10).

This PST reflects personal strategy to achieve the goal 'be exceptionally fit'. As such, the life pathways, personal commitments, support goals, performance measures, initiatives, and tasks reflected on the PST all support achieving only this goal (theme).

We begin by examining the visual component of the Embedded Personal Strategy Map (see Figure 5.11).

Personal Strategic Theme

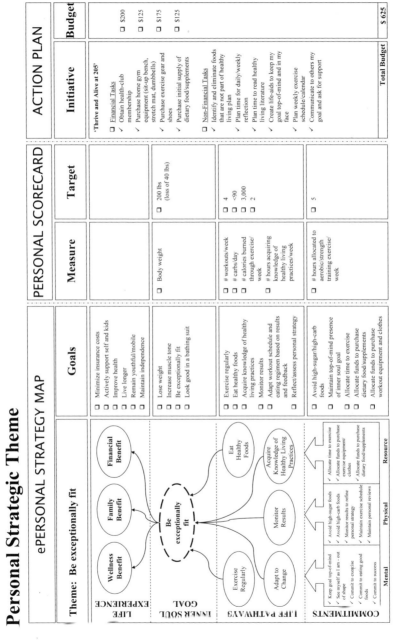

Fig. 5.10

At first glance, we notice that the theme name and the inner soul goal name are the same. This is deliberate, as each

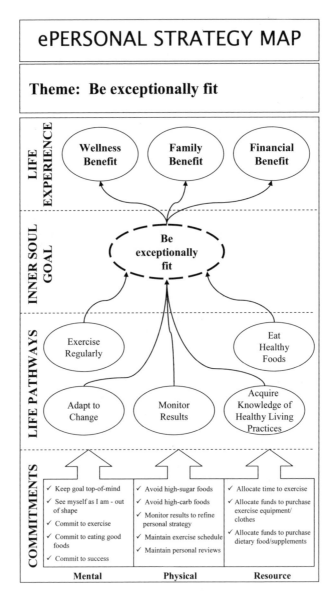

Fig. 5.11

PST reflects only one inner soul goal. We descend deeper, to life pathways, which indicate those activities necessary to achieve our fitness goal:

- Exercise regularly
- Eat healthy foods
- Acquire knowledge of healthy living practices
- Monitor results
- Adapt to change

These activities (i.e., personal processes) work together as a system to effect change, that is, to achieve the goal: exceptional fitness. However, as we learned when discussing PSM's, performing life's pathways is not enough; we need commitment. To sustain the aforementioned activities requires maintaining the following mental, physical, and resource commitments:

Mental:

- Keep goal top-of-mind
- See myself as I am – out of shape
- Commit to exercise regularly
- Commit to eating good foods
- Commit to success (i.e., 'paying the price')

Physical:

- Deliberately avoid high-sugar foods
- Deliberately avoid high-carb foods
- Monitor results
- Maintain exercise schedule
- Maintain personal reviews

Resource:

- Allocate time to exercise
- Allocate funds to purchase exercise equipment/clothes
- Allocate funds to purchase dietary food/supplements

Finally, if we achieve our goal of exceptional fitness, if we maintain commitments, execute life pathways, and course correct personal strategy when needed, we realize several benefits, as indicated in the life experience section:

- Wellness benefits
  - Live longer
  - Improve health
  - Remain youthful/mobile
  - Maintain independence

- Family benefits
  - Actively support family and kids

- Financial benefits
  - Minimize health insurance/life insurance costs

Now, whereas the ePSM provides visual strategy to achieve your inner soul goal, the goals section (of the ePSM) makes strategy explicit with written goal statements which, in turn, facilitates defining performance measures to achieve such goals. The goal statements that appear on an ePSM are 'textual equivalents' of what appears in map form (see Figure 5.12).

Documenting strategy in goal form helps us transition from thinking to doing, from simply defining strategy to implementing strategy. No longer are we just thinking about the 'what' of strategy; we're thinking about the 'how'. And the insights generated from such thinking help form our personal scorecard.

Figure 5.13 illustrates the Personal Scorecard component of our sample PST. In addition to [body weight] serving as our primary measure, five support measures also help indicate progress with achieving our inner soul goal:

- # workouts/week
- # carbohydrates consumed/day
- # calories burned through exercise/week
- # hours acquiring knowledge of healthy living practices/ week
- # hours allocated to exercise/week

Collectively, what this scorecard tells us is that to be exceptionally fit requires doing many things well - eating healthy

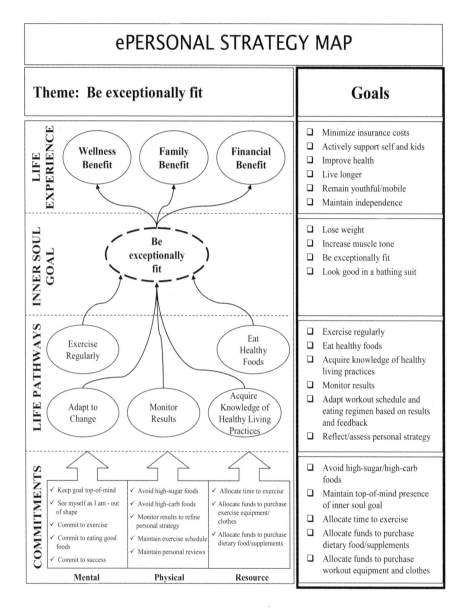

Fig. 5.12

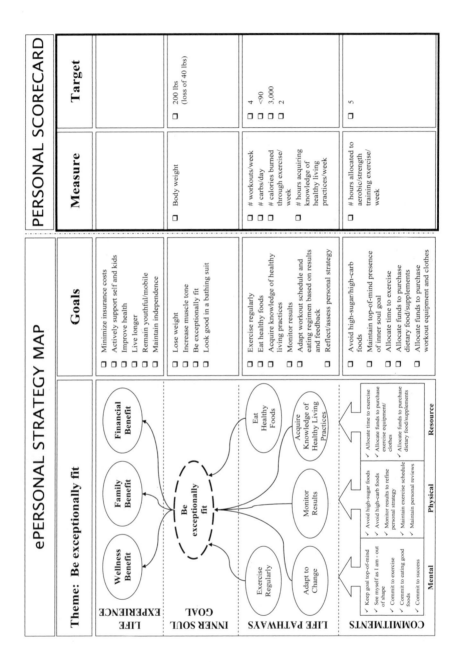

Fig. 5.13

foods, exercising regularly, and increasing knowledge of healthy living practices, among other things. This reinforces what we learned in Chapter 4: that the essence of strategy is to do many things well and integrate them. Table 5.3 defines the significance of each support measure stated above.

It is important to acknowledge that simply having a strategy to achieve a goal does not ensure goal achievement. Goal achievement requires movement from ideas to action. Developing and executing the last component of our PST, an action plan, represents such movement. As discussed, action plans are comprised of initiatives and tasks, with each task representing an 'opening move'. Figure 5.14 indicates 'opening moves' to achieve the goal 'be exceptionally fit':

- Obtain a health-club membership
- Purchase home gym equipment
- Purchase exercise gear and shoes
- Purchase initial supply of dietary food/supplements
- Identify and eliminate unhealthy foods
- Plan time for daily/weekly reflection
- Plan time to read about healthy living practices
- Create life aids to keep our goal top-of-mind and in our face
- Plan weekly exercise schedule/calendar
- Communicate to others our goal and ask for support

Creating a Personal Strategic Theme requires effort. And the more inner soul goals you have, the more effort is required to define personal strategy. Do not let the prospect of work, however, detract you from your ultimate goal, which is to restore and maintain lifelong happiness. The good news is that you will not have to create PST's often, that is, unless your inner soul goals change often. You may, at times, doubt the impact a PST has to achieve a goal or think that the effort required to create and maintain multiple PST's is not worth it. To have such thoughts is normal. The key is not to let such thoughts derail the dream. Defining personal strategy to the level of specificity

Table 5.3

Support Measure	ePSM Section	Significance of Measure
# workouts/week	Life Pathways	Exercise has a direct impact on body weight and degree of fitness. Generally, the more we exercise the more fit we become. Therefore, tracking the number of times exercised per week will not only remind us to exercise, but will also drive our primary measure: body weight.
# carbohydrates eaten/day	Life Pathways	For some people, increased carbohydrate consumption, results in increased weight gain. Consequently, tracking the number of carbs eaten daily will not only remind us to limit carbs but also drives our primary measure: body weight.
# calories burned through exercise/week	Life Pathways	This measure speaks to the quality of our workouts, knowing the more we exert, the more we benefit. Tracking the number of calories burned through exercise weekly also drives our primary measure: body weight.
# hours acquiring knowledge of healthy living practices/week	Life Pathways	As achieving fitness requires lifestyle changes beyond exercise, we record the number of hours spent acquiring knowledge of healthy living practices, as this activity will ensure healthy living remains in our face and top-of-mind. Further, this measure indirectly drives our primary measure: body weight.
# hours allocated to aerobic/strength training exercise/week	Commitments	To drive commitment, we establish a support goal tracking the number of hours we exercise a week. This goal ensures that we exercise as planned and drives our primary measure: body weight.

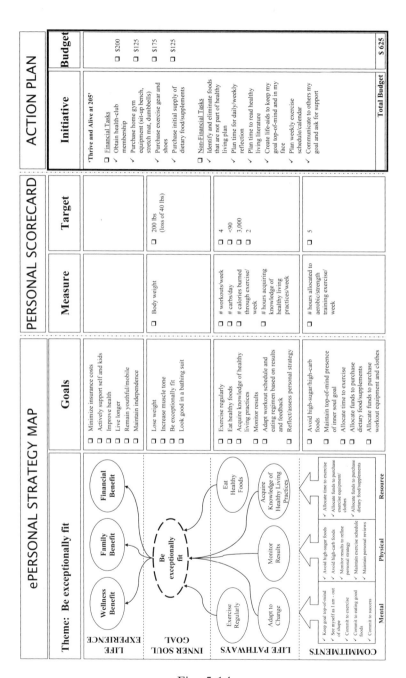

Fig. 5.14

suggested with the PST Framework is necessary to achieve your goals. Without reaching such specificity with our thinking, it is likely any attempt to achieve a goal will be just that, *an attempt*. This is where most people fall down, my (former) self included. The debilitating tendency we all suffer from is a mistaken belief that with a goal, desire, and time, any goal is achievable. These are key ingredients, to be sure, but without an explicit strategy to achieve your goal, mediocre results ensue, eroding both desire and your goal. Why is this? It is because without a personal strategy, our actions will invariably be 'off the mark', leading to goals taking much longer to achieve than necessary, thereby diminishing our enthusiasm, desire, and will to pursue the goal. The result: *goal abandoned*. To create personal strategy requires commitment and, to some people, may seem overly rigorous, but you must endure. Developing personal strategy requires an act of faith that the process and the effort will transform your life for the better, forever.

As we conclude our discussion of PST's, you may still be asking, 'What is it about PST's that enables goal achievement? What is its magic? Why does it work?' The answer to these questions lies in how the components of a PST work together as a system. Figure 5.15 illustrates the systemic relationships that exist between PST components.

ePSM goals dictate both measures (that comprise our personal scorecard) and initiatives (that comprise our action plan). Scorecard measures, in turn, indicate effectiveness of action plan initiatives, which in turn drive achievement of our goals. PST components, when working in isolation, are impotent. However, when brought together to work as a system, something magical occurs; impotent becomes potent; whole becomes greater than the sum of its parts. If you are familiar with "systems thinking", the notion of whole being greater than the sum of its parts will resonate with you. To have a goal (e.g. lose 35 pounds) without a plan to achieve such goal or without measures indicating whether the plan is working is meaningless. Likewise, to track a measure (e.g. # of lbs lost) without the context-setting benefit of

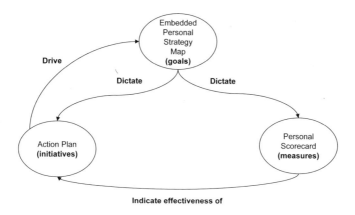

Fig. 5.15

a goal statement or an action plan is also meaningless. Finally, to create an action plan (e.g. 'Thrive and alive at 205') without establishing and measuring plan effectiveness, represents wasted effort. What this tells us is that separately, the parts of a PST offer little, but when brought together to work as a system, achieving any goal is possible.

Chapters 4 and 5 introduced the concept of personal strategy, including introducing the primary tools and frameworks of personal strategy: the Personal Strategy Map and the Personal Strategic Theme. Now, we apply our learnings and use such tools to build *your* personal strategy, next, in Chapter 6 on Building Personal Strategy.

Building Personal Strategy

"If one advances confidently in the direction of his dreams, and endeavors to live the life which he has imagined, he will meet with a success unexpected in common hours."

-Henry David Thoreau

THUS FAR, WE HAVE LEARNED what personal strategy is, what comprises personal strategy, and what tools to use to compose personal strategy. Now, we take these learnings to build <u>your</u> personal strategy. We do this as to build a personal strategy for one's life is to direct one's life; to advance confidently from goal asserted to goal achieved. We begin, as we must, by discussing the process.

The Process

The basic framework of any process is the same whether referring to the process of 'brushing teeth', 'launching a space shuttle', or 'building personal strategy'. There are process inputs, process steps (that add value), and process outputs. In between the bookends of process is where the real work occurs. For our purposes, *the process for building personal strategy begins with defining personal strategy and ends with implementing personal strategy*; these represent the 'bookends' of the process (see Figure 6.1).

Knowing the bookends of process and the major milestones within a process is useful as it scopes our effort; tells us what to focus on to achieve desired output. The process for building personal strategy has five key phases:

- Phase I – Organize for Strategy Development
- Phase II – Define Inner Soul Goals
- Phase III – Develop Personal Strategy Map
- Phase IV – Develop Personal Strategic Themes
- Phase V – Reflect, Refine, and Realize

Each phase consists of steps to perform, outputs to realize, and enablers to leverage (see Figure 6.2). At first glance, this diagram may seem a bit overwhelming. It appears that much is required to build personal strategy. It is true that significant effort is required to build personal strategy, but with an understanding of the steps to perform, outputs to realize, and enablers to leverage, you will move quickly through all phases of the process.

A Few Words before We Begin

(Note: You can download <u>free</u> personal strategy toolbox templates from only1shot.com)

You are about to create a personal strategy for living. Congratulations! This may not be the first time you have attempted such a feat; nevertheless, it is likely this is the first time you have approached the task with as much rigor. Here is what you can expect:

- You will be guided through the process with a rigorous, yet flexible, methodology and set of frameworks along with practical examples, illustrations, and coaching

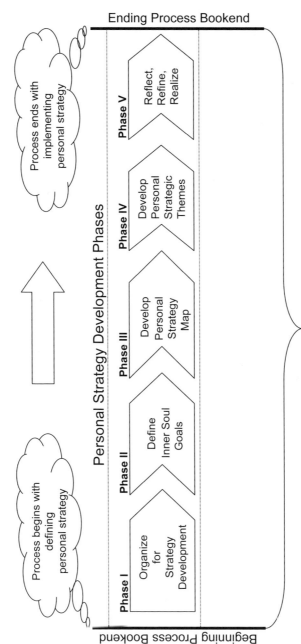

Fig. 6.1

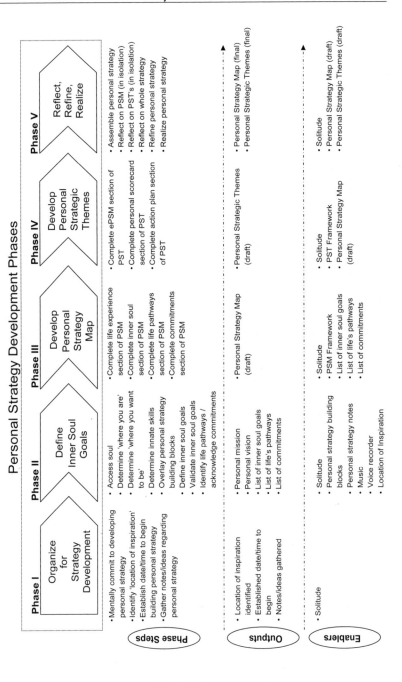

Fig. 6.2

- You will create a Personal Strategy Map reflecting what you want in life and from life at this point in your life
- You will create a portfolio of Personal Strategic Themes to realize what you want in life; to convert dreams into reality
- You will begin to see, will, think, act, and feel differently about self and life; specifically, you will feel liberated to have authored a personal strategy that reflects who you are and want to be on the surface of life
- Your life, forever altered, from defining and implementing a personal strategy for living

Let us begin!

Phase I – Organize for Strategy Development

The essence of Phase I is about mentally (and spiritually) committing to the need for and work of building a personal strategy for living. In other words, having a personal strategy has to make sense to you for you to proceed. Why is this so? It is because building personal strategy takes time. More importantly, it requires sustained, passionate commitment to implement personal strategy. To commit half of one's mind and little of one's soul is to not be committed at all. As you have journeyed this far, I will assume that commitment exists. In addition to committing to building personal strategy, a few other actions characterize this phase.

You need to:

- Identify your 'location of inspiration' to facilitate discovering your inner soul goals
- Establish a date and time to begin building personal strategy
- Gather notes and ideas about your current goals and dreams

You are probably wondering what a 'location of inspiration' is. *The* most important action when building personal strategy is to 'access soul', that is, to converse with soul. As such, there is nothing more important than identifying a solitary place to calm your thoughts; to let the future you 'emerge'. We converse with soul to determine, elicit our inner soul goals, but this requires you 'stop your life'. That is, it requires relaxing self, calming self, stepping outside self to see self. You will have great difficulty 'descending within' in a loud, busy, or otherwise non-solitary place. Consequently, identifying your 'location of inspiration' is about identifying a place where soul can emerge, where you can engage in quiet conversation with soul. Although a hotel room or a conference room in your local library will suffice, the best place to find soul, to converse with soul, is in nature (e.g. Glacier National Park).

To design a meaningful, actionable, soulful personal strategy requires *solitude*. Solitude, you will soon discover, is a common enabler across all phases of the strategy building process. This is deliberate. Solitude is an incredibly generative force, enabling us to:

- Stop our life
- Move from 'doing' to 'reflecting'
- Relax
- Calm ourselves
- Engage in true thinking
- See our thoughts
- Focus our thoughts
- Listen to our thoughts
- Challenge our thoughts
- Get at the truth

Solitude is the gateway to soul, the place from which we derive our inner soul goals – the foundation of personal strategy.

Once you identify your location of inspiration, you need to establish a date and time to begin building personal strategy. Put a stake in the ground. Clear your schedule. Allocate time. Communicate to others that you are busy. How much time should you allocate? I recommend allocating eight hours to 'access soul'. We will discuss this in more detail later. Finally, gather your personal strategy notes, if you have any, along with other supporting notes and ideas, as these will serve as inputs to Phase II.

Let us pause for a completeness check, as we have reached the end of Phase I. You should have accomplished the following:

- Committed to the need for and work of building personal strategy
- Identified a 'location of inspiration'
- Established a date and time to begin
- Gathered personal strategy notes/ideas to facilitate the process

Because your instruction comes from a book rather than a seminar, the tendency is to 'read and continue' without 'stopping and doing'. A word of warning: to get anything out of this book will require active involvement. That is, it will require you to 'stop and do'. Sometimes the pause will last hours, other times days or weeks. Although it may seem unnatural to start and stop your reading to 'do other things', it is proper protocol when reading this book. As such, think of this book as an instruction manual where you alternate 'learning' and 'doing'. If you have completed Phase I work, let us continue to Phase II where we define your inner soul goals.

Phase II – Define Inner Soul Goals

Phase II is arguably *the* most important phase of the process for building personal strategy. Defining one's inner soul goals is about determining what you want in life and from life at this point in your life. Suffice to say, if we do not get this step right, we have nothing right! All of our efforts will be for not as our strategy will be flawed! To prevent such calamity, we pause to reveal wants, to define inner soul goals, in addition to identifying life pathways and commitments to achieve such goals. We begin by defining what is an inner soul goal.

What is an Inner Soul Goal?

Although having made reference to the term on occasion, we have yet to define what an inner soul goal is. An inner soul goal is a deeply felt want, sourced from soul; said differently, it is a *desire of soul*. Inner soul goals represent what we want in life and from life and, thus, are uniquely personal. Lastly, inner soul goals represent substantive goals that are generally long-term and that achieving will make us happy and give life meaning. Some example inner soul goals include:

- Start a business
- Write a book
- Earn a college degree
- Drop five dress sizes
- Quit addiction
- Obtain a private pilot license
- Retire at age 55
- Build a dream home
- Perform volunteer work

Perhaps the most important thing to know about inner soul goals is that they represent the foundation of personal strategy, if not one's life. As such, if we do not get our goals 'right', then we have nothing right. Why is this? The trouble with defining imprecise goals is that our goals trigger significant action on the surface of life, from the activities we perform, to the resources we allocate, to the commitments we keep. Consequently, when we pursue the wrong goals, it results in wasted energy, burned resources, and wavering commitment. Because we rarely achieve lesser goals (effect of wavering commitment), we become apathetic towards setting goals; worse, we become apathetic towards life. Our life becomes a series of 'starts and stops' as we cycle through goals; abandoning one for another in rapid succession. The long-term effect of living this way is a lower quality of life; a life diminished.

In Chapter 3, we discussed the need to meet imperative, seize opportunity. Defining inner soul goals is a precondition to meet imperative and, therefore, seize opportunity. Pursuing goals not inspired by soul only denies imperative, denies opportunity, and perpetuates more of the same. This is not your story, however, as you opted to rewrite story, to define a new life plan reflecting soul; desires of soul. In short, you opted to go the other way. For personal strategy to <u>reflect</u> soul, however, we must first <u>know</u> soul; that is, we must converse with soul, hear what it has to say.

On the Soul

Ralph Waldo Emerson remarked in 1841, "man is a stream who's source is hidden". Today, over 160 years later, this truth remains. That is, we seem to know little more on soul today than in Emerson's day. Of course, this is a failure of our educational system that each of us grows up knowing little to nothing of soul, what it is, how to converse with it, what it's role is in our life. Sadly, it is because of this lack of knowing that most people live diminished lives, unhappy lives. To overcome this failing, we discuss soul; to converse with soul, to learn from soul, to *know soul*.

So, what is soul? For thousands of years, great thinkers have asked this question and the inquiry continues today. We ask this question because we innately know that, somehow, soul is omniscient. That is, we know soul represents, communicates the truth of who we are and were meant to be on the surface of life; it is the authentic being behind the being. Soul represents our essence, before flesh, before bones, before matter. Soul is <u>above</u> such things and, therefore, <u>is</u> all things. Soul is the source of pure intention, of what to do with one's life, of how to increase personal happiness, and of how to reengineer one's life. It is from soul that we <u>seek</u> purpose, <u>discover</u> purpose to <u>realize</u> purpose.

Each of us has purpose, but purpose is locked within soul. Consequently, to reveal purpose requires revealing soul. We reveal soul, learn from soul, through conversation. When we converse with soul, we see what soul sees, to think as soul thinks, to feel as soul feels. We learn soul's thoughts, desires, intention, vision, etc. Most importantly, when we converse with soul, we learn how to live as soul would live. For most people, what _self_ sees and what _soul_ sees are usually two very different things. Consequently, to know soul requires conversing with soul. Now, what most people do not realize is that such conversation does not occur naturally. Self must initiate conversation with soul, as soul lacks faculties to do so. As such, we must view ourselves as an instrument to bring emerging self (soul) forward to learn desires of soul, to craft inner soul goals. But what does it mean to converse with soul? To converse with soul means to have dialogue with soul, a back and forth exchange of words, thoughts, and feelings. To converse with soul is to descend within, to engage in quiet conversation. When I converse with soul, I descend to The Quiet Room. It is eggshell white, with soft-glow light, where soul and I sit just steps from one another, basking in each other's presence, admonishing each other's glow. The atmosphere of The Quiet Room is altogether different when sitting alone. But when self and soul come together to hear what each other has to say, atmosphere changes, smoke clears, enabling pure transmission, clear transmission, *an exchange of the _truth_.*

The importance of conversing with soul is paramount, not only to define meaningful inner soul goals, but also to live a remarkable life. Without knowing soul, desires of soul, you cannot live as soul would live. One does not need to look beyond self to acknowledge this fact. Listed below are reasons why we must converse with soul and the benefits of such conversation:

Reasons Why

- To obtain the truth of who we are and were meant to be on the surface of life

- To learn desires of soul; soul's intent
- To realize authentic self; to live as soul would live
- To reengineer our life
- To create personal strategy reflecting soul
- To rediscover the joy of living
- To set soul free; release spirit within
- To learn what we want in life and from life throughout life
- To reveal the highest form of you; give rise to new form
- To reconnect that which is broken; to operate as whole
- To live a more meaningful, purposeful, and fragrant life experience
- To answer our most pressing personal inquiries
- To establish alignment between self and soul
- To discover emerging you
- To obtain 'wisdom awareness'
- To learn imperative, seize opportunity
- To reorient one's perception from self to soul
- To initiate new cause; to realize new effect
- To align the inner soul with action

Benefits Of

- Ignites divine will
- Results in improved quality of life
- Eliminates disconnectedness; quells the suffering
- We begin to see as soul sees
- We begin to think as soul thinks
- We begin to see clearly our purpose in life
- Removes fragmentation/separation between self and soul
- Enables operating from soul as one's source
- Ensures defining high quality, effective, personal strategy
- Enables living as soul would live

As you can see, the list is long as to why we should converse with soul. Now informed of the benefits, the question becomes, "How does one converse with soul?" For most people, conversing with soul represents unfamiliar territory. Few of us have been schooled in the 'art and practice of descending within' to affect without. As such, there is a need to educate further before making descent.

Descending Within

To 'descend within' is to force reflection of self upon self; to shut down external and ignite internal. Earlier, we learned that human purpose is locked within soul. We also learned that to reveal soul requires engaging soul. However, to engage soul, to discover purpose, requires descending past habitual self to see emerging self; that is, it requires descending past historical seeing, thinking, acting, and feeling. This is at once our problem and our challenge as we cannot see emerging you through historical you; cannot penetrate outer skin once hardness has set in. Consequently, when descending within, we suspend self to redirect our seeing, thinking on *what could be* rather than *what is*. We suspend self; then, we descend within to meet soul, to converse with soul, to hear what soul has to say. Descending within is the mechanism that frees us from our past to realize a more fragrant future. Now, to facilitate, or enable, descending within, knowing that such practice is foreign to most people, we focus our mind's eye on one or more meditative symbols.

Meditative Symbols

It has long been a technique of meditation to focus the mind's eye on one or more symbols to still the mind, enable meditative thought, and descend within. As we attempt to converse with soul, we, too, can focus our mind's eye on symbols to facilitate descending within. Figure 6.3 illustrates five symbols that we will discuss not only because such symbols help facilitate 'descending within' but also because they provide visual context for key themes in this book.

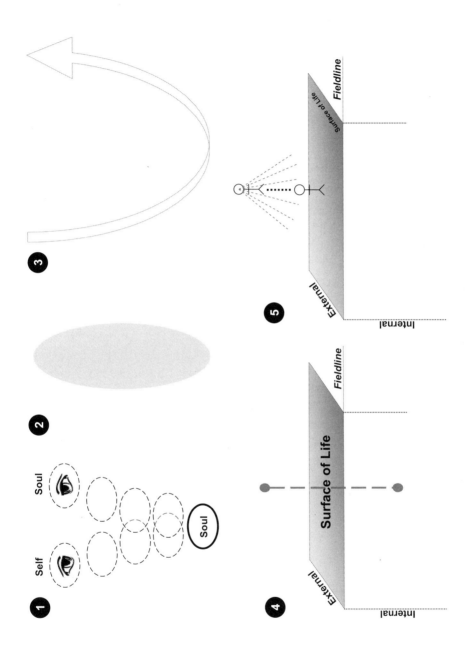

Fig. 6.3

The five symbols we discuss are:

1. Merging Circles
2. The Quiet Room
3. Union or 'U'
4. Surface of Life/Divine Fieldline
5. Rise

The 'Merging Circles' symbol illustrates that when our eyes are open, we exist as two separate entities: self and soul. But, when we close our eyes, parts become whole. That is, self and soul become whole, operating singularly as soul. Try this exercise. Envision your left eye as self, and your right eye as soul. You can <u>feel</u> separation as your eyes are naturally apart. Now close your eyes. Did you <u>feel</u> circles merging? Did you <u>feel</u> parts becoming whole? When we close our eyes, separation subsides, and we <u>feel</u> whole. The image of two circles merging to become One represents what must occur when we descend within. When we descend within, we are trying to collapse boundaries between self and soul. We are trying to widen our space of perception and awareness, such that all that remains when we reach bottom is not two entities with disparate thought, double vision, but One entity with unified thought, single vision; soul. This movement, 'merging circles', is important, as we obtain the truth (of self and life) in proportion to degree of unity between self and soul. In other words, the more circles merge, the more we learn the truth of who we are and were meant to be.

Another image to think about when descending within is an elongated oval. When circles merge to become One, notice how the space common to both circles expands, widens. This elongated 'space' represents The Quiet Room. I think of The Quiet Room as a cocoon, sheltering me, protecting me from outside noise, from the chaos that exists on the surface of life. The Quiet Room enables self to converse with soul; to engage in quiet conversation with soul. It is calming to think of The Quiet Room image as it helps transport us to a better place, a place to see clearly, think clearly, and feel differently; a place to embrace soul, to learn from soul, to alter without from descending within.

This brings us to the next symbol: Union or 'U'. It is instructive to first define the word Union. Union is both a verb and a noun. As a verb, union represents the act of uniting two or more things; about joining fractured elements for a common goal. As a noun, union represents agreement or harmony, a oneness; something made whole.

We are all familiar with the typical uses of the word union, as in these examples:

- Student union
- Labor union
- Mathematical union
- Marriage union
- State of the union

However, what we are not familiar with hearing is union ascribed to individual; that is, we are not used to hearing union represent a uniting of self and soul. Nor are we used to hearing union represent mending separation between self and soul, that is, to make one's self whole. Although too early for you to know, the 'U' symbol symbolizes the journey that is this book. We start our journey descending within (left hand side of U), we slow down, to discover our inner soul goals and design a personal strategy reflecting such goals. Then, we turn up (right hand side of U); we speed up to execute personal strategy on the surface of life. The U is a metaphor for the internal and external work that is this book. As will be revealed later, the U symbol represents the two key movements of life; descending within, rising above. Use of the 'U' symbol to represent these key movements is adapted from the pioneering work of C. Otto Scharmer, a professor of Behavioral and Policy Sciences at MIT, and his landmark book 'Theory U'.

The next symbol, Surface of Life/Divine Fieldline, you have already seen. In Chapters 2 and 3, I introduced this image to distinguish 'our world within' (internal) from 'our world without' (external). In his book 'Theory U', Dr. Scharmer tells of his childhood and how his father, an organic farmer, helped him distinguish between the field on the surface of life and the field below. His father also taught him how both 'fields' co-affect soil quality, co-determine all that emerges. This analogy of 'field above' and 'field below' applies to us as well. Our inner field represents soul, that which lies within; our outer field represents self, that which lies without on the surface of life. Together, the Surface of Life/Divine Fieldline images not only help us visualize descending within, but also makes explicit that descending within requires penetrating the fieldline of life.

The last symbol, Rise, extends the Surface of Life symbol by illustrating self stepping outside of self to see self. It images self rising above self, at 100ft level, to see self operating on the surface of life. When I put this image in my mind's eye, I inherit a feeling of being a part of, yet detached from, self system. To detach self from self is important when conversing with soul, as you need to redirect sight from current you to emerging you, from self to soul. Stepping outside of self to see self facilitates seeing self's interactions, connections with other systems. It allows us to see condition (current thoughts, habits, ways of living), to change condition. Lastly, detaching self from self suspends personal bias, assumptions in the air for challenge, revision. We begin to see with fresh eyes and by seeing in new ways, we are liberated to think, act, and feel in new ways. In short, we are free to *go the other way*.

Together, Merging Circles, The Quiet Room, 'U', Surface of Life/Divine Fieldline, and Rise all help us descend within; to descend past outer to connect with inner. To this day, I keep these symbols in mind when I meditate, that is, when I converse with soul, as such symbols keep me grounded, *keep me connected*. Shortly, you will begin your descent to find soul. One question you may have is, "How far do I go, must I go, to reach soul?" This is an important question, as the quality of the descent affects all that follows.

Quality of the Descent

The first thing that you should know is that the quality of the descent determines the quality of the ascent. That is, how you progress on the inside, the depths to which you crawl, determines how you progress on the outside, all that follows – degree of personal alignment, quality of one's life, happiness with one's life.

There are differing degrees of descent when conversing with soul (see Figure 6.4). What the illustration tells us is that the quality of our descent can be either shallow or deep, of low quality or high quality, with multiple gradations in between. For example, if in the course of meditative thought, you progress only as deep as depth line A, what results from such conversation is both shallow and of low quality. That is, you have not yet entered The Quiet Room, not yet found soul to learn from soul. Descending to depth line B results in higher quality conversation than A, but still suffers from too shallow descent. The same is true of depth line C & D. Only at depth line E, is the descent deep enough, expansive enough, penetrating enough, to produce high quality conversation with soul. The problem with too shallow descents is that they produce shallow goals that do not reflect soul, resulting in diminished thinking, acting, and feeling. Deep descents, on the other hand, produce inspired goals that do reflect soul, resulting in inspired thinking, acting, and feeling. Remaining mindful of quality conversation with soul would not matter if it were not the case that the quality of the descent (self into soul) determines the quality of the ascent (self from soul). But, alas, it does matter. As such, we must remain mindful, as a lesser life results from lesser goals, lesser descents.

Now, while recent discussion illuminates the depths to which one must go to ensure quality conversation with soul, the question that now rises is, "How do I know if I have descended deep enough? That is, how do I know if I have reached soul?"

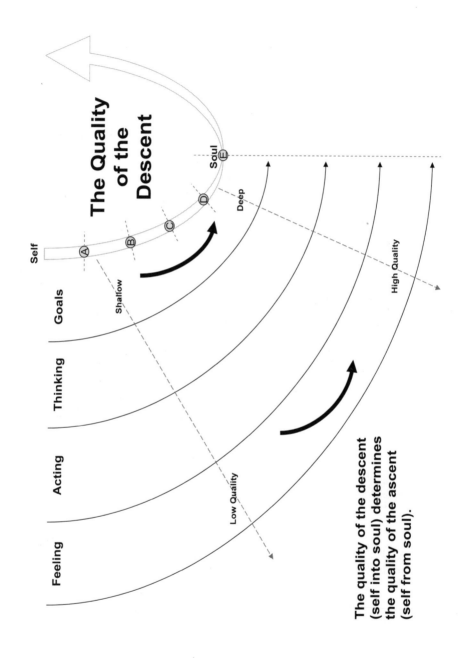

Fig. 6.4

Reaching Soul

It is important to know at the onset that reaching soul, connecting with soul, may take hours, days, or weeks depending on where you currently operate. Do not be discouraged by this fact. To converse with soul takes time; it is a process that cannot, should not, be rushed; coerced. When one reaches soul, there is no <u>deciding</u> 'what to do with your life', as such things come naturally, become obvious. As you descend within, if you are 'deciding' what to do with your life, you have not yet entered The Quiet Room. If **mind** responds to questions asked, you <u>have not</u> yet connected with soul. When we reach soul, begin to converse with soul, the mind has no role, as the conversation is more about *knowing* than deciding; it is more about *feeling* than thinking; it is more a matter of one's *heart* than one's head. Soul does not have voice; its tones are silent. As such, it takes time to hear tones, to develop sensitivity to hear what soul is saying. Thus, do not insist on spoken word, as soul does not respond in this manner; yet, with patience, and despite the apparent lack of dialogue, *we, graciously, miraculously obtain answers to our most pressing personal inquiries.*

Reaching soul is a process, and only when we reach soul, establish connection, can we define inner soul goals. Therefore, to answer the question, 'How do I know if I have reached soul?' the short answer is...**you will feel it**.

The long answer is...

- A profound knowing consumes you. You feel connected to something larger than your-self
- You exist in an 'altered' state; you are not the same person at the end of the conversation, as when entered
- What you see has changed, what you think has changed, life purpose has changed
- When 'what to do' with your life becomes obvious; clarity exists on what to do with remaining time on earth

- You have increased awareness of 1) who you are, and 2) were meant to be on the surface of life
- You are inspired; overcome with excitement; new hope
- Self and soul become One; once operating as parts, now made whole

I still remember when I re-discovered soul, when I once again, heard its sweet sounds. I remember feeling connected to something larger than my-self. I remember existing in an 'altered' state. I remember everything changing – from what I saw, to how I thought, acted, and felt. I remember increased awareness of self and life, of what I needed to do, and who I should become on the surface of life. Suddenly, it became clear to me how to spend remaining time on earth. Finally, I remember nodding my head in private ceremony, tears my only companion, as life destiny became obvious to me. And when this warm feeling consumed me, I felt highest freedom, greatest hope; a feeling of One.

My hope, my wish, for you is to possess similar memories. By descending within, by conversing with soul, by the grace of soul, sun will break, shadows will fade, heart will mend, love will find you. I know this to be true as soul is right beside you, always been with you, <u>all your life</u>.

At long last, with theory behind us, we advance to define your inner soul goals.

Defining Your Inner Soul Goals

Let us summarize what we have learned thus far. We learned:

- What an inner soul goal is
- What it means to converse with soul
- Importance of 'descending within'
- Meditative symbols to facilitate descent
- Quality of descent matters
- The 'signs' of having reached soul

Now, we transition to define your inner soul goals, but before we do, we expand upon, deepen, our understanding of what inner soul goals are. We do this by reframing inner soul goals as 'Seeds of Soul'.

Seeds of Soul

Although inner soul goals represent desires of soul, it is more insightful, instructive to think of them as *seeds of soul*. Why is this? It is because soul, when so directed, is the origin (root) of not only what we see, but also how we will, think, act, and feel; inner directing outer. We know this to be true, as we take our clues from nature where, with *seeds of nature,* that which lies within (seed kernel) determines that which lies without (blooming plant). Therefore, as it relates to personal strategy, we converse with soul to release seeds of soul. Then, with seeds planted (internal action), we apply external action (willpower, life pathways, commitment) to help seeds grow. Such factors represent the sunlight in our growing. This is similar to external factors of water, fertilizer, sunshine, and tilling action, helping nature grow. Figure 6.5 illustrates the two processes at work.

With both processes, we first plant the seed (1). Then, comes external cultivation (2). With external nurturing, comes emergence (3). Finally, what emerges on the surface of life acts on its own behalf to grow faster and more intently (4). The invisible process of reengineering your life, now made visible through this farming analogy, involves four key movements: 1) external intervention (self intervening on behalf of soul), 2) internal cultivation (to determine inner soul goals; *'plant seeds'*), 3) external cultivation (performing actions, maintaining commitments on the surface of life), and 4) emergence (achieving goals, realizing transformation). Shortly, you will plant seeds of soul. Afterwards, the internal work of planting seeds will invert, become external work on the surface of life, as you will then need to cultivate, nourish seeds through willful action. Figure 6.6 illustrates this inversion from internal to external.

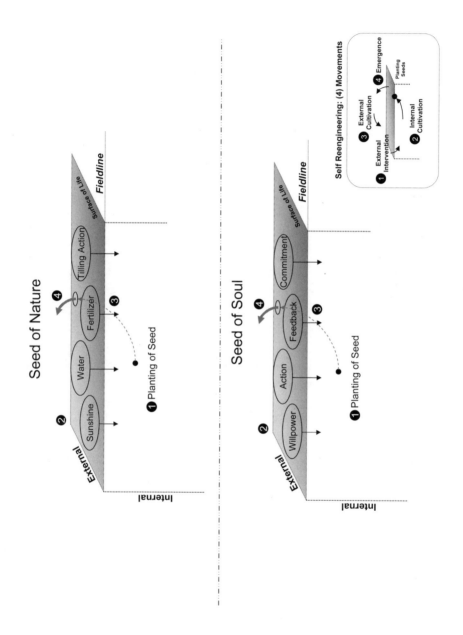

Fig. 6.5

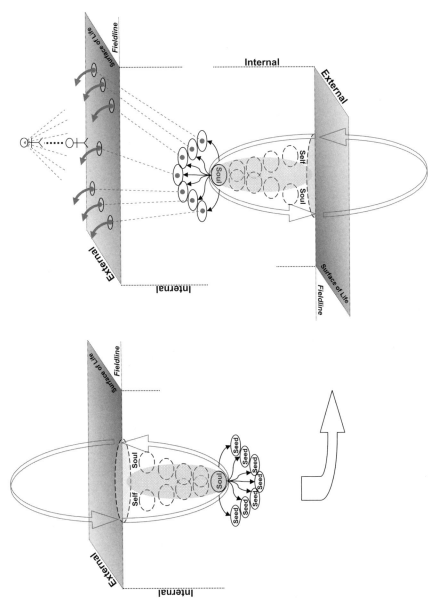

Fig. 6.6

Incorporating meditative symbols, this illustration provides clarity to what is, by default, a hidden process. Defining
one's inner soul goals is the result of self and soul merging to
become One; soul. It is the result of descending to The Quiet
Room, of sliding down the left hand side of the 'U' to converse
with soul. Then, with goals known (planted), we rise mightily
up the right hand side of the 'U'. We pursue our goals on the
surface of life; expose seeds to sun's warm glow. Then, periodically, as we must do, we step outside self to see self, rise above,
to examine where we are relative to where we want to be.

Reengineering one's life is about cultivating seeds of soul,
about *loving them to life*. When I think of seeds of soul, I am
reminded of a quote by the famous 18th century French philoso-
pher, Denis Diderot, who remarked, "Only great passions can
elevate the soul to great things." Know this: an aroused soul can,
<u>if you let it</u>, catapult you to great things.

Now, we learn the process for defining inner soul goals.

Process for Defining Inner Soul Goals

How does one discover his/her inner soul goals? Does it require
an advanced form of meditation? Does it require hypnotherapy?
Does it require extensive deep thinking? As conversing with soul
likely represents unfamiliar territory for you, we address these
questions in this section. It would be just as appropriate to use
the word 'discover' in the heading above as, to 'discover' means
'to reveal' or 'to expose'. That is precisely what we are looking to do. We are looking to uncover, reveal, expose your inner
most wants and make them visible. Now, you may be saying, 'I
already know what I want in life'. Ok. I buy that, to a degree.
Most of us do know what we generally want in life. In many
cases, the problem is not 'knowing' what we want in life; it is a
problem of not 'doing' what we want in life; *the inability to act*.
We will discuss this in greater detail later.

Defining inner soul goals, like all things, is a process (see
Figure 6.7).

Process for Defining Inner Soul Goals

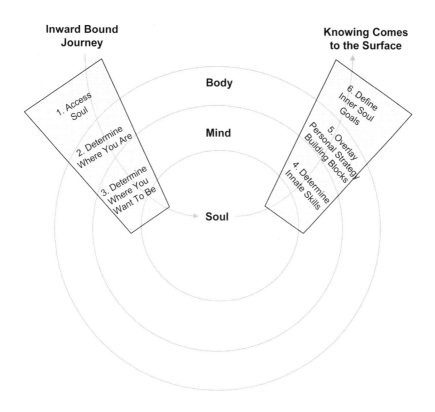

Fig. 6.7

The process for defining inner soul goals essentially describes different conversations we have with soul. The process begins, of course, by accessing soul. Only when in the presence of soul can we converse with soul. With connection established, the next step is to determine where you are. You have already performed this activity. Then comes the important work of determining where you want to be. This step we must get right, as it affects all that follows. Then, we determine our innate skills, those things we are naturally good at and enjoy doing. Innate skills combined with insights of where we are and where we want to be represent the 'raw material' of personal strategy. In the next step of the process, we overlay this raw material on top of the personal strategy building blocks. This step ensures that we create a balanced set of inner soul goals to live a balanced life. Lastly, we define our inner soul goals.

The process for defining inner soul goals is an inward bound journey beyond flesh, beyond mind, into soul, where profound knowing comes to the surface. We begin by accessing soul.

Step 1 – Access Soul

Although past discussions might have mentally prepared you for this step, a question likely remains, 'How do you do it?' Accessing soul is similar to prayer or meditation. With both approaches, the goal is to turn one's attention inward, back onto self. When we do this, it brings us closer to source, *leads to union with soul*. Further, this action brings about innate wisdom; a wisdom awareness. When we pray, meditate, we become aware of current condition to change condition. In this regard, prayer and meditation are enablers, as both create the conditions to access soul. Creating right conditions is important, for if we generate wrong conditions, we generate wrong results (i.e., shallow descent, lesser goals).

To create the conditions to access soul or, as Emerson remarked, to "put myself in an attitude of reception," requires:

- Silence
- Questioning
- Calming your thoughts
- Patience
- Listening
- Remaining open minded
- Closing one's eyes
- Suspending habitual self
- Time

To access soul demands silence. Real communication can take place only where there is silence. To access soul requires questioning self. With each question asked, we descend past self, revealing soul. To access soul requires calming our thoughts. We cannot find soul in a cloud-filled room. To access soul requires patience. Good things come to those who wait. To access soul requires active listening to hear soul's silent tones. To access soul requires keeping an open mind about the process, even if unfamiliar and, therefore, uncomfortable. To access soul requires closing our eyes for when we close our eyes, there is soul. To access soul requires suspending current self to see emerging self. Lastly, to access soul requires time; soul does not respond to forced action.

Now, in addition to these factors creating right conditions, other enablers (as stated on Figure 6.2) help facilitate accessing soul:

- Solitude
- Music
- Voice recorder
- Location of Inspiration

To access soul requires solitude. You must cast away all distractions on the surface of life (work, family, friends, cell phone, Blackberry, laptop, etc.). To access soul, you may want to play music, as music calms the mind, dispelling unwanted storm clouds. To access soul, you may want to use a voice recorder. We use a voice recorder to record our thoughts, questions, and answers when conversing with soul. Recording conversation ensures no insights or revelations escape inquiry. Lastly, to access soul, retire to your location of inspiration so you can be free – free to relax, free to think, free to be. If you use the methods described above, you will create right conditions to access soul.

Okay. We have reached the point in the process where we will begin to access soul. To set proper mood, pause now and break to your location of inspiration.

‹‹ Break to location of inspiration ››

At this point, you should be at your 'location of inspiration' with materials at hand, music on (but set to low), and recorder engaged. If you are in a position to lie down, do so. Get comfortable. You can still read a book while lying down. I hope your 'location of inspiration' is truly inspiring. For me, I would descend into nature or lie on a remote beach somewhere in the Caribbean (St. Martin is nice). You <u>want</u> to feel free, exhilarated, unconstrained. You <u>need</u> to be free, exhilarated, unconstrained as cramped spaces produce cramped results, whereas open spaces produce open results. I hope that you are in an open space.

Because accessing soul is foreign to most people, we discuss the tactical steps to access soul. They are:

- Step 1a – Stop your life
- Step 1b – Get comfortable
- Step 1c – Breath in air
- Step 1d – Listen to your breathing
- Step 1e – Step outside self to see self

To access soul, to converse with soul, requires you deliberately 'stop your life', even if only for a day. It requires you slow down long enough to ask important questions of self and <u>listen</u> for the answer. You have done this. Congratulations! For most people, 'stopping one's life' to reflect on life is an afterthought; *a rare event.* It cannot be, however, when developing personal strategy. Developing personal strategy requires an investment of time to think about self and one's life. Invest the time. Invest in the 'emerging' you. The future you is counting on the commitment of time and energy to this endeavor. Once you 'stop your life', the goal is to, then, get comfortable. Lie still for 60 minutes. Do nothing at all. Breathe in the air. Listen to your breathing. Stop the flow of thought. Step outside self to see self. Let go.

You might be asking, "Why focus on breathing?" The reason we do this is that focusing on one's breath brings mind and matter together; distractions begin to fade; parts become whole; competing interests, now working towards a common goal. Following one's breath is an effective meditation technique to prevent chatter of mind from obscuring soul. So...at this moment...follow your breath, let go.

<< *60 minute rest* >>

Okay. I hope you are relaxed. When was the last time, other than while sleeping, that you took time to do nothing at all, breath in the air, and let go? Feels good, doesn't it? If you are within nature, how did the wind feel coursing across your face and hair? How did the sounds of nature soothe you? If at a beach, how did the sound of crashing waves relax you? How did the ocean breeze ignite soul? Having reached a state of relaxation, you are ready to 'access soul', to converse with soul. Relaxation has enabled descent, opened the door to The Quiet Room for us to converse with soul. All that remains is for us to pass through the door. The mechanism to do this, to penetrate open door, is to ask questions. You may be asking, 'How can questioning of self prompt soul?' It can; trust me. Most people do not recognize the power of questions or of questioning self. Questioning self is powerful because asking questions:

- Stimulates thought
- Facilitates introspection
- Leads to listening
- Demands answers
- Yields insights
- Leads to profound learning

Figure 6.8 highlights the benefits of questioning, in that *the more questions you ask self, the more stimulation of thought that occurs, which leads to greater personal insights about emerging you.*

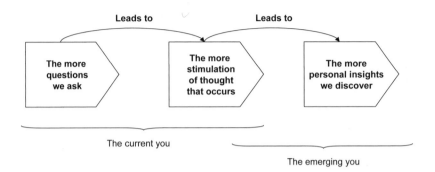

Fig. 6.8

So, what questions do we ask self? Before answering this question, we need to understand key steps of the questioning process (see Figure 6.9).

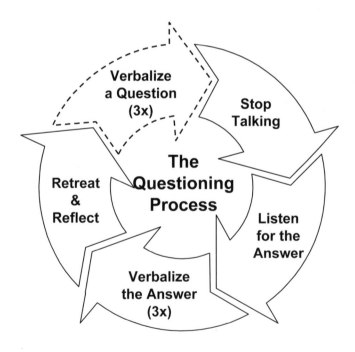

Fig. 6.9

Asking questions, with a goal to discover one's inner soul goals, is perhaps the most important line of questioning in which you will ever engage. When we ask questions of self, we start by verbalizing them. Verbalizing a question makes it real, makes it explicit, and demands an answer. We verbalize each question three times. This ensures that the question penetrates self to reach soul. After verbalizing a question, we stop talking and <u>listen</u> for the answer. The right answer will **not** be one that 'sounds good', but will represent the answer behind the answer - *the real answer*. Please remember, this is not the time to be cavalier with you. That is, this is not the time to bullshit you. You know your own bullshit; get past it. We need truthful answers to hard questions if we hope to discover your inner soul goals. I trust that you will support you. We verbalize our answers in the same manner as when asking. Make the answer heard. Verbalize your answer three times. Let the answer penetrate self *as it reflects soul*. Hear what soul has to say. Upon hearing the truth, as communicated by soul, you can reflect on the truth, ask follow-on 'why' questions, and begin forming inner soul goals. Inner soul goals are not always immediate and, therefore, require nurturing to bubble them to the surface and made visible. By following this process when questioning self, a new you will emerge; soul will emerge in the form of inner soul goals that represent what you want in life and from life at this point in your life.

We are now ready to ask questions of self to learn from soul, to discover our inner soul goals. The questions we ask self are obvious; it is just that we rarely stop our lives long enough to ask them and then listen for the answer. Even though the questions we ask are obvious, their importance is paramount. Getting the right results begins with asking the right questions. Hence, we ask <u>three</u> sets of questions to discover our inner soul goals:

- Baseline
- Innate skill
- Personal strategy building blocks

We begin by asking baseline assessment questions to generate the raw material to form our inner soul goals. Baseline questions help reveal two things: 1) where we are and 2) where we want to be. Then, we ask questions to determine innate skills, those things we are naturally good at and enjoy doing. Finally, we take what we have learned and overlay such insights onto our personal strategy building blocks, asking questions specific to each building block category. Questioning in this iterative manner nets us our true objective: our inner soul goals.

Step 2 – Determine Where You Are

Because this book is adapted from seminar material, the sequencing of activities is slightly modified as you already completed this step in Chapter 2. Despite having given preliminary thought to where you are, much time may have passed. As such, we revisit past questions to validate past conclusions.

Baseline questions are frontline questions into soul. That is, they are direct, probing, and personal. They push our thinking in a direction that facilitates conversing with soul. We ask questions regarding our feelings, our wants, life spirit, and personal mission and vision. The insights we gain from this line of questioning not only help shape our inner soul goals, but also help identify our innate skills.

We ask three primary sets of questions (and several secondary sets of questions) to determine where we are. For each question below, follow the procedure of verbalizing the question, stopping thought, listening for the answer, verbalizing the answer, and reflecting. Take as much time as necessary to resolve each question - 10 minutes, 30 minutes, or 1 hour. With each question, the goal is to turn down and in, to descend within, to understand where you are to reveal where you want to be. Let us begin.

Primary Questions:

On Work

- Are you happy in your current profession and/or role?
- Does your life's work make sense to you?
- Does your life's work reflect your passion?
- Does your chosen profession fulfill you, challenge you, inspire you?
- How do you feel in the morning when embarking on a new day in your chosen profession?
- Are you making the kind of contribution to society, to the world, that is meaningful and makes you proud?
- At the end of your working days, will you recognize what you have accomplished? Will anyone recognize what you have accomplished?
- Will you leave this world a better place because of your life's contributions, your life's work?

On Surroundings

- Are you living in the right location?
- If not, how do you know? What are the signs?

On Life Partner

- Are you with the right life partner?
- If not, how do you know? What are the signs?

Secondary Questions:

On Soul

- What is the state of your soul?
- When you are alone, what does soul say?
- Are you doing what you want <u>in</u> life?
- Are you getting what you want <u>from</u> life?
- Is life meaningful, purposeful?
- Do you desire a new life story?
- Are you living as soul would live?

On Spirit

- What is the condition of your spirit?
- Is spirit alive or sleeping somewhere cold?
- Are you living an inspired existence?
- Is life fragrant, vibrant, full of color?

On Feeling

- What do you feel inside?
- How do you feel about life, living?
- Do you feel alive?
- Are you happy with where you are at personally, professionally, financially?
- Are you happy with your current life story?
- Do you feel inner conflict between <u>where</u> you are and where you want to be?
- Do you feel inner conflict between <u>who</u> you are and who you want to be?
- Are you free?

When we ask these deep, probing questions of self, soul responds. At this time, if not done so already, record soul's responses. Revisit prior questions; use your voice recorder to replay conversation, if needed. This conversation between your self and your soul should have generated significant raw material to begin shaping your inner soul goals. Now, we drop the past to consider a more fragrant future.

Step 3 – Determine Where You Want to Be

Where do you want to be? It seems like a simple enough question to ask self, but for many, it can be one of the hardest questions to answer. No need to worry; *questions will reveal the path which leads home.* Knowing <u>where we are</u> is yin to the yang of knowing <u>where we want to be</u>. Together, such insights represent two-thirds of the raw material we need to determine inner soul goals. As in Step 2, to generate raw material, we ask questions of self, then listen for the answer. The first two questions we ask to determine where we want to be are:

- What is my mission in life?
- What is my vision for self?

As with strategy, we are most familiar with a company developing a mission and vision statement; mission indicating why exist and vision indicating who to be. But just like strategy, having a mission and vision statement is becoming increasingly relevant for individual. Companies create mission and vision statements to provide context for how to operate on the surface of life. It is for the same reason we create a personal mission and vision statement. Creating a personal mission/vision statement provides us context for how we should operate on the surface of life. For example, Mother Teresa's mission statement was "to help the poorest of the poor." Her vision was "to become a change agent, a catalyst, to improve the lives of needy people." With mission and vision providing context, she aligned her thinking, actions, and feelings on the surface of life to achieve mission, realize vision. You and I must do the same. That is, we must create a life mission, life vision to align our thinking, our actions, our feelings on the surface of life. To help you get started thinking about your own personal mission/vision statements, I present my mission, my vision below:

My Mission

To help and enable all people to live up to the extraordinary personal, professional, and financial potential that life offers

My Vision

To become a leading and sought after expert and advocate for developing personal strategy, establishing personal alignment, and maximizing the life experience

---

Another reason to define personal mission, vision statements is that they remind you that you have Only One Shot at
life. To help you craft a personal mission statement, answer
these questions below. The collective response from soul will
reveal <u>what</u> to write in the box below.

- Why are you here on earth?
- What do you value?
- What do you want <u>from</u> life?
- What do you want <u>in</u> life?
- Why do you work?
- What is your purpose in life?
- What is soul telling you to do?
- What will be your legacy from having walked the earth?

My Mission

```


```

Okay. Now that you know your mission, what is your
vision for self? To help you craft a personal vision statement,
answer these questions below. The collective response from soul
will reveal <u>what</u> to write in the box below.

- Who do you want to become on the surface of life?
- How do you want to be remembered?
- Will the world have known your name?
- How will they have known your name?
- What will become of you?

My Vision

```


```

Together, mission and vision provide the context we need to fashion a meaningful, remarkable, and fragrant life experience. Together, they provide us context to design a personal strategy to achieve mission, realize vision. *Together, they determine all that follows.* Mission and vision are born of wisdom, born of that which is whole, born of soul. Mission and vision are born of such things, or nothing at all.

At this point, you have generated much raw material to begin forming your inner soul goals, but before you do, we determine your innate skills.

Step 4 – Determine Innate Skills

We begin by first defining what an innate skill is. Innate skills are those things you are naturally good at and enjoy doing. Some are born with immense innate skill. We call such people 'gifted': the exceptional athlete, the brilliant mathematician, the animated artist, the roused musician, the divine orator. Additionally, some are born with innate knowing; a wisdom awareness, knowing early in life one's destiny (young scientist, public servant, preacher). Most are born not knowing either and must learn, over time, special skill, profound knowing. Knowing one's innate skills is of great importance (and relevance) when designing personal strategy. With such insight, you can define goals that leverage your natural strengths. For example, if you are a naturally skilled communicator with innate problem solving skills and creative abilities, you might be best suited for a role as a management consultant, sales representative, account executive, or corporate trainer. If you are good with your hands, are creative, and enjoy challenges, then, perhaps, you might be best suited for a role as a carpenter, artist, or interior designer. Lastly, if you have a deep connection with nature, enjoy travel, and are physically strong, then, perhaps, you might be best suited for a role as a park ranger, river guide, or hiking instructor. Knowing your innate skills will enable you to identify <u>which</u> professions/ roles cater to and leverage your innate strengths. Without such insight, you might never align native strengths with the right profession/role, leading to deep unhappiness. This is the experience of most people. This was my experience. So, how does one discover his/her innate skills? It begins with identifying your strengths.

Identifying Strengths:

To catalyze your thinking, ask these questions of self:

- What am I naturally good at?
- What have I excelled at?
- What do I enjoy doing on the weekends?
- What do my friends say I am naturally good at?
- What do people complement me on?
- What have my current and former employers said about my strengths?
- What do I enjoy doing that never feels like work?
- What do I enjoy doing when on vacation?
- What did I enjoy doing as a child?
- What are my passions?
- If money were not an issue, what work would I pursue?
- What would I like to do if I could start my career over?

Take time to <u>scan your life</u> when answering these questions. What activities do you remember performing in grade school, junior high, high school, and college at which you *naturally* excelled? Think over your professional career, weekend hobbies, and outside interests for ideas.

Consider these examples:

- Are you a great <u>organizer</u> of people?
- Are you a great <u>communicator</u>?
- Are you skilled in <u>negotiating</u> truces between people?
- Do people confide in you because of your innate <u>listening</u> and <u>empathy</u> skills?
- Are you a <u>risk taker</u>?

- Do you enjoy planning and <u>hosting</u> events?
- Do people naturally defer to you to <u>lead</u> events?
- Are you naturally good at fund raising or <u>selling</u> merchandise?
- Are you naturally <u>creative</u> (e.g. painting, drawing, crafts)?
- Are you a good <u>problem solver</u>?
- Are you skilled with <u>fixing things</u>?
- Do you enjoy <u>teaching</u> others?
- Do you enjoy <u>speaking</u> to others in large group settings?

Review the list in Figure 6.10 for other things you are naturally good at and enjoy doing. Check all that apply.

We always hear how the most successful (in any profession) view their work as 'fun' and 'enjoyable' – never as 'work'. How do we become one of the lucky few who view their life's work as fun, meaningful, and enjoyable? The answer lies in how well aligned your innate skills and abilities are with your chosen profession/role. If you pursue a profession/role that caters to your innate strengths and abilities, it is likely that you will be highly successful and, therefore, happy. The problem is that *most people are not aware of their innate strengths*. As such, they lack needed insight to align strengths with the 'right' profession/role, thereby denying themselves the opportunity to live happily, fragrantly, meaningfully. People who are aligned with the right profession/role are often top performers, experiencing tremendous professional success. Conversely, those misaligned with their profession/role generally do not perform well and experience only mediocre to modest success. When one understands his/her innate skills and abilities, one can <u>precisely define</u> inner soul goals that leverage such strengths. Moreover, to leverage one's innate strengths is to **establish a personal competitive advantage of the highest order**. It is within your control to leverage innate skill; all it requires is knowing innate skill, and now you do.

Identifying Your Strengths

What are you naturally good at and enjoy doing? Check all that apply.

__ Fixing things	__ Risk taker	__ Hosting events	__ Managing property
__ Leading others	__ Sales	__ Caring for the sick	__ Giving massages
__ Writing	__ Painting	__ Outdoor planning	__ Computer skills
__ Negotiation	__ Teaching others	__ Motivating others	__ Cutting hair
__ Problem solving	__ Cooking	__ Caring for children	__ Beautifying yards
__ Speaking	__ Counseling others	__ Photography	__ Organizing
__ Driving/navigating	__ Carpentry	__ Telling jokes	__ Singing
__ Needlework	__ Drawing	__ Listening	__ Reading
__ Typing	__ Flower arranging	__ Inventing things	__ Preaching
__ Shopping	__ Flying airplanes	__ Dancing	__ Extreme sports
__ Planning vacations	__ Telling stories	__ Maintaining fitness	__ Modeling
__ Piloting a boat	__ Leading hikes	__ Housekeeping	__ Growing plants
__ Lawn care	__ Critiquing books	__ Talking on phone	__ Using your hands
__ Other [ ]	__ Other [ ]	__ Other [ ]	__ Other [ ]
__ Other [ ]	__ Other [ ]	__ Other [ ]	__ Other [ ]

Fig. 6.10

Another exercise that may help reveal innate skill/ability involves answering the question: 'If you retired today, what would you do?' (see Figure 6.11)

Another exercise to generate insight regarding innate skill/ability is to list your life awards and/or accomplishments (see Figure 6.12), as this exercise might reveal what you are naturally good at and enjoy doing.

Lastly, as a means to determine innate skill/ability, think back to former times when you were most happy and record what was happening. Record why you were happy, what you were doing, and what was different (see Figure 6.13). Recalling such memories might reveal a new place to start.

Okay. Now we take what you have learned about self and soul and overlay such insights onto the personal strategy building blocks with the goal of refining and shaping your emerging inner soul goals.

Step 5 – Overlay Personal Strategy Building Blocks

Defining one's inner soul goals is an iterative process, requiring refinement. At this point, you have generated significant raw material revealing the 'emerging' you, but our questioning is not yet complete. To complete our questioning of self, we take accumulated insights, consider them from the perspective of each personal strategy building block, and overlay them onto said building blocks. We use the building block categories to spur thought, organize thought, and help brainstorm for what we want in life and from life at this point in our life. Personal strategy building blocks align with the dimensions of the life experience and the categories used to identify life's pathways. This alignment is necessary, as without such alignment, we would miss identifying important inner soul goals, personal processes to achieve such goals, and, ultimately, fail to maximize the life experience (see Figure 6.14).

If you retired today, what would you do?

Travel the world?	Fly airplanes?	Start public garden?
Create custom furniture?	Be public speaker?	Start a ministry?
Start a school?	Write a book?	Become a river guide?
Start a newspaper?	Create art?	Start a magazine?
Start a winery?	Entertain others?	Become a social worker?
Join the peace corp?	Breed horses?	Teach college classes?
Create documentaries?	Own a farm?	Start a not-for-profit?

Fig. 6.11

What have you achieved?

List of accomplishments

List of awards you have received

Fig. 6.12

Remember when...

Fig. 6.13

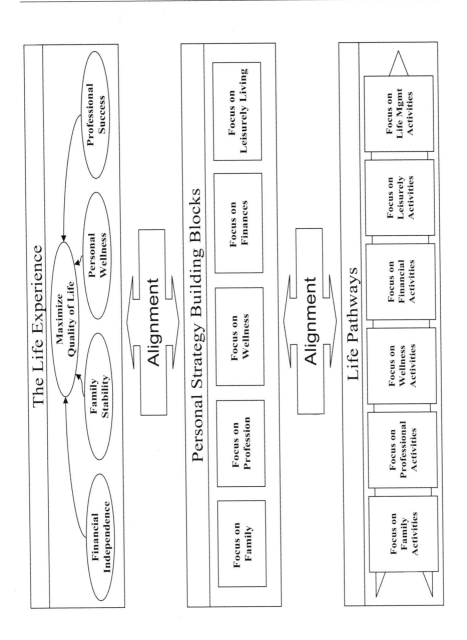

Fig. 6.14

A good personal strategy is a balanced personal strategy, and a balanced personal strategy reflects inner soul goals from each building block category. Therefore, to promote balance, ask these questions of self:

- What do you want to change in your life regarding *family*?
- What do you want to change in your life regarding *profession*?
- What do you want to change in your life regarding *wellness*?
- What do you want to change in your life regarding *finances*?
- What do you want to change in your life regarding *living leisurely*?

Asking the above questions should have prompted new thinking, added to, emerging thoughts about what you want in life and from life. Collectively, all questions in this chapter were designed to generate significant raw material to help you define your inner soul goals (see Figure 6.15). Consequently, all that remains for you to do is define your inner soul goals. We do this next.

Step 6 – Define Inner Soul Goals

Let us recap your conversation with soul:

- You asked questions to determine how you feel, what you want, what stirs soul, and what you aspire to be
- You asked questions to determine personal mission and personal vision
- You asked questions to discover innate skill, those things you are naturally good at and enjoy doing
- You asked questions relative to the building blocks of personal strategy to ensure balance

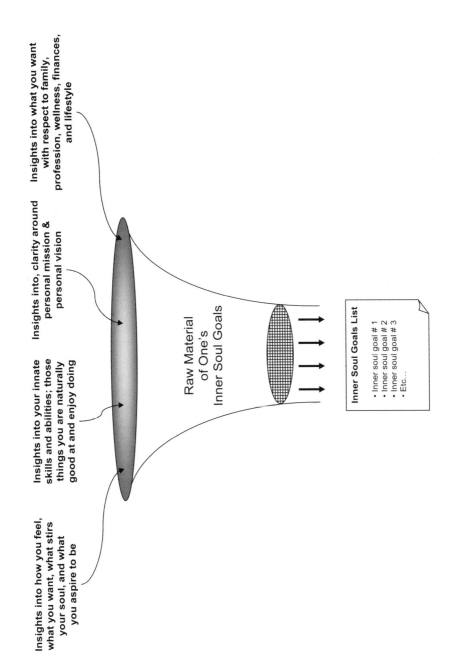

Fig. 6.15

With all this questioning, you should now be able to state your inner soul goals. Having said this, remember to limit your inner soul goals to <u>between five and seven,</u> as any greater number puts you at risk of not achieving any goal.

List your (draft) inner soul goals below:

1. _____

2. _____

3. _____

4. _____

5. _____

6. _____

7. _____

Identifying one's inner soul goals represents a significant milestone when building personal strategy. Congratulations! Inner soul goals serve not only as the foundation of personal strategy, but also one's life. Before identifying life pathways and commitments to achieve new goals, we validate your goals for completeness and quality.

Validating Your Inner Soul Goals

Given the impact inner soul goals have in directing and shaping our life, it is important to perform a quality/completeness check before moving on.

To validate your inner soul goals for completeness is to make sure your goals are mutually exclusive, yet collectively exhaustive, in terms of what you want in life and from life. To perform this check, we use another framework from the personal strategy toolbox (see Figure 6.16).

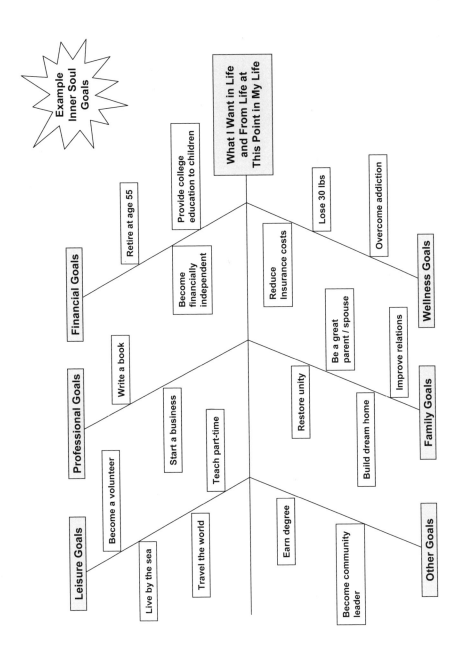

Fig. 6.16

This framework is organized around the personal strategy building blocks. This is deliberate, as we want to define a balanced set of inner soul goals. Although, ultimately, you want only five to seven inner soul goals, you may have generated between ten and twenty goals from previous exercises. Consequently, we use this tool to examine all our 'candidate' inner soul goals and eliminate duplicates. Once you eliminate duplicates, rank and reduce your candidate list to just the top five to seven goals. Refine you inner soul goal list at this time.

Once you have finalized your list, the next thing you do is perform a quality check of such goals (see Figure 6.17).

Inner Soul Goal: _____

Why am I pursuing this goal?

1. _____

2. _____

3. _____

4. _____

5. _____

Fig. 6.17

For each inner soul goal, we ask, 'Why am I pursuing this goal?' Asking this question at this late stage ensures that we have an emotional, spiritual connection to the goal. We validate that each goal is worth paying the price; that commitment exists. If you cannot find compelling reason(s) to pursue a goal, you must drop the goal, as you have no time to waste. As part of this quality check, we pause to reflect on our goals to ensure that they also meet criteria of being a suitable inner soul goal. That is, we validate that each goal is substantive, long-term, meaningful, and represents a desire of soul.

Okay. Now that you have defined and validated your inner soul goals, the question becomes, "How do I achieve them?" To this question, you already know the answer; we achieve our goals via life's pathways.

Identifying Life's Pathways

Knowing what we want in life is necessary, but not sufficient to ensure happiness. Moreover, to say that achieving happiness requires work should come as no surprise. The 'work' I speak of is life's pathways (i.e., personal processes). We have established that achieving our inner soul goals requires knowing which activities to perform. You may be asking, 'How do I know which activities are the 'right' activities to achieve a goal?' To identify the activities to achieve a goal, we use another framework from the personal strategy toolbox (see Figure 6.18).

The framework flows left to right and first requires stating your goal (e.g. 'be exceptionally fit'). Next, we identify the drivers to achieve the goal. Identifying 'drivers' is not difficult, as all that is required of you is to answer the question, 'What do I believe is required to achieve my goal?' The answers to this question reveal 'drivers'. Now, although you may not identify precise drivers, your answers will, at minimum, be directionally correct. Finally, we identify the specific activities (i.e., life pathways) associated with each driver. To identify the activities associated with each driver, we ask, 'What is the activity to accomplish the

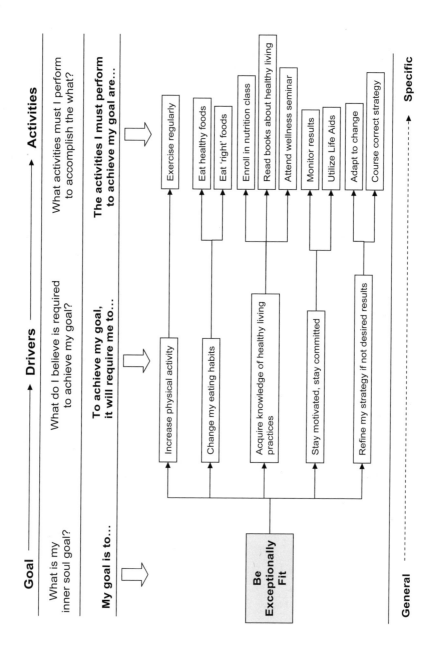

Goal → **Drivers** → **Activities**

What is my inner soul goal?

What do I believe is required to achieve my goal?

What activities must I perform to accomplish the what?

My goal is to...

To achieve my goal, it will require me to...

The activities I must perform to achieve my goal are...

My goal is to...

Be Exceptionally Fit

Increase physical activity → Exercise regularly

Change my eating habits → Eat healthy foods / Eat 'right' foods

Acquire knowledge of healthy living practices → Enroll in nutrition class / Read books about healthy living / Attend wellness seminar

Stay motivated, stay committed → Monitor results / Utilize Life Aids

Refine my strategy if not desired results → Adapt to change / Course correct strategy

General - - - - - - - - - - → Specific

Fig. 6.18

what?' The answer(s) to this question reveals specific activity. This generic framework of [goal → drivers → activities] can be used to identify the life pathways to achieve any goal. At this time, for each inner soul goal, identify the life pathways needed to achieve each goal (see Figure 6.19). Do not obsess about perfection when brainstorming for life's pathways, as you will have opportunity to refine them later when defining your PSM/PSTs.

Life's pathways are the route to results and so to success. Without them, we achieve nothing. With them, we achieve everything. This assumes, of course, that we maintain commitment.

Acknowledge Commitment

Commitment is more than a cornerstone of achievement; it is the *foundation* of achievement. Without commitment, there is no achievement. With commitment, comes achievement. This is undeniable. Commitment is what separates winners and losers. Commitment is what separates achievers from non-achievers. Commitment is what drives life's work. As discussed, there are three forms of personal commitment: mental, physical, and resource. Fully committing to a goal is, itself, a process. At first, we mentally commit to a goal. We decide that a goal is worth paying the price. Then, over time, this commitment deepens into a more formidable type of commitment – physical commitment. We begin to act in the service of our goal combining physical commitment with the follow-on commitment of resources, specifically, time and money. Together, inner soul goals, life pathways, and commitment create an engine of achievement (see Figure 6.20).

Mental Commitment

Defining one's inner soul goals represents the earliest form of commitment, mental commitment. Mental commitment is not only the form from which other forms (of commitment) build; it

Inner Soul Goal: _____

Life Pathway: _____

Fig. 6.19

Fig. 6.20

helps sustain life's work. Therefore, <u>for each</u> life pathway associated with an inner soul goal, identify the mental commitments to sustain life's work. Record mental commitments in the manner illustrated in Figure 6.21. Later, when you create your PSM/PST's, you will need such detail.

Physical Commitment

Achievement requires action. Physical commitment is about action. Consequently, to achieve requires physical commitment – *some form of doing.* Physical commitment is the hardest form of commitment to summon and, therefore, sustain. It is much easier to commit to a goal with one's mind or with resources of time and money. For example, how many times have you said: 'I must lose weight' and you follow this mental commitment with resource commitments of new exercise shorts, shirts, and shoes, only to drop the goal a short time later? It is easy to say, 'I am going to do this or that' and it's easy to allocate money, but only when we physically act in support of a goal do we exhibit physical commitment. As it relates to personal strategy, physical commitment means performing life's pathways. For each life pathway associated with an inner soul goal, identify the physical commitments to sustain life's work. Record physical commitments in the manner illustrated in Figure 6.21. Later, when you create your PSM/PST's, you will need such detail.

Resource Commitment

It almost goes without saying that when one physically commits to a goal with action, one is also, by default, committing resources of time, money, or both. You cannot physically commit to a goal without an equal commitment of resources. For example, going to the gym to exercise requires a commitment of time (to exercise) and money (to pay for gym membership). Likewise, buying the right foods to maintain a healthy diet again requires an investment of time (to shop for food) and money (to buy the food). Finally, learning how to live a healthier lifestyle through self-education requires an investment of time (to read health literature) and money (to pay for a subscription to a health magazine). For each life pathway associated with an inner soul goal, identify the resource commitments to sustain life's work. Record resource commitments in the manner illustrated in Figure 6.21. Later, when you create your PSM/PST's, you will need such detail.

Now that you have identified your inner soul goals, life pathways, and commitments, we pause again to perform a completeness check of your work. Figure 6.22 illustrates the cascading relationship of inner soul goal to life pathways to commitments.

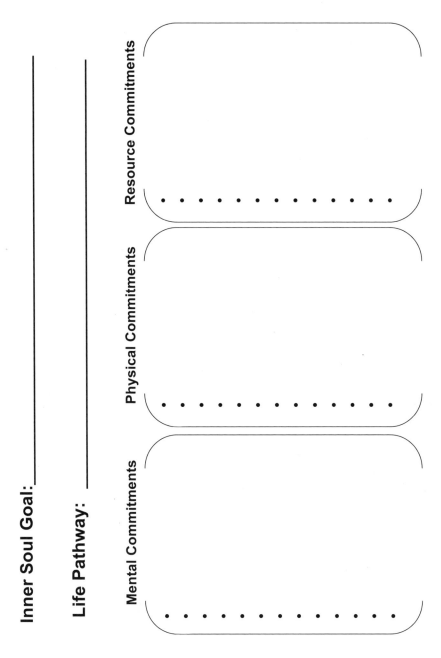

Fig. 6.21

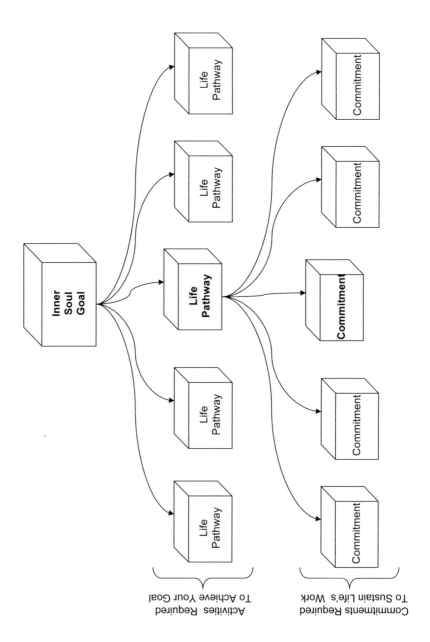

Fig. 6.22

You should have the raw material to create a similar map <u>for each</u> of your inner soul goals. Creating such a map is useful, as it reveals potential gaps in thinking and, therefore, one's strategy. Further, it makes explicit the hidden cause and effect relations that exist between components that enable goal achievement. Lastly, such a map allows us to ensure causality exists from component to component. That is, it allows us the opportunity to verify that stated commitments will drive stated life pathways and life pathways will achieve our inner soul goal. At this time, complete a similar map <u>for each</u> of your inner soul goals.

Congratulations! You have just completed Phase II of building your personal strategy. Before walking into Phase III, you should be walking out of Phase II with the following:

- Personal mission
- Personal vision
- List of your inner soul goals
- List of life pathways to achieve <u>each</u> goal
- List of commitments to sustain <u>each</u> life pathway

The essence of Phase II was about identifying what you want in life and from life at this point in your life. I hope that your inward bound journey produced insights to define a new life plan. Now, we segue to Phase III to document your new life plan in the form of a Personal Strategy Map.

Phase III – Develop Personal Strategy Map

We have completed the first two phases of the process for building personal strategy. With insights from Phase II, you can now create your Personal Strategy Map. As each phase of the strategy development process builds upon work from previous phases, I will assume that you are current through Phase II. The work of Phase III, like previous phases, contains steps to perform, outputs to realize, and enablers to leverage.

Phase III steps include:

- Completing the <u>Life Experience</u> section of the Personal Strategy Map
- Completing the <u>Inner Soul</u> section of the Personal Strategy Map
- Completing the <u>Life Pathways</u> section of the Personal Strategy Map
- Completing the <u>Commitments</u> section of the Personal Strategy Map

Phase III outputs include:

- Personal Strategy Map (draft)

Phase III enablers include:

- Solitude
- PSM Framework
- List of inner soul goals
- List of life pathways
- List of commitments

Phase III is about piecing together the raw material of personal strategy to form a Personal Strategy Map. We build one section of the map at a time while leveraging the enablers listed above. We begin with 'The Life Experience'.

The Life Experience

To define the life experience component of a PSM is to make explicit the type of life you hope to realize. Therefore, to complete this section, we begin by reviewing your list of inner soul goals and define the hoped-for outcomes you expect to realize from achieving <u>each</u> goal. For example, if you had a goal to 'start a business', you would ask, 'what are my hoped-for outcomes from achieving this goal?' You might identify these outcomes:

- Greater personal freedom
- Increased happiness
- Increased meaning in life
- Greater income
- Increased motivation to work
- Greater flexibility

Let us say that your goal was to 'be exceptionally fit'; you might identify these outcomes:

- Live a long life
- Greater self-esteem
- Increased mental health
- Reduced medical expenses
- Greater physical strength
- Reduced life insurance costs
- Improved physical appearance

The purpose of this exercise is to identify how you benefit from achieving your goals. Once you identify hoped-for outcomes for each inner soul goal, the next step is to align each outcome with a dimension of the life experience. Therefore, if an outcome aligns with personal wellness, list the outcome under the personal wellness category. If an outcome aligns with finances, list the outcome under the financial independence category. Continue in this manner until all outcomes align with a specific life experience category. When completing this exercise, remain mindful that achieving a single inner soul goal may benefit multiple dimensions of the life experience. At this time, complete the life experience section of your PSM.

The life experience component of a PSM not only represents a vision for one's life, but also reflects the quality of one's life. In other words, it is both prospective and reflective. It is prospective in that the outcomes we hope for represent a desired future state. It is reflective in that we can assess the quality of our life by examining the current state of each life experience category. In relation to other PSM components, we spend less time defining the life experience, as the life experience represents an outcome and, thus, can only be observed rather than directly acted upon. Instead, we spend most of our time on the factors that 'drive' the life experience. In other words, we focus on those things we can directly act upon (i.e., our thoughts, our actions, and our commitments). The first factor is the inner soul.

The Inner Soul

In Phase II, you identified your inner soul goals – those things you want in life and from life at this point in your life. To complete the inner soul component of your PSM, simply transpose your goals from your inner soul goals list onto the PSM template. When recording your inner soul goals, consider these guidelines:

- State one goal per oval
- Use phrases such as 'Want to...'
- Limit the number of inner soul goals to between five and seven

At this point in the process, it is not important to state your inner soul goals in precise terms. For example, it is ok to state a goal in general terms, such as 'be exceptionally fit' versus the more precise goal 'lose 30 lbs by December 31st'. In Chapter 7, we introduce another framework from the personal strategy toolbox to define one's goals precisely.

Upon completing the inner soul section of the PSM, we document the life pathways needed to achieve our goals.

Life Pathways

We have reached the halfway point in building a Personal Strategy Map. We have completed the life experience component and the inner soul goals component. Now, we document the life pathways needed to achieve our goals. We record this information in the life pathways section of the PSM. You should have identified the personal processes to achieve your inner soul goals during Phase II. With such insights, you can now complete the life pathways component of your PSM. To complete the task, simply transpose each personal process identified during Phase II beneath its related life pathway category on the PSM template. For example, if one of your inner soul goals was to 'be a teacher', and to achieve this goal it required you develop new skills and capabilities, then beneath the <u>profession</u> life pathways grouping, you would record the following personal processes:

- Develop teaching skills
- Acquire knowledge of teaching practices
- Develop teaching capabilities
- Obtain teaching certificate
- Perform job search

It is best to record personal processes in verb-noun format, as this is a crisper way to document needed action. One of the reasons to create a PSM is to identify the high-level processes you need to perform to achieve your inner soul goals. The key phrase here is 'high-level'. The processes recorded on your PSM represent high-level abstractions of the *real work* to perform. At this point, we are just looking to get directionally correct with our strategy, not precise. Later, when we create Personal Strategic Themes, you will have opportunity to identify more specific, tactical actions to achieve each inner soul goal. When finished transposing all personal processes, each life pathway category will contain several processes supporting one or more inner soul goals. Upon completing the life pathways section of the PSM, the last and final step is to document the personal commitments to sustain process work.

Commitments

Nothing of great significance is accomplished in life without commitment. All actions in life require commitment and, usually, require all three forms of commitment we are now familiar with: mental commitment, physical commitment, and resource commitment. When brainstorming for commitments in Phase

II, it is likely that many of the commitments you identified to support one life pathway actually support several, if not all, life pathways. For example, in Table 6.1, several of the <u>same</u> mental, physical, and resource commitments support multiple inner soul goals:

√ Keeping goal top-of-mind
√ Paying the price
√ Monitor results
√ Reflect on results
√ Adapt to change
√ Allocate time
√ Allocate funds

Table 6.1

Inner Soul Goal	Mental Commitment	Physical Commitment	Resource Commitment
Be exceptionally fit	√ **Keep goal top of mind** √ See myself as I am – out of shape √ Commit to exercise √ Commit to healthy eating √ **Commit to paying the price**	√ Eat healthy food √ Exercise regularly √ Read health magazines / articles √ **Monitor results** √ **Reflect on results** √ **Adapt to change**	√ **Allocate time** to exercise √ **Allocate funds** to purchase exercise equipment/ clothes and/or club membership √ Allocate funds to purchase dietary foods/ supplements
Start a business	√ Keep goal top of mind √ Commit to paying the price √ Other… √ Other…	√ Monitor results √ Reflect on results √ Adapt to change √ Other…	√ Allocate time to… √ Allocate funds to… √ Other… √ Other…
Help disadvantaged children	√ Keep goal top of mind √ Commit to paying the price √ Other… √ Other…	√ Monitor results √ Reflect on results √ Adapt to change √ Other…	√ Allocate time to… √ Allocate funds to… √ Other… √ Other…

As you complete the commitments section of your PSM, do not be concerned if many of the same commitments span multiple goals. The two forms of commitment in which we expect redundancy are mental commitment and resource commitment. Mental commitment caters to the same demands of most goals, which is to 1) keep the goal top of mind and 2) pay the price. Resource commitment is principally about committing time and money. Since some goals require an investment of money and all goals require an investment of time, we would expect redundancy here as well. When completing the commitments section on the PSM template, the goal is to document all commitments you identified in Phase II beneath the proper heading (mental, physical, or resource). When completing this task, only record <u>unique</u> commitments even though redundancy may exist across goals.

Congratulations! You have completed your first Personal Strategy Map. You are on your way to realizing the 'emerging' you. As we conclude Phase III, let us summarize what a Personal Strategy Map offers us, tells us, and enables us to do.

A Personal Strategy Map **offers us**...

- A framework to define, organize, document, and communicate what we want in life and from life, throughout life
- A single repository to capture the raw material of personal strategy (inner soul goals, life pathways, and commitments)
- A single document that represents <u>our current life strategy</u> to maximize the personal, professional, and financial potential that life offers

A Personal Strategy Map **tells us**...

- How to achieve our goals by performing specific life's pathways backed by commitment
- No goal or dream is too big, too complex, too out of reach, or too impossible to achieve with a personal strategy

Λ Personal Strategy Map **enables us…**

- To confidently take on the world, rise up, and experience a lifetime of happiness, meaning, and achievement
- To serve as author and lead actor in designing and deploying a new life plan; to realize a different life story
- To seize opportunity and meet imperative

Our goal of developing a personal strategy for living is more than halfway complete. Persevere, my friend; the future you is depending on your current efforts. Now, whereas Phase III was about developing a Personal Strategy Map, of which there is one, Phase IV is about developing Personal Strategic Themes, of which there are many. Let us continue.

Phase IV – Develop Personal Strategic Themes

The first three phases are now complete. Up to this point, we were mostly documenting the 'what' of personal strategy. Now, we document the 'how' of personal strategy. The framework we use to document the 'how' of personal strategy is a Personal Strategic Theme.

Phase IV of the process for building personal strategy represents a movement from thinking to doing and, as in previous phases, has steps to perform, outputs to realize, and enablers to leverage.

Phase IV steps include:

- Completing the <u>Embedded Personal Strategy Map</u> section of the Personal Strategic Theme
- Completing the <u>Personal Scorecard</u> section of the Personal Strategic Theme
- Completing the <u>Action Plan</u> section of the Personal Strategic Theme

Phase IV outputs include:

- Personal Strategic Themes* (draft)
  *Note: We create a PST <u>for each</u> inner soul goal.

Phase IV enablers include:

- Solitude
- PST Framework
- Personal Strategy Map (draft)

Whereas Phase III brought together raw material of personal strategy, Phase IV breaks it apart. We begin by defining strategy to achieve a single inner soul goal.

Building Your ePSM

As our focus now is to develop strategy to achieve a single inner soul goal, we begin by stating a theme for our PST. A theme literally equates to an inner soul goal. In this way, we define personal strategy one theme or one goal at a time. You should have identified between five and seven inner soul goals on your PSM. Each inner soul goal will become its own PST. Thus, if you have six inner soul goals, you will create six PST's. It is best to complete one PST at a time, as each PST requires defining unique strategy. Using the PST template as your guide, record the PST theme name (of your first PST) in the space provided at the top of the ePSM section. Next, record your inner soul goal within the inner soul section. (Note: your PST theme name and inner soul goal should be the same.)

Next, record the personal processes to achieve this goal in the life pathways section of the ePSM. Finally, record the specific mental, physical, and resource commitments to sustain process work. When these sections are complete, specify the dimensions of the life experience (e.g., financial, family, wellness, professional) that benefit from achieving your goal. You should have all the detail you need to complete activities above, as it exists on your PSM. (Note: this is now the time to reexamine life pathways and commitments to ensure that both will drive achieving your inner soul goal.)

At this point, you have defined strategy to achieve a single inner soul goal. Specifically, you have:

- Stated what you want in life and from life (inner soul goal)
- Identified the specific activities to achieve your goal (life pathways)
- Identified the specific commitments to sustain life's work (commitments)
- Identified how your life experience will benefit from achieving your goal (life experience)

Despite this effort, you are not yet finished with defining the ePSM, as you need to complete the goals section.

The goals section (of an ePSM) makes strategy explicit. As we did not define support goals when developing our PSM, this is new territory for us. How do we begin? We approach by identifying support goals on a component-by-component basis within your ePSM, beginning with the life experience component. In Phase III, you completed pre-work for this component by answering the question, 'How will my life experience improve by achieving my inner soul goal?' Using answers to the question above, record your goals for the life experience component. Next, we focus on the inner soul goal component. Generally, the inner soul goal component contains only one or two support goals, in addition to your inner soul goal. For example, if your inner soul goal is to 'be exceptionally fit' your goals might be: 1) lose weight 2) increase muscle tone, and 3) be exceptionally fit. Record your inner soul goal (and related support goals) at this time. Next, we record our goals with respect to the life pathways component. Identifying which goals to represent the life pathways component is not difficult. The life pathways section goals generally represent a restatement of your life pathways themselves. Therefore, at this time, record your life pathways goals.

Lastly, we record our goals for the commitment component. Of the several mental, physical, and resource commitments you may have listed, only a few goals result. The reason for this is that not all commitments (e.g. mental) convert easily to goal form. That is, not all commitments are easily measured. At this time, record your commitment related goals.

Stating one's goals explicitly may seem a redundant exercise (especially in those cases where a goal is simply a restatement of a life pathway or commitment), but there is value in putting goals in writing. We put goals in writing because a written goal:

- Is visible
- Is real
- Indicates priority
- Represents truth
- Inspires us to achieve
- Demands action
- Does not fade due to frail memory or passing of time
- Is fiercely front-and-center
- Is half-achieved

Once you identify your goals, the next step in developing your PST is to identify the performance measures to monitor progress towards achieving such goals.

Building Your Personal Scorecard

Having support goals is necessary but not sufficient to achieve your inner soul goal. It also requires using performance measures to indicate progress; to tell you if you are on track to achieve your goal. Now, just as each goal aligns with a specific component on our ePSM, so, too, does each measure. Having said this, not all support goals require a companion measure. Generally, it is best to limit the number of performance measures on a PST to between five and seven measures. The reason for this is that each performance measure requires effort to collect data, report data, and analyze results. All this activity requires time – *your time*.

As such, the more performance measures you have, the more effort is required to manage personal strategy. A better approach is to identify five to seven indicators that *best serve* as personal progress meters to achieve your inner soul goal. The collection of all measures on your PST represents your personal scorecard. You may be asking, 'How does one identify the vital few measures?' There is no easy answer to this question. Identifying which measures to use is part science, part experience, part art. Your ability to define measures that best predict goal achievement will improve over time. As such, your scorecard will perpetually evolve, as some measures will drop off while others are added. As with most things in life, trial and error is your best teacher. The question we ask to identify performance measures is, 'What vital few measures will serve as reliable indicators to tell me if my strategy is working?' Initially, we rely more on gut feelings than practical experience to answer this question. The characteristics of a good scorecard measure are:

- Aligns with a support goal
- Is specific
- Is measurable
- Data can be obtained easily
- Indicates progress with achieving one's inner soul goal
- Drives achievement of one's inner soul goal
- Indicates effectiveness with performing life's pathways (or)
- Indicates effectiveness with maintaining commitment (or)
- Indicates effectiveness of action plan initiatives/tasks

As you brainstorm for what measures to include on your personal scorecard, remember that not all components (of your ePSM) are created equal. Because life pathways and commitments 'drive' the life experience, it is best to have the majority of your performance measures associate with these components. Lastly, although you can define measures for the life experience component, only rarely is this necessary. Why is this so? We define scorecard measures to achieve our inner soul goal, and if we are successful, that is, if we achieve our goal, then, by default, our life experience improves. Consequently, there is no need to measure how our life has improved, as we already know. At this time, define five to seven performance measures you will use to drive achieving your inner soul goal.

Defining performance measures represents only half your personal scorecard. You also need to define target values for each measure. Target values associate with a specific measure and represent a performance level to which to strive. The purpose of target values is to stretch us, not defeat us. In other words, target values should be attainable, not impossible. For each measure, specify a target value that will stretch you, not defeat you. The most important target value is, of course, the one associated with your inner soul goal measure(s). Achieving your inner soul goal is the reason we create personal strategy. As such, your focus is necessarily on achieving the target value associated with this goal. As you complete your personal scorecard, consider these guidelines:

- Skew your measures such that 80% associate with life pathways and commitment sections and 20% associate with inner soul and life experience sections
- Limit the number of measures on each PST to between five and seven
- Define measures that will drive your inner soul goal
- Define measures that are specific and easily measured
- Specify target values that stretch you, not defeat you

Let us pause to review your progress in creating a Personal Strategic Theme. You have:

- Stated a theme for your PST (inner soul goal)
- Developed a strategy to achieve your inner soul goal (ePSM) including developing support goals
- Defined performance measures (w/ target values) to monitor your progress

Okay. So what remains for you to do? You need to develop an action plan.

Building Your Action Plan

Action plans detail our 'opening moves' to achieve both support goals and our inner soul goal. To identify the right opening moves requires performing a systemic review of all components of your PST:

- Life pathways
- Commitments
- Support goals
- Measures

For the components shown above, we ask the following questions (see Table 6.2), as the answers help reveal the initiatives and tasks that constitute opening moves:

Table 6.2

PST Component	Question to Ask
Life Pathways	What actions/tasks must I perform relative to the personal processes identified in the life pathways section?
Commitments	What actions/tasks must I perform to maintain commitments to sustain life's work?
Support Goals	What actions/tasks must I perform to achieve both my support goals and my inner soul goal?
Measures	What actions/tasks must I perform to measure performance, to indicate if my strategy is working?

Developing your action plan will take time. Many tasks will come to you naturally; others will not. The challenge is to identify the subtle, but vital, actions that hide behind obvious. To identify these hidden actions requires hard thinking. Developing an effective action plan requires you to *push past the obvious to get to the hidden*. Force yourself to be creative, push your thinking to identify the lower-level, tactical actions to achieve your goal. You may feel a certain amount of anxiety when developing your action plan, asking questions such as, 'Have I identified the right opening moves? and 'How do I know if my initiatives and tasks will achieve my goals?' Do not let self-doubt debilitate you. What is important when developing an action plan is that it be 'directionally correct', not precise. If all your initiatives/tasks focus on achieving your goal(s), you can feel confident that you identified the right opening moves. Worst-case scenario, you discover that current actions will not lead you to the Promised Land and you course correct personal strategy accordingly. At this time, detail the actions and tasks that comprise your action plan; that is, constitute your opening moves. Lastly, define budget estimates for those tasks requiring funding.

Congratulations! You have completed your first Personal Strategic Theme. **Remember: you create a PST <u>for each</u> inner soul goal.** As we conclude Phase IV, let us summarize what Personal Strategic Themes offer us, tell us, and enable us to do.

A Personal Strategic Theme **offers us...**

- A framework to define, organize, document, and communicate tactical-level strategy to achieve a goal
- An approach to reduce complexity when developing personal strategy while adding controlled amounts of detail to further refine personal strategy

A Personal Strategic Theme **tells us...**

- How, specifically, to *manufacture* achievement through setting goals, measuring progress, and developing targeted action plans
- The goals that matter most, measures that matter most, and actions that matter most to achieve a single inner soul goal
- What to 'course correct' if our personal strategy is 'off the mark'

A Personal Strategic Theme **enables us...**

- To confidently take on the world, achieve our goals, and live happily
- To view any goal as achievable
- To convert dreams to reality

Developing personal strategy, as you are now well aware, requires considerable effort. It first requires knowing <u>what</u> you want in life and from life then it requires knowing <u>how</u> to get what you want. In the first four phases of the process, we learned how to access soul and identify what we want in life. We also learned how using frameworks such as a Personal Strategy Map and a Personal Strategic Theme can help us define, organize, document, and communicate personal strategy. Upon completing Phase IV, you now have an actionable and balanced personal strategy. You are poised to realize a more meaningful, liberated, and fragrant life experience.

Before we discuss implementing (i.e., realizing) personal strategy, we reflect upon and refine your new life story to ensure that chapters are complete, that storylines are well organized, and that the right themes are considered.

Phase V — Reflect, Refine, and Realize

You have entered the final phase of the process for building personal strategy. The blueprints have been drawn and the foundation has been laid; now it is time to execute. Before implementing your PST's, however, it is important to reflect upon and refine your work from previous phases.

The essence of Phase V is suspension. To suspend is to cease for a period, to pause. Suspension occurs before we execute personal strategy and then, as we will discuss in Chapter 10, occurs periodically throughout our life. Why do we pause? Just as a good carpenter suspends [his cut] to reflect and refine, so, too, do we suspend [implementing personal strategy] to reflect and refine. Phase V, like other phases, has steps to perform, outputs to realize, and enablers to leverage.

Phase V steps include:

- Assemble personal strategy

- Reflect on and refine your PSM
  - Inner Soul Goals
  - Life Pathways
  - Commitments

- Reflect on and refine <u>each</u> PST
  - ePersonal Strategy Map
  - Personal Scorecard
  - Action Plan

- Reflect on whole personal strategy
- Refine personal strategy
- Realize personal strategy

Phase V outputs include:

- Personal Strategy Map (final)
- Personal Strategic Themes (final)

Phase V enablers include:

- Solitude
- Personal Strategy Map (draft)
- Personal Strategic Themes (draft)

You may be asking, "Why must we review entire personal strategy? Have we not developed a comprehensive, actionable, and thoughtful personal strategy?" The primary reason we review our work prior to implementing personal strategy is that much time may have elapsed for you to complete the work of previous phases and your thinking may have evolved. In other words, your inner soul goals may be out of date. Further, you may have identified more precise activities to achieve your goals or commitments to sustain life's work. Above all, we perform a review because our personal happiness and our life experience are at stake. Figure 6.23 highlights the steps to review your personal strategy.

Fig. 6.23

Listed below is a summary of tasks to perform within each step of the review:

Assemble Your Personal Strategy

- Print your PSM and PST's on 11x17 (tabloid) size paper
- Arrange your personal strategy as a book
  - Your Personal Strategy Map is the table of contents of your book
  - Your Personal Strategic Themes are the chapters of your book

Reflect on Your Personal Strategy Map

- Review your PSM in isolation

- When reviewing your PSM, consider these questions:
  - Are the inner soul goals on your PSM still what you want in life and from life at this point in your life?
  - Have any inner soul goals become obsolete due to changes occurring within?
  - Have any inner soul goals become obsolete due to changes occurring without?

- Your PSM should communicate what you want in life and from life throughout life
- Mark necessary revisions on your PSM

Reflect on Your Personal Strategic Themes

- Review each PST in isolation
- <u>For each PST</u>, consider these questions:
  - Will stated activities and support goals drive achieving your inner soul goal?
  - Will stated commitments sustain life's work?
  - Do you have between five and seven performance measures to monitor your progress?
  - Will your performance measures reliably indicate whether your personal strategy is working?
  - Do your performance measures reflect a higher concentration in the life pathways and commitments components than in other components?

- Your personal processes and support goals should drive your inner soul goal
- Your commitments should sustain life's work
- You should have five to seven performance measures to monitor your progress
  - Your performance measures should align more so with the life pathways and commitments components than other components on your PST
- Mark necessary revisions on each PST

Reflect on Your Entire Personal Strategy

- Tape your PSM on a large wall
- Tape each of your PST's beneath the PSM
- Think about the relations between your PSM and subordinate PST's
- View your personal strategy <u>holistically</u> with parts becoming whole
- Consider these questions when reviewing your PSM and PST's together <u>as a system</u>:

  - Do your goals complement one another?
  - Are there holes in your personal strategy?
  - Does your personal strategy reflect your mission, vision?
  - Will your personal strategy help you realize mission, vision?
  - Have you defined too many inner soul goals, putting at risk your entire personal strategy?
  - Have you defined too many performance measures, putting at risk your entire personal strategy?
  - Will your personal strategy deliver the type of life experience you desire?
  - Will achieving your personal strategy make you happy?
  - Does your personal strategy inspire you?

- Your inner soul goals should complement one another; reflect a unified vision for self
- If your personal strategy reflects what you want in life and from life at this point in your life, you should not have any holes in your personal strategy
- Your personal strategy should realize your personal mission, vision; it should drive where you want to be and how you want to operate on the surface of life
- You should have only five to seven inner soul goals
- You should have only five to seven performance measures <u>for each</u> inner soul goal

- Achieving your personal strategy should increase personal happiness
- Your personal strategy should inspire you to begin transformation
- Mark additional revisions on your PSM and PST's

Refine and Realize

- Summarize the revisions to make to your personal strategy
- Update your PSM and/or PST's to reflect current thinking

To realize personal strategy means to execute (i.e., implement) personal strategy, but to execute personal strategy first requires a plan. The good news is you have a plan. That is what your PSM and portfolio of PST's collectively represent. As such, we simply need to know what it means to implement personal strategy.

To implement (realize) personal strategy means:

- Sequencing action plan initiatives
- Executing initiatives
- Collecting scorecard data
- Recording scorecard data
- Allocating resources
- Assessing progress made
- Reviewing personal strategy
- Refining personal strategy
- Developing/utilizing 'life aids'

Designing personal strategy and implementing personal strategy are fundamentally different tasks, but each needs the other. It is not enough to design personal strategy complete with the right goals, activities, commitments, and scorecard measures, as if you poorly implement personal strategy, you will not achieve your goals. We know this to be true, as many companies craft the 'perfect' corporate strategy to increase customer satisfaction, revenue, and profitability, only to mismanage the implementation, resulting in no significant improvement. Hence, to deliver the life experience you desire not only requires having a well-defined personal strategy, but also requires you effectively implement strategy. Know this: the difference between those who succeed with personal strategy and those who do not <u>is a matter of execution</u>. Put bluntly, successful people execute, commit, make the effort, while unsuccessful people do not.

Now, having said this, to sustain effort, requires staying 'in the zone'. The best, most reliable, way to stay 'in the zone' is <u>for you to inspire you</u>. As inspiration is sometimes hard to come by, especially when first implementing personal strategy, there exist a number of 'life aids' one can use to maintain enthusiasm, maintain momentum, and stay 'in the zone'. Life aids are similar in purpose and function to 'job aids' in the workplace. In the same way that people in the workplace develop checklists, cheat sheets, and other job aids to achieve corporate strategy so, too, do we use life aids in our private lives to achieve personal strategy.

Specifically, we use life aids to help us:

- **Remember** *(mission and vision)*
- **Stay motivated** *(to achieve our goals)*
- **Stay enthused** *(to implement personal strategy)*
- **Establish momentum** *(to achieve personal strategy)*
- **Develop consistency** *(in managing personal strategy)*
- **Establish habit** *(of managing our life)*
- **Focus** *(on attaining the prize, personal happiness)*

So, what are examples of life aids? Consider the examples in Table 6.3.

Table 6.3

Example of 'Life Aid'	How It Can Help You Stay 'In The Zone'
Index Cards	You can use index cards to remind self of what to see, how to think, and how to act. For example, you may use index cards to remind self of: • Reasons to pursue your inner soul goals • Quotes that inspire soul • Your personal vision and mission in life
Goal Marker	Goal markers are visual reminders of your goal strategically placed throughout your house, car, and office to keep your goal in your face and top-of-mind. For example, if your goal is to lose weight you might have goal markers (e.g. sticky notes) in the bathroom, in the closet, in the kitchen, in your car, and at your workplace reminding you to lose weight.
Songs (custom-made CD)	Songs can inspire and evoke feelings and emotions that put you in the right state of mind to achieve your goals. Create a custom CD (or MP3 list) with songs that inspire. Play the CD/list every morning on your way to work. Start your day with a dose of inspiration.
Movies	Movies can inspire and evoke feelings and emotions that put you in the right state of mind to achieve your goals. Watch movies that inspire.
Quotations, Books, Articles	Certain books and/or articles can inspire and evoke feelings and emotions that put you in the right state of mind to achieve your goals. Read books that inspire.

Continued on next page

Table 6.3 (Continued)

Example of 'Life Aid'	How It Can Help You Stay 'In The Zone'
Goals Collage	A goals collage is a collection of images of how you want your life to be. Such images inspire us to achieve our goals, to live as soul would live. For example, if your goal is to earn high wealth and live in a tropical paradise, you might have a picture of a beautiful home on the island of Maui. Similarly, if your goal is to be exceptionally fit, you might have pictures of other people exhibiting extreme fitness.
Morning Routine	Establish a :30 minute morning routine to review your goals (index cards), listen to songs that inspire (custom CD), and read inspiring quotes. Develop a morning reflective ritual to put oneself 'in the zone'.
Evening Routine	Establish a :30 minute evening routine to review your day. Identify course corrections to improve personal strategy.
Sunday Routine	Establish a Sunday evening routine to review your goals and progress made during the week. Allocate 60 minutes to the exercise. Converse with soul to discuss all aspects of your personal strategy.
Monthly Routine	Establish a monthly routine to review progress made during the month to achieve your goals. Use your monthly review as an opportunity to course correct personal strategy.
Annual Routine	Establish a tradition of allocating a few vacation days each year to reflect on your personal strategy for living. Review all aspects of your personal strategy. Review your inner soul goals to ensure that they are still what you want in life and from life. Update all objects of your personal strategy. Update/create new life aids to inspire another year of commitment and achievement.

I cannot stress enough the value of using life aids to <u>help</u> <u>you</u> achieve your goals. Even as I write this book, I use all the life aids just described to motivate and inspire me to achieve my goals. I read index cards containing inspirational quotes and other sayings designed to inspire. I listen to a custom-made CD with songs that inspire. I read passages from books that inspire. I watch movies that inspire. I have a goals collage in my home office inspiring me to pay-the-price. I've established morning and evening routines to 'bookend' my day. I've established a routine on Sunday nights to 'bookend my week'. I've established a monthly routine to 'bookend my month'. And I've established a yearly routine to 'bookend my year'. Why do I do all this? Because I need to. Like most people, I possess intermittent will. As such, I <u>need</u> life aids to keep me motivated, keep me inspired, and help me achieve my goals. If I did not review my goals several times a week, if I did not inspire self with songs, movies, and readings, I would not achieve my goals. I know this about myself. Perhaps you are the same. You may not need to use all the life aids I use. Then again, maybe you need more, or different, life aids. At the end of the day, <u>you must inspire you</u>. YOU must do what is needed to help YOU achieve YOUR goals. If this requires using ten life aids, as I do, so be it. There is no shame in relying on life aids to help you achieve your goals. If you are serious about achieving your inner soul goals, and I am confident that you are, then I am also confident that you will find the courage, desire, and creativity for you to inspire you.

We have reached chapter's end. Before you implement your personal strategy, before we conclude Part II, there is one matter to discuss – the practice of keeping score.

Keeping Score

"And I also know how important it is in life not necessarily to be strong but to feel strong, to measure yourself at least once."

- Into the Wild

TO MEASURE YOURSELF, THAT IS THE CALL. The reality is few people measure their lives with the intent of improving their lives. This is not surprising given that we were never taught the need for, or how to, measure our life. Nevertheless, to measure yourself is essential to achieve personal strategy; to live a fragrant life. For without keeping score, we do not know where we are to know what to do to get where we want to go. In Chapter 5, you learned that measuring one's performance, via personal scorecards, is important to achieve one's goals. In Chapter 6, you applied such learning to define your own measures, develop your own scorecards. Now, in this chapter, we build upon recent learnings by discussing how to *keep score* beginning with learning what it means to measure the life experience.

What Does It Mean to Measure the Life Experience?

In Chapter 4, we learned that the essence of personal strategy is to move from present position to a more desirable, but uncertain, future position. To inspire such movement, we use performance measures, as measures inspire performance in addition to providing indication (or comparison) of where we are relative to where we want to be. The act of measuring the life experience has both symbolic meaning and tactical meaning:

Symbolic Meaning

- One is committed to paying-the-price for success
- One is serious about achieving one's goals; about actively working in the service of one's goals
- One understands that what is measured (in life) is what gets done (in life)
- Taking accountability for one's life, being proactive with life, attacking life
- Taking an active interest in achieving one's goals
- To set apart life of old for life anew
- To live rigorously, deliberately
- To establish new patterns for one's life
- To bring about emerging you
- To continually assess one's life
- To compete, to establish competitive advantage
- To establish new rhythm for one's life
- To become intimate with life
- To make explicit one's desire to 'go the other way'

Tactical Meaning

- To measure one's actions, degree of commitment, level of progress
- To explore the hidden side of self, soul, and one's personal strategy

- To establish a basis for comparison; to establish a reference point of where we are relative to where we want to be; to quantify where we are relative to where we want to be
- To ascertain the effectiveness of personal strategy (strategy, goals, initiatives/tasks) to improve personal strategy
- To drive new habits to realize new results
- To evaluate, assess, and improve one's thinking, acting, and feeling on the surface of life to improve one's life
- To achieve one's goals

Hopefully, the list above sheds light on what it means to measure the life experience. For purposes herein, when we talk of measuring the life experience, we are talking about measuring our life performance against expectations – of "doing what we said we would do". We do this, as *there is no commitment to one's goals without an equal commitment to their measurement*. Hence, the need to measure the life experience is revealed.

Knowing <u>what</u> it means to measure the life experience is instructive. What is more instructive, of greater interest, however, is <u>why</u> we should measure the life experience.

Why Measure the Life Experience?

In the last section, we learned what it means to measure the life experience. Now, we learn why we should measure the life experience, and the reasons are many.

As it relates to personal strategy, measuring the life experience:

- Provides needed feedback to assess and improve our life
- Ignites questions; develops a questioning attitude
- Keeps goals in our face and top-of-mind
- Breathes life into a goal, keeps it alive

- Helps us to better understand personal strategy and its capability to deliver hoped-for results
- Enables us to assess effectiveness of personal strategy
- Informs us of when to course correct personal strategy
- Is an antidote to complacency
- Indicates progress
- Makes life performance visible; communicates performance
- Creates momentum
- Maintains momentum
- Drives completion of goals

As it relates to our life, measuring the life experience:

- Helps us to learn how to maximize scarce resources (time, energy, money)
- Serves as a record of accomplishment
- Develops within us a habit of monitoring life performance
- Reinforces (the habit of) monitoring life performance
- Dislodges old to make way for new
- Develops a capability to manage one's life
- Indicates what aspects of our life to improve
- Enables us to succeed in life
- Allows us to live a happy, fragrant, meaningful life
- Helps us to align the inner soul with action

Any of the entries above is reason enough to measure the life experience, but one reason stands above all others: measuring the life experience helps us to align the inner soul with action.

Aligning the Inner Soul with Action

To align the inner soul with action is not only the subtitle of this book; it represents this book's core essence. When I say, "align the inner soul with action", what I mean is to align one's heart, head, and hands around common goals. In Chapter 6, you descended into self to find soul and, in the process, discovered your inner soul goals. However, knowing soul, conversing with soul is not enough to establish alignment. We must act in the service of soul; performing life pathways, maintaining commitment, living as soul would live. When we align our heart (soul), head, and hands around common goals great things happen – *we achieve our goals* (see Figure 7.1).

Now, to achieve our goals, to align intent with action, we measure, 'keep score', as this will ensure our thinking (head) and actions (hands) are aligned with that which matters most (heart). Aligning the inner soul with action is our reason for being; it is all our reasons.

Measuring the Life Experience

With what and why of measuring the life experience behind us, now we focus on <u>how</u> to measure the life experience. Collecting performance data on scorecard measures is the mechanism by which we 'keep score' and although you may know what to measure, questions likely remain as to how to do it.

For example:

- How does one <u>manage</u> the 30-40 measures across all PST's?
- How does one <u>collect</u> data? What method does one use?
- How does one <u>assess</u> data collected? What does one look for?
- How does one <u>report</u> progress with achieving one's inner soul goal and support goals?

These questions represent 'how' aspects of measuring the life experience and, of course, when we speak of 'how', we speak of process.

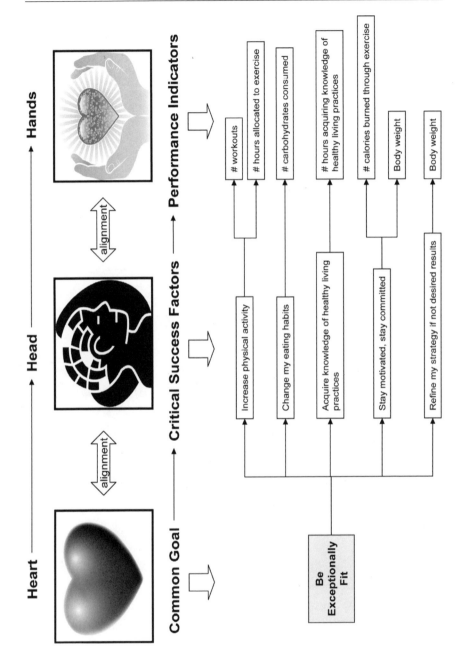

Fig. 7.1

The Process of Measuring the Life Experience

The process of measuring the life experience is comprised of four steps (see Figure 7.2):

1. Define/refine performance measures
2. Develop support tools
3. Implement data collection
4. Analyze results

We begin with Step 1 – Define/Refine Performance Measures.

Step 1 – Define/Refine Performance Measures

Measuring the life experience begins with defining new (or refining existing) performance measures that drive personal strategy; reflect life performance. You have done this. In Chapter 6, you defined performance measures along with target levels to achieve all your inner soul goals. Such measures comprise the personal scorecard section on your PSTs. Once you define aspects of life worth measuring, the next step is to develop support tools that facilitate measurement.

Step 2 – Develop Support Tools

Step 2 involves one primary action: developing support tools to enable 'keeping score'. There are four support tools that enable 'keeping score'.

They are:

- Personal Control Plan
- Inner Soul Goal Timeline
- Personal Dashboard
- Raw Data Sheets

We begin by discussing the Personal Control Plan.

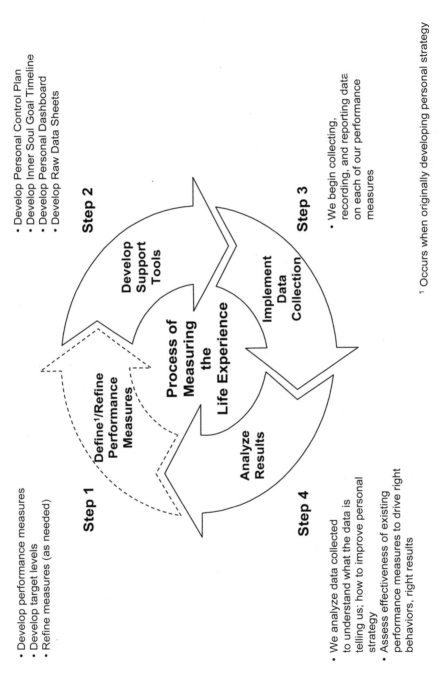

Fig. 7.2

Personal Control Plan

A Personal Control Plan (PCP) is a companion framework to a PST to index <u>all</u> measures contained within a Personal Scorecard (see Figure 7.3).

We use a Personal Control Plan to reduce complexity when managing personal strategy. In the illustration, we see a list of performance measures to drive the goal: 'be exceptionally fit'.

You might recognize these measures as first appearing on the sample PST in Chapter 5. We need a PCP because, although a PST communicates <u>what</u> to measure, it does not offer guidance on <u>how</u> to measure. That is the function of a Personal Control Plan. Therefore, in addition to serving as a container for PST measures and reducing complexity, a PCP offers tactical guidance on how to measure, as the PCP Framework requires, captures additional attributes about each measure. The additional attributes we record are listed in Table 7.1:

Table 7.1

Measure Attribute	Definition
Whether a measure is a leading indicator or lagging indicator	A lagging indicator represents an outcome measure and, therefore, can only be observed (e.g. body weight). Leading indicators, on the other hand, can be acted upon (e.g. # carbohydrates consumed or # calories burned) and, therefore, represent the majority of our scorecard measures.
The target value associated with the measure	Represents the performance level to which to strive for a measure.
What is being measured	The specific action or outcome we are measuring.
How to take a measurement reading	The tool or mechanism used to capture a measurement reading.
The reason to measure (why)	The relevance of a measure; reason to put forth the effort.
Where to record measured data	The tool or mechanism to store a measurement reading.
Frequency of data collection	How often we will take a measurement reading (e.g. daily, weekly, or monthly).
Decision rule / corrective action associated with the measure	Defines the specific actions to take when a measure is off target.

PERSONAL CONTROL PLAN

Theme: [Be Exceptionally Fit]

Measure	Lead or Lag	Target Value	What Measured	How Measured	Why Measured	Where Data is Recorded	Data Collection	Decision Rule / Corrective Action
Body Weight	Lag	200 lbs	Total body weight	Digital scale	Primary outcome measure	Weight Log (Excel worksheet)	Weekly	If [body weight] increases from week to week, assess eating log to determine what foods are responsible for the weight gain and make necessary adjustments; examine workout routine for modification
# Workouts	Lead	4	Total number of times exercised in a week	Count from exercise log	Drives inner soul goal	Exercise Log (Excel worksheet)	Weekly	If [# of workouts] is < 4/week, assess why time cannot be allocated to workouts consistently and make necessary adjustments
# Carbohydrates consumed	Lead	< 90	Number of carbs associated with food and drink consumed per day	Reference carb booklet	Drives inner soul goal	Eating Log (Excel worksheet)	Daily	If [# of carbohydrates consumed] is > 90/day, assess why I was not able to limit/restrict food eaten to maintain daily carb goal; make necessary adjustments to ensure meeting carb intake goal
# Calories burned through exercise	Lead	3,000	Amount of calories burned through exercise in a week	Count from exercise machines/ estimate	Drives inner soul goal	Exercise Log (Excel worksheet)	Weekly	If [# of calories burned through exercise is <3,000/week, assess workout routine and make necessary adjustments to ensure meeting minimum calorie expenditure goal
# Hours acquiring knowledge of healthy living practices	Lead	2	Amount of time allocated to learn healthy living practices in a week	Watch/Clock	Drives inner soul goal	Training Log (Excel worksheet)	Weekly	If [# of hours spent learning healthy living practices] is <2 hrs/ week, review daily planner to understand why I was not able to allocate time; make necessary adjustments to ensure minimum time commitment is met
# Hours allocated to aerobic/ strength training exercise	Lead	5	Amount of time allocated to exercise in a week	Watch/Clock	Drives inner soul goal	Exercise Log (Excel worksheet)	Weekly	If [# of hours allocated to exercise is <5 hrs/week, assess why workouts are being cut short and make necessary adjustments

Fig. 7.3

Defining such attributes provides greater clarity on 'how' to track and record each measure. We obtain our measures and target values from our PSTs; this part is easy. What remains is for us to fill out the other columns within the PCP. We identify whether a measure is a lead or lag measure; most will be lead. Then, we clarify what, specifically, is being measured. As it relates to the measure [# carbohydrates consumed], what we measure is the approximate number of carbohydrates (food/drink) consumed daily. The next question is how to measure. To determine an approximate number of carbohydrates consumed, we might refer to a booklet that contains such information (e.g. Dr. Atkins Carbohydrate Gram Counter). Next, we answer the question, "Why measure?" Aside from our primary measure (e.g. inner soul goal), which measures outcome, all other measures <u>drive</u> outcome, hence the answer to the "why" question. Next, we determine where to record measured data. For illustrative purposes, we record the [# carbohydrates consumed] in an MS Excel Worksheet. Feel free to pursue an alternative approach.

Next, we determine frequency of data collection. Most of your measures will require <u>daily</u> collection, but <u>weekly</u> recording. For example, as it relates to the measure [# workouts], we record workout details daily in an exercise log, but record summary details weekly. We will discuss this in more detail later. Determining frequency of data collection is a personal preference. To minimize busy work, I prefer to record day's events in a journal or logbook (e.g. exercise log, eating log, etc.) and then record summary details weekly. This approach provides me all the data I need, with little effort. The last column to complete the PCP Framework is decision rule/corrective action when a measure is off target. As it relates to the measure [# carbohydrates consumed], if the number of carbohydrates consumed daily exceeds 90, I examine my day, asking why I was not able to limit/restrict my carbohydrate intake, and then make necessary life adjustments. Each of the columns that comprise the Personal Control Plan represents a separate requirement for effective measurement and provides greater clarity on <u>how</u> to measure. What we learned from this discussion is that to measure effectively requires knowing what to measure, how to measure, why we measure, where to record data, how frequently to collect data, and what to do when a measure is off target.

When complete, our Personal Control Plan serves as a single source of record to manage all measures to achieve a goal. Naturally, as we drop measures, add measures, or refine measures, we need to update the Personal Control Plan accordingly. Together, Personal Strategy Maps, Personal Strategic Themes, and the Personal Control Plan establish a Foundation for Living (see Figure 7.4).

A Personal Strategy Map communicates what we want in life and from life. Personal Strategic Themes communicate how to get what we want in life. And Personal Control Plans detail how to keep score to ensure that we get what we want. Establishing such a foundation positions you to achieve your dreams, to live fragrantly, as reflected by the state of the components that comprise the life experience: financial independence, family stability, personal wellness, and professional success. At this time, create a Personal Control Plan for each of your inner soul goals using your PST personal scorecard as the source document.

Now, although creating a PCP is necessary to implement personal strategy, it addresses only one aspect of 'keeping score'. Another way we keep score is by tracking our progress. To do this, we employ two visual frameworks from the personal strategy toolbox: Inner Soul Goal Timeline and Personal Dashboard.

Inner Soul Goal Timeline

Tracking progress (of a goal) is only meaningful within the context of an established timeline. To define and communicate timelines, we use the Inner Soul Goal (ISG) Timeline Framework (see Figure 7.5).

As with the PCP Framework, the ISG Timeline Framework is a companion framework to the PST. It helps us plan achievement (via milestone dates) of each inner soul goal. Further, it helps

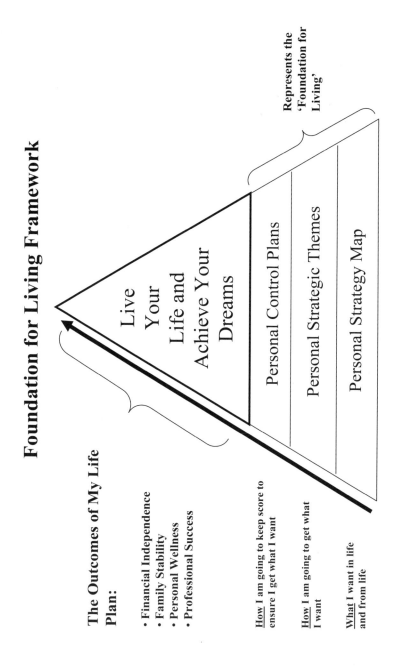

Fig. 7.4

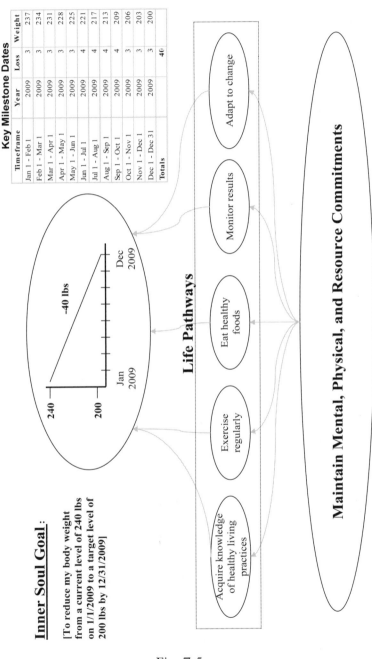

Fig. 7.5

us refine our inner soul goals in more precise terms than originally defined. We discuss first how to refine inner soul goals in more precise terms.

To refine an inner soul goal in more precise terms, do the following:

1. Re-state your inner soul goal using the template below:

[To Reduce/Improve **<Primary Inner Soul Goal Measure>** from <current level> to <target level> by <timeframe>]

For example, if your inner soul goal originally read:

'Be Exceptionally Fit'

You would **redraft** this goal to read:

'To reduce my body weight from a current level of 240 lbs on 1/1/2009 to a target level of 200 lbs by 12/31/2009

The redrafted goal is specific, measurable, and precise. It tells us what is being measured (body weight), what the current level of the measure is (240 lbs), the target value to which to strive (200 lbs), and the date by which to achieve the goal (12/31/09). Upon refining your inner soul goal, you can complete the rest of the ISG Timeline Framework:

2. Specify key milestone dates with intermediate target values to establish a comparative against which to evaluate progress

3. Document the cause and effect relations from commitments, to life pathways, to your inner soul goal

At this time, complete an Inner Soul Goal Timeline <u>for</u>
<u>each</u> of your inner soul goals.

Once you redraft each inner soul goal in more precise, actionable terms, in addition to establishing a timeline for achievement, the next step is to create a Personal Dashboard.

Personal Dashboard

Companies use corporate dashboards to communicate status,
health, and progress of corporate strategy. It is in the same spirit
that we use personal dashboards to communicate status, health,
and progress of personal strategy.

Specifically, we use Personal Dashboards to:

- Communicate progress with achieving our goals
- Keep goals in our face and top-of-mind
- Inspire us to continue to pay-the-price
- Establish a visible connection to our goals
- Bring goals to life
- Establish momentum
- Maintain momentum

Figure 7.6 illustrates a Personal Dashboard (created using
MS Excel) for the Inner Soul Goal: 'be exceptionally fit'.

You will notice that we create one graph per scorecard
measure. Further, we only report measures specific to a <u>single</u>
inner soul goal <u>per</u> dashboard.

Now, to create a personal dashboard requires data and
the tool we use to store data is a Raw Data Sheet. Raw data
sheets are containers to record data associated with a single goal.
Figure 7.7 illustrates two raw data sheets for the goals 'body
weight' and '# workouts'.

Notice in the illustration that the Personal Control Plan,
Personal Dashboard, and Raw Data Sheets are together in a
single MS Excel workbook, each located on different MS Excel

PERSONAL DASHBOARD

Theme: [Be Exceptionally Fit]

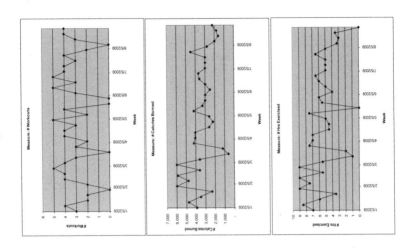

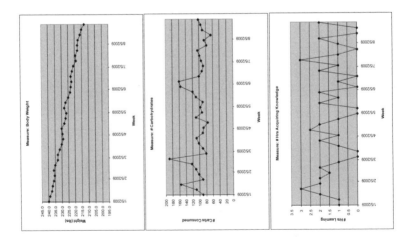

Fig. 7.6

232

Only 1 Shot

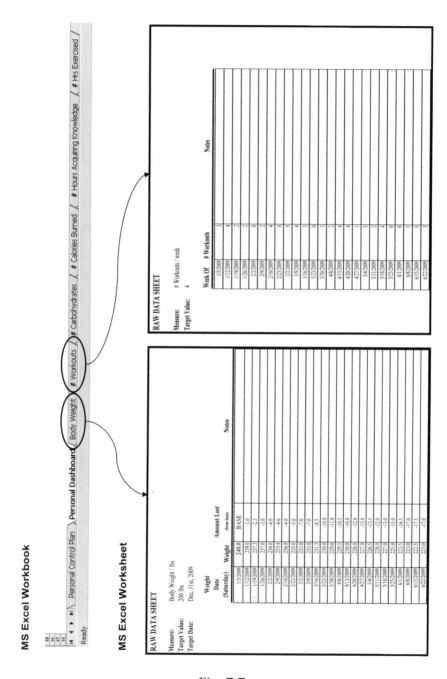

Fig. 7.7

worksheets. This is deliberate, as organizing these support tools in this way reduces complexity when managing personal strategy.

At this time, create a Personal Dashboard and Raw Data Sheets <u>for each</u> inner soul goal. Once you create the means to record and report performance data, the next step is to begin collecting it.

Step 3 – Implement Data Collection

In Chapter 6, we learned that to implement personal strategy partly involves collecting scorecard data. Now that you have created the tools to capture and report scorecard data, the next step is to implement data collection.

You might be asking, "How to begin?" When creating your Personal Control Plans in Step 2, you detailed the what, why, and how of data collection for each measure. As such, you already know how to begin. Therefore, <u>begin collecting data</u> for all measures across all Personal Control Plans. Collect data as prescribed by your Personal Control Plan. Then, record your performance data in the Raw Data Sheets created in Step 2. Upon collecting data, the next step is to begin analyzing it.

Step 4 – Analyze Results

In Step 4, we analyze data collected to understand what the data is telling us. The insights we gain from analyzing results inform us in how to improve personal strategy. That is, how to improve the effectiveness of our personal strategy. Ultimately, what we choose to measure on the surface of life has to be meaningful. That is, such measurements should help us, inspire us, and drive us to achieve our inner soul goal. As such, when we analyze results we are also interested in assessing the effectiveness of existing performance measures for possible refinement. If, upon analyzing results, we learn that better measures exist to help drive right behaviors, right results, then we refine our measures and the process of measuring the life experience repeats; cycles again.

Although the measuring, collecting, and analyzing aspects of 'keeping score' are important, what is of greater importance is to **improve the score**, that is, to improve personal strategy and, therefore, one's performance on the surface of life. We discuss how to adapt personal strategy in Chapter 10. In the meantime, there remains but one thing for you to do, **implement your personal strategy**.

Success in life comes from having both a good strategy and executing it well, and we determine both things by <u>keeping score</u>. 'Keeping score' is tedious but important work to achieve one's goals. Keeping score provides the feedback we need to determine if our personal strategy is working; to course correct personal strategy; to align the inner soul with action. Performance measures are the glue of personal strategy. With performance measures, we achieve goals; without them, we do not. With performance measures, our goals are fiercely front and center; without them, our goals fade as quickly as a high-school romance. Use of a Personal Control Plan, Inner Soul Goal Timeline, Personal Dashboard, and Raw Data Sheet will help you realize your personal strategy for living.

We have reached the end of Part II of this book. From developing goals inspired by mission/vision, to developing detailed personal strategy to achieve mission/vision, to keeping score, you learned how to *align the inner soul with action*. Congratulations! You hold the key (i.e., personal strategy) to re-engineer your life, to rediscover the joy of living. We began Part II learning that personal strategy is a means to an end – achieving one's inner soul goals. This is still true; developing personal strategy is about achieving one's goals. However, we develop personal strategy for a more important, more profound, hidden reason – to achieve *personal alignment*. We discuss this next.

PART III

On Personal Alignment

In Search of Alignment

"An aligned life is a fragrant life."
- Randall Scott Rogers

LET US SUMMARIZE YOUR ACCOMPLISHMENTS to date. Upon learning where you are, you have:

1. Defined new goals inspired by soul
2. Developed a personal strategy to achieve each goal
3. Begun to take action

Your life transformation has begun. This is exciting, because with goals inspired by soul, a personal strategy to achieve each goal, and follow-on commitments to measure and manage life progress, all future outcomes for your life are forever altered. Whatever successes or failures defined you previously now serve as no useful indicator for the future. You are living a new life trajectory. A new life story is being written and you are the author. As you transition from defining goals, defining strategy to pursuing goals, implementing strategy, a subtle, but incredibly powerful change is occurring in the background. You are becoming self-aligned.

What is Alignment?

Before defining what alignment is, let me state from the onset that **alignment is everything**! I make this claim without having provided you proper context to arrive at the same conclusion. For the time being, trust in my words. In time, you will realize that the essence of this book, if not life itself, is about establishing and maintaining personal alignment. So, what is alignment? Alignment is defined as the process of adjusting parts so that they are in proper relative position. Although brief, this definition is useful, as it provides a framework for how to think about and achieve alignment:

- Alignment is a <u>process</u>
- Alignment takes <u>time</u>
- Alignment requires making <u>adjustments</u>
- Alignment of <u>parts</u> is the goal
- Alignment focuses on <u>relations</u> between parts

As the framework above indicates, alignment is both a noun and a verb. As a noun, alignment represents a 'state of being', an end state. As a verb, alignment represents actions to perform, a process. This chapter addresses both forms, in that we are interested in what alignment is (noun form) and the process to achieve alignment (verb form).

To learn what alignment is and the process to achieve alignment, we begin with an example – a car needing a 'front-end' alignment. Using the framework above, we can characterize this example the following way:

- Alignment is a process...
  - A mechanic systematically checks a car's suspension, steering, and wheel systems to ensure that parts are working together as intended to ensure peak performance, riding comfort, and safety

- Alignment takes time...
  - Time to perform diagnostics

- • Time to replace parts
- • Time to perform system tests

- Alignment requires making adjustments...
  - • Adjustments to the suspension system
  - • Adjustments to the steering system
  - • Adjustments to the wheel system

- Alignment of parts is the goal...
  - • Suspension parts
  - • Steering parts
  - • Wheel parts

- Alignment focuses on relations between parts...
  - • Relation of suspension system to steering system
  - • Relation of steering system to wheel system
  - • Relation of wheel system to suspension system

When a car's suspension, steering, and wheel systems are misaligned a number of performance pathologies result:

- • Uneven tread wear in tires
- • Erratic movements of the steering column
- • Pulling to one side or the other
- • Difficult steering
- • Increased risk of accident/injury

Conversely, when such systems are aligned, performance improves, as indicated by:

- • Longer tire mileage
- • Better handling
- • Better fuel consumption
- • Increased riding comfort

What this example illustrates is that the cost of misalignment (e.g. personal injury or death) is far greater than the cost to establish alignment. The same can be said about one's life. The cost of personal misalignment (e.g. sadness, stress, anger, depression, etc.) is far greater than the investment of time and effort to define, deploy, and manage a personal strategy to establish alignment. We can summarize by saying that bad things happen when misalignment exists; conversely, good things happen when we restore alignment. It is for this reason that we discuss personal alignment.

What is Personal Alignment?

So, what is personal alignment and what does it have to do with personal strategy? Up to this point in our journey, our task has been to define and deploy a personal strategy for living. We did this, as having a personal strategy is a means to achieve a more important end. "What end?" you ask. It is, of course, personal alignment. The activities in Part II of conversing with soul, defining mission and vision, determining innate skills, defining inner soul goals, and developing a detailed personal strategy were all about **aligning** one's inner soul with action, *which is the essence of personal alignment*. Together, such activities represent the path to personal alignment (see Figure 8.1).

Through conversing with soul, asking questions of self, and assessing self, alignment emerged in the form of inner soul goals and a personal strategy to achieve each goal. As such, personal alignment is about:

- Aligning all of one's capabilities and resources around common goals
- Everything (seeing, willing, thinking, acting, and feeling) bending towards central purpose
- Creating a context (i.e., vision) for self and then working towards such context
- Establishing and maintaining interconnectedness, 'a conversation' between self and other social systems, in which we are a part
- Eliminating the non-essential in your life (e.g. debilitating thoughts, actions, habits, feelings, acquaintances, etc.) to make way for essential

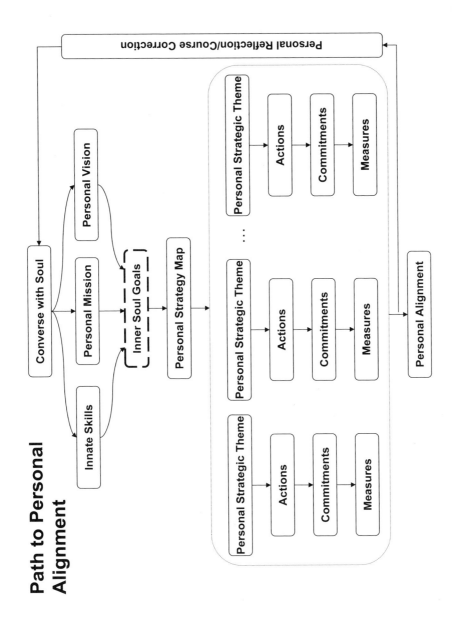

Fig. 8.1

In addition to asking what personal alignment is, you might also be asking, "Why seek personal alignment? Why be aligned?" The reason we seek alignment is that with alignment comes happiness. For example, we are happy due to the greater personal and professional success we realize from having all aspects of our life in balance. We are happy because personal alignment leads to meaningful living and, therefore, increased quality of life. And we are happy because to be aligned is to meet imperative, seize opportunity. Another reason why we seek alignment is that the alternative is misalignment, which results in deep unhappiness; *a life diminished*. While serving as a quality consultant, one of my chief aims was to help companies achieve alignment, from strategy, to operations, to people, knowing that aligning such things can not only increase top line growth, but also decrease bottom line expense. The concept of alignment is just as powerful for individual as it is for company. Just as the full power of alignment is unleashed when a company aligns its resources around common goals, so, too, is the full power of alignment unleashed when we align <u>our resources</u> (e.g. thinking, acting, feeling, time, money, effort) around common goals. For both company and individual, it can be said that when each is aligned, great things happen. All our life we are in search of alignment, *in search of the truth*. Why do we search? It is simple; we desire to be happy, to be free. As you will discover in this chapter, personal alignment is not so much about what we do (although this is important), but about <u>how we feel</u>.

To summarize, we can define personal alignment as both a verb and a noun:

As a noun, personal alignment represents:

- <u>A state of being</u> where one feels internal happiness from having aligned all aspects of one's life with soul

As a verb, personal alignment represents:

- A set of actions, whereby one reengineers one's life (seeing, willing, thinking, acting, and feeling) to live as soul would live

To frame our discussion on personal alignment, we address these questions in the sections that follow:

- What are the dimensions of personal alignment?
- What does personal alignment look like?
- What is the process to achieve personal alignment?
- What are the tools of personal alignment?
- How does one stay aligned?

We continue by learning the dimensions of personal alignment.

Dimensions of Personal Alignment

To achieve personal alignment, it requires aligning *self* with the four dimensions of personal alignment (see Figure 8.2):

- Soul
- Nature
- Family
- Work

Soul is the source of all personal happiness. As such, establishing personal alignment begins with aligning self with soul. Aligning self with soul, in turn, enables aligning all other dimensions of our life: self with work, self with family, and self with nature. Table 8.1 defines the dimensions of personal alignment and their relationship with self:

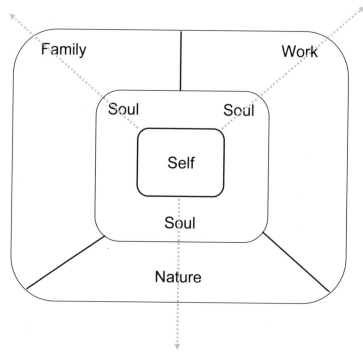

Fig. 8.2

Table 8.1

Alignment Dimension	Definition
Self with Soul	To align self with soul is to pursue one's inner soul goals; to do what you want in life to get what you want from life throughout life
Self with Nature	To align self with nature is to align self with one's surroundings, with mother earth, and with current and emerging societal realities
Self with Work	To align self with work is to align one's passions and innate skills with a profession/role that excites, inspires, and gives life meaning
Self with Family	To align self with family is to align one's goals, priorities, and values with the larger goals, priorities, and values of family

Significant interrelationships exist between self and soul, self and nature, self and work, and self and family (see Figure 8.3).

We call these interrelationships (intersections) our 'boundaries of interest'. Such boundaries establish the 'zone of alignment' between our 'systems of interest' (e.g. self, soul, nature, work, and family). A system, you might recall, is an entity, which maintains its existence through the mutual interaction of its parts. For example, each of us individually represents 'a system'. As humans, we are composed of parts or sub-systems (e.g. nervous system, respiratory system, musculoskeletal system, etc.) and it is only through the mutual interaction of parts that we maintain our existence. If one of our sub-systems breaks down, we break down. The same is true with other systems. With the human body, however, alignment of sub-system to system occurs naturally, whereas other sub-system to system (e.g. self with work or self with soul) alignment does not occur naturally. In Chapter 1, we learned that, with the exception of universe, all systems are sub-systems of some larger system. What this tells us is that soul exists, for example, as a sub-system within the larger system of self, and self exists as a sub-system in the larger systems of family, work, and nature. This is an important revelation, for it implies that if we seek personal alignment, it requires examining and understanding:

- Interactions between systems
- Relationships between systems
- Interdependency between systems

Later in this chapter, we explore each dimension of personal alignment with a focus on understanding the sub-system-to-system interactions, relationships, and interdependencies that drive personal alignment. For now, let us discuss what personal alignment looks like.

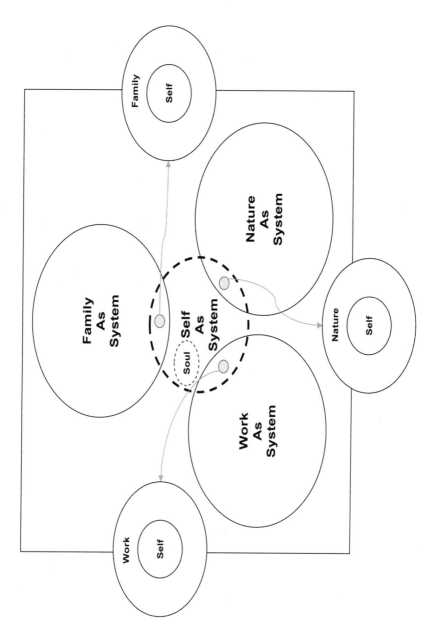

Fig. 8.3

Shapes of Personal Alignment

Personal alignment does have shape. To be more specific, personal alignment has a shape and personal misalignment has a different shape. But, what do we mean by 'shape?' To assess degree of personal alignment, we use a set of diagnostic tools to produce a map, revealing one's 'shape' of alignment. The tools to assess personal alignment are:

- Personal Alignment Profile
- Personal Alignment Map

The personal alignment profile is a survey instrument, the purpose of which is to assess one's alignment (or misalignment) with respect to soul, nature, work, and family (see Figure 8.4).

We complete such survey, as to establish alignment first requires acknowledging misalignment. Then, we plot survey results onto a personal alignment map, thus revealing our 'shape' of alignment. Collectively, both assessment tools are helpful, as they provide a visual and quantitative measure of personal alignment. Knowing which dimensions are misaligned, one can then design/course correct personal strategy with precision and confidence, leading to a happier, more aligned life.

As stated, establishing personal alignment begins with completing a personal alignment profile. The personal alignment profile is comprised of twenty questions, five questions assessing each dimension of personal alignment. The survey asks you to rate your response to each question with answers ranging from 'strongly agree' (.05) to 'strongly disagree' (.10). Thus, each dimension results in a total score from .25 to .50. You might be asking, 'Why do we use a decimal scale?' We use decimals because the soul's scale is One. After answering all questions, you will have the raw data to create your personal alignment map. At this time, complete the personal alignment profile and then plot each dimension's total score on the personal alignment map template (see Figure 8.5). *Note: You can download both*

Personal Alignment Profile

Soul	Strongly Agree				Strongly Disagree
I am doing what I want in life and getting what I want from life at this point in my life	.05 .06 .07 .08 .09 .10				
I feel no internal conflict between the way I am experiencing life today and my vision for how I want to live and be	.05 .06 .07 .08 .09 .10				
To me, life is fragrant, joyful, and full of color	.05 .06 .07 .08 .09 .10				
I am happy with the current quality of my life	.05 .06 .07 .08 .09 .10				
I am living as soul would live	.05 .06 .07 .08 .09 .10				
	Total				☐
Work					
I want to work in my chosen profession, with my current employer, and in the role I currently serve	.05 .06 .07 .08 .09 .10				
My work is interesting, challenging, and I rise each day enthusiastic to perform my work	.05 .06 .07 .08 .09 .10				
My work inspires me and gives life meaning	.05 .06 .07 .08 .09 .10				
I am passionate about my profession/role and view my work as fun and enjoyable	.05 .06 .07 .08 .09 .10				
I am contributing to society, world in a manner that makes me proud	.05 .06 .07 .08 .09 .10				
	Total				☐

Fig. 8.4

Family	
Relations between self and family is positive	.05 .06 .07 .08 .09 .10
My goals, priorities, and values in life are aligned with my spouse/partner	.05 .06 .07 .08 .09 .10
Communication between self and family is open, honest, and frequent	.05 .06 .07 .08 .09 .10
My goals, priorities, and values in life complement rather than contradict the larger goals, priorities, and values of family	.05 .06 .07 .08 .09 .10
I am living with the right life partner	.05 .06 .07 .08 .09 .10
	Total [ ]
Nature	
I regularly upgrade my professional knowledge, skills, and capabilities to adapt to changes occurring in my environment	.05 .06 .07 .08 .09 .10
I have established several sensory outlets to acquire environmental information to aggressively sense, respond, and adapt to change	.05 .06 .07 .08 .09 .10
I regularly allocate time to internalize how changes in my environment affect me and how best to respond to such change	.05 .06 .07 .08 .09 .10
I am living in harmony with host; I am doing what is right for planet	.05 .06 .07 .08 .09 .10
I am living in a location that energizes, inspires, ignites my soul	.05 .06 .07 .08 .09 .10
	Total [ ]

Fig. 8.4 (Cont'd)

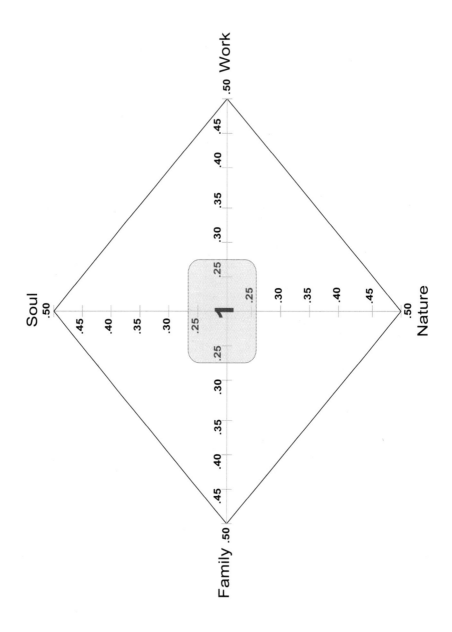

Fig. 8.5

templates from only1shot.com. When finished, connect the dots across the four dimensions to reveal <u>your</u> shape of alignment.

So, how did you do? Does your personal alignment profile indicate personal alignment? Generally speaking, the smaller a dimension's score, the greater the alignment with that dimension. Use Table 8.2 to interpret your personal alignment profile:

Table 8.2

Dimension Score	What the Score Means
.25	You are in total alignment for the dimension
> .25 but ≤ .30	You are near total alignment for the dimension
> .30 but ≤ .35	You are approaching total alignment for the dimension
> .35 but ≤ .40	You are approaching total **mis**alignment for the dimension
> .40 but ≤ .45	You are near total **mis**alignment for the dimension
> .45	You are in total **mis**alignment for the dimension

As you connected the dots, did you notice that your personal alignment map revealed a 'shape'? As mentioned, there are 'shapes of alignment' and 'shapes of misalignment'. Before discussing such differences, however, let us understand the framework that underlies the personal alignment map (see Figure 8.6).

The personal alignment map framework presents a common way to think about and visually depict personal alignment. Personal alignment entails aligning self with soul, self with nature, self with family, and self with work. By depicting all dimensions of alignment on a single map, it provides a more holistic picture of personal alignment. In the pages that follow, we discuss the various 'shapes' of alignment and misalignment. It is important to recognize the patterns of alignment not only to interpret one's personal alignment map correctly, but also to define proper follow-on actions to increase personal alignment.

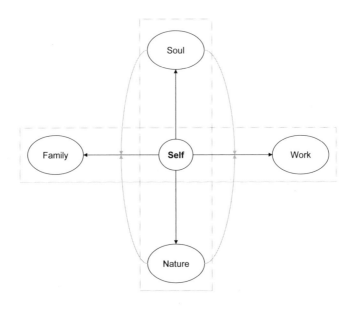

Fig. 8.6

As the patterns of total personal alignment and total personal misalignment are extreme opposites of one another, we begin with a discussion of their shapes. Figure 8.7 illustrates the shape of total personal alignment.

Notice how tight the 'shape of alignment' is around the center of the map. This map communicates total personal alignment of self with soul, nature, family, and work. An individual with this degree of alignment is:

- Pursuing his/her inner soul goals
- Doing what he/she wants <u>in</u> life
- Getting what he/she wants <u>from</u> life
- Living purposefully, fragrantly, happily

Achieving total alignment is the goal, now and forever. Why is this so? It is because total alignment brings happiness, freedom, and joy, whereas total <u>misalignment</u> brings heartache, depression, and sadness. You may be asking yourself, 'Is total

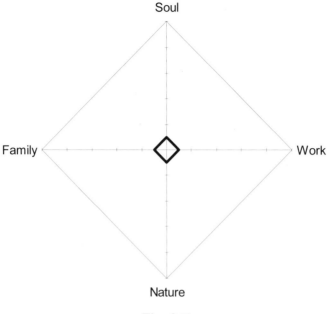

Fig. 8.7

personal alignment possible?' It is possible to achieve total personal alignment if:

- You never change
- Your environment never changes

Of course, neither of these conditions represents reality. Therefore, because we perpetually live in a state of misalignment, trying to become aligned, let us review the patterns of misalignment. Figure 8.8 illustrates the shape of total misalignment.

Notice how this shape is the extreme opposite of total alignment. That is, the shape extends toward the boundaries of the alignment frame rather than clustering near the center. This map communicates total misalignment of self with soul, nature, family, and work. An individual with this degree of misalignment is:

- Not pursuing his/her inner soul goals
- Not doing what he/she wants <u>in</u> life

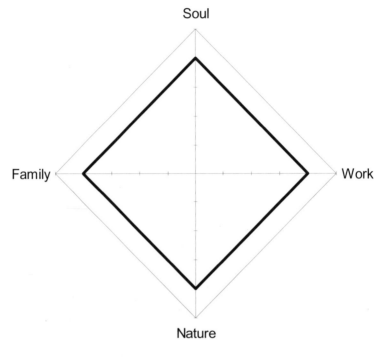

Fig. 8.8

- Not getting what he/she wants <u>from</u> life
- Living with heartache, depression, sadness
- Living a lie

Fortunately, most people are not living a life of total mis-alignment. This good news, however, is short lived as most people are also not living a life of total alignment. This is of great concern, as we have Only One Shot at life, and to live with mis-alignment, in any degree or form, is to not live at all. Wherever you fell on the personal alignment scale, it is likely that you are not completely aligned with what you want in life and from life at this point in life. For if you were, you would not be reading this book. Next, we look at the more common forms of personal misalignment.

Personal <u>mis</u>alignment takes many forms (see Figure 8.9). You can have misalignment of:

- Self with soul
- Self with work
- Self with family
- Self with nature

An individual can be misaligned across multiple dimensions simultaneously. For example, I may work in a profession/role that I do not like, that does not inspire me, and that lacks meaning, in addition to having poor relations with family. This scenario suggests misalignment with work and family.

The shape of misalignment, regardless of dimension, exhibits a 'spear head'-like pattern. The closer the alignment pattern comes to the boundary of the alignment frame, the greater the misalignment for that dimension. Conversely, the tighter the alignment pattern clusters around the center of the alignment frame, the greater the alignment for that dimension. Your degree (and types) of misalignment will determine the resulting 'shape' on a personal alignment map. The personal alignment map, as described, is a diagnostic tool. As such, its purpose is to reveal, inform, and inspire action. For example, if your personal alignment map indicates misalignment with work, this is a sign to establish alignment, that is, to act. Now, you may be saying, 'I understand what alignment is and why it is important to be self-aligned. I even understand the relevance of creating Personal Strategy Maps and Personal Strategic Themes and how both tools enable personal alignment, but what I don't understand is how one becomes self-aligned. That is, what is the process of achieving personal alignment?' We answer this question next.

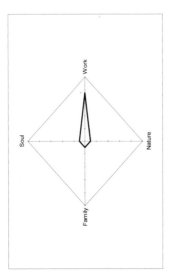

Misalignment of Self with Work

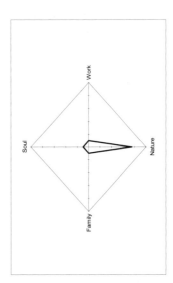

Misalignment of Self with Nature

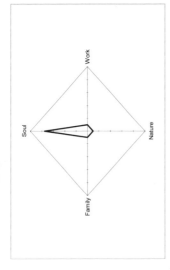

Misalignment of Self with Soul

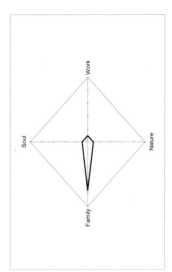

Misalignment of Self with Family

Fig. 8.9

Process of Achieving Personal Alignment

Earlier, we learned that alignment is a process. This is true regardless of what requires aligning. For example, aligning a car's wheel system is a process. Aligning a plane to land is a process. And aligning one's life is a process. Up to now, our discussion has concentrated more on the 'what' of personal alignment. Now, we direct our attention to the 'how' of personal alignment. How does one achieve personal alignment? This is an important question, as personal happiness and the quality of one's life is a function of how well aligned one is with soul, work, family, and nature. Figure 8.10 illustrates the process of achieving personal alignment.

The purpose of this process is straightforward: *to achieve and maintain personal alignment.* We can characterize the process of achieving personal alignment the following way:

- The process is triggered by...
  - Changes occurring within (soul)
  - Changes occurring without (environment)

- Inputs to the process include...
  - Emerging inner soul goals
  - Current/emerging environmental realities
  - Self feedback

- Transformation involves...
  - Aligning Self with Soul
  - Aligning Self with Work
  - Aligning Self with Family
  - Aligning Self with Nature

- Outputs of value include...
  - Increased personal alignment
  - Increased personal happiness
  - Achievement of one's inner soul goals
  - Self feedback
  - Effective personal strategy

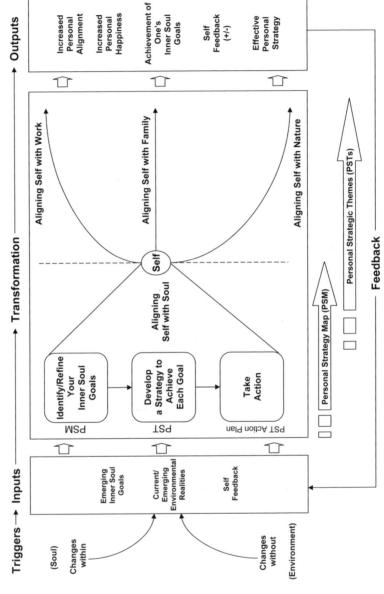

Fig. 8.10

In Part II, we learned that discussions of process usually begin with defining the scope or bookends of process. We do this, as defining the boundaries of a process helps us identify the activities to perform to achieve process goals. As it relates to the process of achieving personal alignment, the bookends are:

The process begins when...	The process ends when...
Changes occur within self or my environment	Actually, the process of achieving alignment never ends

You may be asking, 'Why does the process of achieving alignment never end?' Maintaining alignment, as it turns out, is a lifelong endeavor. There are two primary reasons for this:

- You will change
  - Inner soul goals
  - Priorities
  - Values
  - Mission/vision

- Your environment will change
  - Cultural changes
  - Societal changes
  - World events
  - Climate changes
  - Local changes
  - Family changes
  - Work changes

The common denominator is change! Because change is relentless and infinite, you will always be in a state of achieving personal alignment. Consequently, you may never reach a state of total personal alignment. Do not be discouraged by this fact. This is life. Despite the fact that misalignment is with us, this is no cause for concern, as Figure 8.10 illuminates the path to restore alignment. The path always begins with aligning self with soul.

Aligning self with soul requires:

- Identifying/Refining your inner soul goals (PSM)
- Developing a strategy to achieve each goal (PST's)
- Taking action (PST Action Plan)

Our soul provides the context (via inner soul goals) for what we want in life and from life. With context, we can align all other aspects of our life: self with work, self with family, and self with nature. Without context, all attempts to align our life represent wasted effort; only perpetuate misalignment. What this tells us is that achieving personal alignment must occur in the following way:

1st – Align self with soul

2nd – Align self with other aspects of one's life

- Self with work
- Self with family
- Self with nature

As we are always in a state of 'achieving' alignment, transformation continues indefinitely throughout life. The tools of transformation are Personal Strategic Themes, Personal Scorecards, and PST Action Plans. These tools enable transformation resulting in outputs of value. When discussing process outputs, it is best to delineate outputs from outcomes. Process outputs and process outcomes are equally important. The distinction, however, is that outputs lead to outcomes. Consequently, good output leads to good outcomes and bad output leads to bad outcomes. It is because of this correlation between outputs and outcomes that we use a Personal Control Plan and Personal Scorecard to monitor and manage the outputs from performing life's pathways. The outputs and outcomes for the process of achieving personal alignment are:

- Process Outputs
  - Progress with achieving one's inner soul goals
  - Self feedback (to course correct personal strategy)
  - Progress with achieving personal alignment
  - More effective personal strategy

- Process Outcomes
  - Increased personal alignment
  - Increased personal happiness
  - Achieve one's inner soul goals

Process output is our way of assessing personal strategy and projecting process outcomes. When personal strategy is effective, we see positive outcomes (i.e., goal achievement). Conversely, when personal strategy is not effective, our goals seem farther out of reach. The idea of assessing personal strategy leads us into the final topic of this section, which is the need to collect feedback (see Figure 8.11).

Feedback is necessary for any process to be effective, but especially so for the process of achieving alignment. What Figure 8.11 illustrates is that the outputs of the process 'fold back' as inputs (feedback) to the process. Without feedback, course correcting personal strategy to respond to changes occurring within or without (i.e., work, family, and nature) occurs too slowly or not at all. To ensure achievement of personal alignment, it is imperative that you understand the importance of feedback, sources of feedback, and uses of feedback:

- Importance of feedback
  - Feedback closes the self-assessment loop and ensures that we achieve established goals
  - Feedback provides insights on how to course correct personal strategy when misalignment exists or when circumstances dictate
  - Feedback establishes direction and focus on how to increase personal alignment

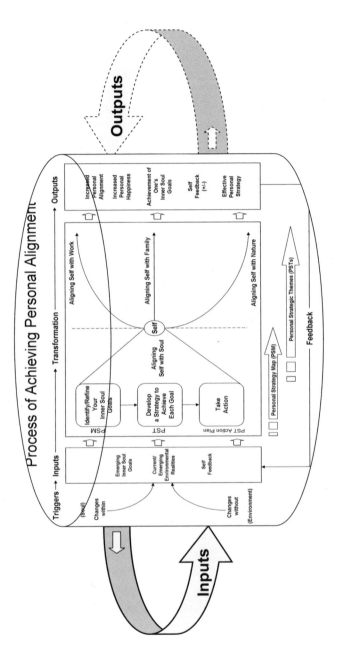

Fig. 8.11

- Sources of feedback
  - Feedback comes from implementing personal strategy (i.e., what is working and not working with personal strategy)
  - Feedback comes from our environment
    - Feedback from one's spouse (or significant other) on good/bad aspects of the relationship
    - Feedback from one's children on the type and level of support needed
    - Feedback from friends and co-workers regarding work or social matters
    - Feedback from one's doctor on personal wellness
    - Feedback from one's priest on spiritual matters
    - Feedback from society on current/emerging realities
  - Feedback from personal reflection/conversing with soul
- Uses of feedback
  - To course correct personal strategy to achieve one's goals
    - Refine inner soul goals
    - Refine single-goal strategies
    - Refine scorecard measures
    - Refine action plan initiatives and tasks
  - To improve the effectiveness of personal strategy
  - To establish/maintain personal alignment

Self-feedback is vital to achieve personal alignment. However, it is only one tool, of many, which we use to establish and maintain personal alignment (see Table 8.3).

Tools of Personal Alignment

Table 8.3

Personal Alignment Tool	How it Enables Personal Alignment
Personal Strategy Map	Provides context (via inner soul goals) to establish personal alignment
Personal Strategic Theme	Provides strategy on 'how' to achieve personal alignment
Personal Scorecard	Identifies the measures to drive/maintain personal alignment
Personal Control Plan	Serves as an index of all measures used to drive personal alignment
Personal Dashboard	Indicates progress towards increasing personal alignment
Data Collection (feedback)	Provides insights on how to course correct personal strategy to ensure personal alignment
Action Plan	Details the initiatives and tasks we perform to achieve personal alignment
Personal Alignment Profile	Provides quantitative indication on how aligned one is with soul, nature, family, and work; reveals what is misaligned in one's life
Personal Alignment Map	Provides visual indication on how aligned one is with soul, nature, family, and work
Sensory Outlets	Provide feedback on changes occurring within one's environment to adapt and respond to; to maintain personal alignment
Personal Reflection	Provides feedback from our most important source to establish alignment: soul

It is important to realize that using just one tool or a few tools in the personal strategy toolbox will not help you achieve personal alignment. It is only when we employ all tools in the toolbox that total personal alignment is possible. Now that we discussed the dimensions, shapes, process, and tools of personal alignment, it is time to deepen our understanding of each dimension of personal alignment beginning with aligning self with soul.

Aligning Self with Soul

Establishing (and maintaining) personal alignment begins with aligning self with soul (see Figure 8.12).

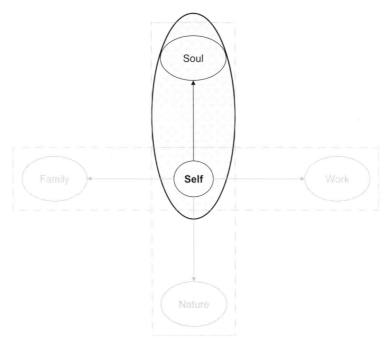

Fig. 8.12

To discuss how to align self with soul, we ask the following questions:

Q: *What does it mean to align self with soul?*
A: To align self with soul means that you believe as soul believes, see as soul sees, and think as soul thinks. In other words, it means aligning one's beliefs, seeing, and thinking around common goals. It means pursuing desires of soul, pursuing one's passions – inner soul goals. Lastly, it means to act in the service of soul, deciding to live as soul would live. Aligning self with soul is not only a prerequisite to align all other aspects of one's life; it is also

a prerequisite for taking effective action. The reason for this is that knowing one's inner soul goals affects all that follows. Consequently, to act in advance of one's goals is tantamount to not acting at all.

Q: *What does misalignment of self with soul mean?*
A: Misalignment of self with soul means that you are not doing what you want in life and, therefore, not getting what you want from life. It may also mean that you are not even aware of what to do in life. Misalignment of self with soul could represent misalignment with one's work, family, surroundings, finances, health, and lifestyle, among other things. It comes down to this: if you are not pursuing desires of soul, self is misaligned with soul.

Q: *How does one align self with soul?*
A: To align self with soul requires:
- Acknowledging misalignment between self and soul
- Conversing with soul
- Determining desires of soul (i.e., inner soul goals)
- Developing a strategy to realize desire
- Taking action

Q: *What does misalignment of self with soul look like?*
A: Holding all other dimensions constant, misalignment of self with soul does have 'shape' (see Figure 8.13). Misalignment of self with soul exhibits a 'spear head'-like shape extending near the boundary of the alignment frame.

Q: *How does self become misaligned with soul?*
A: Self becomes misaligned with soul due to:
- Not conversing with soul
- Not knowing soul
- Not pursuing one's passion in life
- Not reacting to changes occurring within
- Poor strategy to achieve one's goals

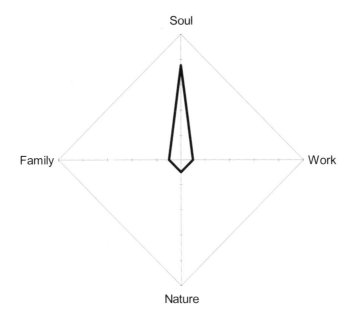

Fig. 8.13

- Lack of strategy to achieve one's goals
- Inability to execute change in one's life

Q: What are the benefits of aligning self with soul?
A: The benefits of aligning self with soul are:

- Greater personal happiness
- Greater internal peace
- Living fragrantly, passionately
- Improved physical health
- Improved mental health
- Personal freedom
- Reduced stress
- Professional success
- Financial independence

You may be asking, 'How can aligning self with soul realize so many benefits?' The reason is simple: when you align self

with soul, you are doing what you love and loving what you do, and there is no more inspired state in which to exist.

Q: *What results when self is misaligned with soul?*
A: When self is misaligned with soul, a number of personal pathologies result (categorized as general and extreme):

General:

- Personal unhappiness
- Problems with spouse (or significant other)
- Problems with other family members
- Poor attitude towards life
- Increased stress
- Feelings of anxiety
- Despondence
- Failed relationships
- Lost friendships
- Disillusionment with life
- Feelings of despair
- Feelings of personal crisis
- Poor performance at work
- Withdrawal/isolation

Extreme:

- Alcoholism
- Drug use
- Poor/failing health
- Erratic behavior
- Severe depression
- Suicide

When self is misaligned with soul, it saps the life force out of you. In a way, you feel that you are living a lie because your life experience and life direction is so at odds with your vision of <u>what</u> you want from life and <u>where</u> you want to be in life.

Q: When is aligning self with soul necessary?

A: The short answer: your entire life. Aligning self with soul is necessary any time you feel internal conflict between what you want to do in life and what you are doing. For example, if you work in a profession/role that no longer interests you, it is time to realign, to pursue a new profession/role that caters to passion. Passions should not lie dormant within soul. As such, **your life will only be as passionate as you allow it to be**, so expose passions to daylight; live passionately. Similarly, if you are in a failed relationship, it is time to realign; to exit gracefully to start anew. Personal alignment equates to personal happiness, so if you are unhappy with life, consider it a sign to realign.

Q: How will I know that I have aligned self with soul?

A: You will feel it. From pursuing goals inspired by soul, you will feel excited, enthused, and renewed, knowing that something good lies just on the horizon. Living one's passion in life whether it be music, carpentry, baking, painting, writing, or teaching is exhilarating. As such, the feelings that result from living passionately are the only indicators you need to know that self is aligned with soul; just as surely as we feel misalignment do we feel alignment. You just know.

Q: How aligned does self need to be with soul?

A: If living a fragrant, colorful, meaningful life is important to you, then self needs to be wholly aligned with soul. If you have Only One Shot at life, why would you choose to live any other way? Know this: the greater the alignment between self and soul, the greater your personal happiness will be in life. The choice is yours and it is a choice.

Aligning Self with Nature

Having aligned self with soul, we now have context to align other aspects of our life. Another dimension of life that requires
aligning is the relationship between self and nature (see Figure
8.14).

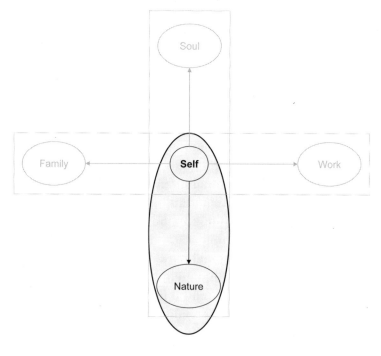

Fig. 8.14

To discuss how to align self with nature we ask the following questions:

Q: *What does it mean to align self with nature?*
A: To align self with nature means to align three things: 1)
   align self with surroundings, 2) align self with mother
   earth, and 3) align self with society. To live in a location

that does not excite the senses, inspire soul, diminishes the life experience. As such, we must seek higher ground to call our home. We must also align self with mother earth. We live in nature and therefore are a part of nature. Take away the buildings, factories, and roads, and we are, once again, walking into the wild. Because we are part of nature, we share common bond, same condition, with blooming flower, buzzing bee, and benign bear. As such, we must align with nature. We must live in harmony with host, do what is right by nature, 'go green'. Lastly, to align self with nature, we must educate self on current and emerging societal realities (e.g. economic, political, and cultural) and use such knowledge to enhance and strengthen all other forms of personal alignment. Regarding this latter point, it also means to identify and implement 'sensory outlets' to collect information from one's environment to rapidly respond to changing conditions. A 'sensory outlet' is any data source (e.g. website, newspaper, magazine, book, blog, news show, radio program, industry conference, etc.) that provides insights on emerging environmental realities relevant to self. An individual who has aligned self with nature is aware of trends and/or shifts occurring in world, nation, and community and understands the effect such changes will have on one's work, family, health, and finances and then responds quickly and adequately to ensure one is ahead of change. At bottom, aligning self with nature is about rapidly responding to the present; in the most ancient of forms, it is about survival of the fittest.

Q: *What does* <u>*misalignment*</u> *of self with nature mean?*

A: Misalignment of self with nature means many things. It could mean that one is out of his element, living in the city when one desires to walk into the wild. It could mean that one has lost relation with nature; such loss going hand-in-hand with the loss of one's own self. To experience, to know, such loss is to:

- See a sunset, and not feel its majesty
- See a rainbow, and not be swept away with its arch
- See animals, and not sense a connection; common bond
- See the ocean, and not appreciate its scale, force
- See the starry sky, and not be reminded how to love

Lastly, misalignment of self and nature could mean that one is out of touch with changes occurring within one's environment that affect work, family, or both. As it relates to this latter point, an individual who is misaligned with nature exhibits the following deficiencies:

- Few, if any, 'sensory outlets' to sense environmental change
- No defined methods to acquire environmental information
- Lack of knowledge regarding current and/or emerging trends
- Slowed reaction to current and emerging environmental realities
- Inadequate response to environmental change
- Inadequate adaptation to environmental change

We are living in competitive times. Today, more than ever, our world represents 'survival of the fittest' or, more precisely, 'survival of the wisest'. In this new world, knowledge is power. And the more knowledgeable you are about current and emerging trends, the more timely and effective you will be with course correcting personal strategy; that is, to self-align. For example, in the 1990's, I programmed computers. My expertise was in creating Windows-based computer programs. Then, the internet became the rage, and the appetite for Windows programming died off. Fortunately, I 'sensed' this shift through reading industry magazines (i.e., 'sensory outlet') that foretold this future. I responded quickly. I adapted to change by developing an expertise for programming internet-based applications. This worked for a while, but then corporate America began outsourcing its programming to India and other countries. Suddenly, another environmental change was threatening my ability to earn an income and provide for my family. Again, through several sensory outlets, I 'sensed' this marketplace shift and responded quickly by developing an expertise in quality improvement. If I did not 'sense' shifts occurring in my environment, if I did not align self with nature, my professional knowledge, skills, and capabilities would have become obsolete without me even knowing it, leading to either limited employment opportunities or unemployment. The moral of this story is this: given the highly competitive world in which we live, it is becoming increasingly important to align self with nature, that is, to remain ahead of change, to 'sense' change. Ultimately, what you choose to 'sense' in your environment is a personal decision. What you feel is important to 'sense and respond' to may not be relevant to what your neighbor, sibling, or friend feels is important to sense and respond to. Sensory outlets are as unique to you as is personal strategy.

Q: *How does one align self with nature?*
A: Aligning self with nature requires:

- Acknowledging misalignment between self and nature
- Determining your location of inspiration and visiting often
- Identifying ways to live in harmony with host, to protect/restore nature
- Immersing oneself in nature, re-connecting with nature
- Defining sensory outlets to 'sense' environmental change, to stay ahead of change
- Taking action

Q: *What does misalignment of self with nature look like?*
A: Holding all other dimensions constant, misalignment of self with nature does have 'shape' (see Figure 8.15). Misalignment of self with nature exhibits a 'spear head'-like shape extending near the boundary of the alignment frame.

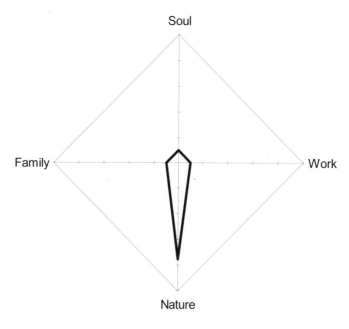

Fig. 8.15

Q: *How does self become misaligned with nature?*
A: Self becomes misaligned with nature due to:

- Not thinking about nature or one's place in nature; not connecting with nature (e.g. visiting national park, zoo, forest preserve, etc.)
- Failure to recognize the importance of sensing and responding to environmental change
- Lack of knowledge about the 'what' and 'how' of establishing sensory outlets

- Failure to respond quickly and/or adequately to changes occurring in one's environment
- Inability to effect change in one's life based on insights obtained from environmental feedback

Q: What are the benefits of aligning self with nature?
A: The benefits of aligning self with nature are:

- Increased happiness and energy from living in one's location of inspiration
- Feeling good about helping earth maintain/restore its health
- Restoring relation with nature; feeling One with nature
- Capitalizing on emerging professions/roles
- Minimizing the possibility of having professional knowledge, skills, and capabilities become obsolete
- Developing the capability to rapidly respond to change
- Developing the capability to self-align
- Staying ahead of change

Q: What results when self is misaligned with nature?
A: When self is misaligned with nature, it diminishes our sense of self, our view of life, and our ability to earn an income, that is, to compete, survive. Regarding this latter point, the impacts to career include:

- Unhappiness
- Growing obsolescence of knowledge, skills, and capabilities
- Missed opportunities
- Lost job(s)
- Lost marketplace value
- Reduced income
- Reduced job prospects
- Missed promotions
- Forced retirement
- Less independence

As the above list indicates, when self is misaligned with nature, it debilitates us, devastates us, and we suffer. Consequently, it is imperative that one remains ahead of change rather than be consumed by change.

Q: *When is aligning self with nature necessary?*
A: The world is changing at an ever-increasing pace, and to stay ahead of change requires each of us align with nature. Aligning self with nature is a pursuit that will never relent. To the extent that you align self with nature, you live. To the extent that you do not, you perish. For this reason, aligning self with nature is a priority of the highest order.

Q: *How will I know that I have aligned self with nature?*
A: You will feel it. You will know that self is aligned with nature when you experience the following:

- Life is joyful; you draw greater energy from inspired surroundings
- You feel connection with nature; appreciate nature
- You possess knowledge, skills and capabilities highly valued in the marketplace
- You identify emerging opportunities quicker than others
- You capitalize on situations that are invisible to most people but for you appear vividly
- You adapt to change effectively
- You rapidly respond to the present.

Q: *How aligned does self need to be with nature?*
A: As with other forms of personal alignment, the degree to which one aligns self with nature is a choice. However, for reasons discussed, it is best to be aligned rather than have to re-align.

Vertical Alignment

We just discussed aligning self with soul and aligning self with nature. Both forms of alignment are important and when considered together, take on even greater significance. Aligning self with soul and self with nature together represent a special form of alignment called vertical alignment (see Figure 8.16).

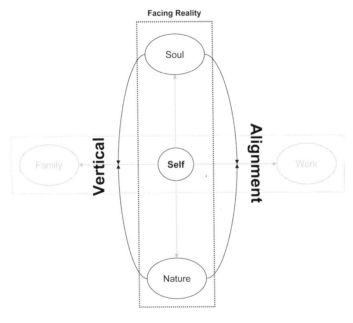

Fig. 8.16

Vertical alignment is important because of what it represents – 'facing reality'. To 'face reality' means:

- To acknowledge and pursue desires of soul (ISG), as this represents <u>the reality of who you are and want to be on the surface of life</u> (aligning self with soul)
- To acknowledge current and emerging realities in one's environment, as this represents <u>the reality of where the world is and how one should respond and adapt to change</u> (aligning self with nature)

Facing reality is a serious matter. You will have great difficulty achieving personal alignment, increasing personal happiness, without pursuing your inner soul goals. Likewise, you will suffer personally and professionally if misalignment exists between self and nature, as the world passes you by. Facing reality is about acknowledging soul; pursuing desires of soul. It is also about 'tuning in' to emerging environmental realities, thereby ensuring alignment between self and work, self and family.

Vertical alignment, like all forms of alignment, has shape. When vertically aligned, the alignment dimensions of soul and nature cluster near the center of the alignment frame (see Figure 8.17).

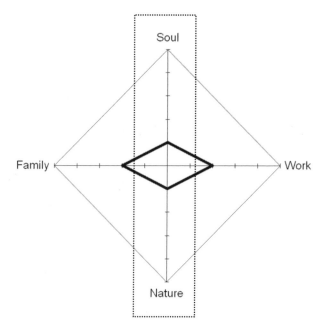

Fig. 8.17

When not vertically aligned, the alignment dimensions of soul and nature extend near the boundaries of the alignment frame (see Figure 8.18).

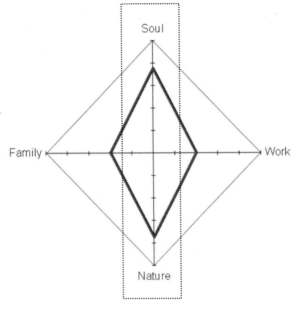

Fig. 8.18

To the extent that we face reality; we live purposefully, fragrantly, happily. To the extent that we reject reality, we do not live at all.

Aligning Self with Work

Another dimension that requires aligning is the relationship between self and work (see Figure 8.19).

To discuss how to align self with work we ask the following questions:

Q: *What does it mean to align self with work?*
A: To align self with work means that you are working in a profession/role that excites you, inspires you, and gives life meaning; it means that you are pursuing your passion(s) in life – doing what you love and loving what you do. It

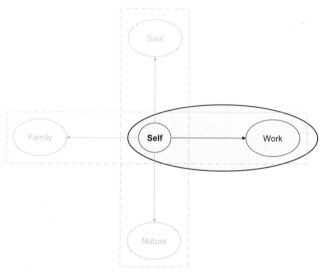

Fig. 8.19

also means aligning your innate skills with your chosen profession/role; leveraging innate skill for personal gain.

Q: *What does <u>mis</u>alignment of self with work mean?*
A: Misalignment of self with work means, quite simply, that you are not doing what you love and loving what you do. It means that you work in a profession/role that does not represent passion and, therefore, does not inspire soul. Misalignment of self with work takes many forms. For example, you may be misaligned with your current role, your employer, your profession, or all three. Regardless of form, when misalignment exists between self and work, it is imperative that you take action, as you have no time to lose and Only One Shot to live.

Q: *How does one align self with work?*
A: Aligning self with work requires:

- Acknowledging misalignment between self and work
- Identifying your passions

- Determining innate skills, those things you are naturally good at and enjoy doing
- Developing a strategy to realize passion, leverage skills
- Taking action

Aligning self with work requires you aggressively pursue your passion in life. For example, if your goal (i.e., passion) requires getting educated, have you enrolled in school? If you goal involves starting a business, have you developed your business plan? If your goal requires downsizing lifestyle to pursue a more fulfilling but lesser paying role, have you downsized lifestyle? Further, are you leveraging your innate skills to establish a personal competitive advantage? Your ability to execute is the only thing holding you back; so just execute! You can accomplish anything you set your mind to. Remember, when pursuing a goal, <u>every day represents movement,</u> and with movement, comes achievement. So just keep going.

Q: *What does misalignment of self with work look like?*
A: Holding all other dimensions constant, misalignment of self with work does have 'shape' (see Figure 8.20). Misalignment of self with work exhibits a 'spear head'-like shape extending near the boundary of the alignment frame.

Q: *How does self become misaligned with work?*
A: Self becomes misaligned with work due to:
- Changed (work-related) inner soul goals
- Failure to pursue one's passions
- Failure to leverage one's innate skills
- Work that is no longer interesting
- Work that is no longer meaningful
- Work that does not represent one's passions
- Slow adaptation to changes occurring within
- Slow adaptation to changes occurring without

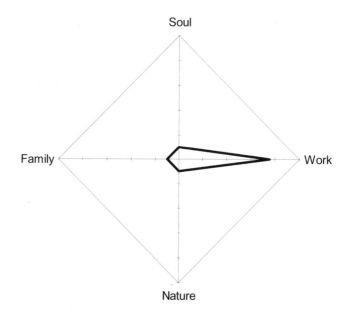

Fig. 8.20

Q: What are the benefits of aligning self with work?
A: The benefits of aligning self with work are:

- Internal happiness
- Sustained motivation, desire, and passion to work
- Professional success
- Increased earnings
- Feelings of performing meaningful work
- Feelings of having purpose in life
- Feelings that work is fun and enjoyable
- Improved attitude towards work and life
- Improved personal performance
- Improved relations with spouse/significant other
- Improved relations with family
- Seizing opportunity from meeting imperative

It is undeniable; when we align self with work, great things happen. Besides feeling that work is enjoyable and fun, aligning self with work positively affects all other aspects of our life.

Q: *What results when self is misaligned with work?*
A: When self is misaligned with work, a number of personal pathologies result:

- Persistent unhappiness
- Aggressive behavior towards co-workers
- Resistant demeanor
- Job-hopping
- Lack of desire to 'go the extra mile'
- Lack of enthusiasm
- Missed promotions
- Mediocre/poor job performance
- Unremarkable performance reviews
- Firings/Lay-offs
- Defeated attitude
- Clock-watching
- Poor family relations
- Poor physical health/sickness
- Poor mental health
- Increased alcohol use
- Increased drug use
- Irritability and fits of rage

Because we spend such a high percentage of our day and life at work, if our work is not right, we're not right. This, too, is undeniable. For this reason, it is critical to align self with work to live happily, meaningfully, joyfully. Most people know when misalignment exists between self and work. You can feel it. You need no other indicator to confirm misalignment.

Q: *When is aligning self with work necessary?*
A: If you cannot pass the 'AM Test' of looking in the mirror every morning and being excited about going to work,

then it is time to realign. Work has to represent more than collecting pay stubs. If you are not passionate about your day-to-day work, you need to find your passion and move aggressively towards living your passion.

Q: *How will I know I have aligned self with work?*
A: You will feel it. No longer will you view work as work, but as enjoyable and fun. Your work will represent passion, which will generate excitement, fuel motivation. Your work will be meaningful. Work will not be about pushing papers, attending meetings, or playing politics, it will represent activity that has meaning, purpose, and inspires soul. Your work will come easy to you as you are leveraging innate skills. You will feel a vibrancy and aliveness that, perhaps, you have never felt before. Lastly, you will feel free because you are free.

Q: *How aligned does self need to be with work?*
A: As work consumes sixty percent of our waking hours and forty percent of our waking life, self must ALWAYS be aligned with work – every day, every week, every month, every year. It comes down to this: when self is not aligned with work, we suffer, which affects our family, our health, our finances, and our quality of life. Therefore, do not accept suffering, to any extent or for any length of time. Do not subject your family, your health, or your future to the ills of misalignment. Live a fragrant life. Live a healthy life. Live *an aligned life.*

Aligning Self with Family

The last dimension that requires aligning is the relationship between self and family (see Figure 8.21).

To discuss how to align self with family, we ask the following questions:

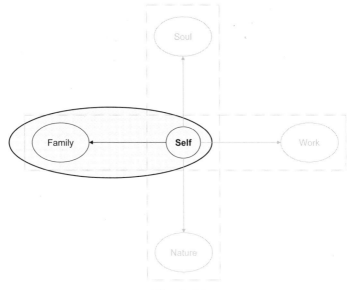

Fig. 8.21

Q: What does it mean to align self with family?
A: To align self with family means to align one's individual goals, priorities, and values with the larger goals, priorities, and values of family.

Depending on your situation, family could represent:

- Your spouse (or significant other)
- Kids
- Siblings
- Parents
- Extended family

Regardless of how you define family, the essence of aligning self with family remains the same, which is to align your interests with the interests of others in a way that is complementary rather than contradictory.

Q: What does <u>misalignment</u> of self with family mean?

A: Misalignment with family, like all forms of self-misalignment, is a personal malady. When self is misaligned with family, it means that your individual life goals, priorities, and values are not complementary to the larger goals, priorities, and values of family. Families reveal a 'life agenda' through priorities, values, behaviors, and actions similar to how an individual reveals a life agenda through priorities, values, behaviors, and actions. The extent that both agendas complement one another determines the degree with which self is aligned with family.

Q: How does one align self with family?

A: Aligning self with family requires:

- Acknowledging misalignment between self and family
- Improving relations with family, communicating more with family
- Understanding the priorities, values, and goals of family to align your priorities, values, and goals accordingly
- Developing a strategy to 'close the gap' and improve relations
- Taking action

Aligning self with family begins with acknowledging that self is misaligned with family. The symptoms of misalignment exist; you just need to acknowledge them. Next, it requires identifying changes that need to be made in your life to restore alignment. Listed below are examples of how one might restore alignment between self and family:

- Devote evenings for 'family time'
- Spend alone time with spouse (or significant other)
- Plan romantic getaways
- Initiate spontaneous getaways (e.g. zoo, beach, city, museum)

- Plan family vacation
- Plan family reunion
- Improve frequency/quality of communication
- Work fewer hours
- Limit work-related travel
- Plan family bonding exercises
- Spend time with kids
- Coach child's sports team

The makeup of your family and the type of relations you have with each family member will determine the types of self-intervention that are necessary to restore alignment.

Q: *What does misalignment of self with family look like?*
A: Holding all other dimensions constant, misalignment of self with family does have 'shape' (see Figure 8.22).

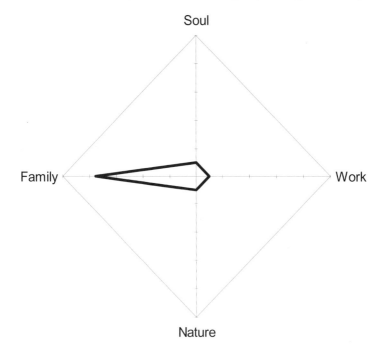

Fig. 8.22

Misalignment of self with family exhibits a 'spear head'-like shape extending near the boundary of the alignment frame.

Q: *How does self become misaligned with family?*
A: Self becomes misaligned with family due to:

- Miscommunication
- Infrequent communication
- Lack of willingness to solve problems, resolve differences
- Lack of willingness to listen, understand others
- Physical distance between family members

Q: *What are the benefits of aligning self with family?*
A: There are several benefits when aligning self with family:

- Internal happiness
- Good relations
- Open communication
- Frequent communication
- Reduced personal conflict
- Meaningful friendships
- Loving friendships
- Meaningful interactions
- Reliable support system
- Reduced stress

Q: *What results when self is misaligned with family?*
A: When self is misaligned with family, several personal pathologies result:

- Little to no communication
- Persistent unhappiness
- Internal sadness
- Stress
- Growing separation
- Hostility towards others
- Lack of participation in family events
- Feelings of isolation

- Erecting of barriers
- Feelings of regret
- Negative impact on work performance
- Increased use of alcohol and drugs

Q: *When is aligning self with family necessary?*
A: As with other dimensions of personal alignment, aligning self with family is necessary all the time. Any time you feel interactions and relations between yourself and other family members is poor, consider it a sign to realign.

Q: *How will I know that I have aligned self with family?*
A: You will feel it. Relations will improve, communication will be frequent, honest, and open, and connectedness will supplant disconnectedness. Lastly, the suffering will subside, which will be the surest indicator of all.

Q: *How aligned does self need to be with family?*
A: The short answer is: it depends. Each of us has our own goals, priorities, and agenda in life; we are different, unique by design. Consequently, aligning self with family is, ultimately, not about having the same goals, priorities, and agenda in life; it is about having an agenda that complements rather than contradicts family.

Horizontal Alignment

We just discussed aligning self with work and aligning self with family. When considered together, both forms of alignment take on even greater significance. Aligning self with work and self with family together represent a special form of alignment called horizontal alignment (see Figure 8.23).

Horizontal alignment is important because of what it represents – the 'work-life' balance. The work-life balance represents:

- Balancing work commitments with family commitments in a way that satisfies both family and employer

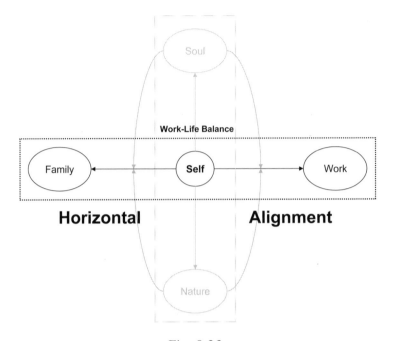

Fig. 8.23

- A mindset that family matters are of equal importance
  with work matters and that work should never
  dominate one's life such that one's physical health,
  mental health, or family is compromised in the process

Maintaining work-life balance is a serious matter. You will have great difficulty achieving personal alignment, increasing personal happiness, if imbalance exists between work and family. Having said this, establishing work-life balance is more about balancing work with family than balancing family with work, as work is generally the cause of work-life <u>im</u>balance. As such, achieving horizontal alignment is largely about addressing work matters. Horizontal alignment, like all forms of alignment, has shape. When horizontally aligned, the alignment dimensions of work and family cluster near the center of the alignment frame (see Figure 8.24).

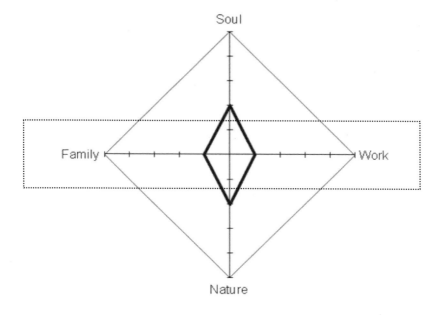

Fig. 8.24

When not horizontally aligned, the alignment dimensions of work and family extend near the boundaries of the alignment frame (see Figure 8.25).

Knowing that one suffers from work-life imbalance enables one to restore balance; establish alignment.

Staying Aligned

You might be saying at this point, 'I understand the forms and shapes of personal alignment (and misalignment) and the benefits of becoming aligned, but what I need to understand now is how to stay aligned once achieved'. The good news is that the process to achieve both is the same (see Figure 8.26).

Step 1 asks us to look for, listen to, and acknowledge misalignment. Whether referring to soul, nature, family, or work, one should always be conscious of signs of <u>mis</u>alignment. For

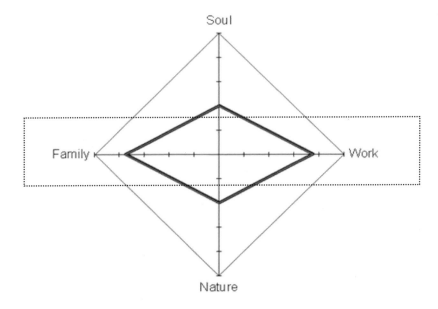

Fig. 8.25

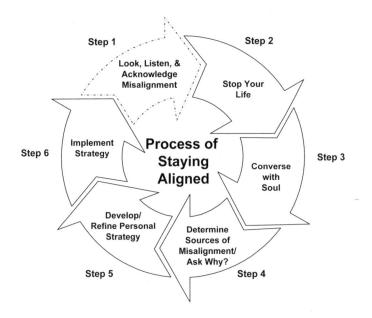

Fig. 8.26

example, what symptoms exist within your workplace that echo misalignment? Perhaps you are irritable with co-workers. Perhaps you lack enthusiasm and passion for your work. Similarly, what symptoms exist regarding your relations with family that might suggest misalignment? Step outside self to see self. Examine your workplace interactions. Examine your family interactions. Examine your connection with nature. Improving your ability to see will, in time, improve your ability to sense misalignment to restore alignment.

In addition to knowing what to look for to maintain alignment, it also requires being a good listener. Since the art of listening is not a developed skill for most people, feedback from one's environment (family, work, nature) usually goes in one ear and out the other. Our task is to listen for clues behind spoken word. For example, as you interact with family and/or your significant other, listen for clues of misalignment. Clues are all around us, yet most of the time we are blind to their existence and deaf to their meaning. Learn to listen for the meaning behind clues, as this will reveal misalignment. Diagnosing personal misalignment requires brutal honesty with self. Few people are members of the total alignment club. Remember this fact as you attempt to declare yourself an honorary member.

With acknowledging misalignment, Step 2 requires stopping your life to examine your life. The key to 'staying aligned' is to interrogate self, to examine one's self throughout life, which requires stopping your life. Stopping your life, in turn, enables Step 3 of conversing with soul to ask important questions of self and listen for the answers. It is through quiet conversation with soul that we maintain personal alignment. Only when we stop our life to ask important questions like, 'Does my work excite me? and 'Are my relations with others healthy? and 'Am I happy living in current conditions?' do we expose and make visible the changes occurring within. With reflection, conversing with soul, we determine, in Step 4, the sources of misalignment. Upon determining sources, in Step 5, we develop/refine personal strategy to eliminate misalignment.

Lastly, in Step 6, we implement strategy. As stated before, achieving personal alignment requires effort. So does maintaining personal alignment. Having said this, the benefits of staying aligned far outweigh the costs. Developing the capacity to self-align is necessary to experience life-long happiness. The good news is that, at this point, you know what to align, how to align, and most importantly why you must align.

Summary – On Personal Alignment

Okay. So, what have we learned about personal alignment? We have learned:

- What personal alignment means
- The dimensions of personal alignment
- The shapes of personal alignment
- The process to achieve personal alignment
- The tools that enable personal alignment
- What it means to align self with: soul, nature, family, and work
- The importance of vertical and horizontal alignment
- How to stay aligned once achieved

We opened this chapter by saying that 'alignment is everything'. I hope, now at chapter's end, that you see the wisdom in this statement. Alignment is a force that is open to all and, therefore, can benefit all. If there is one message to take from this chapter, it is: *to experience true happiness in life, it requires aligning self across all dimensions, not just one or two.* Achieving personal alignment is a process that all can master. With knowledge (of how to become self-aligned), effort, and time, achieving personal alignment is possible. We can summarize personal alignment using the framework presented earlier:

- Personal alignment is a process...
  - The process entails defining one's inner soul goals, developing strategy to achieve each goal, taking action, and course correcting as circumstances dictate

- Personal alignment takes time...
  - Time to define one's inner soul goals
  - Time to develop single-goal strategies to achieve each goal
  - Time to execute action plans and monitor progress
  - Time to adjust plans when circumstances dictate
  - Time to refine the process when a better way exists

- Personal alignment requires making adjustments...
  - Adjustments to one's inner soul goals
  - Adjustments with one's relation with work
  - Adjustments with one's relation with family
  - Adjustments with one's relation with nature

- Alignment of parts is the goal...
  - Self
  - Soul
  - Nature
  - Family
  - Work

- Personal alignment focuses on relations between parts...
  - Relation of self with soul
  - Relation of self with nature
  - Relation of self with family
  - Relation of self with work

Although too early for you to recognize, *developing the capacity to self-align is perhaps the greatest benefit from defining, implementing, and managing a personal strategy for living*. The process of achieving personal alignment is a lifelong endeavor. Indeed, we are constantly in search of alignment. By applying the principles, methods, and tools discussed herein, you will develop a capacity to self align quickly, effectively. Further, by developing this core competency, you will enjoy a personal competitive advantage of the highest order. You will hold the keys to achieve tremendous personal, professional, and financial success; to realize a remarkable life. When you reach this heightened state of living and look back with great profundity and pride on your accomplishments, consider this: personal alignment *has always been with you – always been waiting for you – you just had to go find it.*

Personal alignment is the essence of living. Personal alignment represents a movement from **intellectual alignment** (I know what I want to do with my life) → **spiritual alignment** (I believe the decided path is right for me) → **physical alignment** (I act on my plan to transform my life, to pursue my passion, to live again). As this is a book of truths, a powerful truth exists regarding personal alignment: as personal alignment increases, one's happiness increases, and as personal alignment decreases, one's happiness decreases (see Figure 8.27).

Having a personal strategy is the means to an end: personal alignment. To achieve this end, however, requires we adapt and respond adequately to change. Moreover, we must actively manage change; that is, actively manage personal strategy. Now, because our ability to adapt and respond to change determines our ability to self-align, and because the effectiveness of personal strategy is greatly diminished without actively managing strategy, we address both these topics next in Part IV.

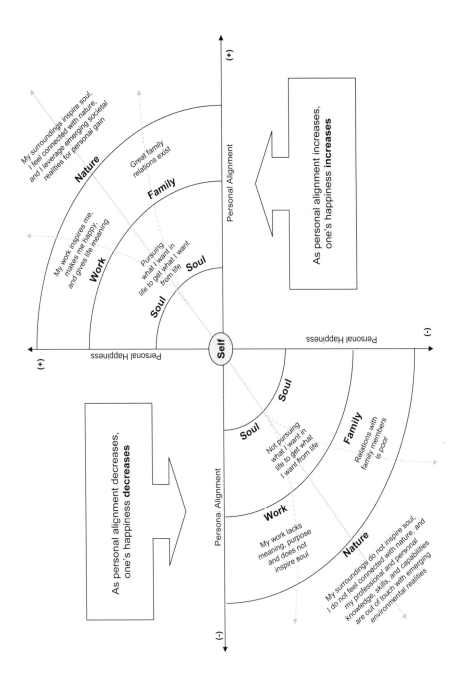

Fig. 8.27

PART IV
Adaptation and Responding to Change

Stumbling Blocks of Personal Strategy

*"Let me tell you the secret that has led me to my
goal. My strength lies solely in my tenacity."*

- Louis Pasteur

BEFORE DISCUSSING THE STUMBLING BLOCKS of personal strategy, let us recap our journey together (see Figure 9.1).

Thus far, we have learned:

- What personal strategy is
- How to define personal strategy
- How to build personal strategy
- How to keep score of personal strategy
- Personal strategy is a means to an end (alignment)

In addition to learning these things, you should have begun implementing your PST action plans and collecting scorecard data. As you implement your new life plan, it is important to understand the stumbling blocks of personal strategy. As such, in this chapter, we discuss how to recognize, overcome, and most importantly, prevent stumbling blocks from sabotaging your inner soul goals. We begin by defining what a stumbling block represents.

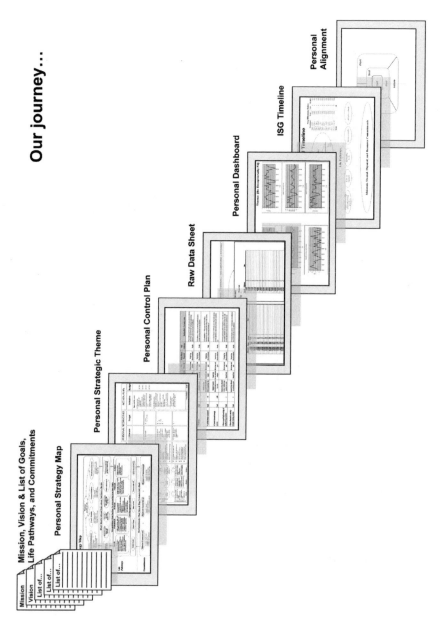

Fig. 9.1

Simply put, stumbling blocks represent <u>any</u> obstacle or impediment to achieving personal strategy, and they come in two forms:

- Stumbling blocks of the Mind
- Stumbling blocks of the Environment

Table 9.1 illustrates the differences between the two forms:

Table 9.1

Stumbling Block's of the Mind	Stumbling Block's of the Environment
Caused by you	Caused by others
Internal	External
More severe	Less severe
Solution requires changing self	Solution requires adapting to change
Issue of self	Issue of self interacting with other systems
Negatively affect personal strategy	Can positively or negatively affect personal strategy
Many symptoms exist	Few symptoms exist

Because stumbling blocks caused by you are more severe and, therefore, more damaging to one's personal strategy, we begin by discussing stumbling blocks of the mind.

Stumbling Blocks of the Mind

Stumbling blocks of the mind refer to *how* <u>*you*</u> *get in the way of* <u>*you*</u>. Often times, you are the barrier to change, and to make progress, it requires getting past you. Therefore, to achieve personal strategy, it is imperative that you recognize, overcome, and prevent stumbling blocks caused by you.

Stumbling blocks of the mind take many forms. Some are more damaging to personal strategy than others, but, regardless of form, all negatively affect your ability to implement and achieve personal strategy. As the list of stumbling blocks is long, we approach by discussing the major 'categories' of internal stumbling blocks:

- Lenses of Life
- Debilitating Tendencies
- Resisting Change
- Dropping the Ball

Lenses of Life

What are the 'lenses of life'? The 'lenses of life' determine what you see when you look at the world. Lens is a metaphor to represent a filter through which we see and interpret events in our life and in the world. Each of us views life and the world through a unique set of lenses (see Figure 9.2).

For example, while some people respond to a layoff from work with destructive behavior and pessimistic thinking, others feel liberated to start their own business. Similarly, while some people view having a personal strategy necessary to achieve their dreams, others do not. So, how is it that two people could view the same event differently? How is it that some people see value in using a personal strategy while others do not? The answer is that each of us looks through different lenses of life. How you view events in life depends on your lenses of life. Many things shape how we look at the world. From early childhood to late in life, we are constantly reshaping, redefining our lenses of life. Every interaction, every life event, every television show watched, every book read shapes our lenses of life. However, not all interactions or life events are created equal. For most people, lenses of life are shaped by the values, beliefs, and teachings of one's parents, but sometimes a grandparent, a college professor, or friend shape our lenses as well. The truth is, all human interaction shapes us in one way or another; it's just that

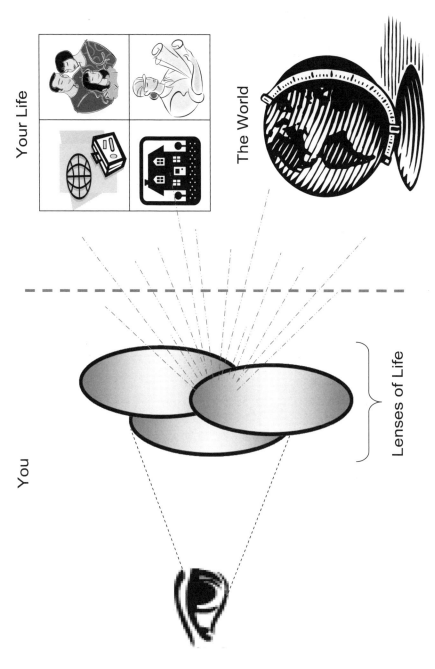

Fig. 9.2

some interactions 'shape' more than others. By the time we reach adulthood, our lenses reflect and are influenced by:

- Our values
- Our beliefs
- Our life experiences

The relevance, connection lenses of life have to personal strategy is that our values, beliefs, and life experiences not only shape personal strategy but also determine whether we achieve personal strategy. Together, such things dictate what you see when you look at the world. And because 'what you see' determines 'how you think,' and 'how you think' determines 'how you act,' and 'how you act' determines 'how you feel,' making visible one's lenses of life is vital to achieve personal strategy (see Figure 9.3)

You might be asking, 'How could one's views affect implementing or achieving personal strategy?' In Table 9.2, consider each situation and pick the view (A or B) that best reflects you:

Table 9.2

Situation	View A	View B
My strategy is not helping me achieve my inner soul goal	Abandon my inner soul goal	Course correct my strategy and implement changes quickly
Collecting scorecard data	Collecting data takes too much time	Collecting data provides insights to improve my personal strategy
Managing one's life	My life does not require 'managing'	Managing my life will help me live a happy, fragrant, and meaningful existence
Measuring one's life	My life does not require 'measuring'	Measuring aspects of my life will help me achieve my goals

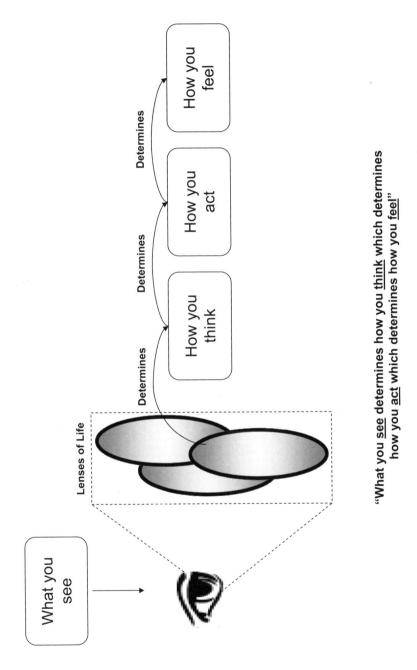

Fig. 9.3

How did you do? Did your responses align more with View A or View B? Clearly, the lenses that reflect View A are much different from the lenses that reflect View B. View A reflects a negative view of personal strategy whereas View B reflects a positive view of personal strategy. What this exercise demonstrates is that the views we hold (i.e., 'what we see') determine all that follows, specifically, how we respond to situations and events. As it relates to personal strategy, we learned that *certain views (e.g. View A) destroy personal strategy while other views (e.g. View B) build up personal strategy.* Viewing the situations above through lens A versus lens B, and vice versa, is a choice. Therefore, what reflects from your lenses of life (i.e., your thinking, your actions, your feelings), is also a choice. Know this: as you implement your personal strategy, success or failure is determined largely by how you think and how you act which, we now know, is determined by what you see.

Another stumbling block of the mind that can affect personal strategy is debilitating tendencies.

Debilitating Tendencies

You are probably wondering what a 'debilitating tendency' is, so let us begin by defining both words. Debilitate means 'to sap the strength or energy of' and tendency means 'a predisposition to think, act, behave, or proceed in a particular way'. Together, both words provide us a definition of a debilitating tendency:

> *"A debilitating tendency is a predisposition to think, act, behave, or proceed in a particular way that saps your strength or energy"*

As defining and implementing personal strategy requires perseverance, this stumbling block is especially debilitating. Consequently, each of us must become aware of our debilitating tendencies, as they sap strength and spirit, not only out of personal strategy, but also our life. With such awareness, the probability of achieving one's personal strategy increases dramatically.

When discussing the 'lenses of life', we learned that how one thinks determines how one acts, which determines how one feels. Interestingly, the same characterization defines a debilitating tendency. That is, a debilitating tendency refers to thinking a certain way which determines how we act (i.e., behave), which determines how we feel (i.e., proceed). As such, the relationship between 'lenses of life' and debilitating tendencies is that 'lenses of life' cause debilitating tendencies. This confirms what we already know, which is *to change how one thinks, acts, and feels, it first requires changing how one sees.* We explore this idea later in the section on preventing stumbling blocks. For now, let us understand the most common debilitating tendencies that destroy personal strategy. They are:

- Manipulate self
- Stinking thinking
- Paralyzed with inaction

To manipulate self means to trick self into thinking and acting a certain way based on a skewed sense of reality. For example, I suffered from a debilitating tendency of looking in the mirror and thinking that I was physically fit when, in fact, I was not fit. But because I <u>saw</u> fitness, I manipulated self into thinking, acting, and feeling the same way. What resulted from this skewed reality is I did not exercise, thereby compounding my weight problem. Equally destructive was my willingness to eat sweets, thinking I could do so because I was 'fit'. I manipulated self into thinking that I was fit based on what my lenses of life reflected. Since I saw fitness, I thought fitness. This example illustrates how 'what we see' influences 'what we think'. Manipulating self is a highly destructive and common debilitating tendency that from which many people suffer. As achieving one's inner soul goals requires 'facing reality', this stumbling block can be especially debilitating. Debilitating tendencies distort our thinking, which undermines our ability to do, and as achieving personal strategy is all about 'doing,' if we are not 'doing', we are also not 'achieving'. For this reason, it is important to 1) understand debilitating tendencies and 2) identify those that afflict you. Later in this chapter, we discuss how to recognize, overcome, and prevent this stumbling block of personal strategy from occurring.

Stinking thinking is yet another debilitating tendency. Stinking thinking, like manipulating self, indicates debilitating thought, hence the name. Stinking thinking is another debilitating tendency I suffer from. I became aware of this years ago while selling insurance. It represents a tendency to view events or situations from a negative point of view. Because of the intangible nature of insurance, and because of its commodity status, selling insurance can be difficult. Consequently, an insurance salesperson must endure many rejections before getting a sale. Over time, these rejections build up, afflicting many with a case of stinking thinking. When I sold insurance, I suffered from stinking thinking. At times, during the five years I sold insurance, I thought:

- I am a bad salesperson
- My products are not competitive
- Sales is no fun
- There is too much competition
- No one buys insurance
- I will never make money selling insurance
- My territory is dry
- Sales is too hard
- People do not care about insurance

Each of the examples above reflects stinking thinking. The debilitating part of stinking thinking is that how we think dictates how we act. Therefore, if one thinks negative thoughts, it usually leads to negative behavior. This was my experience. Because of stinking thinking, I did not work as hard; I did not prospect for sales leads as diligently as I should have; I stopped learning how to become a better salesperson, and ultimately, the company forced me out. It was not a pleasant experience, but it did teach me that negative thoughts breed negative behavior while positive thoughts breed positive behavior.

Stinking thinking crippled my ability to sell. It can also cripple personal strategy. Table 9.3 details how stinking thinking can affect personal strategy:

Table 9.3

Example of Stinking Thinking	Effect to Personal Strategy
"Achieving my inner soul goals takes too long"	Abandon personal strategy and your inner soul goals
"Collecting scorecard data requires too much effort"	No data collection leads to few insights into one's personal strategy, which leads to no refinement of personal strategy, thereby diminishing personal strategy
"Defining personal strategy requires too much effort"	Personal strategy is never implemented and inner soul goals lie dormant forever
"My life is too busy, too complex to have a personal strategy"	Personal strategy is never implemented and inner soul goals lie dormant forever
"Only people with screwed up lives need a personal strategy"	Personal strategy is never implemented and inner soul goals lie dormant forever

Stinking thinking destroys goals. This is a fact. To prevent stinking thinking from affecting personal strategy, it requires 1) recognizing stinking thinking as it occurs and 2) working yourself out of such thoughts quickly. Later in this chapter, we discuss how to recognize, overcome, and prevent this stumbling block of personal strategy from occurring.

Paralyzed with inaction is yet another debilitating tendency. What does this mean? Paralyzed with inaction refers to situations when you want to do something (e.g. implement personal strategy), but for a myriad of reasons, cannot. Like all debilitating tendencies, this is a stumbling block of the mind. Part of you is saying 'go', but a bigger part of you is saying 'no'. Not all people suffer from this tendency, but for those who do this stumbling block is especially debilitating. Paralyzed with inaction can take many forms. Examples include:

- Fear of failure
- Fear of success

Fear of failure is perhaps the most common cause for inaction. For those who suffer from this paralysis, their fear is that they will never achieve their goals so why bother? Why put forth the effort? Whatever the cause, fear halts progress; we stop 'doing' because we fear failure with the task. A common indication of those who suffer this debilitating tendency is that they endlessly tweak personal strategy, fearing implementing personal strategy. To define personal strategy is easy; the hard part is implementing it and some people, upon defining personal strategy, are so overcome with anxiety that they find reason to tweak, knowing the longer they tweak the longer they delay. As this example demonstrates, fear of failure can destroy personal strategy. Equally destructive, but perhaps lesser known, is a fear of success.

I first encountered the notion of someone 'fearing success' when I was in insurance sales. I worked with an individual who was a good salesman, a rising star. Nevertheless, once he reached a certain sales volume, he seemed to go no further. It appeared as if he was afraid to go to the next level. For him, the fear of success was real. He wanted to attain the next level, wanted to be more successful, but was paralyzed with inaction. Many people, I believe, suffer this debilitating tendency. To some extent, I suffer from this tendency. Part of me always strived to climb the next rung of the corporate ladder, but another part of me remained fearful of actually achieving the next rung. I, too, was paralyzed with inaction. Although not as prevalent as other debilitating tendencies, this stumbling block can nevertheless impede one's goals.

Debilitating tendencies are a part of us, part of our DNA. Consequently, each of us suffers from one or more debilitating tendencies. The good news is, once you know what you suffer from, you can eliminate or minimally reduce such tendencies. For example, earlier I mentioned how I suffered from a debilitating tendency of manipulating self (e.g. seeing and thinking 'fitness' when none existed). Now that I am aware of this tendency, I can manage this tendency; that is, I can quickly prevent manipulation of self. Individually and collectively, debilitating tendencies destroy personal strategy. Equally destructive to personal strategy is when we resist change, which is another stumbling block of the mind.

Resisting Change

The essence of personal strategy is change. Just as the essence of writing is rewriting, so, too, is the essence of personal strategy revised strategy. From defining personal strategy, to implementing personal strategy, to managing personal strategy, change happens. Consider how you have changed (seeing, thinking, acting, feeling) since first opening this book:

What you see...

- Opportunity and imperative
- A new vision for self
- A new life trajectory

How you think...

- Your priorities (i.e., inner soul goals)
- Your purpose in life
- What gives life meaning

How you act...

- The activities you perform
- The activities you do not perform
- The commitments you keep
- The resources you allocate

How you feel...

- Your life experience
- Your personal happiness
- Your quality of life

Some people embrace change; others do not. To implement personal strategy, however, requires developing a capacity to change. For most people, designing and implementing personal strategy, as described in this book, will demand greater effort, greater rigor, and greater personal change than any past attempt at defining personal strategy. As such, many will resist change and respond with self-imposed stumbling blocks.

For those who resist change, implementing and living by a personal strategy will be difficult, if not impossible, to achieve. If 'managing your life' or 'measuring your life' are concepts too rigid for you to accept, this mental stumbling block will likely prevent you from achieving your inner soul goals. Later in this chapter, we discuss how to recognize, overcome, and prevent this stumbling block of personal strategy from occurring.

Another stumbling block of the mind that can affect personal strategy is 'dropping the ball'.

Dropping the Ball

To *drop the ball* means to 'quit prematurely', to 'proceed lethargically', or to 'miss an opportunity'. As it relates to personal strategy, there are several ways that people 'drop the ball':

- Stop conversing with soul
- Stop collecting scorecard data
- Stop refining personal strategy
- Stop caring about personal strategy
- Stop exerting necessary commitments
- Stop performing life's pathways
- Stop allocating necessary resources

Each of the examples shown above destroys personal strategy. Dropping the ball of one's strategy is especially debilitating as it indicates lost enthusiasm not only to live by personal strategy, but also to achieve one's goals. It is difficult to resurrect personal strategy when the well of enthusiasm goes dry. In Chapter 6, we learned the importance of conversing with soul. Conversing with soul is the means by which we learn desires of soul, stay connected with soul, learn to live as soul would live. Consequently, if you cease communicating with soul, you cease to know soul, resulting in:

- Outdated personal strategy
- Flawed personal strategy
- Lost interest in having a personal strategy
- Lost momentum to drive personal strategy
- Increased personal <u>mis</u>alignment

Conversing with soul is crucial to achieve your inner soul goals. Equally crucial is collecting performance data on scorecard measures. Collecting performance data reveals whether our strategy is working and helps identify which aspects of personal strategy require course correction. When you stop collecting performance data, you lose visibility into:

- How to improve personal strategy
- How to drive achievement of your inner soul goals
- What aspects of personal strategy require tweaking
- The cause and effect dynamics underlying personal strategy
- How to best measure your life experience

What the above suggests is that with data, we can drive our new life plan with confidence. Without data, we are blind, unable to chart proper course. Perhaps the most important reason to collect performance data is that it enables refining personal strategy, which is another way we 'drop the ball'.

Refining personal strategy is just as important as defining and implementing personal strategy. Now, since you and I are having an intimate conversation, let me be the first to tell you that your personal strategy is flawed and will require refining. You may discover, for example, that your current strategy will not achieve your inner soul goal, your performance measures drive the wrong behavior, or your action plan initiatives are 'off the mark'. Do not be alarmed; this is typical. You will get better at perfecting personal strategy over time, but this does assume, of course, that you refine your personal strategy over time. As stated in Part II, personal strategy is a living, breathing entity and as we change, as we obtain feedback from self and environment, so, too, must our personal strategy change. Consequently, if you stop refining personal strategy, if you stop using feedback from scorecard measures and sensory outlets, your strategy stops evolving, stops improving, and ultimately, stops working. When this occurs, one might falsely conclude that having a personal strategy is meaningless and not worth the effort, as it is incapable of delivering desired results. This could not be further from the truth, but this scenario does reveal the importance of continually refining one's personal strategy over time. When we think our personal strategy is not working, it changes our attitude from caring about personal strategy and achieving goals to not caring about personal strategy and achieving goals. This attitude shift represents yet another form of 'dropping the ball', which is, itself, a cause for not exerting necessary commitments, not performing life's pathways, and not allocating necessary resources.

The majority of people will, in the words of Henry David Thoreau, "live a life of quiet desperation". Said differently, the majority of people on earth will not live a fragrant, meaningful, or happy existence. Why is this so? Well, a lot has to do with not having a personal strategy, not pursuing one's inner soul goals, and not living as soul would live, but in addition to that, living a fragrant life requires a caring attitude. When I think of such things, it reminds me of a line from the movie, 'The Shawshank Redemption,' about the need to "get busy living or get busy dying". To live as soul would live, to pursue goals inspired by soul, reflects an attitude of 'get busy living,' whereas to not live as soul would live, to not pursue goals inspired by soul, reflects an attitude of 'get busy dying'. Inner soul goals give our life direction, purpose, and meaning. They fill us with hope, excitement, and reason to live. Without them, life ceases to have direction, ceases to have purpose, and ceases to have meaning, resigning one to live a life of quiet desperation.

You may be thinking, 'With all the stumbling blocks of mind that exist, how can I ever achieve my inner soul goals?' Well, I am here to tell you that you can overcome each of the stumbling blocks of personal strategy just discussed. However, stumbling blocks of the mind are not all that is standing in your way of personal happiness. There also exist stumbling blocks of the environment.

Stumbling Blocks of the Environment

Stumbling blocks of the environment refer to *how your environment gets in the way of you achieving your goals*. Stumbling blocks of the environment take many forms, and unlike stumbling blocks of the mind, they can affect personal strategy in either a positive or negative way. Therefore, it is important to become familiar with the most common stumbling blocks caused by others. Stumbling blocks of the environment emanate from four primary sources:

- Stumbling blocks caused by **work**
- Stumbling blocks caused by **family**
- Stumbling blocks caused by **society**
- Stumbling blocks caused by **nature**

Together, work, family, society, and nature represent our external 'environment'. In Part III, we learned that we cannot control our environment; we can only 'sense and respond' to events and/or changes occurring beyond our control. Our environment influences every aspect of our life. Work influences our soul, our mind, and our body. Family, society, and nature also influence our soul, mind, and body. Consequently, to achieve personal strategy requires knowing how our environment can interfere with personal strategy. First, we discuss stumbling blocks caused by work.

Stumbling Blocks Caused by Work

Work can affect personal strategy in a myriad of ways. 'Work,' in this context, means:

- <u>Where</u> one works
- <u>What</u> one does at work
- <u>How</u> one works
- The <u>environment</u> in which one works
- The <u>people</u> with whom one interacts at work

Based on recent discussion, we know that stumbling blocks of personal strategy <u>distract</u> personal strategy. Therefore, when thinking about work, we are interested in learning how work distracts us from implementing and achieving personal strategy. Table 9.4 provides examples of how work can distract personal strategy.

Table 9.4

Distractions to Personal Strategy Caused by Work System
• Operating condition of the company (i.e., company health)
• Cultural issues
• Corporate downsizing
• Corporate reorganization
• Physical working environment
• Unexpected promotion
• Sabotage from others / corporate politics
• Changes in valued knowledge, skills, and capabilities
• Corporate fraud (e.g. Enron, Arthur Andersen, WorldCom, etc.)
• Unexpected opportunity
• Competition from other companies within same industry
• Business trends (e.g. outsourcing, globalism, automation)
• Company relocation

It is important to recognize distractions in the workplace, as they affect all our inner soul goals, not just our profession-based goals. Distractions from the workplace can be good or bad. Most distractions shown above are bad, but some are good, like 'unexpected promotion' and 'unexpected opportunity'. Good or bad, distractions cause us to reevaluate our personal strategy and, in some cases, modify personal strategy based on events occurring beyond our control. For example, upon graduating from Northern Illinois University with a Master's Degree in MIS, I worked for one of the big four consulting firms in Chicago, a prestigious company that paid well. Shortly after arriving, I discovered the culture, and the people, to be very elitist in nature. This rubbed me the wrong way. I did not come from a wealthy family, nor did I attend an Ivy League school, and adopting an 'elitist' mindset was unsettling. I earned my way to work for a top employer, but now *the environment* I was working in, *the culture* I was forced to adopt, conflicted with not only my personal values and sensibilities, but also proved too much a distraction to my personal strategy. How did I respond? I started my own consulting firm and never looked back.

Stumbling blocks caused by work are not the only stumbling blocks in your environment of which you should be aware. You also need to be aware of those caused by family.

Stumbling Blocks Caused by Family

Like work, family can affect personal strategy in a myriad of ways. 'Family' in this context means:

- Immediate family (spouse or significant other, including kids)
- Extended family (parents, siblings, aunts, uncles, etc.)

When thinking about family, we are interested in learning how family distracts us from implementing and achieving personal strategy. Table 9.5 provides examples of how family can distract personal strategy.

Table 9.5

Distractions to Personal Strategy Caused by Family System
• Unexpected tragedy (e.g. death, illness)
• Unexpected blessing (e.g. pregnancy)
• Erratic behavior of others (e.g. drug use, criminal activity, etc.)
• Personal injury caused by others (e.g. physical, mental abuse)
• Unexpected heartache (e.g. affair by spouse, trickery, deceit)

It is important to recognize distractions occurring in one's family, as they affect all our inner soul goals, not just our family-based goals. As with work, family distractions can be either good or bad. Most distractions shown above are bad, but some are good, like 'unexpected blessing'. Good or bad, distractions cause us to reevaluate our personal strategy and, in some cases, modify personal strategy based on events occurring beyond our control. For example, only months into writing this book, I discovered that I was going to be a father. This unexpected blessing caused me to reevaluate and refine my strategy to write and publish this book. Suddenly, writing took a back seat to parenthood. I did finish the book, of course, but this example illustrates that when events occur in the family system, they can affect your personal strategy. In my case, I did not abandon or change my goal of writing this book, only my strategy for *when and how* I would write.

In addition to stumbling blocks caused by work and family, you also need to be aware of those caused by society.

Stumbling Blocks Caused by Society

Society can affect personal strategy in a myriad of ways as well. 'Society' in this context means:

- Local & national culture (of where one lives)
- Neighbors, friends, and acquaintances
- World events

When thinking about society, we are interested in learning how society distracts us from implementing and achieving personal strategy. Table 9.6 provides examples of how society distracts personal strategy.

Table 9.6

Distractions to Personal Strategy Caused by Society System
• Unexpected tragedy (e.g. 9/11, SARS virus, Anthrax attacks)
• Changes in world stability
• Changes in economic stability (e.g. recession, housing crisis)
• Changes in political stability
• Changes in societal norms
• Life altering book
• Life altering movie
• Life altering acquaintance
• Unexpected business opportunity

It is important to recognize distractions occurring in society, as they can affect all your inner soul goals. As with work and family, societal distractions can be either good or bad, causing us to reevaluate our personal strategy and, in some cases, modify personal strategy based on events occurring beyond our control. For example, the impetus to write this book was the result of over fifteen years of consulting to industry, and observing (i.e., 'sensing') that many people were unhappy with their work. Most people I encountered felt that their work provided little meaning to their life other than by providing the necessities of food, clothing, and shelter. And as most people felt disempowered to change their situation, they, in effect, resigned themselves to live a life of quiet desperation. The more I encountered these troubled souls, the more compelled I was to write this book to liberate such people from the hopelessness and despair that accompanies a life of quiet desperation. This societal 'distraction' affected not only my personal strategy, but also my life mission, life vision. Sometimes, distractions can profoundly affect one's life, as in my case; other times, the effect is less dramatic. In any case, the key is to adapt and respond adequately to such change.

Finally, we need to be aware of stumbling blocks caused by nature.

Stumbling Blocks Caused by Nature

Events of nature can affect personal strategy as well. When thinking about nature, we are interested in learning how nature distracts us from implementing and achieving personal strategy. Table 9.7 provides examples of how nature distracts personal strategy.

Table 9.7

Distractions to Personal Strategy Caused by Nature
• Natural disaster (e.g. Hurricane Katrina, Indonesian Tsunami)
• Global warming
• Climate shifts
• New appreciation for nature

It is important to recognize distractions occurring in nature, as they can affect all your inner soul goals. As with distractions caused by work, family, and society, distractions caused by nature can be either good or bad, causing us to reevaluate our personal strategy and, in some cases, modify personal strategy based on events occurring beyond our control. For example, although I always felt a connection with nature, when I reached adulthood, I lost touch. Then, a few short years ago, I fell back in love with nature, which deeply affected not only my personal strategy, but also how I wanted to operate on the surface of life. I revaluated everything – where I wanted to live, where I wanted to vacation, and what hobbies I wanted to pursue. As with the societal example just discussed, such distraction from nature changed all that follows.

Stumbling blocks of the environment can be every bit as disruptive or damaging to personal strategy as stumbling blocks of the mind. As you implement your personal strategy, it is important to recognize how work, family, society, and nature are affecting your strategy. Moreover, it is vital that you respond adequately and quickly to change. For example, you may find that simple course correction is all that is needed to get on track. Other times, you may find that changes occurring beyond your control prompt a wholesale readjustment of personal strategy, including defining new mission, new vision, and new inner soul goals. None of us can 'control' our environment. We are but cogs in a bigger wheel. Thus, the best we can do is 'sense and respond'. But, for those who develop a capacity to do so, they will possess a personal competitive advantage **of the highest order**. All the more reason to become familiar with the stumbling blocks of personal strategy.

To recognize, overcome, and prevent stumbling blocks of personal strategy from occurring, first requires knowing what they are. At this point, you do know the types of stumbling blocks that affect personal strategy. However, simply *knowing* the stumbling blocks that affect personal strategy is not enough. To minimize the effects stumbling blocks have on personal strategy, it is vital that you *recognize* them as they occur.

Recognizing Stumbling Blocks

Recognizing the stumbling blocks of personal strategy first requires knowing what to look for. This step is relevant, becomes significant when one considers that *knowing what to look for enables one to see*. At this point, you do know what to look for; you can see, as we discussed the most common types of obstacles that affect personal strategy. And to recognize the stumbling blocks of personal strategy, *to see the symptoms*, enables one to overcome and prevent stumbling blocks from affecting one's goals (see Table 9.8).

Table 9.8

	The Symptoms	
Stumbling Blocks of the Mind	**Lenses of Life**	
	• View personal setbacks as negative • View slow progress with achieving one's goals as negative • View collecting scorecard data as a waste of time • View managing one's life as not worth the effort • View measuring one's life as providing little value	
	Debilitating Tendencies	
	• Tendency to view things differently than they are • Tendency to adopt a poor attitude • Inability to take action • Fear of failure • Fear of success	
	Dropping the Ball	
	• Stop reviewing personal strategy • Stop refining personal strategy • Stop collecting scorecard data • Stop performing life's pathways • Stop allocating resources • Waning commitment • Stop caring about one's goals • Stop conversing with soul	
	Resisting Change	
	• Little effort expended to define personal strategy • Little effort expended to implement personal strategy • Little to no progress with achieving one's goals	
Stumbling Blocks of the Environment	**Work**	
	• Declining company performance • Misalignment with company culture • Company reorganization/reengineering • Changing business trends/industry trends • Changes in what your company values in terms of knowledge, skills, and capabilities	
	Family	
	• Changed behavior of family members • Changed condition of family members	
	Society	
	• Changing societal norms • Changing economic conditions • Changing political conditions	
	Nature	
	• Changing climate patterns • Changed relation with nature	

Recognizing stumbling blocks of personal strategy is important, as without acknowledging condition one cannot overcome condition. Now that we are aware of the symptoms, given that we now see, let us discuss overcoming the stumbling blocks of personal strategy.

Overcoming Stumbling Blocks

Overcoming stumbling blocks of personal strategy requires knowing:

- What the stumbling blocks of personal strategy are
- How to recognize stumbling blocks as they occur
- The process and tools one can use to mitigate stumbling blocks

We have discussed the first two items above. What remains is to understand the process and tools we can use to overcome stumbling blocks of personal strategy. We begin with process.

The Process

The process to overcome stumbling blocks of personal strategy consists of five phases (see Figure 9.4).

Phase I – Acknowledge an Obstacle Exists

The first step of the process to overcome stumbling blocks of personal strategy is to step outside self to see self looking for symptoms that an obstacle (i.e., stumbling block) exists. If symptoms exist, we brainstorm for potential causes as to <u>why</u> the obstacle exists. When finished brainstorming, we group causes by category, eliminating duplicates. Lastly, we document our findings in a Cause and Effect Diagram. To enable Phase I work, we use the following tools from the personal strategy toolbox:

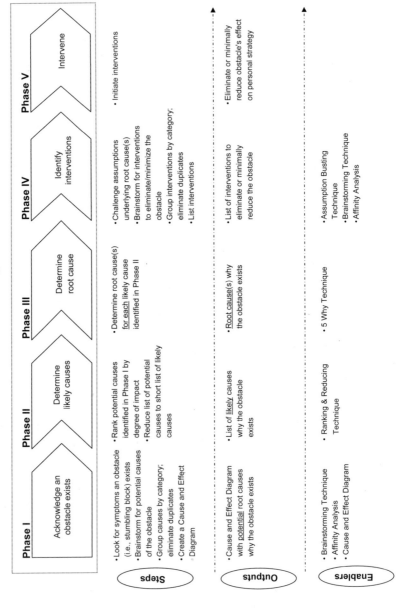

Fig. 9.4

- Brainstorming Technique
- Affinity Analysis
- Cause and Effect Diagram

Together, these tools help us identify the root causes of a problem in a mutually exclusive, collectively exhaustive way. They help push our thinking; to think around a problem, to consider all angles and causes, not just those that seem most obvious. As these tools may be unfamiliar to you, an example follows:

1. Look for symptoms that an obstacle exists
   - Step outside self to see self
   - State the obstacle
     - Ex. *'Belief I won't achieve my goals even with a personal strategy'*

2. Brainstorm for potential causes of the obstacle
   - Record each cause on a sticky note and affix notes onto a wall to visualize the complete list (see Figure 9.5)
   - Try to identify between 10-20 potential causes
   - When brainstorming, focus more on quantity than quality. The more we brainstorm, the more likely the 'real' cause(s) will surface

3. Group causes by category and eliminate duplicates
   - With a list of potential causes identified, the next step is to group causes by category and eliminate duplicates (see Figure 9.6)
   - Grouping causes by category helps identify gaps in one's thinking and usually leads to identifying additional causes
   - Grouping causes by category represents performing an Affinity Analysis

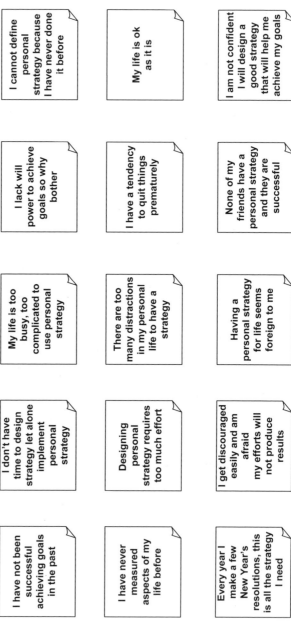

Fig. 9.5

Group Causes and Eliminate Duplicates

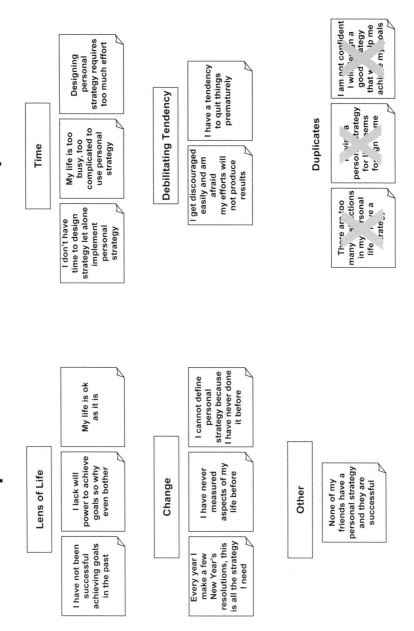

Fig. 9.6

4. Create a Cause and Effect (C&E) Diagram
   - Having categorized several potential causes, we document our findings on a Cause and Effect Diagram (see Figure 9.7)

   - Record the obstacle (problem) in the right-most box on the template. Next, record the major categories identified during Affinity Analysis in the boxes at the top and bottom of the template (e.g. 'lens of life', 'time', 'change', etc.). Finally, record each brainstormed cause under the appropriate category

   - Review the diagram for completeness and refine as needed

A Cause and Effect Diagram helps push our thinking beyond symptoms (i.e., causes that sound good but which are not true causes) to reveal root cause. The diagram also provides needed structure to our brainstorming exercise. Upon completing the Cause and Effect Diagram, you are finished with Phase I. At the end of Phase I, you should have between 10-20 (or possibly more) potential causes of the obstacle affecting your personal strategy. The next step is to rank and reduce your list of potential causes to only the 'vital few' likely causes.

Phase II – Determine Likely Causes

In Phase II, our focus is to reduce a long list of <u>potential</u> causes to a short list of <u>likely</u> causes. We do this by ranking each potential cause on a scale of 1 to 10 where 1 represents the symptom and 10 represents the likely cause. Once you rank each potential cause, sort the list from high to low. At this point, you have a ranked list of potential causes of your problem. Next, reduce this list to only the <u>top five</u> causes. Once you identify the top five, update your Cause and Effect Diagram, as illustrated in Figure 9.8, to reflect this knowledge.

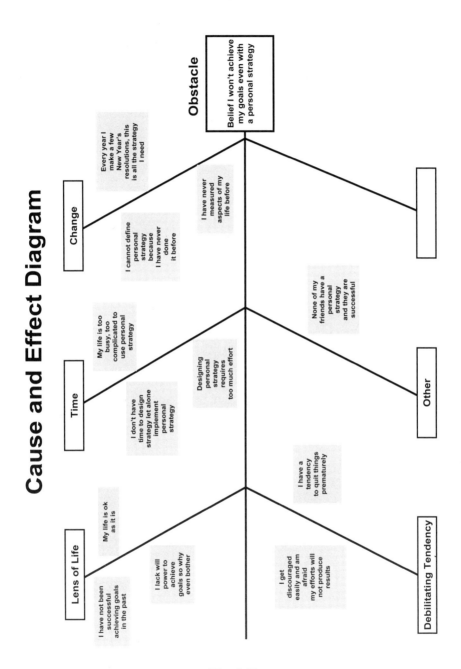

Fig. 9.7

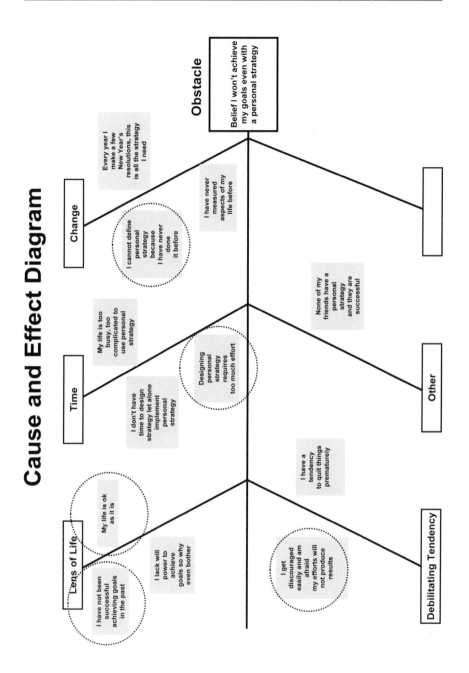

Fig. 9.8

We focus on the top five causes, as these are likely responsible for greater than 80% of the problem (i.e., Pareto Principle). When complete, this ranking and reducing exercise should produce a list similar to that shown in Figure 9.9. Having identified the likely causes to your problem, the next step is to decompose each likely cause to its root cause.

Phase III – Determine Root Cause

Knowing likely causes (to a problem) is good, but if this is as far as we go, it is likely that any intervention identified in Phase IV will not eliminate the problem. In other words, your interventions might be directionally correct, but imprecise, and imprecise solutions lead to the problem resurfacing. To prevent this situation from occurring, we dive deep to determine the root cause associated with each likely cause. To perform this task, we use another tool from the personal strategy toolbox: '5 Why' technique.

The '5 Why' technique is a simple problem-solving technique that pushes likely cause to root cause, quickly. The technique begins by stating the obstacle. Then, we state one of the likely causes identified during Phase II. Then, we ask, 'Why does this cause exist?' Very often, the answer to the first 'why' will prompt another 'why,' and the answer to the second 'why' will prompt another, and so on; hence, the name '5 Why'. Figure 9.10 illustrates the use of the '5 Why' technique as described below:

The Process of '5 Why'

1. State the obstacle
   - Ex. 'Belief I won't achieve my goals even with a personal strategy'
2. State a likely cause of the obstacle
   - Reference your top-five list of likely causes
   - Ex. 'I have not been successful achieving goals in the past'

Obstacle

Belief I won't achieve my goals even with a personal strategy

Top 5 List of <u>Likely</u> Causes

1. I cannot define personal strategy because I have never done it before

2. I have not been successful achieving goals in the past

3. I get discouraged easily and am afraid all my efforts will not produce results

4. Designing personal strategy requires too much effort

5. My life is ok as it is

Fig. 9.9

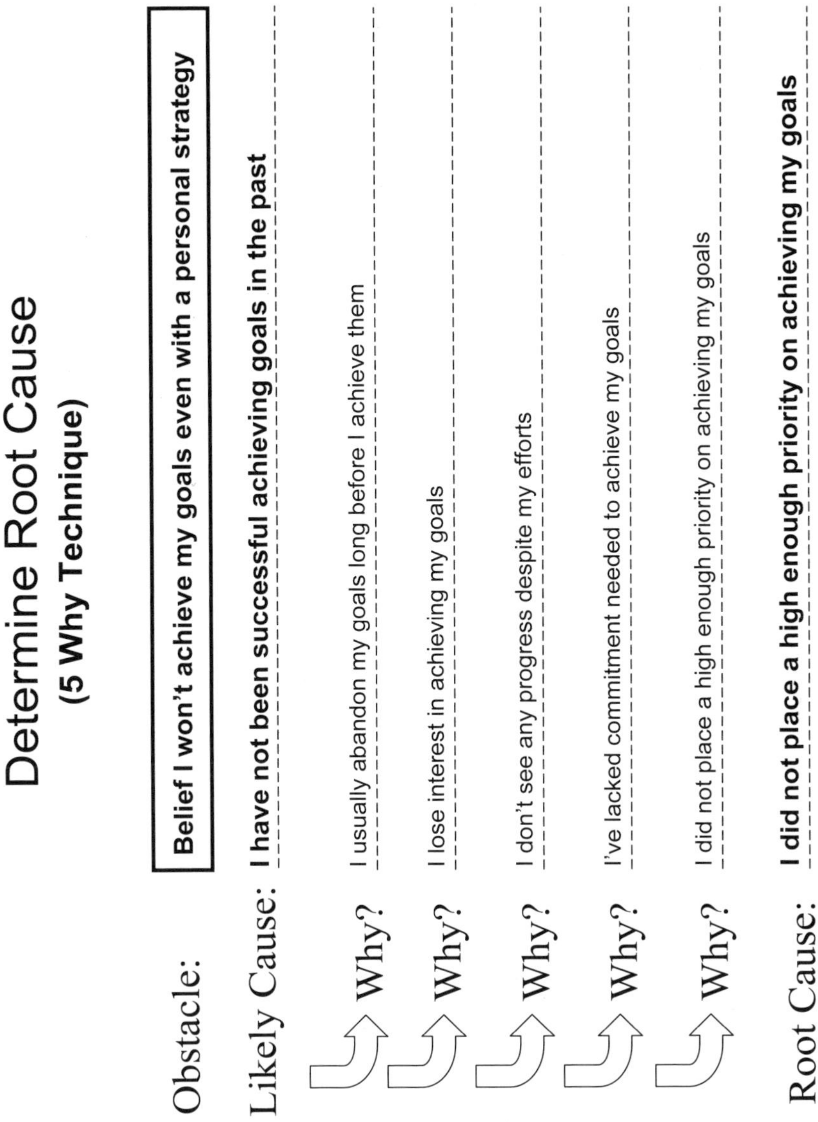

Determine Root Cause
(5 Why Technique)

Obstacle:

Likely Cause: **I have not been successful achieving goals in the past**

Why?   I usually abandon my goals long before I achieve them

Why?   I lose interest in achieving my goals

Why?   I don't see any progress despite my efforts

Why?   I've lacked commitment needed to achieve my goals

Why?   I did not place a high enough priority on achieving my goals

Root Cause: **I did not place a high enough priority on achieving my goals**

Fig. 9.10

Belief I won't achieve my goals even with a personal strategy

3. Ask Why
  - Ask, 'Why does the cause exist?'
      1. Ex. '**Why** have I not been successful achieving goals in the past?'
          - Answer: I usually abandon my goals long before I achieve them
  - With each successive answer, ask why again (up to 5 times)
      2. Ex. '**Why** do I abandon my goals?'

      3. Ex. '**Why** do I lose interest?'

      4. Ex. '**Why** don't I see progress?'

      5. Ex. '**Why** have I lacked commitment?'
  - Continue in this manner until you feel you've reached the root cause

    <u>Root Cause:</u> I did not place high enough priority on achieving my goals
  - There is nothing sacred about 'asking why' 5 times. You may reach the root cause after only two or three 'whys.' Sometimes, you may have to go beyond five 'whys' to determine the root cause.

4. State the root cause
  - A root cause is something that ***feels right*** and is ***within your control***; something that <u>you</u> can act on (e.g. assign higher priority to my goals)

Using the '5 Why' technique can help you identify root cause(s) of an obstacle. In the example above, the root cause of [I have not been successful achieving goals in the past] is that [I did not place a high enough priority on achieving my goals].

This root cause not only feels right, it is something on which I can act. Once you identify the root cause, you can address it by identifying interventions to eliminate or minimally reduce the effects the obstacle has on personal strategy.

Phase IV – Identify Interventions

With knowing root cause(s), the next step is to identify interventions. Knowing how to intervene partly depends on which stumbling block is causing the problem. For example, eliminating stumbling blocks of the mind might require: changing the lenses through which one views the world, adjusting one's attitude, or overcoming fear, etc. Stumbling blocks of the environment, however, might require: changing one's vocation, reevaluating one's priorities in life, or adapting to new economic realities. As each scenario is unique, so, too, are interventions unique. This is not cause for concern. To intervene, all that is required of you is to converse with soul, assess the situation, and use the process and tools described herein to design interventions that <u>you believe</u> address the root cause in the most effective and responsible way. To help identify interventions, we use another tool from the personal strategy toolbox: Assumption Busting.

Assumption Busting is a technique we use to overcome stumbling blocks of the mind. As such, Assumption Busting challenges what one sees and how one thinks. Earlier, we established that how we <u>act</u> is the result of how we <u>think,</u> which is the result of what we <u>see</u>. Therefore, to overcome stumbling blocks of the mind, we must begin by challenging what we see. Figure 9.11 illustrates the high-level process of Assumption Busting as described below.

The Process of Assumption Busting

1. State the obstacle
   - Identify what is distracting you from achieving your goals.

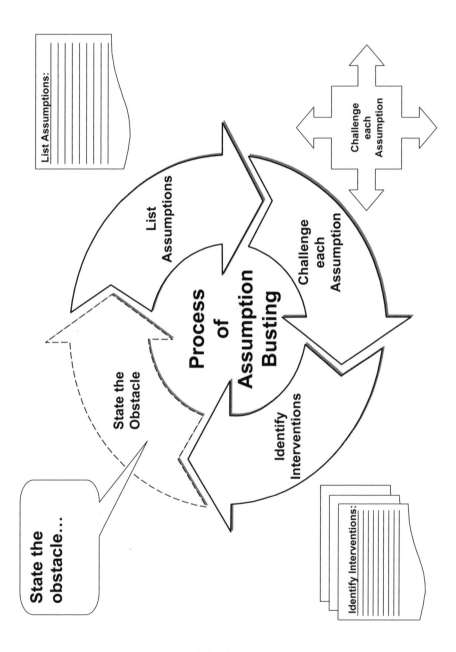

Fig. 9.11

2. List assumptions
   - Look at the obstacle before you. What are the assumptions you are making about it? What seems so obvious that you would not normally think about challenging it?
3. Challenge each assumption
   - Test each assumption. Pick it apart. Look at it from every angle. Ask under which conditions it would <u>not</u> be true.

   - You will start to make assumptions as you challenge some assumptions; simply add these to the list, and challenge them as well.
4. Identify interventions
   - Design interventions to change what you see and therefore how you think with regards to the obstacle before you.

Figure 9.12, demonstrates how to use Assumption Busting to dissolve a stumbling block of the mind.

Assume that the following mental obstacle is interfering with your personal strategy:

- I have not been successful achieving goals in the past

To overcome this obstacle, you need to challenge the <u>hidden</u> assumptions driving such thinking, such as:

- I am incapable of achieving my goals
- I cannot define a good strategy to achieve my goals
- My past is the only indicator of my future
- I cannot be successful in life

Each of these hidden assumptions severely diminishes one's mental capacity to achieve personal strategy; as such, it is necessary to 'bust' (i.e., replace) each debilitating assumption with an inspiring assumption. For example, we bust the

Assumption Busting Technique

Obstacle:

> **I have not been successful achieving goals in the past**

Assumption: I am incapable of achieving my goals

Busting: With a plan, I can achieve any goal

Assumption: I cannot define a good strategy to achieve my goals

Busting: With guidance, I can define a strategy to achieve my goals

---

Assumption: My past is the only indicator of my future

Busting: My past does not dictate my future; I dictate my future

---

Assumption: I cannot be successful in life

Busting: With a personal strategy, I can maximize the personal, professional, and financial potential that life offers

Fig. 9.12

debilitating assumption, 'I am incapable of achieving my goals' with an inspiring assumption, 'With a plan, I can achieve any goal'. Please note: <u>this is not a mental game to trick your mind</u>. Assumption Busting is a powerful technique because it makes visible the hidden assumptions that underlie our thinking. By making hidden assumptions visible, you can challenge such assumptions and replace them with more formidable and inspiring assumptions. As assumption busting may be unfamiliar to you, consider these examples:

Obstacle: **My life is too busy to develop a personal strategy**
Assumption: Developing personal strategy takes a long time
Busting: With guidance, I can develop precise personal strategy, quickly

Obstacle: **I'm too old to have a personal strategy for living**
Assumption: Pursuing goals is something only young people do
Busting: I still have dreams and much to accomplish in life

Obstacle: **I won't achieve my goals, even with a personal strategy**
Assumption: Personal strategy cannot drive goal achievement
Busting: With precise personal strategy, I can achieve any goal

Obstacle: **Collecting scorecard data requires too much effort**
Assumption: There is little value in measuring the life experience
Busting: Measuring aspects of my life will inform what is working with personal strategy and what I need to course correct to improve strategy to achieve my goals

Obstacle: **New Year's resolutions are all I need**
Assumption: The life experience does not need managing
Busting: Managing my life will ensure living a remarkable life

Obstacle: **I am already living a good life**
Assumption: Improving one's life is not possible
Busting: I can transcend 'good living' for 'remarkable living'

Assumption Busting is a powerful technique to identify meaningful, impactful interventions. To intervene means 'to involve oneself in a situation so as to alter or hinder an action or development'. Therefore, when brainstorming for interventions, our goal is to identify actions to alter (i.e., minimize) or hinder (i.e., eliminate) the root cause(s) of our problem. Without 'busting' debilitating assumptions prior to brainstorming for interventions, it is likely that your interventions would have little to no effect in eliminating your problem. The steps to brainstorm for interventions are the same as those when brainstorming for causes, only now, our focus is on how to eliminate or minimally reduce such causes from affecting personal strategy. For each root cause identified in Phase III, brainstorm for interventions (see Figure 9.13).

The question we ask self when brainstorming for interventions is, 'What must I do and/or change (seeing, thinking, acting) to eliminate the root cause of my problem?' Most, if not all, interventions represent changes in how one sees, thinks, or acts. By addressing root cause, you will identify interventions that are precise, substantive, and impactful. Once you identify interventions, the next step is to group interventions by category and eliminate duplicates. This step will reveal gaps in your thinking and help identify even more precise, substantive interventions (see Figure 9.14).

You will notice in Figure 9.14 that most of the intervention categories align with some component of personal strategy. This

Brainstorm for Interventions

Root Cause: I did not place a high enough priority on achieving my goals

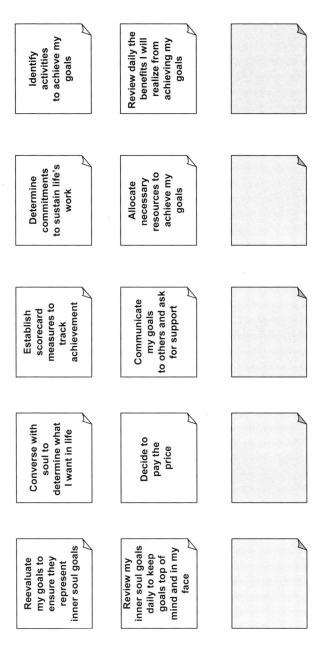

Reevaluate my goals to ensure they represent inner soul goals	Converse with soul to determine what I want in life	Establish scorecard measures to track achievement	Determine commitments to sustain life's work	Identify activities to achieve my goals
Review my inner soul goals daily to keep goals top of mind and in my face	Decide to pay the price	Communicate my goals to others and ask for support	Allocate necessary resources to achieve my goals	Review daily the benefits I will realize from achieving my goals

Fig. 9.13

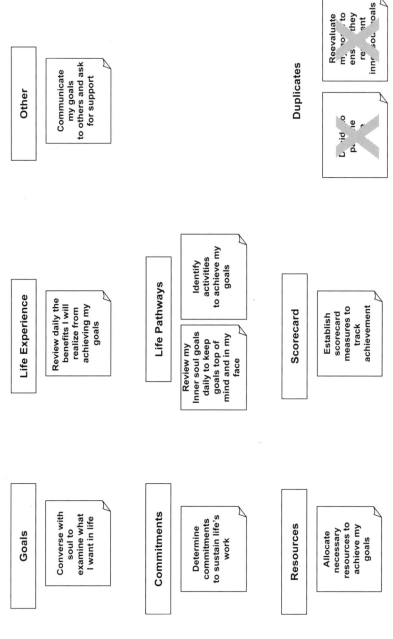

Fig. 9.14

is deliberate. As you encounter obstacles to personal strategy, and as you identify interventions to overcome such obstacles, some, if not all, interventions will require modifying some aspect of personal strategy. When finished, summarize your interventions in list form (see Figure 9.15).

Producing a list of precise, targeted interventions is the primary <u>output</u> of the process to overcome stumbling blocks of personal strategy. The primary <u>outcome</u> of the process is, of course, to eliminate our stumbling block. Now that you brainstormed for potential causes, determined root-cause, and designed interventions, all that remains is to intervene.

Phase V – Intervene

To intervene should not be difficult. At this point, you know what constrains you, but you also know the interventions that will set you free. You are in an empowered state; so just execute. You must intervene (on your behalf), as no one else will. You must learn, as I did, that *when implementing personal strategy, there is only one person looking out for you, and that is you.*

Throughout life, you will encounter an endless variety of stumbling blocks affecting personal strategy. Your challenge is to:

- Recognize a stumbling block when it exists
- Determine the root cause(s) of why the stumbling block exists
- Design interventions to eliminate or minimally reduce the effects each stumbling block has on personal strategy
- Intervene

By following the process as summarized in Figure 9.16, you will develop a capacity to overcome any stumbling block of personal strategy and achieve your goals.

Developing a capacity to overcome stumbling blocks is important, but this is tantamount to 'fighting fires' as opposed to

Obstacle/Root Cause

I did not place high enough priority on achieving my goals

List of Interventions

1. Converse with soul to examine what I want in life

2. Review daily the benefits I will realize from achieving my goals

3. Identify activities to achieve my goals

4. Determine commitments to sustain life's work

5. Allocate necessary resources to achieve my goals

6. Establish scorecard measures to track achievement

7. Review my inner soul goals daily to keep goals top-of-mind and in my face

8. Communicate my goals to others and ask for support

Fig. 9.15

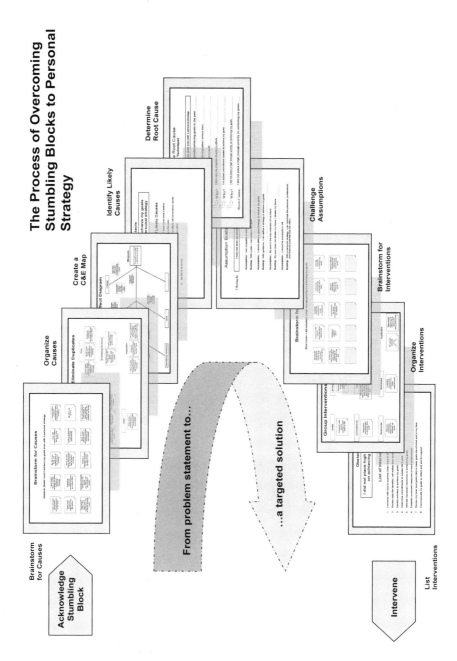

Fig. 9.16

'preventing fires'. For the record, our goal should not be to get better at overcoming stumbling blocks as they occur ('fighting fires'), but instead, should be to develop a capacity to prevent stumbling blocks from occurring in the first place ('preventing fires'). We discuss preventing stumbling blocks next.

Preventing Stumbling Blocks

To prevent means to keep from happening. This is precisely what we want to do; we want to prevent stumbling blocks of personal strategy from happening. There are three keys to doing this:

- Develop an optimistic mindset
- Observe self and environment
- Intervene quickly

Preventing stumbling blocks from occurring begins with adopting a mindset (and an attitude) that no obstacle is big enough or formidable enough to prevent me from achieving my goals *(e.g. I am the master of my destiny; I am the author of my life's plan, and I will achieve my inner soul goals.)* To maintain an optimistic mindset, I repeat the following items morning, noon, and night. Perhaps repeating these statements will work for you as well:

- I am determined to make my success happen.
- I am operating from soul, the highest form of me.
- Never doubt success. Deliberately focus my mind on something good coming up.
- Everyday represents movement. Just keep going.
- The best way to predict the future is to create it.
- I can do anything I set my mind to.
- I've got a vision. I am steadily building towards my vision.
- I have Only One Shot to seize opportunity, meet imperative.

The most successful people in any profession develop a mindset of optimism, success, and achievement. They develop a mental picture and then go to work materializing that picture in all its form; they <u>steadily build</u> to achieve their goals. This is what we do when we implement personal strategy; we steadily build to achieve our goals. Developing the right mindset is vital to prevent stumbling blocks from occurring. But, developing the right mindset, as we learned, first requires changing how one sees. Therefore, as you implement your personal strategy, remember that to prevent stumbling blocks of personal strategy from occurring it first requires changing how you look at the world. How does one do this? It is not as difficult as you might first think. To change <u>what you see</u> when you look at the world, perform these steps:

1. Decide which <u>views</u> are no longer compatible with who you are and want to be and replace them with new views
2. Brainstorm for events/situations that might/do trigger undesirable views and undesirable actions to appear
3. Isolate such events/situations in your mind and be on alert for their occurrence
4. Acknowledge an event/situation *when it occurs*
5. During the event/situation, forcibly replace an undesired view with a new view, new thinking, and new actions
6. Evaluate your response to the event/situation and how to improve

By following the steps above, changing one's mindset, while difficult, is possible. In addition to having the right mindset, to <u>prevent</u> stumbling blocks from occurring, it also requires keen observation. Sherlock Holmes said it best when he said, 'although almost all of us *see*, few of us *observe*'. Because most people are too consumed with 'living life' to spend time 'working on' their life, items of interest go unnoticed. In other words, very little 'observing' of self or environment takes place. However, to prevent stumbling blocks from occurring, it requires observing

self and one's environment. Specifically, it requires training self
to observe self, *to train oneself to notice what one sees*. Based
on previous discussion, you should have a good idea of what
to look for to determine if you are getting in the way of you.
Observation is a form of literacy, whereby one 'reads' information from self and environment. How literate are you when it
comes to observing self and environment? You might now be
asking, 'What should I observe?'

Items of interest include:

- Observing your thoughts
- Observing your assumptions
- Observing your actions
- Observing events occurring in your workplace
- Observing events occurring in society
- Observing events occurring in your family
- Observing events occurring in nature

By observing self and environment, you will obtain clues
to facilitate, enable prevention. We obtain clues by seeing our
thoughts, suspending our assumptions, observing our actions,
and sensing our environment. Such clues will enable you to intervene quickly, which is the third key to preventing stumbling
blocks of personal strategy from occurring.

The road to goal achievement is long. As such, there are
many opportunities to distract self, or be distracted, along the
way. In this chapter, we learned how each of us and our environment obstruct personal strategy. Using the process, tools, and
techniques discussed herein will help you overcome any obstacle
to achieve your goals. Now, having said this, recognizing, overcoming, and preventing stumbling blocks of personal strategy,
while necessary, is not sufficient to achieve your goals; to deliver
the life experience you desire. It also requires that you manage
your personal strategy. As such, we discuss this topic next.

Managing Personal Strategy

"That which we persist in doing becomes easier, not that the task itself has become easier, but that our ability to perform it has improved."

- Ralph Waldo Emerson

IN THE PREVIOUS CHAPTER, we learned how self and environment can distract personal strategy. That is, left unchecked, self and environment can debilitate personal strategy. As such, there is need to manage personal strategy to minimize disruption to ensure we achieve our goals. But what does it mean to manage personal strategy? Perhaps the best way to answer this question is to describe the essence of managing personal strategy.

The essence of managing personal strategy is:

- More effective personal strategy
- Better understanding of personal strategy
- Deeper relation with soul
- Increased ability to manage personal strategy
- Increased likelihood of achieving one's goals

In Part II, we learned how to build personal strategy using the PSM and PST Frameworks. We created such documents not only to achieve our inner soul goals, but to <u>enable</u> personal alignment. Now, when managing personal strategy, our goal is to <u>achieve</u> personal alignment (see Figure 10.1).

In Part III, we learned that alignment is everything; nothing has changed, alignment is still the end to which personal strategy enables. We also learned that we are always in a state of 'achieving' alignment, as life is dynamic. Consequently, to achieve alignment, to maintain alignment, requires managing the means to establish alignment. As such, in this chapter, we discuss the what, why, and how of managing personal strategy. We begin by discussing what it means to manage personal strategy.

To manage personal strategy requires three key actions:

- <u>**Document management**</u> – managing the *objects* of personal strategy
- <u>**Physical management**</u> – managing the *implementation* of personal strategy
- <u>**Content management**</u> – managing the *effectiveness* of personal strategy

First, we discuss how to manage the objects of personal strategy.

Managing the Objects of Personal Strategy

Managing personal strategy partly entails managing the objects of personal strategy. To refresh, let us review the objects of personal strategy that require 'managing' (see Figure 10.2):

- Personal Strategy Map
- Personal Strategic Themes
  - ePSM
  - Support Goals
  - Personal Scorecard
  - Action Plan

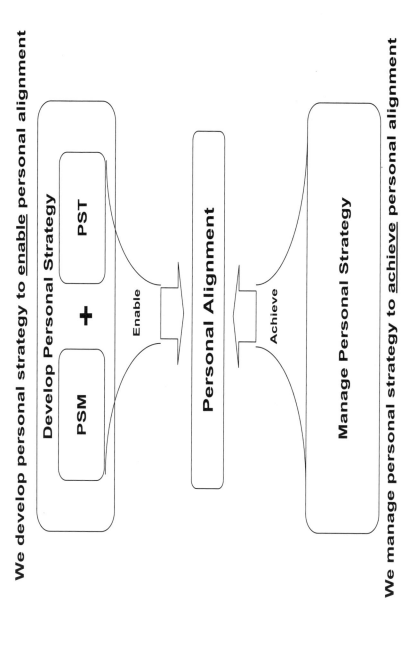

Fig. 10.1

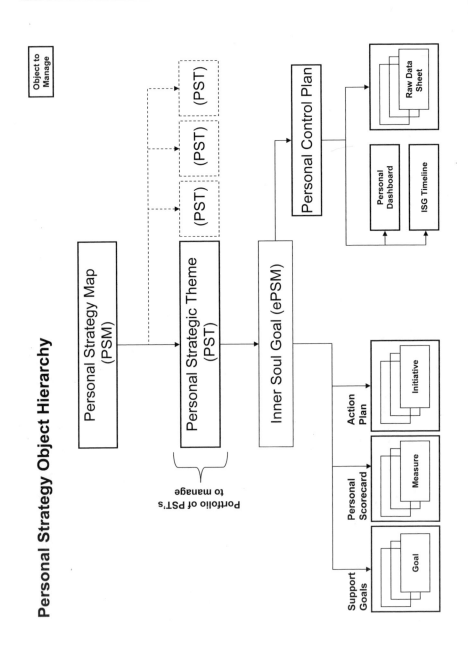

Fig. 10.2

- Personal Control Plan
- Personal Dashboard
- Raw Data Sheets
- ISG Timeline

As first suggested in Part II, personal strategy reads like a book where our PSM represents the table of contents and each PST represents a chapter. Thinking of your personal strategy this way, makes it easier to visualize, and therefore manage (i.e., organize), personal strategy. Because each object of personal strategy results in creating one or more documents, managing such documents can be a challenge. To reduce complexity, consider organizing your personal strategy using designated folders as illustrated in Figure 10.3.

Notice how I organized the documents of personal strategy. The PSM has its own folder and each subordinate PST gets its own folder. By organizing your personal strategy this way, you will maintain order while reducing complexity. Now, as having a personal strategy is a lifelong endeavor, so, too, is managing personal strategy a lifelong endeavor. As such, it is important to organize the documents that comprise personal strategy, as they will be with you your entire life. If you prefer to maintain your strategy in hardcopy form, as I do, consider organizing your documents as chapters in a book using a portfolio organizer. Managing the objects of personal strategy is important. Of greater importance, however, is managing the implementation of personal strategy.

Managing the Implementation of Personal Strategy

Managing the implementation of personal strategy is about managing one's ability to get things done. Tactically, it represents a movement from ideas to action. At first, we define personal strategy, which can take days, weeks, or months, and is 70% intellectual, 30% physical. We spend most of our time thinking about the components of personal strategy (inner soul goals,

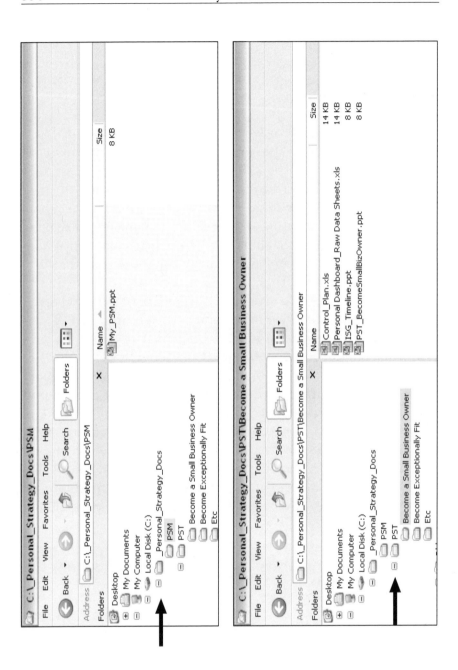

Fig. 10.3

life pathways, commitments, measures, action plan initiatives). The physical represents documenting personal strategy. Once we define personal strategy, however, the percentages invert as we spend 70% of our time doing (i.e., implementing) and only 30% of our time thinking. This reversal is necessary. For, without more doing, and less thinking, we cannot achieve our goals. In Chapter 6, we learned what it means to implement personal strategy. We repeat the message here, as managing personal strategy requires occasional tweaks; consequently, implementing personal strategy is always with you.

Having said this, managing the implementation of personal strategy is no guarantee that you will achieve your inner soul goals. It also depends, of course, on having an effective personal strategy.

Managing the Effectiveness of Personal Strategy

Managing the effectiveness of personal strategy means *to improve personal strategy; to increase precision, probability of achieving one's goals.* The question is, what do we manage? To improve personal strategy, increase its effectiveness, we need to manage the parts (i.e., content) of personal strategy, as a system; a unified whole (see Figure 10.4).

As with all systems (and personal strategy *is* a system), only when we bring parts together to operate as One can a system achieve its goals. Consequently, managing the effectiveness of personal strategy means to manage the interdependencies, cause and effect relations, between and within the parts of personal strategy. By focusing on the whole of personal strategy, you will improve the effectiveness of your personal strategy. More importantly, you will achieve your goals.

The preceding discussion provides us a good overview on what managing personal strategy means. However, before we get too deep, let us discuss *why* manage personal strategy.

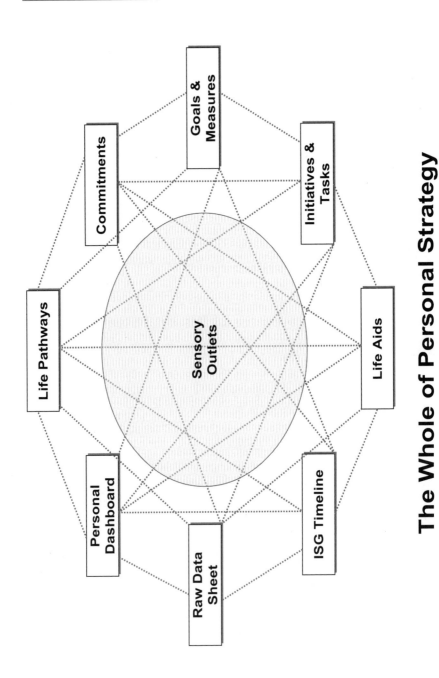

Fig. 10.4

Why Manage Personal Strategy?

Although you now know what it means to manage personal strategy, perhaps, you are still wondering *why* manage personal strategy. It is easy to believe that by defining goals and a personal strategy to achieve each goal success is eminent. Nothing could be further from the truth. There are many reasons why we need to manage personal strategy (see Table 10.1).

Table 10.1

Reason to Manage Personal Strategy	Benefit of Managing Personal Strategy
You will change	Your personal strategy always reflects what you what in life and from life throughout life
Your environment will change	Your personal strategy addresses/reflects emerging realities
To achieve goals quicker and with less effort	Accelerates personal alignment, personal happiness
Stumbling blocks exist	Overcome and prevent obstacles from impeding your goals
To maintain momentum	Keeps personal strategy in your face and top-of-mind
To develop a mindset and habit of measuring and managing one's life	Develop new habits, new behaviors, new capabilities that support personal strategy
Overcome weak, intermittent will	Ensures we implement personal strategy
Our quality of life is at stake	Maximize the personal, professional, and financial potential that life offers
To ensure personal alignment	To live meaningfully, fragrantly, happily
To improve personal strategy	More precise, effective personal strategy
Life is hard (and getting harder)	You direct your life, life does not direct you
The world is becoming ever more competitive	Establish a personal competitive advantage of the highest order
To be happy	Rediscover the joy of living

Just as instructive as knowing why manage personal strategy is knowing what will happen if we do not manage personal strategy. When we do not manage personal strategy, it affects personal strategy and our life in the following ways:

- Fewer insights on how to refine personal strategy
- No improvement of personal strategy
- Personal strategy becomes outdated
- Failure to achieve one's inner soul goals
- Lost enthusiasm for having a personal strategy
- Lost momentum in driving personal strategy
- Continued personal misalignment
- Diminished life experience

What this list indicates, is that managing personal strategy is necessary to achieve your goals and realize a higher quality life. However, to do this effectively, efficiently requires a process. As such, we discuss the process of managing personal strategy next.

The Process of Managing Personal Strategy

Up to this point, we have discussed what and why of managing personal strategy. Now, we get into how. The process of managing personal strategy has six phases (see Figure 10.5).

Phase I – Implement Personal Strategy/Course Corrections
Phase II – Obtain and Record Feedback
Phase III – Analyze and Interpret Results
Phase IV – Evaluate Effectiveness of Personal Strategy
Phase V – Identify Course Corrections
Phase VI – Update Objects of Personal Strategy

The process of managing personal strategy has several distinct characteristics:

- Represents a closed-loop process
- Highly iterative
- Demanding
- Seamless

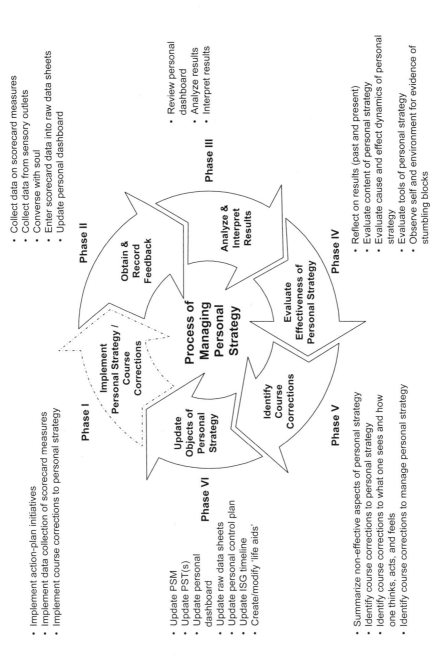

Fig. 10.5

'Closed-loop' is a term used to describe a system with an active feedback loop. Your personal strategy represents 'the system' and the process of managing personal strategy represents the feedback loop. A key activity when implementing personal strategy is to collect feedback as only when we do this do we know if our personal strategy is working (or not working) to achieve our goals. Feedback, in this regard, 'closes the loop'. Without feedback, without a closed-loop process, we lack data, insights to know what aspects of personal strategy to course correct to improve performance.

The process of managing personal strategy is also highly iterative. Whereas some (personal) processes cycle only a couple times a month (e.g. pay bills) or once a year (e.g. pay taxes), the process of managing personal strategy cycles several times a year. In fact, you may find that you are cycling through the six phases of the process <u>weekly</u>. This is expected. As many factors affect personal strategy and as you collect feedback from your scorecard measures and environment, it is often necessary to make frequent course corrections to ensure personal strategy is 'tuned' to drive goal achievement.

The process of managing personal strategy is demanding. That is, much effort is required of you to perform process work. For example, Phase I requires <u>you</u> to implement personal strategy/course corrections. Phase II requires <u>you</u> to collect and record data on scorecard measures. Phase III requires <u>you</u> to analyze and interpret scorecard results. Phase IV requires <u>you</u> to evaluate the effectiveness of personal strategy. Phase V requires <u>you</u> to identify course corrections to improve personal strategy. Finally, Phase VI requires <u>you</u> to update the objects of personal strategy.

Before you get too distraught over the rigor required to manage personal strategy, please know that the process of managing personal strategy is seamless. That is, each phase of the process segue's nicely into subsequent phases. For example, once we implement personal strategy (or course correct existing strategy), we segue seamlessly into Phase II, where we collect and record feedback from our environment and scorecard measures. Once we collect feedback, we segue seamlessly into Phase III where we analyze and interpret performance data, and so on. Over time, the phases of the process become transparent. As each phase is logically linked to the next, little thought or effort is required to segue from phase to phase; it just happens.

With this introduction, let us explore each phase of the process beginning with Phase I.

Phase I – Implement Personal Strategy/Course Corrections

Phase I is about implementing personal strategy, the first time, and for subsequent course corrections to existing strategy. Technically, we only implement personal strategy one time. Afterwards, all subsequent implementations represent course corrections to improve strategy. To implement personal strategy means to implement action plan initiatives in addition to initiating data collection on scorecard measures. To implement course corrections, on the other hand, means to implement:

- New/modified inner soul goals
- New/modified life pathways
- New/modified commitments
- New/modified initiatives
- New/modified data collection methods
- New/modified sensory outlets
- New/modified 'life aids'

Upon implementing personal strategy/course correcting existing strategy, we transition to Phase II of obtaining and recording feedback.

Phase II – Obtain and Record Feedback

Obtaining and recording feedback on our personal strategy is what facilitates, enables us to manage personal strategy. Specifically, we obtain and record feedback to generate insights into personal strategy, our environment, and soul.   The data sources we draw from to obtain such insights are:

- Scorecard measures
- Sensory outlets
- Conversing with soul

Such data sources tell us not only how effective our personal strategy is to achieve our goals, but also what parts of our personal strategy require tuning. For example, data from scorecard measures tell us if our commitments are driving the right behavior to achieve right results. Further, such data tells us if we are performing the 'right' life pathways to achieve both support goals and our inner soul goal. Lastly, scorecard measures tell us if our action plan initiatives/tasks are 'off the mark'. Scorecard measures provide the insights we need to improve personal strategy to achieve our goals. Having said this, obtaining feedback from scorecard measures is not sufficient to manage personal strategy effectively, as we also need feedback from sensory outlets.

Sensory outlets, you might recall, are the 'listening posts' of life that we use to collect data from within our environment: society, work, family, and nature. As our environment has great influence on our life and therefore our personal strategy, it is imperative that we monitor our environment to know how it's changing and how such changes will affect our life. As with scorecard measures, collecting feedback from our environment helps shape and refine personal strategy; helps us improve personal strategy. However, obtaining feedback from both scorecard measures and from our environment is still not sufficient to manage personal strategy effectively, as these data sources reflect only that which is external. To be sure that our personal strategy is directionally correct, we must also seek data from an internal source: soul.

The importance, relevance of conversing with soul, as it relates to managing personal strategy, should be clear. It is only from quiet conversation with soul that we access soul, to hear what it has to say. Obtaining such feedback ensures that our personal strategy always reflects what we want in life and from life throughout life.

Together, feedback from scorecard measures, sensory outlets, and soul help us manage personal strategy; together, such data sources help us adjust personal strategy to changes occurring within and without. To operate a personal strategy without feedback is just as ineffective as one trying to operate a sailboat without sails. Just as a sailboat needs sails to establish direction, drive performance, so, too, does personal strategy need feedback to establish direction, drive performance.

Now, some of the feedback we obtain can be applied immediately (e.g. feedback from our environment and from soul) to improve personal strategy. However, some feedback comes to us as raw data and, therefore, is not immediately accessible or useful. Only when we convert data into information (via charts and graphs) do we generate insights to improve personal strategy. The way we generate information, derive insight, is by:

- Entering scorecard data into raw data sheets
- Updating our personal dashboard to reflect progress

Monitoring progress is key to manage personal strategy effectively. To monitor means to observe, record, or detect. The tools we use to observe, record, and detect our progress are personal dashboard and ISG timeline. A personal dashboard contains graphs and charts that indicate performance over time. As such, it helps establish a performance baseline from which to advance, in addition to communicating the effectiveness of personal strategy. The ISG timeline, on the other hand, helps us interpret dashboard results relative to our inner soul goal. For example, your ISG timeline helps determine if you are on schedule, behind schedule, or ahead of schedule to achieve your goal. Think of recording feedback as the yang to the yin of obtaining feedback. To manage personal strategy requires both actions. Without obtaining feedback and recording results, we have neither the data nor the information we need to properly analyze and interpret such results.

Phase III – Analyze and Interpret Results

To manage personal strategy effectively requires analyzing and interpreting results. Why must we do this? We analyze and interpret results to improve results. That is, to improve our performance on the surface of life. Depending on how frequently you collect data will determine the frequency with which you analyze and interpret results.

The essence of this step is to determine, reveal the following:

- How we are doing; where we <u>are</u> relative to where we want to <u>be</u>
- If our personal strategy is working as intended
- If current/recent changes made to personal strategy are improving performance
- Where problems exist with personal strategy
- How personal strategy can help us achieve our goals
- How to detect early signs of trouble
- What solutions work

For example, one of my inner soul goals is 'be exceptionally fit'. When I implemented my personal strategy and began analyzing and interpreting results, I learned what foods to avoid and what threshold of carbohydrates I could eat to maintain (and lose) weight. I learned, for example, that bananas cause me weight gain and apples make me bloated. I learned that eating organic bread helps me lose weight while other types of bread cause me to gain weight. And I learned that drinking low-carb beer does not affect me but drinking wine does. Prior to analyzing and interpreting such data, I was unaware of such insights. Additionally, I learned that watching what I eat, limiting carb intake, was not enough to tip the needle of performance. I needed to exercise 4x/week and take a dietary supplement. Lastly, I learned that tracking certain factors on my personal scorecard had no impact on weight loss and therefore could drop the measure. Perhaps, my greatest learning, however, from analyzing and interpreting results was that I became aware of the hidden relationships, interdependencies between actions, measures, and results. I would not have acquired such insights without collecting, analyzing, and interpreting performance data. Performing these activities enabled me to operate from a source of intelligence in determining how to change my life to improve my life. This example highlights only tip-of-the-iceberg benefits one can realize from collecting, analyzing, and interpreting life data. As you implement your personal strategy and begin collecting and analyzing data, look for the hidden relationships, interdependencies between actions, measures, and results. Such insights represent the real benefit from measuring one's life. To the extent that you understand the hidden cause and effect dynamics that underlie your personal strategy, determines the effectiveness of your personal strategy.

Phase IV – Evaluate Effectiveness of Personal Strategy

Evaluating the effectiveness of personal strategy is *the* most important step when managing personal strategy. We know this to be true, as <u>not</u> managing the effectiveness of personal strategy results in:

- Flawed personal strategy
- Goals taking longer than expected to achieve
- Wasted time, money, and effort
- Lost interest in having a personal strategy
- Lost enthusiasm to drive personal strategy
- Goals dying on the vine

Earlier, we learned that to manage the effectiveness of personal strategy is to manage, evaluate the <u>content</u> of personal strategy. To do this, we descend within, converse with soul, to:

- Reflect on results (past and present)
- Evaluate content (commitments, life pathways, support goals) of personal strategy
- Evaluate cause and effect dynamics that underlie personal strategy
- Evaluate tools (life aids) of personal strategy
- Observe self and environment for evidence of stumbling blocks

We observe, reflect on, and evaluate such things to reveal things about our personal strategy. That is, we seek to understand the effective and non-effective aspects of our personal strategy.

Many factors may be responsible for you not achieving your goals, and one of those factors may be the content of personal strategy. If your personal strategy (i.e., PST) is not producing intended results, not driving your inner soul goal, it is likely that some or all of your personal strategy is amiss. Table 10.2 describes what aspects to consider, what questions to ask, and what to look for when evaluating the effectiveness of your personal strategy.

Of all the things we do when evaluating personal strategy, perhaps the most important is to evaluate the cause and effect dynamics that underlie and drive personal strategy. Cause and effect refers to how one action or event results, or triggers, another action or event. Each component of a PST is involved in one or more cause and effect relations. For example, commitments drive life's pathways. Life pathways drive our inner soul goal. And scorecard measures drive all three. What these examples indicate is that every part of your personal strategy affects and influences every other part (see Figure 10.6).

Table 10.2

Aspect of PST to Consider	Questions to Ask	What to Look For
Life Pathways	Am I performing the right activities to achieve my goal? Am I wasting energies performing the wrong activities? Is there a better way?	Missing and/or wrong activities
Commitments	Have I committed mentally to achieve my goal? Have I committed physically to achieve my goal? Have I committed necessary resources to achieve my goal? Are my commitments driving life's pathways?	Missing and/or wrong commitments
Support Goals	Are my support goals driving my inner soul goal? Are my support goals driving life's pathways? Are my support goals helping sustain commitment?	Missing and/or wrong support goals
Personal Scorecard	Are my scorecard measures driving both my support goals and inner soul goal? Am I measuring the wrong activities, wrong behaviors? Are my scorecard measures driving the wrong behavior? Are my target values aggressive enough? Do my scorecard measures adequately report progress with action plan initiatives?	Missing and/or wrong scorecard measures
Action Plan	Are my action plan initiatives and tasks driving my support goals and my inner soul goal? Do my action plan initiatives and tasks reflect life's pathways? Are my action plan initiatives and tasks inspiring commitment?	Missing and/or wrong tasks

Cause and Effect Dynamics Within a Personal Strategic Theme (PST)

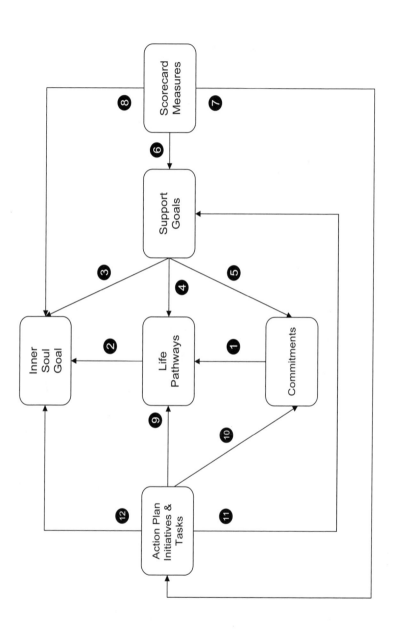

Fig. 10.6

1. Commitments drive life pathways
2. Life pathways drive our inner soul goal
3. Support goals drive our inner soul goal
4. Support goals drive life pathways
5. Support goals drive commitments
6. Scorecard measures drive support goals
7. Scorecard measures drive action plan initiatives and tasks
8. Scorecard measures drive our inner soul goal
9. Action plan initiatives and tasks drive life pathways
10. Action plan initiatives and tasks drive commitments
11. Action plan initiatives and tasks drive support goals
12. Action plan initiatives and tasks drive our inner soul goal

Figure 10.6 illustrates the web of cause and effect that underlie personal strategy. Knowing the interdependencies that underlie personal strategy is necessary to improve personal strategy. If your personal strategy is ineffective, it is likely that one or more cause and effect relations are defective. For example, you may discover that certain action plan initiatives do not drive life pathways in a meaningful way. Similarly, you may discover that certain scorecard measures drive the wrong behaviors. So informed, you can then resolve such problems by introducing new initiatives, new measures. By evaluating the hidden cause and effect relationships between the *parts* of personal strategy, you can improve the *whole* of personal strategy, thus enabling goal achievement.

Evaluating the effectiveness of one's personal strategy is vital to achieve personal strategy. Without assessing what is working/not working with personal strategy, it stops improving, stops evolving, and ultimately stops working. The good news is, as Voltaire confidently asserted, *"no problem can withstand the assault of sustained thinking."* What this tells us is that there is no challenge, no defect of personal strategy that you cannot resolve. As you create personal strategy, so, too, can you improve personal strategy.

Of course, the primary benefit one gains from evaluating personal strategy is that it provides insights on how to course correct personal strategy.

Phase V – Identify Course Corrections

To 'course correct' means to change direction, as in, changing the direction of one's personal strategy. There are many reasons to change, to course correct one's personal strategy. Examples include:

- Personal strategy is not achieving one's inner soul goal
- Need to adapt to changes occurring within (soul)
- Need to adapt to changes occurring without (environment)

Developing the capability to 'course correct' personal strategy represents a ***personal competitive advantage of the highest order.*** Few people have a well-defined personal strategy, and fewer still have developed a capability to improve personal strategy, that is, to rapidly respond to the present. It is important that each of us becomes athletic with change, whether change emanates from within or without. Becoming agile with change ensures that personal strategy is tuned to deliver what you want in life and from life throughout life.

You may have to 'course correct' personal strategy often when initially implementing personal strategy. Over time, as you learn how the parts of personal strategy work together as a system, fewer course corrections will be needed; until such time, be prepared to 'course correct' personal strategy often. Upon exiting Phase IV, you should have identified what aspects of personal strategy to improve. As such, the first step in Phase V, is to summarize non-effective aspects of personal strategy. As you perform this step, consider organizing 'corrections' along these axes:

- Corrections to components of your personal strategy
- Corrections to what you see and how you think, act, and feel
- Corrections on how to manage personal strategy

Organizing corrections this way will reveal gaps in your thinking. What this list indicates is that course corrections extend beyond simply correcting content of your personal strategy. Course corrections may require adjusting what you see and how you think, act, and feel about personal strategy. Corrections of this type address stumbling blocks of the mind. Finally, course corrections may require altering how you manage personal strategy. Table 10.3 highlights sample course corrections to personal strategy.

Table 10.3

Component of Personal Strategy to Course Correct	Sample Course Corrections
Personal Strategy Map	• Add new inner soul goal(s) • Modify existing inner soul goal(s) • Delete existing inner soul goal(s)
PST – ePSM	• Add new life pathway(s) • Modify existing life pathway(s) • Delete existing life pathway(s) • Add new commitment(s) • Modify existing commitment(s) • Delete existing commitment(s) • Add new support goal(s) • Modify existing support goal(s) • Delete existing support goal(s)
PST – Scorecard Measures	• Add new measure(s) • Modify existing measure(s) • Delete existing measure(s) • Change target value of measure(s)
PST – Action Plan	• Add new initiative(s) • Modify existing initiative(s) • Add new task(s)
Personal Control Plan	• Add new measure(s) • Modify existing measure(s) • Delete existing measure(s)
Personal Dashboard	• Add new graph(s) • Modify existing graph(s) • Delete existing graph(s)
ISG Timeline	• Modify goal timeline • Modify inner soul goal
Life Aids	• Add new life aid(s) • Modify existing life aid(s) • Drop existing life aid(s)

As you identify course corrections to personal strategy, you may find yourself asking these questions:

- 'How do I know if I am correcting the right things?'
- 'How will I know if my corrections are working?'

Let us address each question in turn. If you thoroughly evaluated personal strategy in Phase IV, you should have identified potential problem areas based on instinct alone. It is my experience that 'the gut' rarely misinforms self. Assessing and reflecting on your personal strategy will likely confirm what you already know. Further, you will know course corrections are working, as your personal dashboard will show improvement, your attitude will improve, and your enthusiasm will restore.

Before implementing course corrections, there is one final step to perform – update objects of personal strategy.

Phase VI – Update Objects of Personal Strategy

The last phase of managing personal strategy is to update objects of personal strategy. Why must we do this? It is important that your personal strategy <u>always</u> reflects what you want in life and from life, as your personal strategy is your roadmap to improve your life.

The type of course corrections will determine which objects require updating. For example, if you have new or changed inner soul goals, it will require updating your PSM and updating/creating PST's. More than likely, changes to personal strategy will be to one or more PST's, your Personal Control Plan, Personal Dashboard, Raw Data Sheets, and your ISG timeline. Updating the objects of personal strategy also includes updating and/or creating 'life aids'. As your personal strategy should always reflect what you want in life and from life, this phase should always precede implementing course corrections.

Managing personal strategy is vital to achieve personal strategy. Just as poor management of corporate strategy yields poor corporate performance, so, too, does poor management of personal strategy yield poor life performance. To ensure achieving your goals, we discuss the keys to managing personal strategy next.

Keys to Managing Personal Strategy

Before discussing the keys to managing personal strategy, let us review what we have learned. We have learned:

- The essence of managing personal strategy
- What it means to manage personal strategy
- What managing the objects of personal strategy means
- What managing the effectiveness of personal strategy means
- Why we need to manage personal strategy
- The benefits of managing personal strategy
- How to manage personal strategy (i.e., the 'process')

With all this learning, you now possess knowledge to effectively manage personal strategy and achieve your goals. To ensure success, let us now summarize the keys to managing personal strategy. The keys to manage personal strategy can be grouped in the following categories:

- Key Prerequisites
- Key Tools
- Key Enablers

A prerequisite is something that is required in advance. To manage personal strategy effectively, the following prerequisites must exist:

- Understand the parts of personal strategy and how they work together as a system to achieve one's goals
- Understand the essence of managing personal strategy
- Willingness to pay-the-price for success

A key prerequisite to manage personal strategy effectively is to understand the parts of personal strategy and how they work together as a system to achieve your goals. The reason PST's are effective in helping people achieve their goals is because of the underlying cause and effect dynamics between the parts of personal strategy. Therefore, knowing what cause and effect means and how it relates to personal strategy is key to manage personal strategy effectively. Another prerequisite is to understand the essence of managing personal strategy.

We started this chapter learning what the essence of managing personal strategy is. Knowing the essence of managing personal strategy ensures course corrections to personal strategy are directionally correct, that is, reflect essence. Having said this, understanding the essence of a task is meaningless if one is not prepared to pay-the-price to perform the task. Consequently, paying the price is also a prerequisite to manage personal strategy effectively.

Not all people who will read this book will achieve their inner soul goals. Only the most dedicated, persistent, and determined individuals will reach the Promised Land. Why is this so? It is because few people will pay-the-price for success. Most people see only the prize (of success) and not the price. For example, when we see the successful actor, musician, athlete, business owner, executive, or author all we see is the prize (big home, fancy car, and fat wallet). However, most successful people will tell you that they paid the price for success. Donald Trump paid the price. Tiger Woods paid the price. Eminem paid the price. Harrison Ford paid the price. Albert Einstein paid the price. What we do not see, or to be more precise, what we fail to acknowledge is that *success has a price and all must pay*. How instructive and inspiring it is to know back-story. That is, to know that the successful actor, for example, lived in near poverty for years while perfecting his craft, or that a successful business owner filled orders out of a dingy basement until success arrived, or that a famous author sold books from the trunk of a car before hitting it big. Short of winning the lotto or being born into money, success demands a serious investment of time and effort. The moral: success has a price, and unless you are willing to PAY-THE-PRICE, your dream to live a remarkable life is just that: a dream. A question I ask myself and others when personal strategy fails to deliver intended results is:

'Have you paid the price OR are you paying the price?'

When managing personal strategy, people fall into one camp or the other. Either you have *paid-the-price* through time and effort to manage personal strategy effectively, or you are *paying-the-price* through lack of effort and personal strategy is faltering. To manage personal strategy effectively, requires serious investment of time and effort. This should come as no surprise, as I have stated several times that defining, implementing, and managing personal strategy is hard work. Know this: to pay-the-price (by actively managing personal strategy) is to achieve your goals. If, however, you decide not to pay-the-price, your personal strategy does not stand a chance and neither do your goals.

Another key to manage personal strategy effectively is to utilize the tools from the personal strategy toolbox.

In the course of defining, implementing, and managing personal strategy, we use several tools from the personal strategy toolbox:

- Personal Strategy Map
- Personal Strategic Theme
- Personal Control Plan
- Personal Dashboard
- Raw Data Sheet
- ISG Timeline
- Problem Solving Tools
  - Cause and Effect Diagram
  - Brainstorming
  - Affinity Analysis
  - 5 Why
  - Assumption Busting
- Life Aids

As you implement and refine your personal strategy, it is important you use such tools continually. Continued use of the frameworks and tools described herein will not only provide structure and organization to personal strategy, but will also deepen your understanding of how to use (and augment) such tools over time.

In addition to having the right tools to manage personal strategy effectively, it also requires leveraging certain key enablers:

- Conversing with soul
- Positive thinking
- Being resourceful
- Getting angry, passionate, fanatical
- Personal creativity

Managing personal strategy demands that you converse with soul. In Part II, we discussed the need to establish morning and evening routines to review personal strategy. By allocating 'quiet time' to review each day, you can 'tune' personal strategy to achieve your goals. We also discussed the need to establish monthly and annual conversations with soul. We use these latter conversations to reflect on the weeks and months of effort spent implementing personal strategy. It is with these conversations that we 'stop our life', to ask hard questions of self and listen for the answer. As I've said before, without engaging soul, personal strategy ceases to be effective, ceases to exist; and when personal strategy ceases to exist, so, too, do your inner soul goals.

Another key enabler to manage personal strategy effectively is positive thinking. This revelation is hardly shocking, but is worth mentioning. Nearly twenty years ago, I came across a phrase that affected my life profoundly. The phrase:

'Your <u>attitude</u> and not your <u>aptitude</u>, determines your <u>altitude</u>'

There will be days, perhaps weeks, when you think that having a personal strategy offers little. There will be times when collecting scorecard data will seem more a chore than something to value. And there will be times when you think that managing personal strategy requires too much effort. How do I know this? It is because I have felt these feelings, and I know you will too. However, these feelings emerged only because I let them emerge. And what do we call situations when we let negative thoughts affect our attitude? You guessed it: 'stinking thinking'. Therefore, dismiss such thoughts, quickly, as they are debilitating. Instead, adopt a mindset and an attitude that:

- A better life awaits me
- A sense of urgency exists
- Personal alignment is everything
- Personal happiness is the goal
- I have Only One Shot at life

Thinking positive thoughts, however, is just the beginning to manage personal strategy effectively. It also requires being resourceful.

To manage personal strategy effectively you must become your own best resource. Know this: achieving your inner soul goals is your imperative and yours alone. No one else is, nor should be, responsible for you achieving your goals. Your goals are your own as the life experience is your own. As such, the responsibility for achievement, for living a fragrant, meaningful, and colorful life rests squarely with you. This imperative is captured in the following phrase:

'If it is to be, it is up to me'

To meet this responsibility, to rise to the challenge, requires anger, passion, and fanaticism. I am angry that I did not pursue my inner soul goals years ago. You should be too. I am passionate about not just living a 'good' life but living a remarkable, fragrant life. You should be too. I am fanatical about achieving my goals. You should be too. Anger, passion, and fanaticism <u>fuel</u> personal strategy. With them, we achieve our goals. Without them, we do not. As anger, passion, and fanaticism are products of your own creation, you hold the key to leverage these enablers.

Lastly, to manage personal strategy effectively requires personal creativity. Creativity to:

- Innovate one's personal strategy
- Enhance the frameworks and tools presented herein
- Develop new tools, approaches, methods to achieve your goals

By following the process of managing personal strategy as outlined in this chapter, and by leveraging the tools and enablers just described, your ability to manage personal strategy rises dramatically. Before presenting summary thought, we discuss how to improve your ability to improve.

Improving Your Ability to Improve

By actively managing personal strategy, you will achieve your goals. This is undeniable. Having said this, some people achieve faster than others. To accelerate achievement, we discuss how to improve your ability to improve personal strategy.

So what does improving one's ability to improve mean? It means developing, refining key skills that, if mastered, provide one a significant competitive advantage to improve personal strategy quickly to achieve one's goals. We improve our ability to improve by developing, refining these skills:

- Observation
- Deduction
- Intuition
- Documentation
- Preparation
- Collaboration

- Dedication
- Explanation

Observation is key to improving personal strategy. It is from observing self and environment that we obtain the raw material we need to course correct personal strategy to improve strategy. Most things in life are not invisible, they are simply unnoticed. However, to manage personal strategy effectively, happenings in your life and environment must not go unnoticed. No longer can you use the excuse that you don't know what to look for; no longer are you illiterate to the stumbling blocks or the challenges of managing personal strategy. Based on prior discussion, you do know what to look for, which enables you to see, think, act, and feel in ways that build up personal strategy rather than tear it down (see Figure 10.7).

To improve your ability to observe self and one's environment requires:

- Conversing with soul
- Training self to notice what one sees
- Developing capability of seeing self outside of self
- Developing awareness of one's environment
- Improving sensitivity to look for the 'right' things
- Developing meaningful sensory outlets
- Reminding self what one is looking for

By developing your observation skills, you will improve your ability to improve. Another skill to develop is deduction.

Deduction is the process of drawing a conclusion, of listing alternative explanations and eliminating all but the 'vital few'. This process should ring familiar, as deducing is about determining cause and effect, which we learned how to do in Chapter 9 to overcome stumbling blocks of personal strategy and in this chapter to evaluate the effectiveness of personal strategy. By improving our ability to deduce cause and effect, the faster we can course correct. And, the more proficient we become at course correcting personal strategy, the more likely we are to achieve

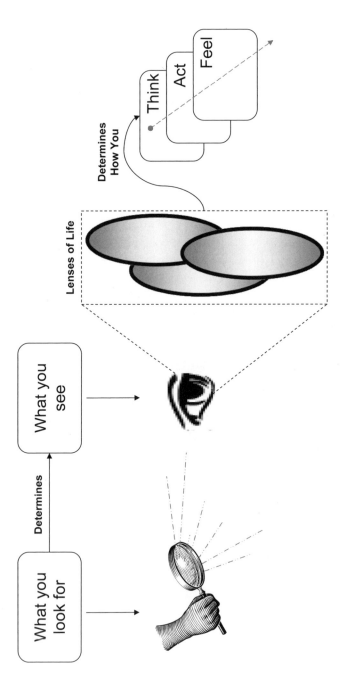

Fig. 10.7

personal strategy. Another skill, which if developed, could improve your ability to improve is, intuition.

Intuition is the act of knowing or sensing something. Intuition lies between observation and deduction. Earlier, I used the phrase 'trust your gut' to reflect situations when you instinctively know what requires course correcting with personal strategy. Trusting one's gut is a matter of intuition rather than scientific method. By following your intuition, by <u>trusting</u> your own wisdom awareness, you will improve your ability to improve. *Together, observation, intuition, and deduction provide the basis to improve personal strategy quickly to achieve your goals.* Documentation is yet another skill, which if developed, could improve your ability to improve.

It is important to keep accurate record of personal strategy. Earlier, we learned how to organize personal strategy. Staying organized gifts us more time to implement personal strategy than manage personal strategy. In addition, good documentation helps reduce complexity, which is key to achieve personal strategy. Along with documenting personal strategy well, we must prepare well when implementing personal strategy.

Of all the learnings you take from this book, I hope that one of them is that preparation, (as in prepare to define, implement, and manage personal strategy), is vital to achieve your goals. It has been said, "Chance favors the prepared mind". I could adapt this to say, "<u>Life</u> favors the prepared mind," as life is chance, played out daily. Now, how you prepare for the chances of life is up to you. The contrasts, however, are stark: for the prepared – *a fragrant life*, for the unprepared – *a life diminished*. With preparation, whether to review personal strategy, course correct personal strategy, or converse with soul, you will improve your ability to improve.

Developing the habit of collaborating with others is another important skill when defining, implementing, and managing personal strategy. Whether family member or friend, collaborating with others helps improve our ability to improve.

Specifically, collaborators:

- Provide feedback on personal strategy
- Push our thinking
- Identify gaps in our thinking
- Motivate us to keep going
- Support us; to stay with the program

By collaborating with others, the probability of achieving your goals rises dramatically. Collaboration also means collaborating with self. The better you become at conversing with soul, penetrating your inner chamber, the greater the probability you will achieve and maintain personal alignment. Improving collaboration with self and others will improve your ability to improve as will dedicating yourself to achieving personal strategy.

Dedicating oneself to one's personal strategy is essential to achieve personal strategy. But what does it mean to dedicate oneself to personal strategy? It means:

- Believing in the need for and purpose of personal strategy
- Believing that a personal strategy will help you achieve your goals
- Utilizing the frameworks, tools, and instruction herein to define, implement, and manage personal strategy
- Meeting imperative, seizing opportunity
- Paying the price
- Actively managing one's personal strategy

To live by a personal strategy should never result in internal struggle. Defining, implementing, and managing personal strategy is its own reward. We live to achieve personal strategy, to achieve our inner soul goals; our glory, profound pride, comes from sequence of goal defined, stumbling blocks overcome, goal achieved. To dedicate means to devote wholly and earnestly to some purpose. We dedicate ourselves to something because we want to not because we have to. Maintaining your dedication to personal strategy will improve your ability to improve. The last skill, which if developed will improve your ability to improve, is explanation.

Managing personal strategy is about self-discovery, self-explanation; about *getting the story of you (and your personal strategy) right*. When we define personal strategy, we use the PSM and PST's to explain to self (and others) what we want in life and from life. As you communicate personal strategy to self (and others), you clarify personal strategy; you begin to understand personal strategy; of how component parts work together to achieve a goal. Improving explanation skills, like all skills discussed, will also improve your ability to improve.

To advance, improve defines our species, as we always strive to do things better, to improve upon the latest process, the latest technique, the latest technology. The eight skills just described, if mastered, will improve personal strategy, if not your life. But developing certain skills is not the only tactic we can use to improve personal strategy. We can also improve by reading topics related to personal strategy (see Table 10.4).

Table 10.4

Reading Topic	Relevance to Personal Strategy
Systems Thinking	Systems thinking underlies both personal strategy and personal alignment
Performance Management	Performance management encompasses the tools: Personal Scorecard, Personal Dashboard, and Scorecard Measures
Scientific Method	Scientific method reflects underlying essence of managing personal strategy
Total Quality Management (TQM)	The problem solving tools of TQM help eliminate the stumbling blocks of personal strategy; help us find root cause
Strategy Maps/Balanced Scorecard	Personal Strategy Maps and Personal Strategic Themes were adapted from Strategy Maps and The Balanced Scorecard

The methods, tools, and techniques described in this book have roots, foundation in the topics shown above. Therefore, if you are interested in theory behind approach, I recommend reading the leading books within each of the topical categories. In addition to outside readings improving your ability to improve, modeling others (in terms of what, why, and how) is also a recommended technique. By learning what works for others, we can modify personal strategy to reflect clearer sight, better thinking, and more effective action. There is nothing shameful about modeling the vision, thinking, and actions of others. The fact is, we can accelerate our progress by:

- Modeling what they do (life pathway's)
- Modeling their commitments (mental, physical, resource)
- Modeling how they keep score (measures)
- Modeling their initiatives and tasks

Therefore, if you want to be a successful business owner, model the activities, commitments, measures, initiatives, and tasks of a successful entrepreneur. If you want to be a successful teacher, model a top educator. If you want to be a star athlete, model a world-class athlete, etc. Keep in mind that as you seek a life mentor you are not limited to 'the living'. It is possible to model those who have departed. Do research, become resourceful, learn all you can. Modeling others will improve your ability to improve.

By actively managing personal strategy, you will improve personal strategy. This is certain. And, as we learned, you can accelerate achievement by developing key skills, reading related works, and modeling others.

Managing Personal Strategy: In Summary

Managing personal strategy is not an exact science. As each person is unique, so, too, is managing personal strategy unique.

What we learned in this chapter is that managing personal strategy is as much about adopting the right mindset as it is about performing right action. Moreover, managing personal strategy is a necessary follow-on to implementing personal strategy. To conclude our learnings, Table 10.5 highlights several leading indicators to know if you are doing a good job managing personal strategy:

Table 10.5

You are managing personal strategy well if...	You are managing personal strategy poorly if...
• You are collecting, recording, analyzing, and interpreting scorecard data • You are regularly conversing with soul (daily, weekly, monthly, annually) • You deepen your expertise of the tools within the personal strategy toolbox • You allocate time to evaluate the effectiveness of personal strategy • Your 'course corrections' advance personal strategy • You update your personal strategy as you change and your environment changes • You implement course corrections quickly	• You do not collect scorecard data or go long periods of time without collecting scorecard data • You rarely converse with soul • You do not use the tools within the personal strategy toolbox • You do not evaluate the effectiveness of personal strategy • Your 'course corrections' hinder personal strategy • Your personal strategy is outdated; does not reflect what you want in life and from life • You implement course corrections slowly, if at all

Managing personal strategy, like living by a personal strategy, is a choice. You can <u>only benefit</u> from managing personal strategy. Hopefully, this chapter provided you enough of the what, why, and how of managing personal strategy to accept this wisdom.

In Part IV of this book, we learned how to adapt and respond to change. Now so armed, we segue to Part V, where we learn how to set a course for personal excellence.

PART V

Setting a Course for Personal Excellence

New Ways to See, Think, Act, and Feel

"Without freedom from the past, there is no freedom at all, because the mind is never new, fresh, innocent."

- Krishnamurti

YOU HAVE REACHED THE POINT in our journey where you should be seeing, thinking, acting, and feeling differently about your life experience. You are not captive to past views, past thinking, past actions, and past feelings. You have set a new course for personal excellence by defining, implementing, and managing a personal strategy for living. As you implement your new life plan, it is important to keep that which is new, fresh, innocent top-of-mind. To ensure that this occurs, we review in this chapter new ways to see, think, act, and feel, and as what we see influences all that follows, we begin by discussing new ways to see.

New Ways to See

Changing what one sees when viewing self and world can be difficult given the years of conditioning and reinforcement of beliefs, values, and habits that occur from simply living life. Regardless of how thick your lenses of life are, however, views can change. For example, prior to reading this book you may not have viewed the life experience as an opportunity to seize, with imperative to meet. I will assume that since you have read this far, your views have changed to reflect the fact that we do have Only One Shot at life and, therefore, should seize opportunity, should meet imperative. However, as we learned in Chapter 3, to do this requires establishing purpose, direction for one's life. Consequently, in Chapter 6, in an effort to drive new seeing, we defined personal mission, personal vision, which spawned new inner soul goals, thus making new vision explicit. Now, although these actions helped you see in new ways, to maintain new, to realize vision, requires reorienting your lenses of life.

Lenses of life, you might recall, largely determine what we see when we look at the world. From the moment we become aware to our last days on earth, we view, interpret, and evaluate life through our lenses of life. Although this innate behavior does not change when implementing personal strategy, it is likely that you will change *how* you view, interpret, and evaluate events when you look at the world. This is as it should be. The mental models that defined your past are not those that now drive your future. If you are having difficulty breaking free from past views, consider life through a toddlers' eyes (see Table 11.1).

Table 11.1

Seeing with Toddlers' Eyes	Seeing with Tired Eyes
• See opportunity	• See failure
• See possibility	• See obstacles
• See wonder of life	• See repetitiousness of life
• See grandness of life	• See blandness of life

When viewing life through a toddler's eyes, anything is possible. Toddlers' see only opportunity, never failure. They see only possibility, never obstacles. Moreover, they see life as wondrous and grand, not repetitious and bland. This is how we must be; see life. We must reorient our lenses of life to reflect emerging self (seeing with toddlers' eyes) not current self (seeing with tired eyes). Only by seeing life through toddlers' eyes can we 'go the other way', lest we perpetuate 'more of the same'. Seeing in new ways also means seeing the price (of success), not only the prize.

In the last chapter, we discussed how easy it is to see only the prize and not the price of success. It is easy to say, upon seeing someone drive a luxury sports car, how great it would be to drive such a car, not knowing that it took the driver **twenty years of hard labor** to afford such a prize. Likewise, it is easy to say, upon driving through a neighborhood of multi-million dollar homes, how great it would be to live in such a neighborhood, not knowing that it took most people in the community a **lifetime of employment** to make such purchase. The moral is this: to achieve anything in life requires paying the price. There are no shortcuts. Achieving your inner soul goals will take time, and if your goals are of a substantial nature, it may take years to achieve one goal, let alone all your goals. It is ok to focus on the prizes of life, but <u>you must focus equally</u> on the price to achieve the prize. If you acknowledge only the prize and not the price, you will fail to achieve your goals. Why is this so? Because achieving goals requires patience and time, two investments that someone focused only on prize **will not** fund. Because success takes time, one who is only focused on the rewards of life will quickly grow impatient and abandon personal strategy and, therefore, one's goals. Fortunately, life does not have to play out this way. In other words, you have a choice.

Success rarely happens overnight. Consider Einstein. It took him ten years of concentrated study to perfect his equations on general relativity. Did success happen overnight for Einstein? No. Consider Tiger Woods. He spent twenty years perfecting his skills to win big on the PGA Tour. Did success happen overnight for Tiger? No. Consider Sam Walton, the founder of Wal-Mart. He spent several years operating a small convenience store before expanding his operations and creating an empire. Did success happen overnight for Sam? No. Consider Harrison Ford, the famous actor. Harrison did not become famous until nearly age forty; toiling for twenty years to make a name for himself in Hollywood. Did success happen overnight for Harrison? No. Finally, consider JW Marriott, the founder of Marriott Hotels. JW spent several years running an A&W fast food franchise before getting into the hotel business. Did success happen overnight for JW? No. Name any successful businessperson, athlete, or scientist throughout history and there is likely a back-story of struggle, perspiration, and years of toiling behind their success. You should take comfort in this. I do. It tells me that I can be just as successful and can acquire the same prizes in life as others by following the same model – that is, *by paying the price.* Let the prizes in life inspire you to pay the price in life. By seeing the price and the prize, you will, in time, enjoy all that life has to offer. Now, in addition to seeing the price and prize, to achieve personal excellence also requires seeing the need to design and manage the life experience.

The majority of people traverse life without design, that is, without a personal strategy and with no design for one's life comes no desire to manage one's life. Indeed, it is because most people do not see life as something to design, to manage that so many live in quiet desperation. Sadly, life does not come with an instruction manual. Mother does not present 'The Guide to Fragrant Living' upon exiting womb. The good news is, we can design an instruction manual for life; it's called your personal strategy and you are the author. And with personal strategy comes the ability to manage one's life; no longer does life direct you, you direct life.

Collectively, when you <u>see</u> opportunity and imperative, when you <u>see</u> life through toddlers' eyes, when you <u>see</u> price and prize, and when you <u>see</u> life as something to design and manage, you will be seeing in ways to maximize the personal, professional, and financial potential that life offers. Moreover, by seeing in new ways, you will begin to think in new ways.

New Ways to Think

Seeing in new ways gives rise to thinking in new ways. This is the real benefit of changing what we see, as it changes how we think. For example, by seeing the imperative that exists from having Only One Shot at life, you will begin to change your thinking to reflect this orientation. This change will be most apparent with how you think about your life's work. Suddenly, you may find, for example, that your current vocation is misaligned with mission and vision; does not reflect true passion. Subsequently, you may find yourself pursuing a new role within your company or pursuing an entirely new career. This is what you should be doing. This is how you should be thinking. Once you define purpose in life, many things will change, career being just one of them. Another important change in thinking occurs when we begin to see the value of having a life plan.

It is easy to traverse life without a plan. In fact, most people operate this way. A common saying in the financial services industry is, "people do not plan to fail, they fail to plan". Now, while this saying refers to one's ability to manage one's retirement effectively, it also applies to the life experience. That is, if you do not have an explicit plan for living, then, by default, you have no plan, and not having a plan for something as important as your life experience will result in the following personal pathologies:

- Working in a profession/role long past the point of caring
- Missed opportunities
- Delayed and/or denied success in life
- Lost years
- Personal misalignment
- Deep unhappiness

When we see value in having a life plan, in designing the life experience, our thinking changes to reflect this orientation. This change in thinking becomes most apparent in how you govern your life – utilizing personal strategy versus settling for default.

Another new way to think is to establish and maintain personal alignment. For most people, personal alignment does not happen automatically, and when combined with a lack of knowledge about personal alignment or how to establish alignment, it results in great suffering. This is not your fate, however. You understand personal alignment, and more importantly, those areas of your life that are misaligned; *require alignment*. The moment that you stopped your life to ask questions of self, to hear what soul had to say, was the beginning of personal alignment. By implementing personal strategy, you will achieve alignment. In time, you will realize, as I did, that alignment is everything.

Yet another new way to think as you execute your new life's plan is to think long-term. So many of us think and act in the moment (i.e., short-term). Unfortunately, this type of thinking contradicts the notion of having a personal strategy. Why is this so? It is because our inner soul goals represent substantive, <u>long-term goals</u>. Earlier, I described how Einstein, Tiger Woods, and other world-class achievers took years to accomplish their goals. So, *how will it be different for you*? The short answer: it won't be different. Short of winning the lotto or developing the next killer product, you can expect achievement to take years. This is life. Thinking long-term sets proper expectation for self. This is important, especially if you suffer from the debilitating tendency of giving up when the going gets tough. Mitigate this tendency by setting realistic expectations with self. Train self to be patient and remember that every day represents movement.

Another new way to think is that it is okay to downsize lifestyle to achieve your goals. Downsizing lifestyle means making changes in your life to facilitate new beginnings. For example, you may have an inner soul goal that results in taking a lesser-paying, but more meaningful, job. You swap your meaningless $100k job where you pushed paper, played politics, and accomplished little with a meaningful job whose purpose is to improve the human condition. You might now be saying, 'What about the money?' I need money. My lifestyle needs money. I have a thirty-five hundred square foot house and two cars in the driveway. How can I downsize my lifestyle? Believe me; you can downsize your lifestyle. Many people do it. If downsizing lifestyle will enable you to live your passions, to live a happier, more fragrant life, do it. Swallow your pride; check your ego at the door; the step back is only temporary. Do not trade the superficiality that comes from living a certain 'lifestyle' with personal happiness. Few people, at life's end, express regret for not having another car, diamond ring, or vacation house. Regrets mostly have to do with living a happier, more meaningful life. When determining whether to downsize lifestyle, remember mission, vision. Ask yourself, 'What matters most?' If you are like most people, you want to pursue passion, want greater happiness, but feel trapped by current condition. Know this: when we downsize lifestyle, it affords us the opportunity *to take risks*; to do what we have longed to do, to live free.

Sometimes, taking a step backward (with earthly possessions) is necessary to take two steps forward (with personal happiness). Downsizing lifestyle takes courage and faith, but your inner soul goals are at stake. Your personal happiness is at stake. Nay, your life experience is at stake. Do not make the mistake of thinking that the bigger home or more luxurious car will provide lifelong happiness. It is likely that you have already learned this life lesson. If so, do something about it. To suffer through life, to live with unhappiness, is to not live at all. Therefore, make the change. Chances are, your increased personal happiness from living your passion will lead to far greater success and riches than you have today. When you have established personal alignment, then the time will be right for you to upgrade lifestyle, and how glorious life will be for you then. My advice: take a step backward so you can take two steps forward. The common refrain from those who downsize lifestyle is that it was a difficult adjustment to make at the time, but they would never go back. Make the change; you will be glad you did.

The last new way to think is in terms of [y = f(x)]; "*y is a function of x*". No, I am not asking you to re-learn algebra, but this formula does have application to live a happy and fragrant life. The [y] part of the formula represents your life experience. The [f(x)] part represents the 'levers of life' that drive the life experience. When applied to personal strategy, the [y] represents the life experience component of your Personal Strategy Map and the [f(x)] represents your Personal Strategic Themes, as life pathways, commitments, measures, and initiatives individually represent the 'levers of life'. It is from performing <u>certain</u> activities, applying <u>certain</u> commitments, measuring <u>certain</u> aspects of life, and executing <u>certain</u> initiatives that we achieve our goals. Consequently, knowing <u>which</u> activities to perform, commitments to make, measures to introduce, and initiatives to execute is key. Over time, through trial and error, we not only learn which levers in life will help us achieve our goals, but also in which direction (up or down) to tweak levers. Your 'levers' will be different from your family's, friends', and neighbors. This is expected; as we are unique, as our personal strategy is unique, so, too, are the levers of life unique. In summary, thinking in terms of y=f(x) is important for the following reasons:

- Gets us to think in terms of cause and effect
- Provides the context for tweaking personal strategy
- Focuses our efforts on optimizing the 'vital few' levers of life
- Provides us insight on how to maximize our life experience
- Provides us the defining equation to achieve personal excellence

When we <u>think</u> about pursuing passions, utilizing personal strategy, achieving personal alignment, in addition to thinking long-term, that it is ok to downsize lifestyle, and that our quality of life is a function of the levers of life, it leads to acting in new ways.

New Ways to Act

The mind controls the body. Therefore, thinking in new ways gives rise to acting in new ways. This is true of personal strategy as inner soul goals (new thinking), spawn new action. Minimally, having a personal strategy will require you act in these new ways:

- Measuring your life
- Managing your life
- Conversing with soul
- Observing self and environment
- Acting with urgency

It is likely that prior to reading this book, you did not measure many aspects of your life. Likewise, you probably did not actively manage your life. Lastly, it is likely that you conversed little with soul. I do not make these statements to condemn, only to highlight the before and after actions that come with implementing personal strategy. Living by a personal strategy requires all the actions stated above, especially acting with urgency, as we have Only One Shot to meet imperative, seize opportunity.

When we are seeing in new ways, thinking in new ways, and acting in new ways, it leads to feeling in new ways.

New Ways to Feel

Few things produce greater feelings of aliveness than to set, pursue, and achieve a goal. The satisfaction and sense of pride we feel when we plan and achieve is unparalleled. Whether cleaning the house, cutting the lawn, or executing personal strategy, we love to achieve. However, the feelings we experience, the gush of emotion we exert when executing personal strategy, are of a much higher order. We feel:

- Inspired
- Excited
- Empowered

- Hopeful
- Motivated

We feel inspired because personal strategy reflects soul; desires of soul. We feel excited because we are pursuing passion. We feel empowered because we have a detailed, precise strategy to realize passion. We feel hopeful because we know that something good lies just on the horizon. Lastly, we feel motivated because...we are inspired, desire happiness, long to be free.

Remember, anything you conceive, you can achieve. All that is required of you is to see in new ways, think in new ways, act in new ways, and feel in new ways (see Figure 11.1). However, to do all this requires will. As such, we discuss next a matter of will.

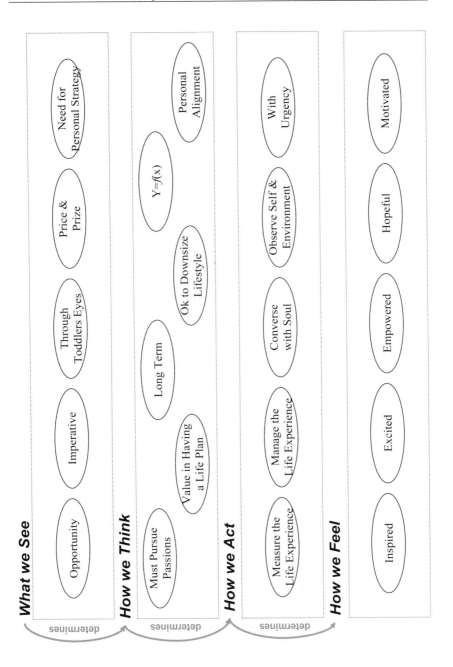

Fig. 11.1

A Matter of Will

*"There can be no driving force, except through
the conversion of the man into his will, making
him the will, and the will him"*
- Ralph Waldo Emerson

THE HUMAN WILL! WHAT IS IT? We have all heard or said phrases such as, "I have no will power" or "so and so is a strong willed person," but do we really know what will is? This chapter provides such insight. The will, as you will soon learn, is *the key* to goal achievement and, therefore, this chapter represents, in many ways, the most important chapter of this book. Put bluntly, with will, we achieve our goals; without it, we fail. You will learn that while having a personal strategy is necessary to achieve a goal, it is not sufficient, as one also needs will. Most people know little of the human will, how to develop it, and most importantly how to utilize it for personal gain. Thus, given our knowledge gap, perhaps the best way to introduce a matter of will is to first define will.

Defining Will

There are many ways to define will, the simplest of which is, *doing what you plan*. You establish a goal and through planning and action (i.e., 'doing'), you achieve your goal. Although this definition reflects the essence of will, it lacks substance. Therefore, a better definition of will is:

- The power of self-direction
- The power to control one's mind, impulses, and actions
- The power to execute one's decisions, wishes, or plans

The common element of each definition above is the word 'power'. It is my hope that by chapter's end, you will recognize the power that is <u>your will</u>, and how will can help you achieve your goals. For now, let us understand each component of the definition of will.

To exert will means to control your direction in life, to be self-directed; it means that you direct your life rather than life directing you. However, to direct self properly requires a plan, a personal strategy. You have a personal strategy and, therefore, are empowered to self-direct your life.

To exert will also means to control your mind, your impulses, and your actions. For example, if your goal is exceptional fitness, will directs and controls your mind and body to eat the right foods, exercise regularly, and acquire knowledge of healthy living practices. This is the power of will.

Lastly, to exert will means to execute your decisions, wishes, and plans. You have already demonstrated your ability to do this, as you have a new life plan and are executing said plan.

Will is an energy source that we draw from for strength and resolve, as desire alone is not enough to achieve our inner soul goals. Perhaps the best way to vision will is that it is a filter, a protective layer, for self and soul to block desires of mind, body, and environment from influencing mind, allowing only desires of soul to pass through to direct one's thinking, one's actions (see Figure 12.1).

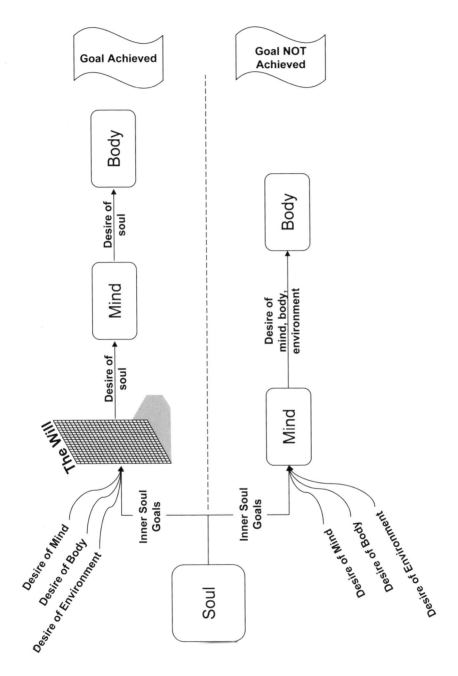

Fig. 12.1

Notice how desires of mind, body, and environment compete for will's favor, seek mind's attention. This is our challenge.
Desires are always with us; every hour, every day, every week,
every month, every year. The question is, 'Is will present, <u>at</u>
<u>attention</u>, to block debilitating desires from corrupting mind?'
When will is strong, desires of mind, body, or environment do
not sway will. ***Will takes direction only from soul, hears only
soul's tones.*** Desires of soul must prevail over lesser desires for
you to achieve your goals; realize vision for self. Because of
the important role will plays in helping us achieve our goals, in
the pages that follow, we discuss several characteristics of will
including strength of will, quality of will, and power of will.
However, before we do, let us first discuss the essence of will.

Essence of Will

Essence, you might recall, is what remains when the immediate passes; therefore, what can we say remains upon exerting
will? Earlier, we learned that the function of will is to direct and
control our life. Consequently, if 'directing/controlling' represents the 'immediate' of will, then the 'passing' (essence) of will
represents:

- Soul exercising self-direction
- Personal alignment
- Stronger will
- New habits
- Self-control
- Stronger mind
- New thinking, new actions, and new feelings

As this list indicates, essence of will represents many things.
When we exert will, soul is exercising self-direction. Will is our
commander within, not only reminding us of what soul desires,
but also executing what soul desires. The long-term effect of

applying will, of having will direct and control the mind, is to establish and maintain personal alignment. There is little more important in life than to establish and maintain personal alignment. Every time we exert will, whether resisting temptation or exercising at the gym, we strengthen will. More importantly, when we exert will, right thinking, right actions prevail. And when we are thinking right, acting right, and strengthening will, something unbeknownst occurs: we develop new habits. Developing new habits represents the core essence of will, and as we replace debilitating habits with habits that inspire, we develop greater self-control. Self-control, in turn, helps develop a stronger mind, enabling you to achieve your inner soul goals, increase personal happiness, and realize a more fragrant life. Lastly, when we exert will, we force new thinking, new actions, and new feelings upon current self to realize emerging self. It is because of the cascading effect of will that we must now update an earlier illustration to reflect 'willing' action as a response to 'seeing' in new ways and as a driver to 'think, act, and feel' in new ways (see Figure 12.2).

Although what we will influences how we think, act, and feel, our ability to will depends largely upon our desire to engage in willing action. That is, it depends on strength of will. We discuss strength of will later in this chapter.

Now that we defined essence of will, let us discuss will's relation to soul, mind, and body.

Soul – Will – Mind – Body

To utilize will for personal gain requires understanding the connection between soul, will, mind, and body. Each entity plays a distinct, yet interconnected, role in achieving one's goals, establishing personal alignment, and increasing personal happiness (see Table 12.1).

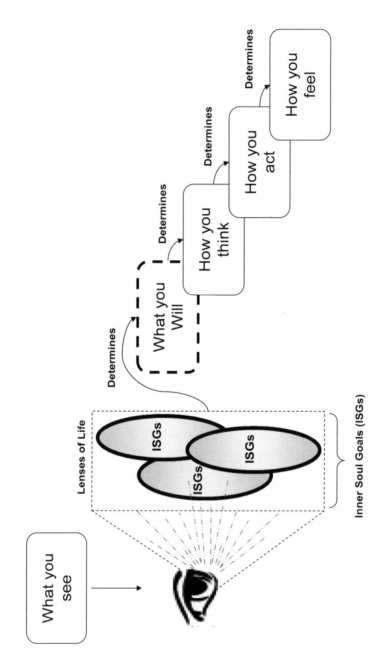

Fig. 12.2

Table 12.1

Entity	Role
Soul	Soul is the source of our inner soul goals; those things we want in life because pursuing them will make us happy and give life meaning. **Soul directs will.**
Will	Will represents our commander within, directing and controlling mind to execute soul's desires (i.e., ISG's). **Will serves soul.**
Mind	Mind is an instrument of will. Mind receives commands from will to direct self and body to support soul. **Mind serves will.**
Body	Body takes direction from mind to execute soul's desires. **Body serves mind.**

Although each entity individually plays an important role in achieving goals, establishing personal alignment, and increasing personal happiness, it's the <u>system of relationships</u> between entities that determine whether we achieve such things (see Figure 12.3).

To ensure that you understand how soul-will-mind-body interact for goal achievement, we examine these key relationships:

- Soul – Will
- Will – Mind
- Mind – Body
- Soul – Will – Mind – Body

Now, as soul represents the source from which all else emanates, we begin by discussing the relationship between soul and will.

The [Soul – Will] Relation

Soul and will are separate and distinct, but each needs the other. Soul provides direction (for our life) and will executes direction. Together, they determine our life experience (see Figure 12.4).

Without soul and the content (i.e., ISG's) it provides, we drift aimlessly through life and without will to execute what soul desires, we achieve nothing. Therefore, the relationship between soul and will is clear:

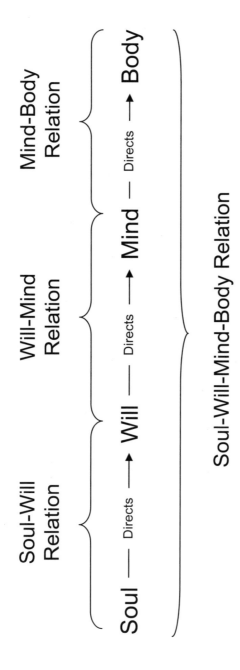

Fig. 12.3

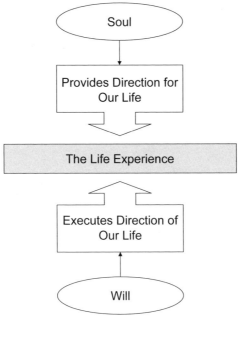

Fig. 12.4

Soul directs will and
will executes what soul desires

What this relationship reveals is that soul and will are One. That is, soul is will and will is soul. Soul communicates what we want in life and from life as represented by our inner soul goals. Our ISG's, in turn, provide the context will needs to drive right thinking, right action to achieve such goals (see Figure 12.5).

As personal strategy is comprised of inner soul goals and as inner soul goals derive from soul, will exists to serve personal strategy. Therefore, if soul desires exceptional fitness, it is will, as servant, who makes it happen. Likewise, if soul desires the freedom that comes from entrepreneurship, it is will, as servant, who makes it happen. At this point, it is important to distinguish divine will from self will. When desires of soul direct will,

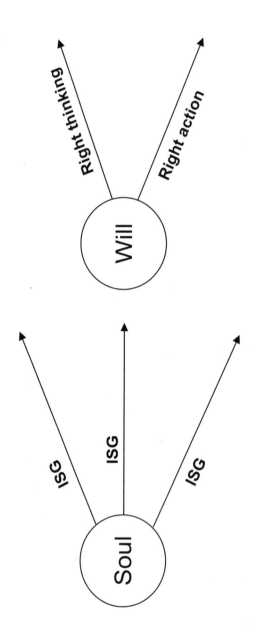

Soul directs will using inner soul goals as context to drive right thinking, right action to achieve such goals

Fig. 12.5

we call this divine will. When desires of self, body, or environment direct will, we call this self will. For purposes herein, unless otherwise stated, when we speak of will, we speak of divine will. Now, depending on the source from which you operate (self vs. soul) determines who will takes orders from. Sadly, for most people, desires of mind, body, and environment direct will as opposed to soul directing will. When this occurs, goals fizzle and die. Table 12.2 describes the effects to the goal [be exceptionally fit] when soul drives will versus mind, body, or environment driving will.

Table 12.2

When soul drives will...	When mind, body, or environment drive will...
• You resist eating wrong foods • You exercise regularly • You focus on your goal • You maintain self-control • You achieve your goal	• You give in to temptation • You exercise sporadically • Your focus is easily distracted • You lack self-control • You abandon your goal

The purpose of this example was to make the point that you will achieve far greater success in life when soul directs will than when mind, body, or environment direct will. When desires of mind, body, and environment direct will, there is no lasting commitment to goals, no lasting commitment to act, and, therefore, no lasting commitment to achieve. Why is this so? It is because desires of mind, body, and environment are fleeting, of the moment, and, therefore, incapable of sustaining long-term achievement. However, when passion (i.e., desires of soul) directs will, we are inspired to commit, inspired to act, inspired to achieve. Passion is fertile ground from which achievement rises. To have vision for self but lack will to realize vision is tragic. To ensure that this does not happen to you requires remaining conscious of soul and soul's relation to will (see Figure 12.6).

Never lose awareness, consciousness of what soul desires – *of what you desire*. Remember, the life experience is not about satisfying desires of mind or body; it is about satisfying desires of

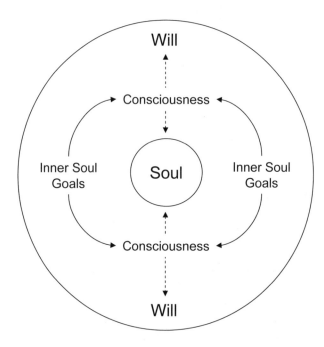

Fig. 12.6

soul; of doing and living by what soul wants, not by what self or body want. We are not here on earth to satisfy desires of mind or body or to indulge desires from our environment; we are here to realize soul's desires. For when we do and live by what soul desires, we experience lifelong happiness, the result of having met imperative, seized opportunity.

The will, <u>your will</u>, is *the* vehicle to realize emerging you. The emerging you reflects soul and, therefore, you are soul and soul is you. And as soul is also will, it follows that you are will (see Figure 12.7).

To understand the relation between soul and will is to utilize will to achieve mission, realize vision. However, to do this requires alignment beyond [soul and will] it also requires alignment between [will and mind].

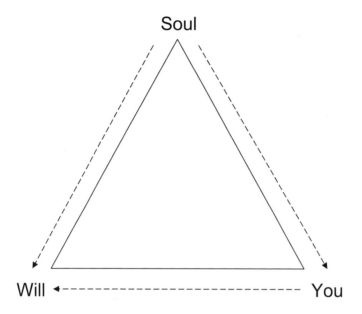

Soul is you. Soul is will. You are will.

Fig. 12.7

The [Will – Mind] Relation

We learned that the relation between soul and will is such that soul directs will and will executes what soul desires. Now we extend our discussion to include the relation between will and mind.

To achieve desires of soul, mind must align with soul; that is, it must support soul. Thus, a key function of will is to establish such alignment by directing mind to execute what soul desires. Thus, the relationship between will and mind is this:

Will directs and controls mind and
mind executes what soul desires

Although the basic relationship between will and mind is described above, the exact relationship between will and mind is multi-faceted:

- Will is a conduit between soul and mind
- Will creates alignment between self and soul
- Will filters thoughts of mind
- Will communicates commands of soul to mind
- Will maintains mind consciousness of soul

As the relationship between will and mind is vital to achieve one's goals, we explore each aspect of this relationship next.

The majority of people traverse life deeply wanting one thing or another but, in apparent opposition to soul, do something else. In other words, most people never pursue their passion in life. Why is this? How is it that someone could work their entire professional career without pursuing their true passion in life? One reason is that soul and mind are misaligned in thought, purpose, and spirit. Soul is saying and wanting one thing, and mind is saying and wanting another. Over my fifteen plus years consulting to business, I encountered many people, with occupations ranging from computer programmer, to accountant, to project manager, to lawyer, who were very unhappy with their role, their job, their career. For them, their job lacked purpose, lacked meaning and it was affecting every aspect of their life. I would ask them, 'What do you really what to do with your life?' and 'What are your passions?' Invariably, I would get answers like, "I want to make custom furniture" or "I want to open a photo studio" or "I want to teach". It was heartbreaking to see people not living their passions, as I saw how deeply it affected their attitude, their ambition, and their view of life. Pursuing passion does not have to be a 'wish;' it can be 'reality'. The problem is, when will is not present to direct mind, not only do our passions fade away, so, too, do our goals fade. Hence, the need for will, as it provides a conduit between soul and mind, to align thought, align vision. Soul communicates passions to will and then will directs mind to pursue such passions. This linkage from soul to will to mind is vital for goal achievement (see Figure 12.8).

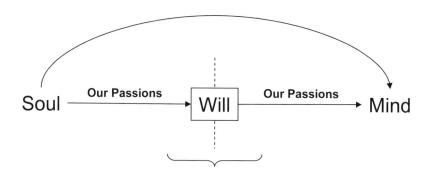

Will is a conduit for aligning thought,
aligning vision (passions) from soul to mind

Fig. 12.8

With such linkage, we achieve our goals; without it, we fail. With such linkage, we pursue and live our passions; we become the furniture maker, we become the entrepreneur, we become the teacher. In short, we become who we were meant to be on the surface of life.

Aligning self with soul is the essence of living. It is what we were meant to do and what we should always strive for in life. To do what you want to do, to live the way you want to live is the key to personal happiness and our will plays a central role in establishing such alignment. We exert will to direct and control thoughts in our mind to achieve our inner soul goals. Without will filtering thoughts of mind, we succumb to desires, impulses, and motives of mind, body, or environment. Why is this so? It is because we are inherently weak. As such, the influencing, controlling, and filtering roles will plays are crucial for goal achievement, as we encounter multitudinous distractions from our environment and our mind that could derail our goals. For example, suppose one of your goals was exceptional fitness, and to achieve this goal you swore off eating sugar, among other things. You arrive at work one day to discover that a co-worker brought two dozen Krispy Kreme donuts. What do you do? A distraction from your environment is challenging your goal, challenging resolve, tempting wrong action. Your dilemma: do you give in to temptation or do you exert will and resist. Will exists to filter desires, impulses, and motives that oppose soul, that oppose your inner soul goals. In this case, the proper course of action, obviously, is to exert will and resist temptation. Later, we discuss strength of will and quality of will, two characteristics of will that determine whether you eat the donut or resist. What the example above tells us is, for will to influence and control mind requires persistent communication, commands of soul, from will to mind.

You might be asking, 'What does it mean for will to communicate commands of soul to mind?' Let us answer this question in parts. Firstly, commands of soul represent our inner soul goals, desires of soul. Once we determine our inner soul goals, it is the function of will to communicate such goals to mind, relentlessly and continuously. Such communication keeps our goals in our face and top-of-mind; helps us remain conscious of soul. Now, just as soul directs, informs will of what matters most by communicating inner soul goals, so, too, does will direct, inform mind of what matters most by issuing commands of soul (see Figure 12.9).

Will directs mind on which desires to placate, and more importantly, which desires not to. These communications from will to mind represent commands of soul. With persistent communication from will to mind of what soul desires, the power of will, once dormant, rises to take control. In time, will comes to dominate mind, and when this happens, when will and mind are aligned in thought, purpose, and spirit, great things happen.

Achieving inner soul goals is difficult, largely because most people lose consciousness of their goals when tempted with

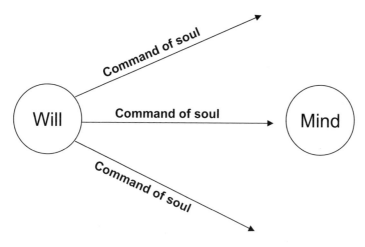

Will directs mind by issuing commands of soul

Fig. 12.9

desires from mind, body, and environment. For a moment, we forget we swore off eating sugar, we forget we committed to exercise every day, we forget we committed to never smoke again. We're caught up in the moment, satisfying desire of mind, body, or environment, and we relent. Most of us are masters at tuning out and tuning in our goals depending on circumstance. The problem with these mental lapses is that to achieve any goal in life, especially inner soul goals, requires keeping your goal top-of-mind and in your face AT ALL TIMES, not only when it is convenient. The temptations of life are numerous, frequent, unrelenting, and ever-present. Believe me; I know! Just like you, I have had my own challenges resisting temptations of mind, body, and environment. However, divine will, when present, banishes such desires, impulses, and motives from one's consciousness, thereby clearing mind, purifying mind of all except for desires of soul.

The relationship between will and mind is central to goal achievement. Without will directing, controlling, and filtering mind, achieving one's goals is impossible. Having said this, aligning will and mind in thought, purpose, and spirit is still not enough to ensure achieving your goals; it also requires aligning mind and body.

The [Mind – Body] Relation

In prior sections, we learned that soul directs will and will directs mind. Now, we extend our discussion to include relations between mind and body.

As discussed, will is a conduit between soul and mind, whereby will issues commands of soul to mind of what soul desires. With such direction, mind then directs body, through willing action, to support soul, that is, to execute what soul desires (see Figure 12.10).

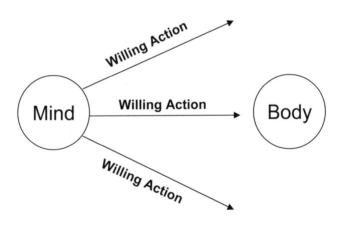

Mind directs body through willing action

Fig. 12.10

Thus, the relationship between mind and body is this:

Mind directs body through willing action and body executes what soul desires

Of the relationships discussed, the relationship between mind and body might be the most obvious. However, our focus is not so much *that* mind directs body to act; it is *how*, the <u>source</u> from which mind directs body to act. Because mind takes direction from will and will represents soul, when mind directs body mind is driving right action to execute personal strategy and achieve our goals. However, when mind and body are misaligned in thought and purpose, we fail to execute personal strategy and, therefore, fail to achieve our goals. To the extent that you view, consider mind a servant of will, a servant of soul, will determine your ability to drive right action, right results. This is our challenge. This is our goal.

Thus far, we have considered paired relations between soul, will, mind, and body. Now, we consider <u>all</u> relations, together, as a system.

The [Soul – Will – Mind – Body] Relation

Figure 12.11 illustrates the cascading relationship and interdependency that exists from soul to will to mind to body.

The cascade begins with soul directing will to pursue desires of soul. Then, will directs mind to act in accordance with soul. Finally, mind directs body to perform actions to realize what soul desires. The soul-will-mind-body relationship represents a system of thought and action aligned around common goals. What we see, what we will, how we think, how we act, and how we feel are all aligned in thought, purpose, and spirit. When this degree of internal alignment exists, you can achieve any reasonable goal in life. Few people are aligned in this manner, but for those who are, their achievements are legendary. Tiger Woods set goals for himself at an early age to eclipse the

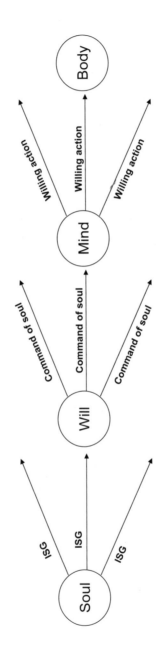

Soul directs will using inner soul goals as context and will directs mind by issuing commands of soul and mind directs body through willing action

Fig. 12.11

achievements of his idol Jack Nicklaus. Tiger set goals, exerted will, controlled his mind, and directed his body to act in accordance with soul. The result? Tiger is on pace to become the greatest golfer in history. The same can be said regarding the achievements of Walton, Marriott, and Einstein. Each of these men exemplify the success one can enjoy when soul-will-mind-body are aligned. More than luck, more than good fortune, more than good timing, each of these men exerted great will to achieve their dreams. This should comfort you, as it indicates that to achieve the same degree of success in life, all that is required is for your soul, will, mind, and body to be aligned in thought, purpose, and spirit. You have the innate components (soul-will-mind-body) to be successful. Success will follow. How do I know? Your will, will make it so.

Now, although each of us has the ability to will, strength of will varies considerably among people. Because strength of will determines whether we succeed or fail, whether we rise or fall, whether we achieve new or perpetuate old, we discuss this matter next.

Strength of Will

The human will is an internal force that enables people to achieve great things. In fact, all the achievements throughout history, good and bad, are the result of men and women exerting will. We have all heard stories of how someone overcame poverty to amass great wealth or how someone overcame disability to achieve remarkable success or how someone overcame addiction to lead a more inspired life. The common denominator with such people is that they exerted great will to overcome great odds, to achieve their goals. To have a goal, desire, and a personal strategy to achieve each goal is not enough. To achieve your goals in life requires strong will. Strength of will is *the deciding factor.*

There are three different intensities or will strengths:

- Strong will
- Intermittent will
- Weak will

You may have strong will, such that once you set your mind to a goal, you advance mightily and relentlessly until goal achieved. On the other hand, you may exhibit intermittent will, where you still advance towards your goal, albeit slowly and discontinuously. Finally, you may have weak will, in which case repeated slips result in you abandoning your goal altogether. Table 12.3 provides an overview of the different will strengths.

Table 12.3

Will Strength	Meaning	Indicators
Strong will	• Will is present at all times • Will is fixed on achieving one's inner soul goals • Will rarely succumbs to desires, impulses, or motives of mind, body, or environment	• Achievement of goals • Invincible determination • Attitude that failure is not an option • No backsliding • Self-control
Intermittent will	• Will appears in spurts rather than in persistence • Will occasionally relents to desires, impulses, or motives of mind, body or environment	• Goals take longer to achieve • Indulge old habits occasionally • Occasional backsliding • Moderate self-control
Weak will	• Will is non-existent • Will always relents to desires, impulses, or motives of mind, body, or environment	• Goals abandoned quickly • Indulge old habits often • Significant backsliding • Little self-control

Given the above, what type of will do you have? Do you pursue goals with reckless abandon or do you indulge desires of mind, body, or environment? Does your will sway with the varieties of life, or does your will stay focused on the goal? Know this: with a strong will, you will achieve your goals and realize a happier, more fragrant life. Conversely, with an intermittent will, it is unlikely that you will achieve your goals and with a weak will it is certain that you will not achieve your goals.

You might be saying, 'I agree having a strong will is necessary to achieve my goals but what determines strong will? In other words, what must I focus on to develop strong will?' We answer these questions next.

Determinants of Will Strength

There are several factors or determinants of will strength (see Figure 12.12):

- Strength of willing action
- Emotive state
- Strength of mind
- Presence of will
- State of mind

Strength of willing action is an indicator of will strength. The purpose and function of will, as discussed, is to direct and control the mind through willing action. Therefore, the strength of willing action, the intensity with which we 'direct' and 'control' our mind, indicates whether our will is weak or strong. Table 12.4 describes the effect on will strength based on strength of willing action:

Table 12.4

Determinant of will: *Strength of willing action*		
Strong Will	**Intermittent Will**	**Weak Will**
• Commands to direct and control mind are forceful, relentless	• Commands to direct and control mind are forceful at times and weak at other times	• Commands to direct and control mind are weak

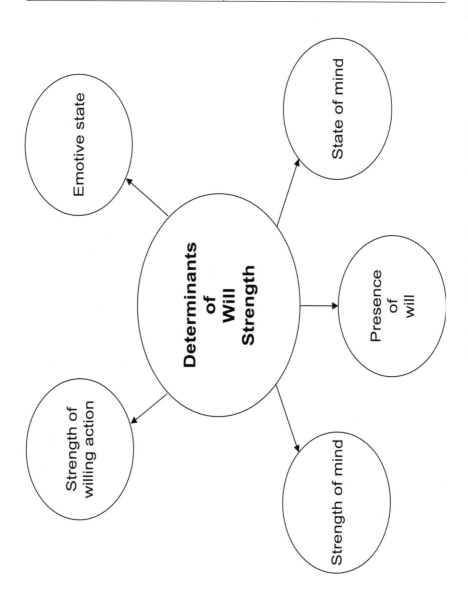

Fig. 12.12

As Table 12.4 indicates, there is great difference in will strength based on strength of willing action. Another factor or determinant of will strength is emotive state.

The emotive state of an individual refers to <u>what</u> drives will. The emotive states that determine will strength are:

- Our moods
- Our passions

When our moods drive will (i.e., self will), will strength is much weaker than when passion (i.e., divine will) drives will. Why is this? It is because moods are transparent, fleeting, and unpredictable. Passions, conversely, are substantive, formidable, and predictable. Know this: your ability to achieve in life is a function of what drives your life. Are you driven by mood or are you driven by passion? It is because of the fleeting and unpredictable nature of moods that such emotive state is incapable of helping us achieve our goals. We need a more formidable foundation built of strong emotion, feeling, and desire to achieve our goals. Now, because passions emanate from soul, they provide a more formidable base upon which to rally our thoughts, actions, and life experience around. Table 12.5 describes the effect on will strength when mood drives will versus passion driving will:

Table 12.5

Determinant of will: *Emotive state*		
Strong Will	**Intermittent Will**	**Weak Will**
• Thinking and actions driven by passion • Consistent, predictable behavior • Desire to achieve is strong	• Driven by passion but corrupted by mood • Inconsistent behavior, actions • Desire to achieve vacillates	• Thinking and actions driven by mood • Unpredictable behavior • Desire to achieve is weak

As Table 12.5 indicates, there is great difference in will strength depending on emotive state. Another factor or determinant of will strength is state of mind.

State of mind refers to a <u>willingness</u> to exert will. Although all are endowed with will, few people utilize will to its full potential. Why is this? It is because *you have to <u>want</u> to will for will to work*. Will directs mind and body to act in accordance with will but before will can perform this function, mind and body must allow willing action to occur. What this implies is that *to achieve your goals in life you must surrender mind and body to will*. Surrendering mind and body to will requires changes in not only how one thinks, but also how one acts. When we surrender mind and body to will, desires of soul direct our thoughts and actions versus desires of mind, body, or environment directing our thoughts and actions. To the extent that we surrender self for soul we increase self discipline, self control, and will intensity (see Figure 12.13).

When our mental state is such that we would rather indulge desires of mind, body, and environment than pursue desires of soul, our will intensity is weak. However, when we develop new resolves for our life, sourced from soul, will strength intensifies. But, having purpose in life does not, on its own, create strong will. A strong will only exists if you let it exist. Table 12.6 describes the effect on will strength when mind and body surrender to will:

Table 12.6

Determinant of will: *State of mind*		
Strong Will	**Intermittent Will**	**Weak Will**
• Mind and body serve will • Will forcefully directs/ controls mind • Ability to will is strong • Mind is strong	• Mind and body serve will but are corrupted by desires of mind, body, and environment • Will intermittently directs/ controls mind • Ability to will vacillates • Mind is lazy	• Mind and body serve desire • Will does not direct/control mind • Ability to will is weak • Mind is weak

As Table 12.6 indicates, there is great difference in will strength depending on state of mind (degree of surrender).

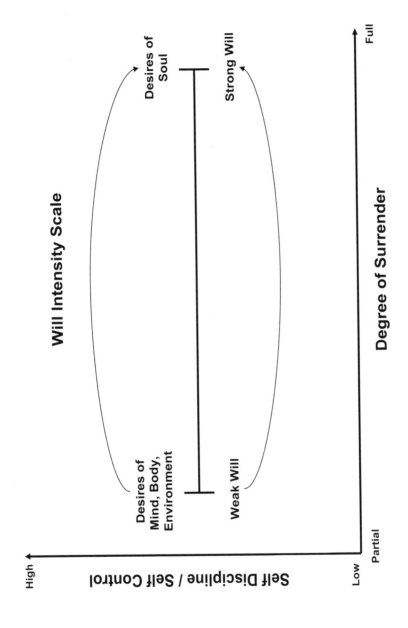

Fig. 12.13

Another factor or determinant of will strength is strength of mind.

Strength of mind is a key determinant of will strength because without a strong mind, it is impossible to will yourself to will. For example, to will yourself to lose 40 pounds, start a new business, quit smoking, or exercise five days a week all require a strong mind. To have a strong mind, is to believe failure is NOT an option. A strong mind is too controlled, too disciplined, too determined to accept defeat. Table 12.7 describes the effect on will strength based on strength of mind:

Table 12.7

Determinant of will: *Strength of mind*		
Strong Will	**Intermittent Will**	**Weak Will**
• Firm resolve • Strong ability to exert will • Fanatical belief in one's goals • Thoughts that failure is not an option	• Wavering resolve • Weak ability to exert will • Positive thinking and defeatist thinking co-habit the mind	• Weak resolve • Inability to exert will • Defeatist thinking dominates the mind

As Table 12.7 indicates, there is great difference in will strength based on strength of mind. The last, and most significant, factor or determinant of will strength is presence of will.

Presence of will is *the* most significant factor in determining will strength, for if will is not present, it cannot help us achieve our goals. Have you ever wondered why you can set a goal and then seemingly lose interest in the goal or adopt an attitude of 'I just don't care' only a short time later? Have you ever asked yourself, 'Why do I fail to achieve my goals' or 'Why do I not do what I want to do?' These are important questions, each with the same answer. *It is because <u>will</u> was not present.* When will is present, it directs mind and body to act in accordance with soul. When it is not, we succumb to desires of mind, body, and environment. A present will focuses mind to achieve our inner soul goals. It keeps our goals in our face and top-of-mind while

preventing debilitating thoughts and actions from derailing chosen course. Your will must never relent at any time during your
lifetime; it must always be present; "at attention". For when
will fades, goals fade, and in time, the path that you have chosen
for your life will fade as well. Table 12.8 describes the effect on
will strength based on presence of will:

Table 12.8

Determinant of will: *Presence of will*		
Strong Will	**Intermittent Will**	**Weak Will**
• Will is present at all times • Effort to maintain will's presence is strong • Will's presence never relents	• Will is sometimes present • Effort to maintain will's presence varies • Will's presence relents occasionally	• Will is rarely present • Effort to maintain will's presence is non-existent • Will's presence relents often

As Table 12.8 indicates, there is great difference in will
strength based on presence of will.

It should be clear that strength of will, as determined by
the factors just described, is vital to achieve one's goals. Without
strong will, we achieve little. With strong will, we can achieve
anything. Remember: will strength is a choice. If you do not
have a strong will, it is because you choose to have a weak or
intermittent will. Later in this chapter, we discuss how to grow
will. To summarize strength of will, Table 12.9 describes characteristics of each strength type:

Table 12.9

Strong Will	**Intermittent Will**	**Weak Will**
• Fanatical belief • Driven by passion • Laser focus • Strong mind • Strong commitment • Unwillingness to settle • Great achievement	• Transparent belief • Succumb to desire • Lost focus • Lazy mind • Little commitment • Moderate achievement	• No belief • Slave to desire • No focus • Weak mind • No commitment • No achievement

The degree of success and achievement we enjoy in life hinges on *strength of will* and *quality of will*. We discussed the importance and relevance of a strong will; now we discuss quality of will.

Quality of Will

As with strength of will, one's actions indicate quality of will. We determine quality of will by two factors:

- Force of will
- Persistence of will

Force of will refers to the intensity with which one exerts will. Simply put, the more you exert will, the greater your force of will. For example, suppose your goal is exceptional fitness and to achieve this goal requires exercising five times a week. How many times you exercise each week is an indicator of force of will. If you average only two trips to the gym each week, you exhibit low force of will. If, on the other hand, you average five or six trips to the gym each week, you exhibit high force of will. To achieve anything significant in life requires great force of will. To achieve your personal strategy will require great force of will. Force of will is an indicator of quality of will, in that greater force correlates with higher quality. We also determine quality of will by persistence of will.

To persist means to continue steadfastly or firmly in some state, purpose, or course of action. A persistent will is a present will. As with force of will, a persistent will is evidenced through one's actions. For example, if force of will represents how many days we exercise a week, then persistence of will represents how many weeks we exercise a year. Our inner soul goals represent substantive goals that could take months, if not a lifetime, to achieve. Because such goals are long-term by design, achieving them will require persistent will. Every day, every week, every month, every year, will must be present; it must persist. Persistence of will is also necessary to remain conscious of soul, to block desires of mind, body, and environment from corrupting one's thoughts. Without a persistent will, achieving personal strategy will be difficult, if not impossible, to achieve.

Together, force of will and persistence of will indicate quality of will. By developing high quality will, you will achieve any goal you set for yourself. This is certain! The greatest achievers throughout history exhibited great force of will, in persistence, and so can you!

Now, to exhibit forceful will, to maintain persistent will, represents manifestation of will. We discuss this topic next.

Manifestation of Will

To manifest means to make clear or evident. Thus, to exert will means to manifest will. Every time you exercise, you manifest will. Every time you resist foods from the 'bad list', you manifest will. Every time you resist smoking, you manifest will. Manifestation of will indicates:

- Willingness to pay the price
- Motivation to achieve
- Commitment
- Drive
- Desire to live passionately
- Desire to achieve personal strategy

When we manifest will, we are demonstrating desire to live passionately, to execute personal strategy, and to pay the price for success. We know this to be true, as our actions tell us so.

Manifestation of will exists as:

- A single act
- A series of acts

As a single act, manifestation of will represents exercising for a day, or avoiding sugar for a day, or not smoking for a day. On a more serious note, it may take the form of a parent rescuing a child from a life-threatening situation or a firefighter rescuing people from a burning building (e.g. 9/11). As a series of acts, manifestation of will may take the form of exercising every day, never smoking again, or dedicating one's life to saving others. Life renders both forms. However, from our discussion on quality of will, we learned that success comes not from exerting will occasionally, but from exerting will repeatedly. We achieve fitness not by exercising one day a week, but by exercising five days a week. We build a business not by exerting will some of the time, but all of the time. In short, achievement is not the product of instance, but of repetition, and with repetition comes habit.

Habit and Will

We are our habits. The habits we hold not only define us; they shape our life experience. Thus, to change who we are, our direction in life, we must first change our habits.

Habits represent fixed tendencies to think and act in predictable ways. To be human is to develop habits, good and bad. Our daily lives are an amalgam of habits. For example, our morning routine is habit, our work routine is habit, our evening routine is habit, and to a large extent, our weekend activities are habit. Most of us do the same thing, at the same time, in the same way every day. This is life. Now, although habits represent fixed tendencies of mind and body, they are not permanent tendencies. That is, you can change habit. What this indicates is that we are not slave to habit. Having said this, most of us are slaves to habit because we choose to be. For the longest time, I was a slave to sugar. My typical day consisted of eating two bowls of sugary cereal in the morning followed by mid-morning and mid-afternoon snacks from the vending machine (Snickers bars), concluding with a heaping bowl of ice cream after dinner.

These daily habits (choices) did not support my goal of exceptional fitness and were preventing me from making real progress. To what are you a slave? How do your current habits impede your inner soul goals? It is best to <u>think of habits as servants</u>, servants to your goals. When viewed this way, habits either support your goals or they do not. By thinking of habits as servants, you will begin to develop and nurture habits that support personal strategy and eliminate those that do not.

Habits are what remain from exerting will. At first, we exert will in a deliberate attempt to force new thinking, new behaviors, and new actions. However, over time, habit forms, and exerting will becomes automatic; what was new becomes standard (see Figure 12.14).

When repetition of new thinking, new behavior, and new action requires little willed effort, habit exists. This is the power of will. This is also good news in that to achieve our goals, we need only exert will until new behaviors, new actions become habit. Having said this, as your personal strategy contains five to seven inner soul goals, you will likely need to make several new behaviors habit, and, therefore, will always need will.

Now, for will to develop new habits, it must first overcome existing habits. This is where many people fall down. People start on a course of new thinking, new behaviors, and new actions, hoping to establish new habits, but because changing habits takes time and great resolve, most become frustrated with slow progress and quickly abandon the course upon which they decided. To ensure that this does not happen to you, it is important to realize that habits are tendencies *burned into the brain* through repeated thinking, repeated behavior, and repeated action. Thus, to establish new habit requires you undo such history, undo repetition.

To overcome existing habits requires you do two things:

- Keep your goal(s) in your face and top-of-mind
- Think about the consequences of yielding (to temptation)

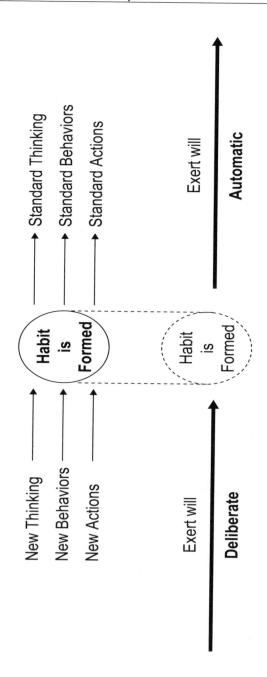

Fig. 12.14

For example, suppose your goal is exceptional fitness, and to support this goal you resolve to eliminate sugar from your diet; no more ice cream, no more candy, no more sugary cereal. With such resolve, when tempted by desires of mind, body, or environment, you must respond accordingly:

Step 1 - Voice goal to self (3x)
Step 2 - Think of the consequence of yielding

By voicing your goal, you regain consciousness of soul to direct right thinking, right action. Additionally, by thinking of the consequence of eating the hot fudge sundae, (i.e., <u>four hours</u> on the treadmill), you will provide self compelling reason to resist temptation. Voicing goal to self and thinking of the consequences of yielding has saved me on multiple occasions from betraying my goals.

At this point, you might still be wondering, 'How does will establish habit?' As with all things in life, it is a process (see Figure 12.15).

The process begins when soul directs will to pursue inner soul goals. This step represents resolution of will of what matters most in life. Then, will takes over by driving necessary mental, physical, and resource commitments to achieve each goal. This step represents presencing of will; rise of divine will. Next, commitments drive action. This step represents persistence of will to achieve one's goals. Finally, action drives habit. This step represents repetition of will; repetition of new thinking, new behavior, and new action until habit formed.

Although overcoming habit is difficult, it is possible. You must remain steadfast in your resolve to direct a new course for your life. We are not slaves to habit. We are above habit. We know this to be true, as all that is required to change habit is to think differently, behave differently, and act differently <u>as directed by will</u>. Such wisdom is reflected in this phrase:

"The Habit which is not indulged in Dies"
                                              - Frank Haddock

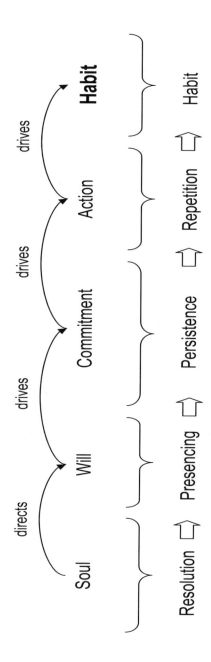

Fig. 12.15

For example, if you stop drinking soda and/or coffee, your dependency on caffeine will die, as will your habit. Similarly, if you stop smoking, your dependency on nicotine will die, as will your habit. Habits equate to action, and as the totality of our actions determine our life experience, it follows, then, that the habits we hold determine the life we live. Consequently, to re-engineer your life requires you adopt new habits. It begins with designing a personal strategy reflecting new thinking, new behavior, and new actions for one's life. Then, with will and time, new habits form, the accumulation of which result in a new life experience (see Figure 12.16).

Good habits not only help us realize a better life, they help us develop a personal competitive advantage. The highest achievers in any profession display <u>different habits</u> than do non-achievers. For example, the habits of Tiger Woods, Donald Trump, and Eminem are different from the non-achievers in their respective professions. Each of these professionals exhibit different thinking, different behavior, and different actions that others do not exhibit, and it is these differences which give them each a distinct competitive advantage within their profession and within life. When selling insurance, one lesson I learned was that successful people do things unsuccessful people do not want to do. I learned that to be successful, for example, I must work sixty-hour weeks. I must prospect relentlessly and I must continually practice and refine my sales skills. By doing these things, I quickly became a top salesman for two different companies. Sadly, in my five years as an insurance salesman, I saw over fifty sales reps come and go. Why did so many fail? It was because they did not do what successful salespeople do. Their <u>habits</u> were different from my own and other successful people. Habits made all the difference.

Table 12.10 illustrates the effect habits have on achieving the goal [exceptional fitness]:

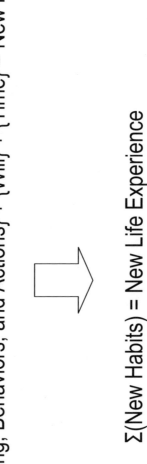

{New Thinking, Behaviors, and Actions} + {Will} + {Time} = New Habit

Σ(New Habits) = New Life Experience

Fig. 12.16

Table 12.10

I achieve my goal of exceptional fitness with habits of...	I do not achieve my goal of exceptional fitness with habits of...
• Exercising daily • Reading fitness magazines • Keeping my goal top of mind and in my face • Watching what I eat • Monitoring progress • Adapting to change	• Exercising sporadically • Not learning how to live a healthy lifestyle • Not keeping my goal top of mind and in my face • Not watching what I eat • Not monitoring my progress

Each of the actions in the example above represents habit. As you can see, one set of habits promotes achievement while the other promotes failure. As you implement your personal strategy, consider whether your current habits promote achievement or promote failure. Engaging in new thinking, new behaviors, and new actions to support personal strategy is a choice.

Therefore, resolve to:

- Demand new thinking of self
- Demand new behaviors of self
- Demand new actions of self
- Demand new habits of self

When you demand these things of self, achievement will come! How do I know? Because your will, will make it so. To conclude prior sections, Table 12.11 summarizes 'what will is' and 'what will is not':

Table 12.11

Will Is...	Will Is Not...
Reflection of soul	Desire
Executor of soul's desires	Emotion
Conduit between soul and mind	Habit
Voice of soul	Executor of lesser tasks
Filter of mind	Mood
Force of energy	Feeling
Mind over matter	Temporary enthusiasm
Commander within	Optimism
Soul	Promises
You	Resolutions

Personal Strategy and Will

Designing and implementing personal strategy usually triggers great change in one's life, as the goals that comprise personal strategy are significant, substantive, and may take years, if not a lifetime, to achieve. Another way to describe such goals is that they are challenging. Consequently, to achieve our inner soul goals, we need help. What we need is will.

Prior to reading this book and developing personal strategy, would you have viewed your inner soul goals as too reaching, too impossible to achieve? I ask this question because what we see determines what we will. Moreover, what we will determines how we think, act, and feel. Consequently, if the goals that comprise your personal strategy are significant, great challenges may lie ahead of you, as to achieve such goals will likely require not only developing new habits, but also seeing, willing, thinking, acting, and feeling in remarkably new ways.

Consider this sample goal and the effort required to overcome current condition to achieve the goal:

The Goal:

- Be exceptionally fit
- Lose 60 pounds

The Means:

- Stop smoking
- Exercise 5x a week
- Learn healthy living practices
- Modify diet/eating patterns

The Challenges:

<u>Current **habits**:</u>

- Eating foods high in sugar
- Smoking (before and after meals)
- Not exercising
- Sedentary living

Current **views**:

- Diet is acceptable
- Quitting smoking is too hard
- Healthy living magazines are boring
- Exercise requires too much effort
- No time to exercise

Current **tendencies**:

- Avoid exercise
- Smoke
- Consume large amounts of sugar
- See fitness, not obesity
- Abandon goals

The list of challenges could expand in a myriad of ways, but let us limit our discussion to those shown above. To achieve this fitness goal, such person will have to overcome several debilitating habits, replace several debilitating views, and mitigate several debilitating tendencies. Now, let me ask you, doesn't this goal seem formidable given these challenges? It does to me. The challenges such individual faces are significant, and without exerting strong will, such individual has no hope of becoming exceptionally fit. Now, consider your inner soul goals. What habits, views, tendencies do you have that will challenge your ability to achieve? Use the template in Figure 12.17 (**Note: you can download a free template from only1shot.com.**) to make explicit the challenges you face, and subsequently must overcome, to achieve each of your inner soul goals.

To achieve your goals in life, to realize personal strategy, will require *you overcome you.* Many of your existing habits, views, and tendencies will have to change for you to transform your life. It is possible, but requires persistently strong will. Whatever your goals in life, whether starting a new business, losing weight, or writing a book, each goal will require significant effort, significant change, and plenty of will. At this point,

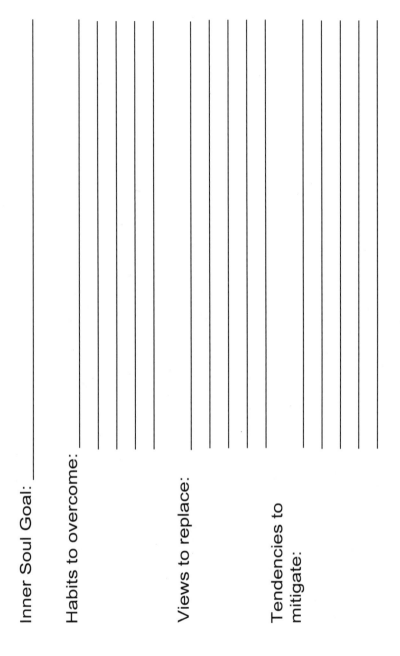

Fig. 12.17

I hope that you understand the need for will to achieve personal strategy. To ensure that you understand the role of will concerning personal strategy, let us briefly review the process of developing and implementing personal strategy using will (see Figure 12.18).

In Step 1, we define inner soul goals to drive our new life plan (PSM). In Step 2, we design strategy (PST's) to achieve each goal. Will enters at Step 3. In Step 3, we implement strategy, by exerting will. We continue exerting will in Step 4 as we manage personal strategy until we achieve our ISG's in Step 5. Exerting will does not end, however, upon achieving <u>current</u> goals, as we define <u>new</u> goals to achieve. In fact, at no point in life do we relent, either with using personal strategy or with exerting will, as utilizing both ensures we live a happy life, full of achievement.

When your purpose in life is to achieve desires of soul (using will) and not about satisfying desires of mind, body, or environment, you will begin to live a much richer and meaningful existence. You will begin to see the colors of the world again. You will rediscover the joy of living. Exercise your right to live joyfully. Exercise your right to live remarkably. When you demand such things of self and life, they arrive. Remember, no obstacle, no debilitating habit, no view, no tendency can withstand the relentless assault of will, <u>your</u> will. You are endowed with a mighty will; you simply must let it out.

To conclude this section, Table 12.12 summarizes role of will in achieving personal strategy:

Table 12.12

Role of Will in Achieving Personal Strategy
• Directs mind and body to execute personal strategy
• Drives new habits, new views, and new tendencies to support personal strategy
• Helps sustain mental, physical, and resource commitments
• Blocks desires of mind, body, and environment from sabotaging personal strategy
• Helps overcome stumbling blocks of personal strategy
• Ensures that we actively manage/refine personal strategy

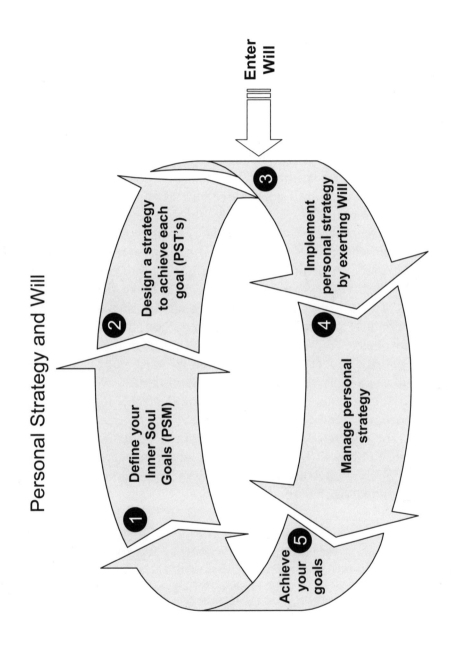

Fig. 12.18

Now, despite recent discussion, questions might remain such as, 'What do I do if I lack will power? and 'How can I achieve my goals if I have weak will?' These questions demand answers. If you believe that you have a weak or intermittent will, and fear you will not be able to achieve your goals, do not fret; help is here. You can grow will.

Growing Will

Given previous discussion on the need for strong will to achieve one's goals, you might find yourself deeply unsettled if you possess a weak or intermittent will. Do not lose enthusiasm; you can grow will. <u>The key to growing will is surrendering to will.</u> The difficulty in doing this is that our [self] is a powerful force to overcome. I must admit that I have struggled over the years to suppress mind and body in favor of will. Perhaps you have as well. The reason we struggle is that we never learned how to harness the power of will. Consequently, self dominates, becomes all-powerful. Thus, the challenge you and I face is to overcome self dominance to unleash soul's dominance. It is possible to overcome self in favor of soul. What is required is to supplant self's interests for soul's interests consciously, deliberately, forcefully. You will struggle at first; and the struggle may last days, weeks, or months, but will, that is, soul, will prevail; mind and body will surrender to will. And when this occurs, when we surrender mind and body to will, something remarkable happens: *we awaken will.*

Although each of us is endowed with will, few have been endowed with great will. What this means for most people is that to exert great will first requires developing will. Surrendering mind and body to will awakens will for growth. A power, once dormant, now rises to attention. Awakening will is really about awakening you to the potential of will. Your task is to learn how to grow it further, to take a weak or intermittent will and make it strong. So, how do we grow will? It is a process.

Growing will is a process that begins with taking small steps. Just as a toddler takes small steps to learn how to walk, so, too, does growing will require taking small steps. To grow will, we must exercise will. How do we exercise will? It begins with identifying your most deeply ingrained habit. If you had to quit something this moment, what would be the hardest for you to quit? Is it smoking, eating chocolate, consuming soft drinks, taking drugs, eating fast food, or drinking alcohol? Whatever would be the hardest habit for you to kick, identify it now. Okay. Now, at this moment, resolve <u>not</u> to indulge this habit for 24 hours. Believe it or not, this small act of will grows will. Admittedly, it will take longer than 24 hours to replace the debilitating habit, but *being forceful for a day leads to being forceful for a lifetime*. Growing will occurs not with dramatic, infrequent acts of will, but with small, frequent, acts of will.

Another exercise you can perform to grow will is to do something each day that you do not want to do. Remember, <u>every act of will</u>, no matter how insignificant to you, <u>strengthens will</u>. Strengthening or growing will is a process. A wine does not reach its full potential overnight, and neither does will. It is going to take time. It is going to take several small acts of will, repeated often, to grow will. Do not discount small acts of will. Each small act of will (:30 minute walk on the treadmill) leads to bigger acts of will (120 minute walk). I once had a habit of drinking the equivalent of twelve cans of cola each day. Every day, every week, every month, every year, I consumed excess amounts of cola. For me, this was a deeply ingrained habit to overcome. What did I do to overcome this habit? I did what you must do; I took small steps; I exercised small acts of will. I started with not drinking soda for one day. Then, one day turned into a week. Then a week turned into a month. Then, a month turned into six months. Although I occasionally enjoy soda today, I am no longer a slave to habit. When I took first steps, my will was weak. Now, I have a strong will, the result of exercising several small acts of will.

There is no shortcut to grow will. As such, you must be patient. Once you conquer one debilitating habit, conquer another, and then another, until <u>all</u> your habits support personal strategy rather than tear it down. A strong mind can overcome and conquer several debilitating habits at once. Until you have developed invincible will, focus on eliminating one debilitating habit at a time. You should be able to eliminate any habit within 90 days. Still, questions might remain such as, 'What do I do when I slip?' and 'How do I prevent backsliding?' These are important questions, and let me be the first to tell you that you will slip; you will backslide. I did, and so will you. Fortunately, there is a process to deal with 'Moments of Weakness' (MoW).

Moments of weakness represent any situation when the temptation to oppose soul is as strong as or stronger than willing action. For example, you attend a dinner party where an all-you-can-eat dessert tray is served. A condition of your fitness goal is to avoid sugar. However, everyone is taking samples from the tray and telling you how delicious they are. What do you do? Do you give in to temptation or do you exert will and resist temptation? The number of inner soul goals you have and the nature of each goal will determine the <u>situations</u>, <u>events</u>, and <u>circumstances</u> that could lead to a 'moment of weakness'. Although mind can conjure moments of weakness by convincing self that it is ok to indulge in a debilitating habit, our environment presents the greatest temptation to will. Indulging temptation will occur from time to time, but we must do our best to resist temptations of mind, body, and environment. We must remain fortified in our commitment to our goals if we hope to achieve our goals. In short, we must overcome moments of weakness.

To overcome a MoW, requires intervention. Who intervenes? You do. Only you can stop you from succumbing to debilitating habit or to temptations of mind, body, or environment. In moments of weakness, follow the process outlined in Figure 12.19.

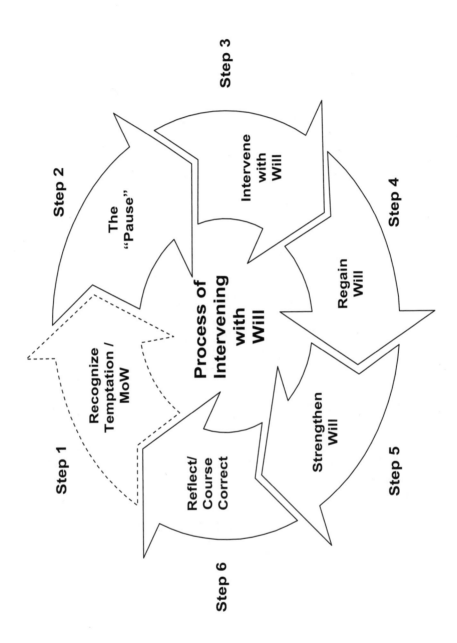

Fig. 12.19

By internalizing these six steps each time a moment of weakness occurs, you will strengthen will, thereby growing will. Step 1 is to recognize temptation; acknowledge a moment of weakness *as it is happening.* If you are actively pursuing your personal strategy, then you are constantly thinking about your goals and how best to achieve them. Keeping one's goals top-of-mind increases sensitivity to detect/recognize situations or conditions that represent a moment of weakness. This is good. Our sensitivity to recognize moments of weakness strengthens with time. Still, it is possible to succumb to temptation if one is not conscious of the moment; thus, we 'pause', which is Step 2. The 'pause' represents opportunity to <u>summon</u> will to block debilitating desires from corrupting mind.

Specifically, the 'pause' affords us opportunity to:

- Voice our goal to self (3x)
- Reflect on the consequences of yielding
- Filter out desires of mind, body, or environment
- Intervene with right thinking, right actions
- Establish new habit
- Strengthen will
- Grow will

It is in the pause that Steps 3, 4, and 5 occur. We intervene with will in Step 3 by filtering out desires of mind, body, and environment. We regain will by intervening with right thinking, right action. And we strengthen will by banishing temptation from mind. Step 6 occurs during our end of day (PM) routine, when we review the events of the day as they relate to our personal strategy. At such time, we reflect on how we handled MoW and, if needed, devise/refine our strategy of how best to handle such situation(s) in the future.

Temptation is all around us. As such, expect moments of weakness to occur daily. At first, you may not recognize that a moment of weakness has occurred until the event passes. There have been many times when I have eaten sweets without even thinking of my fitness goal, let alone the consequences of yield-ing. Do not let occasional infractions get you down. Learn from moments of weakness, and over time, your ability to detect and mitigate these situations will improve dramatically. There will come a day when Steps 1 through 5 will occur so fast that it could be considered reflex. Until that day arrives, however, it might be best to create a life aid (e.g. index card) to remind self each day (e.g. AM routine) how to handle MoW.

Just as taking small steps to exercise will grow will, so, too, does the process of intervening with will grow will. However, growing will does not rely on these actions alone. There are three requirements to grow will.

They are:

- Fixed aim
- Pursue passion
- Willing mood

There needs to be some constancy in goals for us to stabilize new thinking, new behaviors, and new actions. That is, constancy is required to develop new habits. If your goals change weekly or monthly, developing new habits to support such goals will be an exercise in futility as you constantly change gears. By fixing your aim on the main thing (i.e., inner soul goals), you awaken will for growth.

Pursing one's passions is also a requirement to grow will. Power of (divine) will only reveals itself when passion drives will. Therefore, to grow will requires pursuing desires of soul versus desires of mind, body, or environment. Our passions bring out the best in us. We are more inspired, more energetic, more com-mitted when pursuing passion. To pursue one's passion, whether it be teaching, hiking, wood-working, antiquing, or writing cre-ates a sense of aliveness and connection with life. The raw ener-gy generated from living with purpose is precisely what enables will growth to occur.

Lastly, to grow will requires a willing mood. At bottom, *you have to want to will to will.* It is that simple. If you do not command mind to exert will, then you have no will. Hopefully, your inner soul goals reflect passion and, therefore, generate strong will naturally. The excitement that comes from pursuing inner soul goals should be enough to generate and sustain a willing mood throughout life. If you are not excited about your goals in life, then you have the wrong goals. Pursue passions, and a willing mood will follow.

Now, as growing will depends on our ability to intervene with will in MoW and as temptation of mind, body, and environment is all around us, we need to understand better the forces working against us. That is, we need to understand diseases of will.

Diseases of Will

Soul, will, and mind occupy the same space (see Figure 12.20).

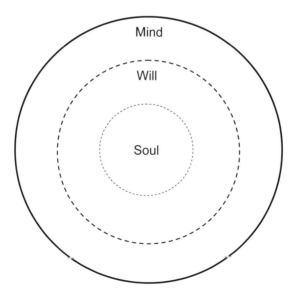

Fig. 12.20

Now, for will to function properly, that is, to filter thoughts of mind, mind must make it so. Although soul provides right direction to perform right action, if mind does not surrender to will, will succumbs to temptation of mind, body, and environment (a.k.a. 'disease of will'). Because will deals with matters of execution (i.e., doing), it is susceptible to weakness, complacency, and disease. As soul is will and will is soul, disease of will represents any thought or action that opposes soul, opposes our inner soul goals. When mind and body surrender to will, we act in ways that support rather than debilitate personal strategy. Disease of will, at bottom, represents disease of self; it is about self dealing, exalting self interests above soul's interests.

It is because we do not exert strong will, in persistence, because we allow mind, body, and environment to control us, manhandle us, and infect us that we:

- Are weak
- Do things we know we should not do
- Don't care about our goals at times
- Abandon goals
- Oppose soul
- Fail will

Know this: *disease of will only exists because you let it.* As such, you must decide whether divine will, will direct your life. You must decide whether to utilize will for personal gain. You must decide whether to awaken will. History proves that one cannot achieve his/her inner soul goals when afflicted with disease of will, as there is no will to drive new thinking, new actions, or new habits. The following statement reflects this truth:

Know will. Know achievement.
No will. No achievement.

Will is the oxygen of achievement, of purposeful living. With will, we live; without it, we die. Sadly, most people are not living, as within most people, will is dormant; lying in wait.

The long-term effect of dormant will is self confusing mediocrity with achievement. Do not let mediocrity define your life. Another long-term effect of disease of will is that it weakens will. Each time you slip, each time you succumb to desires of mind, body, or environment, you weaken will. Ultimately, the slips become more and more frequent, at which point you abandon your goals altogether. Consider that every time you indulge sugar, when your goal is to avoid sugar, you weaken will. Consider that every time you smoke, when your goal is to quit smoking, you weaken will. Consider that every time you find excuse to avoid exercise, when your goal is to exercise, you weaken will. To help you recognize disease of will, Table 12.13 highlights symptoms of disease:

Table 12.13

Symptoms of Disease of Will
• Succumbing to desire of mind, body, or environment
• Slipping more and more frequently
• Losing consciousness of soul
• Experiencing a moment of weakness
• Succumbing to debilitating habit
• Feeling guilt for betraying soul
• Progressing slowly in achieving goals
• Abandoning goals

Most of the symptoms shown above are obvious. The fact is we know when we betray soul, betray our goal. When you recognize a MoW, intervene with will. At first, intervening will be difficult, unnatural. In time, as with any action performed repeatedly, intervening will become habit, automatic.

A key to eliminating disease of will is to avoid conditions that breed disease. Table 12.14 highlights known conditions that breed disease of will.

Table 12.14

Condition that Breeds Disease	Explanation
• Use of alcohol	Alcohol softens the mind, weakening will, thus opening the door for desires of mind, body, and environment to corrupt mind, betray soul. Avoid alcohol and you avoid disease.
• Location of temptation	Going to a fast food restaurant is not what you want to do if your goal is exceptional fitness. Similarly, going to a bar is not what you want to do if trying to curb addiction. Avoid location(s) of temptation, and you avoid disease.
• Inappropriate company	Certain company may not support the emerging you. That is, certain people may instigate wrong behavior, wrong action. Avoid inappropriate company and you avoid disease.

To live a remarkable life, to achieve your inner soul goals requires a strong mind, invincible determination, and an almighty will. Few people throughout history have demonstrated to the world that they possess all three traits. Will you be one of these rare spirits? It is within your capability. You have the ability to develop a strong mind, develop invincible determination, and grow an almighty will. Resolve today, **NOW** to develop these qualities. Demand these qualities of self. Demonstrate to self and world that you are rare, strong, invincible, and almighty.

Will is *the* differentiator between success and failure. Will is *the* difference between achieving and not achieving. Will is *the* determinant of all that follows. In short, will is power. Let us explore power of will.

Power of Will

In this chapter, we have discussed several aspects or character-istics of will that contribute to power of will. For example, we discussed strength of will, determinants of will intensity, and quality of will. Each of these discussions hinted at power of will. Additionally, we discussed how (power of) will drives develop-ing new habits that help us achieve our goals. Despite these discussions, you might still be wondering what power of will is. We started this chapter with a quote from Emerson: *"There can be no driving force, except through the conversion of the man into his will, making him the will, and the will him."* Consider Emerson's choice of words. He observed will as a "driving force" of man with the key word being *force*. In the pages that follow, I will attempt to describe this very powerful, yet hidden, force we call will.

Will is a profoundly important human force. Every signifi-cant event in human history is the result of willed action, willed effort. On one level, you could say that will is responsible for every action we perform in life. For example, I will myself to get out of bed in the morning and go to work. I will myself to en-dure a job that no longer interests me because I need to pay the bills. I will myself to go to the store to buy food to feed myself and others, etc. Although it would be difficult to argue against will playing some role in directing these actions, will exists for a higher purpose. The role of will is not to drive the mundane of life, but to elevate us to greatness, to help us live a remarkable life. Consider the (willed) effort required to quit addiction (e.g., smoking, alcohol, drugs), start a new business, or force oneself to exercise five days a week versus the effort required to get out of bed in the morning. There is no comparison, as anyone who has attempted these goals would tell you. However, even these examples pale in comparison to the highest potential of will, as when, for example, a nation's people declared independence for itself, or when it ended slavery, or when it came together in solidarity following a terrorist attack. Power of will elevates individuals, communities, nations; all of humanity. It is a force that elevates good to great and great to remarkable.

The dictionary defines *force* as:

- Physical power or strength possessed by a living being
- Strength – Power – Energy – Intensity
- Mental strength
- A capacity for affecting the mind or behavior
- A powerful effect or influence

Each element of this definition tells. That is, describes will. Will is a power that all possess. Will provides us strength, power, energy, and intensity to pursue challenging goals and achieve them. Will represents mental strength; the ability to never relent until goal achieved. Will has the capacity to affect mind and behavior, as already discussed. Finally, will has the power to influence, to drive new thinking, behaviors, and actions, to form new habits, to effect a better life.

Force of will resides within; it is a construct of mind and, therefore, intangible, hidden from view. Thus, perhaps the best way to describe power of will is by example. Many people throughout history have demonstrated power of will, probably without even knowing that it was will that was responsible for their achievements. To demonstrate power of will, one need not look beyond the adversity and achievements of these remarkable people:

- Rafer Johnson
- Chris Gardner
- Eminem
- Og Mandino
- Abraham Lincoln

Consider the adversity and achievements of Rafer Johnson:

He overcame adversity...

- Poverty
- Racism
- Few resources
- Few opportunities

...To achieve greatness

- Olympic silver medal
- Olympic gold medal

Consider the adversity and achievements of Chris Gardner:

He overcame adversity...

- Homelessness
- Jail
- Few resources

...To achieve greatness

- Entrepreneur
- Self-made millionaire
- Philanthropist

Consider the adversity and achievements of Eminem:

He overcame adversity...

- Poverty
- Lack of education
- Drug addiction
- Transient
- Attempted suicide

...To achieve greatness

- 80+ million records sold
- Music producer / Founder of music label
- Academy award
- Actor
- 8 Grammy Awards
- 13 MTV Music Awards
- 6 American Music Awards
- Self-made millionaire

Consider the adversity and achievements of Og Mandino:

He overcame adversity...

- Homelessness
- Unemployment
- Alcoholism
- Disintegration of family
- Contemplated suicide

...To achieve greatness

- Successful author and lecturer
- Author of 19 books
- 50+ million books sold worldwide
- President, Success Unlimited magazine
- Inducted into National Speakers Association Hall of Fame

Consider the adversity and achievements of Abraham Lincoln:

He overcame adversity...

- Defeated for IL state legislature (1832)
- Failed in business (1833)
- Sweetheart died (1835)

- Had nervous breakdown (1836)
- Defeated for IL House Speaker (1838)
- Defeated for nomination for Congress (1843)
- Rejected for land officer (1849)
- Defeated for US Senate (1854)
- Defeated for nomination for Vice President (1856)
- Defeated for US Senate again (1858)

...To achieve greatness

- Elected 16th President of United States (1860)
- Abolished slavery
- Preserved the union

Each of the individuals described above pursued a dream against great odds. Each pursued their passions in life with great resolve and indomitable will. There are countless stories of ordinary people rising up, using will to live extraordinary lives. This is my hope for you, to rise up and live not just a good life or a great life, but *a remarkable life.* Why accept anything less? Despite your current circumstances, you can rise. Although we may enter the world with back against the wall, we can rise. It is within us all to rise. Each of the individuals profiled had their back against the world and, still, they rise. If you are living an ordinary life, ascend to a good life. If you are living a good life, ascend to a remarkable life. How do I know that such transformation is possible? Because your will, will make it so.

Consider your achievements in life. Have you:

- Graduated high school?
- Earned a college degree?
- Lost significant weight?
- Started your own company?
- Earned a promotion?
- Learned how to play an instrument?
- Overcome disease?
- Beat addiction?

- Stopped smoking (even for a short time)?
- Completed a marathon?
- Bought a home?

Whatever your achievements, the point is *you achieved*. Such achievements are the result of exerting will. Your life story is far from complete. There is still much to accomplish in your life, and force of will, will make it happen. Physical strength is weak compared to force of will. Physical strength does not enable man to lift a car; it is will which makes it so. Intellect is weak compared to force of will. If you review human history, the great accomplishments of man are more a function of will than intellect. Consider this: one can possess the intellect to earn a degree from Harvard, Princeton, or Yale and yet not achieve anything significant in life because of intermittent will. Yet a high school dropout with invincible will can be among the top 1% earners and achievers in the world. How is this possible? Because will moves mountains; intellect does not. It was will that propelled Chris Gardner, from 'Pursuit of Happiness' fame, to rise from homelessness and despair to build a multi-million dollar company, not intellect. It is will that enables the smoker to become smoke free, not intellect. It is will that drives the obese to become exceptionally fit, not intellect. It is will that enables the addicted to shake addiction, not intellect. In short, it is will that drives achievement, not intellect. Admittedly, intellect plays a role; but more than intellect, it is will that makes it so.

Power of will is a mindset, reflecting two resolves:

- Invincible determination
- The belief that failure is NOT an option

Adversity is all around us. To be human is to experience adversity. It is also human to overcome adversity. Each of the individuals profiled earlier experienced adversity and yet they rise. Adversity awakened will and will helped each rise above current condition, rise above adversity, rise to greatness. When faced with adversity, humans rise. It is part of our DNA to do so. Some rise faster, longer, and more intently than others, but all can rise. *The* factor determining how fast, how long, or how intently you rise is <u>willing mindset</u>. Previously, I mentioned how early in my professional career I learned that it is not your *aptitude* (to do something) that determines your success in life, but your *attitude* or *mindset* towards what you do that determines success. A willing mindset enables us to overcome adversity, to rise, to achieve.

Power of will is real! Its effects are profound at an individual level and greater still on a global level. My advice: embrace will. Use will. Benefit from the power of will as many before you have benefited. Rise from current condition to live a more colorful, joyous, and meaningful life experience. Choose to live remarkably. Choose to live passionately. Choose to live purposefully. Choose these things, as you will have Only One Shot to do so!

Now, having said all this, increasing power of will, won't happen overnight. Developing will, as discussed, takes time; it could take weeks, months for you to experience power of will. Just as determined you are to drive a new life plan, be determined to develop will. Developing will and driving a new life plan go hand in hand. Practice growing will. Remember that each small act of will, strengthens will. In time, presence of will, will become habit. Be patient. Once you develop power of will, you can then set your sights on ascending to the highest state of will: *the perfect will*.

The Perfect Will

What is the perfect will? Does it exist? Can one acquire or develop a perfect will? Developing will, as discussed, is a process. Consequently, to develop a perfect will first requires knowing what to develop. Thus, we conclude this chapter by discussing the characteristics and enablers that make for the perfect will (see Table 12.15).

Table 12.15

The Perfect Will is...
1.   Strong
2.   Present
3.   Invincible
4.   Persistent
5.   Driven by passion
6.   Focused on fixed aims
7.   Free
8.   Self-controlling
9.   Focused on ends not means
10. Aligned (heart, head, hands)

1. A perfect will is a strong will. It is not swayed by desires, impulses, or motives of mind, body, and environment, but by soul.
2. A perfect will is a present will. Only when will is present can it direct mind and body to achieve desires of soul. It is the function of will to maintain will.
3. A perfect will is invincible. Never does will relent in its role as filter for the mind. Never does will relent in driving right thinking, right actions. Never does will relent in focusing mind and body to achieve desires of soul.
4. A perfect will is a persistent will. A persistent will directs mind and body to achieve desires of soul every day, every week, every month, every year.
5. A perfect will is driven by passion. Passions (i.e., inner soul goals) derive from soul; as such, soul is the only suitable source to direct will. When passion drives will, great things happen.
6. A perfect will focuses on fixed aims. Inner soul goals reflect 'fixed aims'; provide context and constancy to direct will.

7. A perfect will is free. A free will is not slave to desires of mind, body, or environment. A free will exists only when inspired by that which <u>offers</u> freedom, <u>speaks</u> of freedom, and <u>desires</u> freedom: *soul*.

8. A perfect will is self-controlling. A perfect will maintains its own presence, roots out disease, and develops a habit of 'willing' action.

9. A perfect will focuses on ends rather than means. Together, will and personal strategy represent means to achieve a more important end, personal alignment.

10. A perfect will implies alignment. A perfect will exists when heart, head, and hands are aligned in thought, purpose, and spirit.

By developing these ten characteristics of will, you will develop a stronger, more effective will, capable of elevating your life experience. A perfect will is the goal. Even if you come up short, you have gained. The closer we come to developing a perfect will, the more capable and likely we are to execute personal strategy, achieve our goals, and sustain personal happiness. No longer must will lie dormant, its powers hidden from view. Know this: **as will rises, so, too, will you rise.** We know this to be true, as the saying goes, *"all things are possible to he who wills."*

Thus far in Part V, we discussed new ways to see, think, act, and feel in addition to learning about almighty will. With these discussions behind us, and considering all discussion that preceded it, we can bring together the whole of this book (thus far) to discuss as One entity, One message, One story.

Bringing It All Together

*"We spend most of our time and energy in a kind
of horizontal thinking. We move along the surface
of things...[but] there are times when we stop. We
sit still. We lose ourselves in a pile of leaves or its
memory. We listen and breezes from a whole other
world begin to whisper."*

- James Carroll

I CHOSE THE QUOTE ABOVE because it represents where we are;
where humanity is. That is, we are so busy living life that we
spend little time working on our life. Rarely do we stop our life,
sit still, and lose ourselves in thought. Rarely do we slow down,
ask questions, and listen to what soul has to say. Rarely do we
examine that which lies within, to affect that which lies without.
This is tragic, as only when we stop our life to converse with soul
can we <u>see</u> what soul sees, <u>think</u> as soul thinks, to <u>live</u> as soul
would live. In short, it is only when we lose ourselves; listen to
the breezes from our world within, that we see clearly what to
do with our life.

We have discussed much over the course of this book; many topics, many concepts, and many tools. Now, we pause, sit still, to reflect on past discussion, bringing together all the elements that comprised our journey. We bring together the story of OOS (Only One Shot); to consider as a whole. Then, we bring together all that emerged from OOS along the way. Lastly, we bring together the tools of OOS that enable personal excellence. To provide context for latter discussions, we begin by summarizing the story of OOS.

The Story of OOS

To summarize OOS, to bring it all together, requires we consider all parts of OOS as forming a whole. We do this, as we can only understand this book's true purpose by examining its content in its entirety. Thus, we bring together the whole of OOS to examine it as a complete entity, as an unfolding story (see Figure 13.1).

Our journey together began by discussing where the world is. Then, we discussed a more intimate matter, where you are. From there, we discussed the opportunity that befalls us all and the fact that we have **Only One Shot** at said opportunity. Later, we learned that with opportunity comes imperative. And from discussing imperative, opportunity, and you, we established context, obtained insight, to define personal mission, personal vision. Consequently, we defined mission, defined vision; by challenging, asking, refining what we see and how we think, act, and feel about self and life, resulting in a new set of resolves (inner soul goals). Then, we discussed how to achieve resolve by creating personal strategy. And as having personal strategy means little if we do not implement it, we discussed how to deploy personal strategy, how to 'keep score', and later how to manage (i.e., adapt) personal strategy to changes occurring in self and environment. With vision and means to achieve vision in hand, we possessed the tools and insights to realize an im-

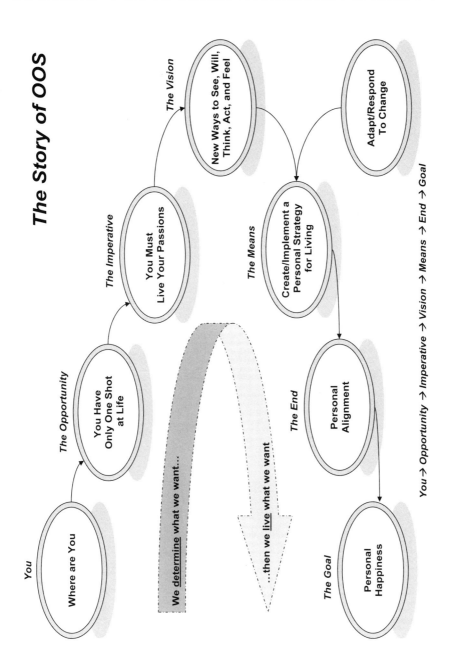

Fig. 13.1

portant end: personal alignment. Lastly, and at various points throughout OOS, we learned the true intent of OOS, the goal to which end enables: *personal happiness.*

Together, the parts of OOS provided us space, opportunity, and occasion to assess self, recognize opportunity, understand imperative, craft vision, develop means, realize an end, and achieve a goal. The story of OOS, however, was not about these activities singularly, as they represent 'how' aspects of a more important 'what.' No, the focus of this book has always been to help you discover what you want in life and from life at this point in your life; to help you increase personal happiness. We endured the parts (of OOS) to realize the whole. This was necessary, as each part played a role in light of the purpose for which the whole exists. Having said this, only by applying the whole of OOS can one improve condition and experience true happiness. The reason for this is that the story changes, weakens when we consider parts independent of whole. In this regard, the whole of OOS is much greater than the sum of its parts. We know this to be true, as to assess self but not acknowledge opportunity means little. To acknowledge opportunity but not understand imperative is tragic. To understand imperative but lack vision is misguided. To have vision but lack means (to achieve vision) is wasteful. To know the means but not the end is uninformed. Finally, to know the end but not the goal is regrettable.

Together, the parts of OOS ignited a *system of change* to help you:

- Reengineer your existence
- Design an effective personal strategy and
- Rediscover the joy of living

Like all books, OOS has a story to tell. The OOS story is one of personal transformation and the main character is you. OOS is also a story of hope, of opportunity, of reuniting self with soul to reclaim, restore that which has been lost since youth: happiness. My intent for OOS was to catalyze, to inspire, to educate, and to coach **you** with *reengineering your existence* by *designing an effective personal strategy* with the hope that you could live a more passionate, purposeful, and meaningful existence; to live a fragrant life, full of color. Above all, my intent for OOS was to help you *rediscover the joy of living*.

Throughout OOS, each successive topic (or level) provided context for future discussion, deeper inquiry, and greater personal discovery (see Figure 13.2).

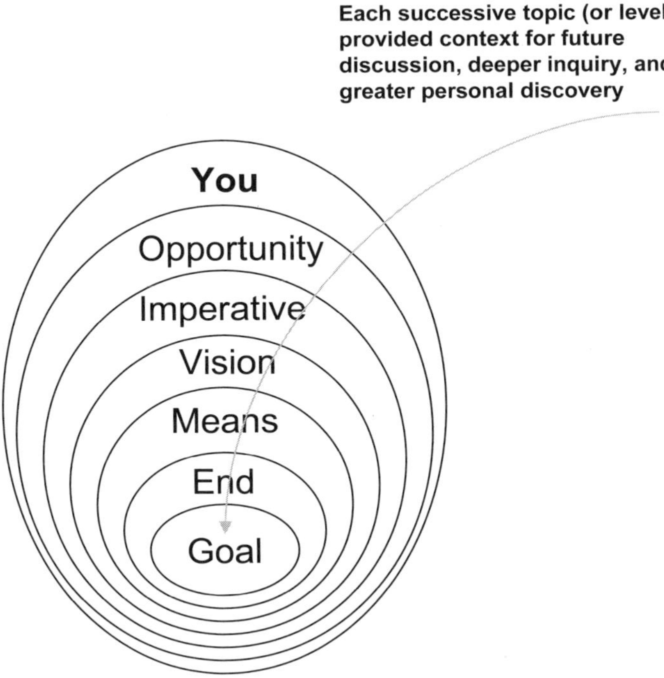

Each successive topic (or level) provided context for future discussion, deeper inquiry, and greater personal discovery

You

Opportunity

Imperative

Vision

Means

End

Goal

Fig. 13.2

In this chapter, we summarize past discussions, relate separate inquiries, and reveal what emerged along the way. At bottom, the story of OOS is about finding soul and pulling it forward, into the present, onto the surface of life, for self to live as soul would live. It is a true story, the whole story; *the only story that matters*. And when we speak of truth, when we speak of wholes, when we speak of that which matters most, we reveal essence.

The Essence of OOS

To get to essence (of anything) requires one to go beyond the immediate of an object to penetrate into the object. For example, if the object is this book ('immediate'), then to get to essence we must look beyond physical aspects of cover, paper, and ink, and penetrate into it. We must even look beyond content, beyond printed word. Specifically, it requires examining intent, of understanding purpose prior to intent giving rise to form. This is our inquiry; the point from which we begin.

So, what is the essence of OOS? Is OOS simply about developing a personal strategy for one's life? Is it about establishing personal alignment? Or is it about maximizing the life experience? Truth be told, OOS is all these things. However, the purpose of OOS is far more than creating personal strategy or learning of personal alignment. No, the purpose of OOS is fundamentally about discovering who the real you (the 'emerging you') is, and then, through designing and implementing personal strategy, realizing the emerging you. OOS was a journey into self to find soul. It was the vehicle for self to converse with soul, to learn from soul, for self and soul to come together in thought and action to realize emerging you (see Figure 13.3).

Nearly all of us, through no fault of our own, become disconnected from soul at some point in life. For most, this separation occurs early in life and continues to life's end; unresolved. The result of separation is a life denied; denied happiness, denied opportunity, denied freedom. The purpose (essence) of OOS is to close this gap; to restore self's relation with soul. It is about shifting perspective from seeing self and soul as separate to seeing self and soul as One. It is about operating from a new center,

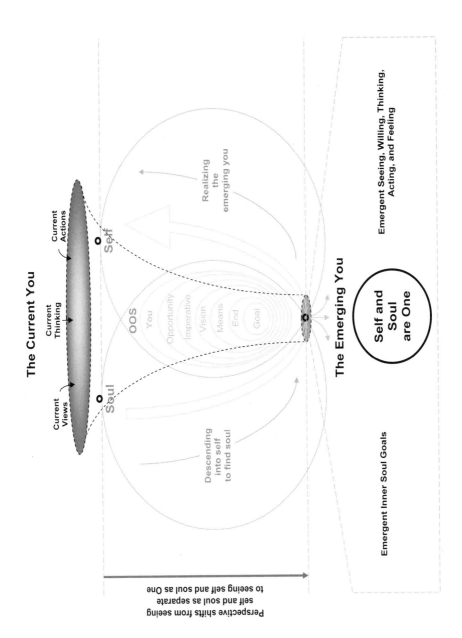

Fig. 13.3

a new source, a new plane, *soul*, versus operating from self as most people do.

With each chapter, each topic, each paragraph, you descended deeper into self to find soul. Ultimately, this 'below ground' activity, this downward movement into self, helped reveal emerging you, the authentic you, as evidenced by: 1) new inner soul goals (which reflect soul) and 2) new ways to see, will, think, act, and feel (which support soul). Sadly, most people spend little to no time cultivating or performing 'below ground' activities, thus the authentic self never emerges in their lifetime. Only when self and soul become One do we reach a point of clarity, the point at which what to do with your life becomes obvious; the point at which you discover **who** you really are. Upon discovering emerging you, began the external process of realizing emerging you by designing, implementing, and managing a personal strategy for living. Moreover, these 'above ground' activities, this upward movement, supplanted current views, current thinking, and current action with emergent views, emergent thinking, and emergent action; old gave way to new; background (soul) became foreground; what was invisible became visible.

Therefore, to summarize the essence of OOS, we observe that which remains when OOS passes by. What remains is:

- A vision for self (i.e., inner soul goals) reflecting soul
- A personal strategy to realize vision
- New ways to see, will, think, act, and feel that support soul
- Freedom, purity, and hope
- Beginnings of true happiness
- Self and soul as One
- Emerging you

These remnants, 'leave behinds', represent essence of OOS. Throughout OOS, we sought to discover who you really are and how you want to live. Your descent within was necessary to develop an authentic understanding of how to direct your life; to become more and more adequate to actuality, to soul. Essence has, indeed, given rise to new form, and that new form is the emerging you, replete with new vision, new resolves, and new imperative for your life.

To understand how parts contributed to whole, reflect essence, we briefly review each part of the OOS story beginning with the end in mind: (emerging) you.

You

Your journey began by assessing you; assessing where you are mentally, emotionally, spiritually, and physically with regards to soul, work, family, and nature. This was necessary, as before you could remove discontent, it first required *sourcing* discontent. By viewing self as system, interacting with other systems, you gained insight, visibility into underlying structure of your life (i.e., relations with soul, family, work, and nature). Knowing structure prompted you to examine key interrelationships driving current condition. This, in turn, helped you identify, clarify those aspects of your life (a.k.a. 'leverage points') that require attention, improvement. Finally, identifying key leverage points provided the basis for you to craft effective personal strategy (see Figure 13.4).

By examining the interconnectedness, or lack thereof, between self and soul, self and work, self and family, and self and nature, you obtained insight into your life to reengineer your life.

From assessing self in Chapter 2, I hope that you were able to articulate to self 'where you are'. I suspect that many symptoms existed, indicating misalignment, indicating disconnectedness, reflecting suffering. Whether symptoms indicated disillusionment with life, tension with family, or unhappiness with career, I hope that you are in a better place today; mentally, physically, spiritually, and emotionally from reading this book. Your past, and all that defines your past, is now no useful indicator for your future. Part I of your life experience is complete. Part II began the moment you stopped your life to converse with soul, to assess self, to identify your inner soul goals, and to

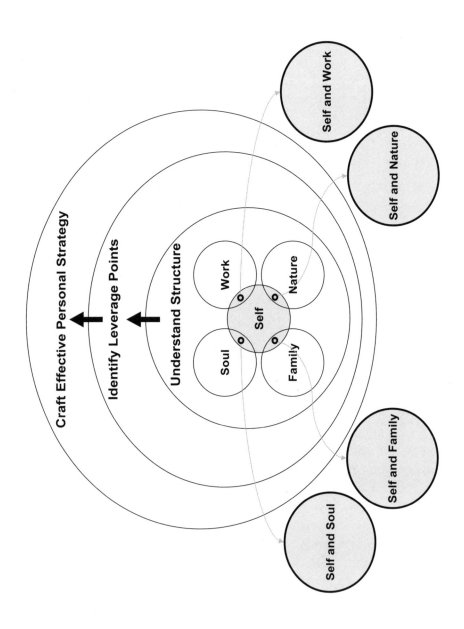

Fig. 13.4

define a personal strategy to achieve each goal. The 'current' you gave way to 'emerging' you; how glorious it is for the 'real' you to finally emerge.

You sensed change inwardly (through soul) and outwardly (through expression), and you had the courage to reveal emerging you to self and world. Sadly, most people never muster such courage; never initiate personal transformation. Despite experiencing great unhappiness, it seems that unhappiness is not enough to compel the masses to transform self; to transform one's life. This is baffling. Why do people accept unhappiness? Why would anyone, with the power of choice, choose to endure heartache for a day, let alone a lifetime? Perhaps it is because people fail to acknowledge the fact that we have Only One Shot at life. Perhaps it is because of a lack of courage. Perhaps it is both. I am glad that you had courage. I am glad that you exercised choice. I am glad that you acknowledged opportunity.

By assessing you, you developed an understanding of 'where you are', which provided needed contrast to articulate 'where you want to be'. The insights you obtained provided the basis from which to close the gap between current you and emerging you, which is how discussing [you] not only contributed to the whole of OOS, but also helped realize its true purpose, its essence. It also led us to consider opportunity.

Opportunity

None of us asks for life; we just arrive. And with arriving, comes opportunity and responsibility. What is the opportunity? It is the life experience. What is the responsibility and with whom does it rest? The responsibility is to maximize the personal, professional, and financial potential that life offers, and it rests with you. I am nearly forty years old as I write this chapter. Only a few years earlier, did I acknowledge the opportunity that is the life experience. Only a few years earlier did I realize that I, too, could maximize the personal, professional, and financial potential that life offers *if I chose to*. I regret having lived half my life without first establishing mission, vision, and a personal strategy. I regret not pursuing my passions earlier in life. Not all is lost, however, as there is still time. Time to pursue passions, time to feel the sun's warm glow, time to experience happiness as I once knew it. I now acknowledge the fact that I have Only One Shot at life, Only One Shot at opportunity, Only One Shot at happiness. I hope that you, too, acknowledge this fact. Your purchasing this book tells me that you do.

Acknowledging opportunity, as you do, is a profoundly powerful state to live in. The majority of people, my (former) self included, traverse life without ever thinking about the great opportunity that befalls us or that such opportunity will come but once. The importance of acknowledging opportunity is that it changes our perspective from simply living life to attacking life, from accomplishing little, to accomplishing achievements of a lifetime. When one acknowledges opportunity, suddenly, there is no time to waste. Suddenly, one cannot act with greater urgency to live a happier, more fragrant life.

Society tells us that when presented with opportunity, seize it. Run as far, as long, and as hard as you can, as opportunity may come but once. Yet, most do not apply this mantra to the greatest of all opportunities: the life experience. Therefore, do not squander the life experience by working in a profession/role that lacks purpose, lacks meaning, and does not inspire soul. Similarly, do not endure a relationship lost of love, as this represents false hope. We do not have a second chance at living a _more_ purposeful, _more_ meaningful, and _more_ inspired existence. When considering the life experience, there simply is no such thing as second chances. The life experience affords each of us opportunity to dream big and to achieve our dreams. It affords us opportunity, for example, to advance the knowledge of mankind, to improve the human condition, or to serve others by becoming:

- An inventor
- A writer
- An artist
- A fireman or policeman
- A scientist
- An astronaut
- A musician
- A teacher
- A business owner
- A public servant

Opportunity is with us our entire life. Take comfort in this. Achieving your goals may take years, but achievement will come; happiness will arrive. For example, to write this book required four years of effort, five days a week, two to four hours a day. I persevered. I endured. I achieved. Now, I am happy. You are capable of the same. I chose to endure; I chose to persevere because I knew that with persistent action comes achievement, and with achievement comes happiness. The greatest thing you can do for self and soul is to recognize and acknowledge the opportunity before you. Only by doing both will you make the commitment, summon will, and exert energy needed to realize emerging you. You can be what you choose to be. **Your time is now. The present is your servant.**

Thinking of opportunity, as I have described it, achieved many things:

- Provided you context and perspective to transform your life; to rise above current condition to realize better condition
- Caused you to act with urgency
- It catalyzed new ways to see, will, think, act, and feel about the life experience
- It inspired you to develop, implement, and manage a personal strategy to seize opportunity; to maximize the personal, professional, and financial potential that life offers

Only by acknowledging the opportunity before you, will you exert needed discipline, perform right actions, and make proper choices to increase personal happiness; realize emerging you. In this way, thinking of [opportunity] not only contributed to the whole of OOS, but also helped realize its true purpose, its essence. It also led us to consider imperative.

Imperative

It is a fact. Opportunity, as I have defined it, will come but once; therefore, we must live our passions. To do this requires redirecting how we view and think about the life experience. It requires shifting the source from which we operate, *from self to soul*. When this shift occurs, no longer do we see and interpret life through mind's eye, but through soul's eye. No longer do thoughts reflect self-centeredness; they reflect soul-centeredness. No longer do we live as self lives; we live as soul would live. Each of these shifts, redirections is necessary to experience true happiness. Why is this so? It is because only soul sees clearly our intended purpose in life. Only soul knows the truth of what will make us happy. Only soul can express to self how to meet imperative, how to seize opportunity. To realize the emerging you is to realize soul's intent; it is about bringing soul to the surface of life, from background to foreground, so self can live as soul would live.

To meet imperative, to seize opportunity, requires ending your current life (a life directed by self) in favor of a new life (a life directed by soul); said differently, **self must die for soul to rise**. To achieve this requires a determined shift in mindset and attitude to pursue and live one's passions, desires of soul. The moment we redirect mind and attitude to live our passions, to live passionately, is the moment we begin to reengineer our existence. It is the moment when we begin to operate from soul (as our center) versus operating from self. Most people do not live passionately. This is largely due to the fact that most people do not know what their passions are and even for those who do know, few pursue them. In Chapter 3, you contemplated these questions:

- What will be my life accomplishments?
- What will be my contribution to the world?
- How will the world remember me?

For those resolved to live a life of quiet desperation, asking these questions is pointless. However, for a determined, willful life participant like you, I suspect these questions have meaning. They do for me. I want to accomplish achievements of a lifetime. I want to contribute to the world. I want the world to have known my name. What do you want?

As previously discussed, over the course of my consulting career, I encountered dozens of people who were hurting inside. How did I know? I could see it in their faces. As face reflects the soul, when soul suffers, it shows. Often, I asked people if they enjoyed their work, if their work was meaningful, if their work represented passion, if their work inspired soul. In nearly all cases, and whether someone served as programmer, analyst, accountant, manager, secretary, or security guard, the answer to all questions was no. Upon further inquiry, I learned of their true passions, like: building custom furniture, building bicycles, teaching, studying the stars, collecting antiques, photography, building custom bird cages, archeology, and preaching the gospel.

While I conducted these impromptu interviews, I must confess, I, too, was hurting inside. For years, I consulted to industry, helping companies improve their operations, when what I really wanted to do was help people improve their lives. For me, helping one entity provided meaning, established purpose, and catered to passion, while helping the other lacked meaning, lacked purpose, lacked passion. The same was true for those I privately surveyed. What I discovered then, and now know and feel with all my being is this:

You will only know true happiness by living your passions; <u>all other pursuits</u> will deny you the happiness you crave

Imperative, as we learned, is something that demands attention or action; it is an unavoidable obligation or requirement. Therefore, let us restate your imperative: **you must always live your passions.** Be the custom furniture maker, be the photographer, be the writer, be the personal trainer, be the teacher, be the social worker, be the scientist, be the antique dealer. In short, *be you; authentic you.* To do otherwise is to waste the life experience, to deny self true happiness. This sounds harsh, but soul knows the truth. Each of us has an obligation to self and soul to live passionately, and to live one's passions demands attention, your attention. As such, the imperative is yours and yours alone. Do not let this indictment intimidate you, as you have a personal strategy designed to meet imperative. Trust in your goals, trust in your strategy, trust in (emerging) you.

The extent to which you live your passions determines the quality of your life as indicated on 'The Spectrum of Life' scale (see Figure 13.5). The good news is that you do not have to live a diminished life or even a good life. You can live a *remarkable* life. And although few can claim to have lived a 'remarkable' life, you can be among such company. You see, to live a diminished life or to live a remarkable life is a matter of choice; **a different decision one makes.** It may be hard to believe, but the difference between living in squalor and living in a beachfront mansion is choice; a <u>single</u> decision exercised by you to realize a better life.

It has been said, there is no destiny, only different choices one makes. To pursue imperative is to choose passion. To pursue passion is to choose happiness. And to pursue happiness is to choose emerging you. In learning about [imperative] you learned to make different choices for your life, which not only contributed to the whole of OOS, but also helped realize its true purpose, its essence. It also led us to consider vision.

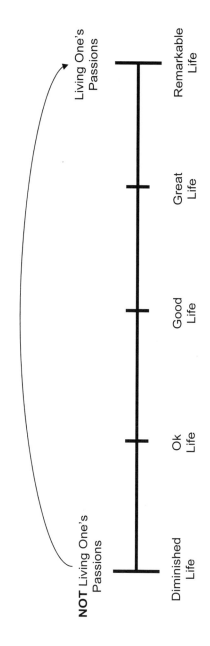

Fig. 13.5

Vision

A personal vision provides context for the life experience; it provides foundation from which to realize happiness; realize emerging you. We defined personal vision two ways: 1) as a set of inner soul goals and 2) as an explicit statement of self.

Few people ever develop a personal vision for their life, whether as inner soul goals or as an explicit statement of self. Most follow the standard life design, which is to complete high school and then either enter the workforce or complete a college degree and then enter the workforce. From there, we collect forty-five years of pay stubs. Then, we retire. This pattern describes the life experience of most people. At no point do we define what we want in life and from life. We rise, go to work, drive home, eat dinner, watch TV, and go to bed, only to do the same thing the next day; each day redundant, each day routine, each day boring! This is no way to live, but it does reflect what happens when we do not develop and execute a personal vision for self.

Developing personal vision requires seeing, willing, thinking, acting, and feeling in new ways. For many years, prior to writing this book, I felt internal restlessness that I could not articulate. All I knew was that I was not happy; something was amiss. Unfortunately, like most people who suffer from this condition, it affected all aspects of my life. I was following the standard life design, collecting pay stubs, and I was miserable. What I did not realize then, but in hindsight now do, is that I was beginning to see self and the life experience in new ways. I was beginning to think, act, and feel in ways uncharacteristic to current self. My inner soul, my authentic self, was beginning to emerge. I was not satisfied with the standard life design. I wanted more in life and from life. For me, the life experience had to represent more than collecting forty-five years of pay stubs and then retiring. I needed more! Perhaps this is how you feel. By seeing in new ways, I began to think in new ways. I began to think about what I wanted to do with my life. I began to converse with soul to determine passions; to obtain clarity of what to do with my life that only soul can provide. I began to define my inner soul goals; to define vision for self. With goals established, I took action; quick, determined, willful action. Among other things, I began to write this book. And with new actions came new feelings. Suddenly, I felt free because I was free. In liberating soul, I liberated self; I was beginning to realize emerging me. By defining vision and a personal strategy to realize vision, you too are on the path to freedom; to realizing emerging you. And with freedom, with realizing emerging you, comes happiness.

Defining [vision] not only contributed to the whole of OOS, but also helped realize its true purpose, its essence. It also led us to consider means (to achieve vision).

Means

To develop means, within the context of OOS, is to develop personal strategy. We develop personal strategy because it is the surest and most exact way to achieve our goals. As most people can attest, just to declare to self and world that one has a goal means little in terms of actually achieving the goal. For example, how many times have you declared to self and world, 'I am going to lose weight, exercise more, or start a business,' only to have the goal die on the vine a short time later? If you are like most people, the (former) me included, the answer is, "often". The reason we fail with such regularity is that to achieve a goal requires a plan, a strategy. Developing and implementing a personal strategy does more than help you achieve goals, however. It helps realize emerging you. Throughout life, each of us continually evolves in a kind of unfolding pattern – As soul evolves, so, too, does self evolve. In this regard, self and soul are never static. This, I suspect, is where you are. That is, you are in a state of unfolding; current you is giving way to emerging you and you responded. You responded with not only new inner soul goals that reflect emerging you (i.e., soul), but also a personal strategy to realize emerging you. Your response is timely and needed. Without acknowledging emerging you, without responding to unfolding soul, disconnectedness would be with you; suffering would consume you.

In addition to developing personal strategy to achieve goals
and to realize emerging you, we also develop personal strategy
to achieve that which we crave most: happiness. In Chapter 1,
we learned of humanity's suffering; that the world is full of unhappy people; so many troubled souls, lost souls. This is heartbreaking, as upon arriving on earth, the whole aim and purpose
of life is to be happy. Personal happiness underlies all aims, all
purposes one might have in life. We know this to be true, as to
have riches but not happiness is to have no riches at all. To have
power but not happiness is to have no power at all. To have life
but not happiness is to have no life at all. OOS provided space,
opportunity, and occasion to restore happiness to your life. By
developing goals that reflect unfolding soul and a personal strategy to achieve each goal, you can be happy. You possess the
tools, capabilities, and almighty will to make it happen; it is now
a matter of executing. With faith, courage, and enthusiasm, you
can be what you choose to be, you can realize emerging you.
Happiness is your birthright and it is in sight.

Learning of [means] not only contributed to the whole of
OOS, but also helped realize its true purpose, its essence. It also
led us to consider End.

End

When developing and implementing personal strategy, the desired end state is personal alignment. Defining goals to reengineer one's life can be difficult. As such, anything that can provide
clarity, context when performing this task is helpful. In addition
to insights from assessing self helping establish context to reengineer our life, discussing personal alignment also provided
context for what to improve, pursue in life. As such, discussing
personal alignment helped refine not only your goals, but also
your personal strategy to restore alignment. The utility, usefulness in discussing personal alignment, however, is not limited to
defining personal strategy, as it also serves as a good indicator
of personal happiness; of realizing emerging you. The extent to

which we <u>align</u> self with soul, self with work, self with family, and self with nature not only reveals the degree to which the real you has emerged, but also dictates the degree of happiness that is possible in your life.

The reason we seek personal alignment is that it gives rise to personal happiness. The correlation is clear: as personal alignment increases, so, too, does personal happiness increase (see Figure 13.6).

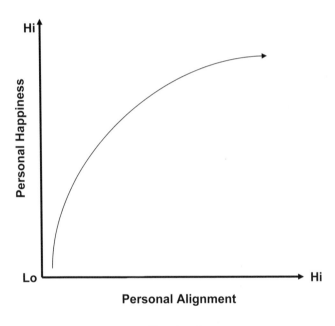

Fig. 13.6

It is because of this relationship, correlation that we say *alignment is everything*. Personal alignment is the result of pursuing the right goals and having the right strategy to achieve each goal. And although personal alignment comes in pieces, *it must come* to experience true happiness in life. When we make personal happiness our goal in life, knowing what to align and keep aligned becomes obvious. Having said this, and as much as personal happiness is the goal, *you must first make personal alignment the goal.* In other words, personal alignment is the goal before the goal.

Learning [end] not only contributed to the whole of OOS, but also helped realize its true purpose, its essence. It also led us to consider the Goal.

Goal

Aristotle declared, "Happiness is the meaning and purpose of life, the whole aim and end of human existence". Sadly, many people are not happy; not happy with occupation and career, not happy with relations, not happy with finances, not happy with looks or health, among other things. We started OOS with the end in mind. That is, we began the OOS journey by discussing You. The goal was clear: articulate to self what to change in your life to increase personal happiness and then implement change. Starting with the end in mind provided reason, cause to reengineer your existence, to transform self and life. It provided motivation and impetus to converse with soul to learn from soul. Finally, it provided the standard against which to define goals, develop personal strategy, and rediscover the joy of living.

In the end, my goal for writing this book and your goal for reading this book is the same: to increase YOUR personal happiness. OOS provided space, opportunity, and occasion for the emerging you to peek through, from future to present, to inform your life, to direct your life, to elevate your life. In short, to live happily, just as Aristotle advised us to do. In learning from the future, as it were, you began to see, will, think, act, and feel differently about self and life. Not only did your expectations of the life experience change, so, too, did the goal change. You awoke to opportunity and imperative and to merely exist would not do. You discovered what Thoreau remarked about long ago, and that is, *"To be awake is to be alive".* This was my experience as well. I, too, wanted to live, to feel alive, and when soul entered my life, it showed me what was right, which changed everything!

OOS presents an unfolding story, and like most stories, can only be understood when considering whole. Although presented in parts, the whole of OOS remains intact, with single intent; common goal. I hope that summarizing the parts of OOS helped reveal how each part contributed to the whole of OOS if not its essence.

Now that we brought together the story of OOS, we can discuss, bring together, all that emerged along the way. We do this by summarizing OOS from a systems perspective. Specifically, we summarize OOS as: a 'system of thought', a 'system of learning', and a 'system of alignment'; together, representing a system of emergence (see Figure 13.7).

You might be asking, 'Why summarize OOS as a system?' It is because to have a systems discussion, to think in systems terms, <u>is the most revealing of understanding</u>, of fostering understanding. Only by examining a system (e.g. OOS) can one understand the system, that is, to know what emerges from the system, and what emerged from OOS was extraordinary.

OOS: A System of Thought

Many times throughout this book, we discussed the notion of system and how a system can only be understood by considering its parts, together, as a whole. This book is a system comprised of chapter parts. As such, to understand this book is to consider its chapters as forming a whole. We discussed many distinct, yet related, topics ranging from personal assessment, to personal strategy, to personal alignment. Now, we must bring these discussions together as a whole; as a set of interactions; as a 'system of thought'.

Throughout OOS, many different thoughts came together in a kind of swirl of interaction, and it is from this swirl of thought that new thoughts emerged; that new thinking emerged. Throughout OOS, each successive topic (or level) provided context for future discussion, deeper inquiry, and greater personal

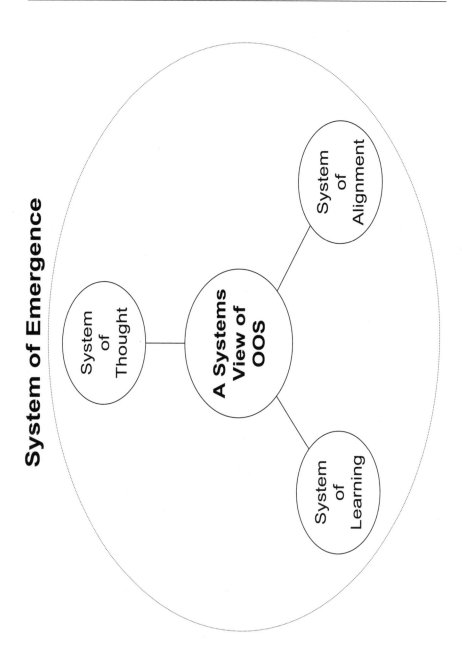

Fig. 13.7

discovery. With each subsequent discussion, not only did you become more aware of the whole of OOS, you became more aware of the whole of you; the emerging you.   You became more aware of what you want in life and from life at this point in your life. Moreover, from such awareness, you began to see, will, think, act, and feel in ways that increasingly served emerging you.

Figure 13.8 reflects OOS as a system of thought, where current thinking gave way to emergent thinking in an ongoing swirl of cognitive refinement.

With each subsequent topic, you descended deeper into self to find soul. This descent created an opening or gateway to converse with soul *to see as soul sees and think as soul thinks*. And upon meeting soul, you exist in altered state; with changed perspective, different orientation, new thinking, resulting in increased clarity, understanding, and awareness of who you really are and how you should operate on the surface of life. Let us understand how you got here.

In Chapter 2, you thought about current condition to change condition. You began to think of self as a 'system', interacting with and relating to other social systems like family, work, and nature. You began to think about life objectively by stepping outside of self to see self; to assess where you were relative to where you wanted to be, and this thinking led you to identify potential changes to make in your life to improve your life.

In Chapter 3, you thought about the opportunity and imperative that befalls us all. You thought about the meaning of life, the quality of your life, and the fact that you will pass this earth but once. This thinking led you to question what to do with remaining time on earth. Moreover, asking this question, among others, got you thinking about imperative that accompanies opportunity and how to respond appropriately. Finally, all this thinking culminated in the realization that you have no time to waste and, therefore, should take quick, determined, willful action to live happily, joyfully, purposefully each and every day.

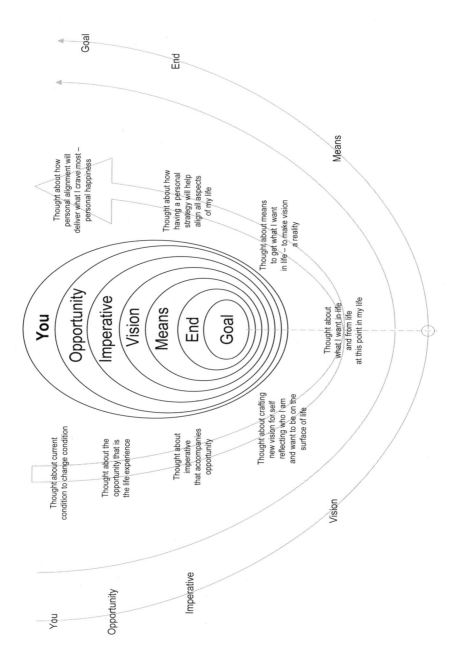

Fig. 13.8

When thinking about self combined with thoughts of opportunity, what emerged from these intersecting thoughts were <u>new</u> thoughts of:

- Wanting to seize opportunity
- Wanting to maximize the personal, professional, and financial potential that life offers
- Urgently changing condition; improving condition
- Not wanting to waste time
- What can be accomplished in my lifetime, as there is still time

I hope that these thoughts are still with you. Later, as you thought about imperative combined with thoughts of self and opportunity, it is likely that you once again began to refine your thinking. For example, it is likely that these thoughts began to emerge:

- I must pursue my passions
- I must live my passions
- I must know the priorities in my life
- I must know what I value in life
- I must know how to increase personal happiness

I hope that these thoughts are still with you. Later, in Chapter 6, you began to think about new vision for self; a vision reflecting who you are and want to be on the surface of life. You thought about crafting a new life plan designed to inject passion, purpose, and meaning into your life. This thinking, in turn, spawned new thoughts about what you want in life and from life at this point in life. Ultimately, such thinking spawned your inner soul goals, thus making vision explicit. From thoughts when crafting vision, combined with thoughts of self, opportunity, and imperative, your thinking changed yet again. For example, these thoughts began to emerge:

- I do have a vision for self and life
- Having a personal vision is necessary to meet

imperative, seize opportunity
- I know what I want in life and from life at this point in my life
- I know what my inner soul goals should be
- I know who I am, at core, within soul

I hope that these thoughts are still with you. In Chapters 4, 5, 6, 7, 9, and 10, you thought about how to realize vision. You thought about how to design personal strategy to achieve your goals and later how to manage and adapt personal strategy to changes occurring in self and environment.

From the thinking that occurred when developing means (personal strategy), combined with thoughts on self, opportunity, imperative, and vision, your thinking changed once again. For example, these thoughts began to emerge:

- How to design a personal strategy to achieve my goals, meet imperative, and seize opportunity
- How my personal strategy will help realize vision
- How to course correct personal strategy as I change and my environment changes
- How to overcome obstacles when implementing personal strategy

I hope that these thoughts are still with you. In Chapter 8, you began to think about personal alignment and the meaning behind the statement, "Alignment is everything". You began to think about the degree of alignment that exists between self and soul, self and work, self and family, and self and nature. This thinking led you to identify what was misaligned in your life and how such misalignment was affecting you and others.

When thinking of end (personal alignment), combined with thoughts of self, opportunity, imperative, vision, and means, your thoughts changed yet again. For example, these thoughts began to emerge:

- I know which aspects of my life are misaligned and how my personal strategy will restore alignment

- To establish alignment is to meet imperative
- Personal alignment is necessary to seize opportunity; to maximize the personal, professional, and financial potential that life offers
- I understand how being aligned would improve my life, increase personal happiness
- Personal alignment is everything

I hope that these thoughts are still with you. Finally, in Chapters 11 and 12, if not throughout the whole of OOS, you began to think about how to see, will, think, act, and feel in ways to achieve the goal: a happier you.

When thinking of the goal combined with thoughts of self, opportunity, imperative, vision, means, and end, your thoughts changed yet again. For example, these thoughts began to emerge:

- The path to happiness is sourced by soul
- Understanding opportunity and imperative only amplifies the need and urgency to establish and maintain personal happiness
- Vision should reflect that which will make me happy
- Means should align all energies (seeing, willing, thinking, acting, and feeling) to establish and maintain personal happiness
- Personal alignment is the key to sustained personal happiness

I hope that these thoughts are still with you. I hope that each discussion, beginning with assessing 'where are you', led to deeper inquiry, broader insight, and greater personal discovery. Each subsequent discussion resulted in intersecting thought, and as thoughts collide, new thinking emerged; new thinking, better thinking, holistic thinking. Collectively, this thinking generated deeper awareness of who you are and want to be. With increased awareness of who the 'real' you is, you are now empowered to direct all aspects of you (seeing, willing, thinking, acting, and feeling) to bring emerging you to the surface. I wrote OOS as a system of interconnected topics where the whole of OOS means more, represents more, than the sum of its parts. Together, the parts of OOS provided us space, opportunity, and occasion to deepen our sense of self through connected, inspired, and cascading dialogue. However, to say that OOS was just a 'system of thought' or just an opportunity to engage in dialogue discounts your true accomplishments, as much occurred over these pages; you not only engaged in much thought, you engaged in much learning.

OOS: A System of Learning

Thinking enables learning. As we think, it leads to more thinking, which, in turn, inspires yet more thinking, which collectively enables learning. Consequently, the system of thought just discussed naturally gave rise to a 'system of learning' (see Figure 13.9).

For example, when discussing **you**, you learned:

- That to change condition requires stopping your life to observe condition
- That you are a system (of One), and to understand self-disconnectedness, self-suffering requires examining the interactions that exist between self and other social systems
- Where you are mentally, physically, emotionally, and spiritually with regards to soul, work, family, and nature
- What to change in your life to improve your life

When discussing **opportunity**, you learned:

- That the life experience is an opportunity to maximize the personal, professional, and financial potential that life offers

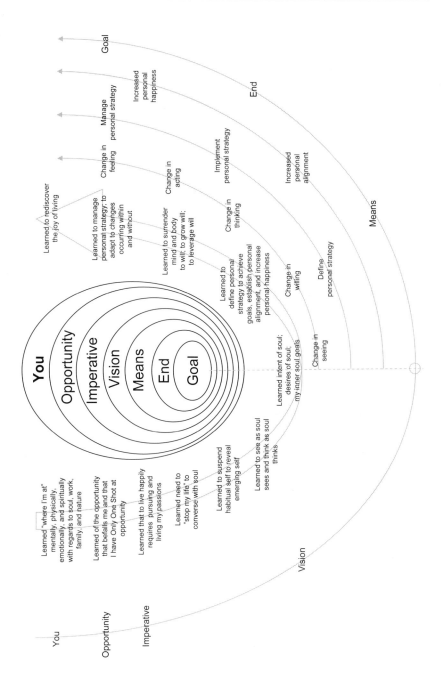

Fig. 13.9

- That opportunity will come but once
- That you still have time to be whoever you want to be; to seize opportunity
- That the majority of people do not seize opportunity, but live in quiet desperation
- That the great achievers recognize opportunity and seek to maximize the life experience; to achieve accomplishments of a lifetime

When discussing **imperative**, you learned:

- That to be happy requires pursuing and living your passions
- That passions come from within; are sourced by soul
- That to seize opportunity first requires meeting imperative
- That to meet imperative is your responsibility and yours alone

When discussing **vision**, you learned:

- What it means to create a vision for self and life
- To be still; to embrace silence, as silence is the gateway to soul; facilitates hearing soul
- How to converse with soul; to ask questions of self for soul to respond
- To see as soul sees and think as soul thinks
- The "truth," as only soul knows it
- To suspend current self, habitual self, to reveal emerging self
- How to translate vision into new resolves; inner soul goals
- How to represent your goals on a Personal Strategy Map
- That your personal strategy represents 'emerging you'

When discussing **means**, you learned:

- How to define single goal strategy via Personal Strategic Themes
- How to define support goals, performance measures, and initiatives to achieve each inner soul goal
- That you must change your seeing, thinking, acting, and feeling to support personal strategy
- How to manage your personal strategy to reflect changes occurring within and without
- How to surrender mind and body to act in accordance with will

When discussing **end**, you learned:

- The dimensions of personal alignment
- That your personal strategy should help restore personal alignment
- That to achieve personal strategy is to achieve personal alignment
- That personal alignment enables personal happiness
- That only by becoming self-aligned can you meet imperative, seize opportunity
- That establishing personal alignment begins with aligning self with soul which then enables aligning all other aspects of your life
- The meaning behind the statement "Alignment is everything"

Lastly, you learned that OOS is not about means or even end, but about a more important issue, a more immediate issue, a private issue: increasing personal happiness.

You have indeed learned much, but you did more than learn about self and soul, you aligned self <u>with</u> soul.

OOS: A System of Alignment

If you are like most people who bought this book, misalignment
is with you; affecting you, debilitating you. The days of personal
<u>mis</u>alignment, however, are diminishing. With a personal vision
to direct your life and a personal strategy to realize vision, you
are positioned to restore alignment to your life. Throughout OOS,
you experienced a swirl of thought and learning, and together both
enabled alignment to occur. First, you aligned self with soul. Now,
with implementing personal strategy, you are aligning all other aspects of your life: self with work, self with family, and self with nature (see Figure 13.10).

OOS was the vehicle that enabled self and soul to come
together, to align, to become One. What began as inner work
to align self with soul became outer work of aligning self with
work, family, and nature. Together, both efforts helped realize
the subtitle of this book: *aligning the inner soul with action*. To
achieve personal strategy is to achieve personal alignment. As it
stands, both tasks remain unfinished, as it may take months and
years to achieve personal strategy, achieve personal alignment,
depending on your inner soul goals. Do not be discouraged by
'the waiting', as each day represents movement.

From the moment you began assessing self, to the moment
you defined personal strategy, to now, much has been emerging.
Emergence is the real story of OOS; it is the undercurrent that
defines our journey together. As such, we conclude this section
by summarizing OOS as a 'system of emergence'.

OOS: A System of Emergence

The term 'emergence' represents a gradual beginning, a coming
forth of new properties. Emergence is a process that refers to
something 'becoming visible'. Using these definitions, one can
observe that from the moment you began reading this book,
emergence was occurring (see Figure 13.11).

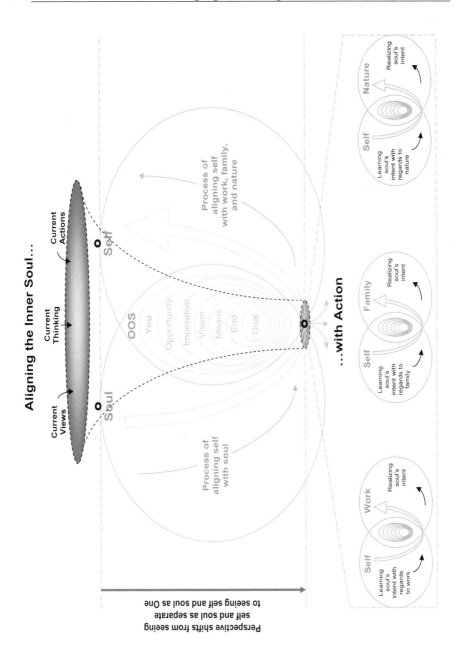

Fig. 13.10

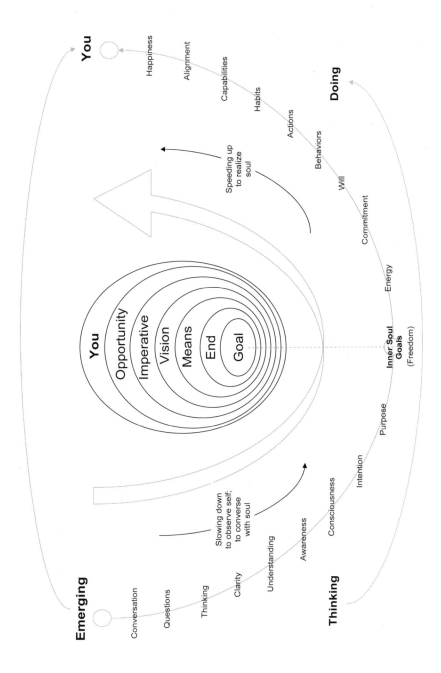

Fig. 13.11

What emerged first was conversation. OOS provided space, opportunity, and occasion for self to reunite with soul; to converse with soul. And within the stillness, amidst the darkness, questions emerged. Questions asked by self, but responded to by soul, revealed 'where you are'. From questioning self, new thinking emerged: thinking about self, about life, about where you are, and more importantly, where you want to be. Moreover, with questioning, constant thinking, clarity emerged: clarity regarding the cause of discontent in your life; the dimensions of your life which were misaligned and, therefore, responsible for current condition. Ultimately, by assessing self, what emerged was a deeper understanding of you. And with understanding, came awareness. You stepped outside self to see self, and in the process, became aware of your thoughts, feelings, and actions; you descended past habitual self to reveal emerging self.

From awareness emerged new consciousness. You became conscious of what to do in life, how to direct your life. You possessed insights to begin transformation, to start life anew. From such consciousness emerged intention. From deepening conversation between self and soul, you revealed intention's of soul; desires of soul. Moreover, from revealing intention, emerged purpose. Suddenly, what to do with your life became obvious. And from purpose emerged inner soul goals; freedom. You were free to live as soul would live.

Freedom, in turn, spawned new energy. Pursuing passions has a way of energizing us, inspiring us, like nothing else can. With new energy emerged new commitment. And from commitment emerged (divine) will. From applying will, what later emerged were new behaviors. And with new behaviors, emerged new actions; new habits. With swapping old behaviors, old actions with new behaviors, new actions, you began to replace debilitating habits with habits that inspire; habits to drive personal strategy. And, from implementing and managing personal strategy, what emerged were new capabilities. You developed the capability, for example, to converse with soul, to surrender mind and body to act in accordance with will, to overcome stumbling blocks of personal strategy, and to adapt personal strategy to changes occurring in self and environment. In short, you developed the capability to manage you. And, alas, with new capabilities, with implementing personal strategy, what emerged was alignment. By first aligning self with soul, you initiated, cleared the way, to align all other aspects of your life. Lastly, and most importantly, with increased personal alignment, what emerged was increased personal happiness.

Now, of the various forms of emergence that occurred along the way, the most important thing that emerged was the authentic you, the 'real' you: soul. For without realizing authentic you, one cannot experience true happiness. The system of emergence that occurred throughout OOS represented a movement from thinking to doing; from slowing down to observe self, to converse with soul, to speeding up to realize soul. The essence of OOS was about bringing emerging you to the surface of life. By conversing with soul, you discovered who the real you is. Then, with action, you realized emerging you. Although it may take years to achieve your goals, at least the authentic you 'emerged'; at least you have begun the process.

Thus far, we brought together the story of OOS and that which emerged along the way. Now, in the final section of this chapter, we bring together the frameworks, tools, and actions of OOS that not only formed our approach to reengineer you, but also enabled Total Personal Excellence.

Approach to Reengineering You

Over the course of this book, you performed many actions, utilized several frameworks, and applied numerous tools from the personal strategy toolbox. Now, we bring these actions, frameworks, and tools together to present in unified form. We begin by summarizing the key actions, 'approach', to reengineer you.

A key 'how-to' goal of OOS was to help you reengineer your life; to inject new breath into what was, perhaps, a stale existence. There are many reasons why someone would want to reengineer their life: wrong career, wrong partner, wrong surroundings. To reengineer self, however, requires a strategy, an approach. To be specific, it requires performing certain key actions: *1ˢᵗ order actions* (see Figure 13.12).

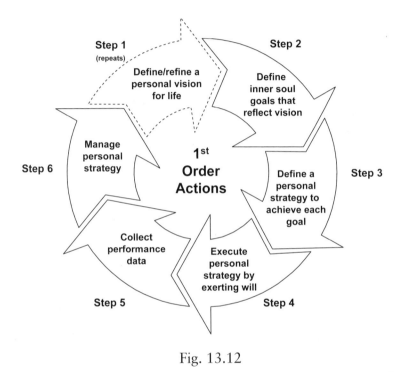

Fig. 13.12

To reengineer (anything) first requires a plan or vision. You defined vision. With vision, you set the wheels of change in motion. Next, it was necessary to define new resolves, a set of inner soul goals that reflected vision. You defined goals. Knowing destination but lacking a map, the next step was to define strategy to achieve each goal. You developed strategy. With strategy in hand, the next step was to execute strategy; to begin realizing emerging you. You have begun executing strategy. To ensure effective strategy, the next step was to monitor performance using support goals and performance measures to provide feedback.

Finally, with feedback, you could manage personal strategy. Now, although performing 1st order actions is necessary to reengineer one's life, on their own, they are insufficient. As such, it requires performing ***2nd order actions*** (see Figure 13.13).

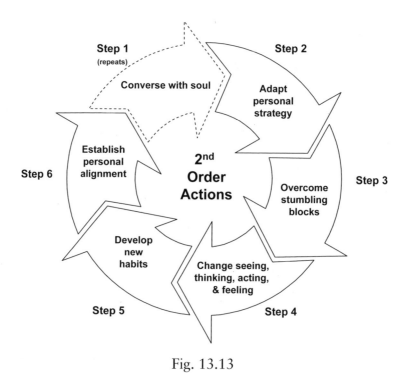

Fig. 13.13

If 1st order actions represent defining and deploying personal strategy, 2nd order actions represent course correcting personal strategy. Life is an unfolding process. Just as nature follows a cycle of birth, death, and re-birth, so, too, do we follow such a cycle. In our case, however, what is dying is not external but internal; outdated goals and the strategy to achieve such goals. Consequently, as soul unfolds to reveal itself anew, self responds. Fresh seeing, fresh thinking, fresh actions replace current seeing, current thinking, and current actions. Our unfolding soul triggers 2nd order actions; which we perform n times throughout life.

Living by a personal strategy is a lifelong endeavor. Consequently, as your environment changes, as you change, so, too, will your personal strategy change. Because personal happiness is a moving target, because desires of soul change over time, we must adapt strategy to reflect such changes; otherwise, we jeopardize our happiness; become misaligned. By managing change, whether internal to self or external in environment, your vision, goals, and personal strategy will <u>always</u> reflect emerging you; unfolding soul.

Together, 1st and 2nd order actions do more than form an approach to reengineer you, they enable Total Personal Excellence.

Total Personal Excellence

Total personal excellence (TPE) is, at once, a goal and a state of being. It represents a place to which to strive. It is a place characterized by:

- Total personal alignment
- High achievement
- Deep internal happiness
- Maximizing the life experience

The TPE Framework (see Figure 13.14) is a way to visually depict the components that enable total personal excellence. What is illustrated is that the TPE Framework is comprised of a series of building blocks; *interconnected steps*. We discuss the components of the TPE Framework next.

Components of the TPE Framework

We can divide the components of the TPE Framework into two categories:

- Foundational elements
- Key actions

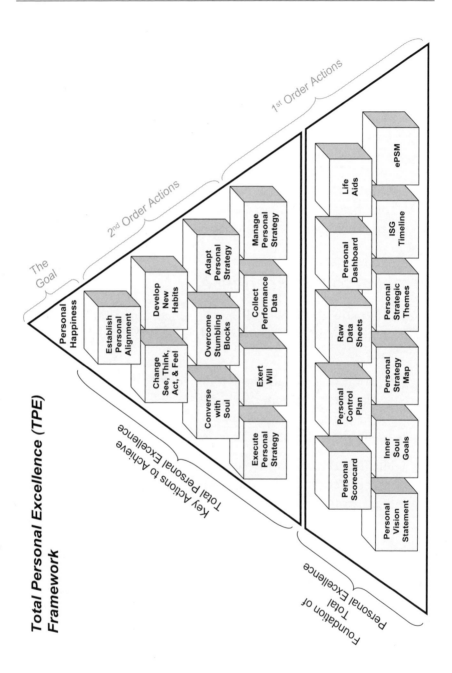

Fig. 13.14

Foundational elements represent those things that ensure personal excellence – however you define it. Foundational elements include:

- Developing a personal vision statement
- Crafting goals that reflect vision
- Developing a personal strategy composed of:
  - Personal Strategy Map
  - Personal Strategic Themes
    - ePSM
    - Personal Scorecard
- Raw Data Sheets
- ISG Timeline
- Personal Control Plan
- Personal Dashboard
- Life Aids

We build a life of achievement and happiness from these foundational elements. Although foundational elements may change with the years, they are always with us. Personal vision may change, personal strategy may change, the life aids we employ may change, but they remain – helping us realize The Goal.

Establishing the foundation of personal excellence represents only design work. Consequently, what remains is to execute design. We execute design by performing these key actions:

- Converse with soul
- Change how we see, think, act, and feel
- Collect personal performance data
- Execute personal strategy
- Manage personal strategy
- Overcome stumbling blocks
- Adapt personal strategy
- Exert will
- Develop new habits
- Establish personal alignment

Collectively, these actions determine whether we achieve total personal excellence; achieve The Goal. As such, we need to perform all actions as just performing one or a few actions will not do. Each action plays a role in helping us achieve our goals, establish personal happiness, and live a remarkable life. And when we combine persistent, focused action with thoughtful design, great things happen. To understand how greatness occurs, we discuss the TPE model at work.

The TPE Model at Work

It is most instructive to think of the TPE model as a set of integrated gears (see Figure 13.15).

At first, we engage gear one, which consists of developing vision, establishing goals for your life, and developing personal strategy. We have movement. Next, we engage gear two, which consists of executing personal strategy, exerting will, collecting personal performance data, and managing personal strategy. With engaging gear two, gear one is now moving with greater intensity and force. Lastly, we engage gear three, which consists of conversing with soul, changing how we see, think, act, and feel, overcoming stumbling blocks, adapting personal strategy to changes in self and environment, and developing new habits. When engaging gear three, gear two moves with greater intensity and force, which again increases the momentum of gear one. Now, just as a car engine requires fuel to keep the engine going, so, too, does the TPE engine need fuel. The fuel this engine requires, however, is will. Only with will, does engine engage, gears turn. The good news is that this fuel source is abundant, if you want it to be. Together, such gears produce a powerful engine of change to establish personal alignment, restore personal happiness, and achieve total personal excellence. Perhaps the most profound and powerful outcome that results from combining key elements with key actions is that it establishes tremendous leverage over the life experience.

Fig. 13.15

Leverage over the Life Experience

Leverage is an incredibly powerful force. Leverage is defined as having positional advantage; the power to act effectively. It also means to have control. As it relates to personal strategy, it means having the power to realize any goal. Can you imagine wielding so much power, possessing so much leverage over the life experience that achieving ANY goal is possible? It is exciting to think of such power; the great things you will do; the remarkable accomplishments you will achieve. Such power lies before you in the form of this book. How is this so? Power originates from applying the tools of OOS onto the place of highest leverage for personal change – *the space between inner and outer; the fieldline of our life* (see Figure 13.16).

The <u>place</u> of highest leverage to effect change in our life is the *narrow band* between inner and outer; the *shared space* above and below the fieldline of life. We refer to this space as the physical interface as it straddles the 'plane' of the life experience. Because the physical interface encompasses both outer and inner, that which occurs within affects that which occurs without, and vice versa, hence revealing why the physical interface is the highest leverage point to transform our life. Because the physical interface is *the* key leverage point to affect our life, we direct all our energies (i.e., tools, actions, frameworks of OOS) onto such interface. It is because most other efforts/approaches to transform one's life consider only outer, neglect inner that they fail. The TPE model works because it encompasses both spheres in which we operate.

The tools we utilize on the surface of life (physical tools) include:

- Utilize life aids
- Manage strategy
- Overcome obstacles
- Collect data

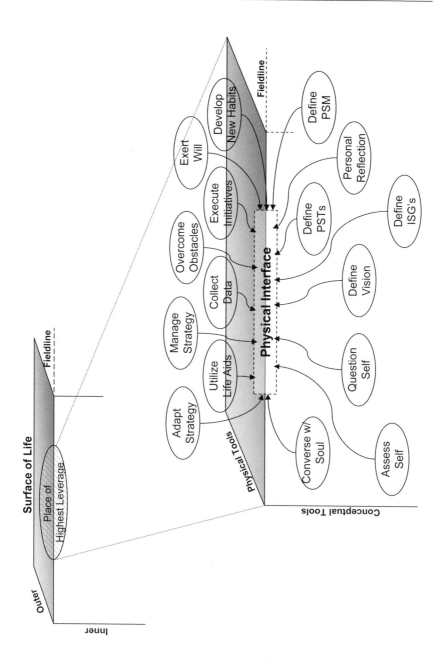

Fig. 13.16

- Execute initiatives
- Exert will
- Develop new habits
- Adapt strategy

The tools we utilize below the surface (conceptual tools) include:

- Converse with soul
- Assess self
- Question self
- Define vision
- Define ISGs
- Define PSM
- Define PSTs
- Engage in personal reflection

It is important to discuss the interface that lies between outer and inner, because the extent to which you attend to, nurture, and cultivate the physical interface determines success or failure with reengineering you; with achieving personal excellence. The interface that joins both spheres in which we operate is the highest leverage point to alter/shift one's reality. As such, the tools we apply to such interface, when used properly, can transform your life; can establish significant leverage over the life experience.

Ultimately, increasing one's leverage over the life experience depends on the degree with which one manages the factors that drive the life experience (see Figure 13.17). Three factors drive the life experience:

- Ability to manage that which lies within
- Ability to manage that which lies without
- Ability to establish competitive advantage

Managing that which lies within represents a major milestone in establishing leverage over the life experience. Having said this, simply knowing innate skill or desires of soul is not enough. It is equivalent to knowing the winning lotto numbers without buying a ticket; in other words, such knowledge, on

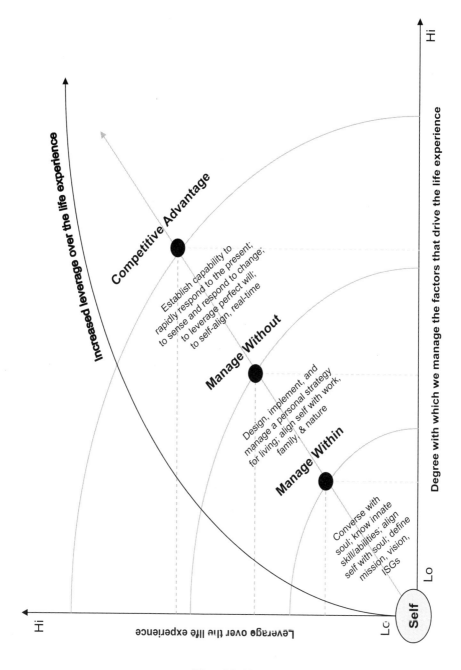

Fig. 13.17

its own, does us no good. It requires taking action; managing without.

When we develop a capacity to manage that which lies without we experience a step increase in our leverage over the life experience. This more advanced form of personal management delivers a heightened state of living that few individuals ever experience, not because of a lack of ability, but because of a lack of commitment. For those who pay the price to experience this heightened state, there exists an even higher plane to ascend. If your goal is to live a world-class life; a life so fragrant, so colorful, so meaningful that your life becomes a model for others to emulate, there exists an even more advanced form of personal management to which one can aspire. To ascend to this most refined state of living, requires one to develop and manage the following capabilities:

- Ability to rapidly respond to the present
- Ability to sense and respond to change
- Leverage perfect will
- Ability to self-align, real-time

With these capabilities, the world is yours for the taking. No goal will be too out of reach, as you will have developed a competitive advantage of the highest order; advantages, I might add, few people possess.

In this chapter, we brought together the elements of OOS to present as a whole, as an unfolding story. From my perspective, Only One Shot represents an intervention; an intervention to transform you and your life. I hope that the intervention worked. That is, I hope that you have begun personal transformation. We do not ask for life, but having arrived, the aim and purpose of life is happiness. Make it your immediate and life-long goal to be happy. Take the necessary steps; continue with your personal transformation. You can be happy; it is within your control, and therefore **it is possible**. How do I know? I know because not long ago, I intervened to transform my own life. I took necessary steps to establish personal alignment and restore happiness to my life. Although my transformation is far from complete, it is now my immediate and lifelong goal to be happy. I could not live any other way. I suspect that this is your story as well.

Part V of this book was about setting a course for personal excellence. We now know that this entails seeing, thinking, acting, and feeling in new ways. It also entails using power of will to direct all aspects of self and life. Lastly, it entails attacking life with new approach, new expectations, and new attitude. Now, we transition to the last section of this book (Part VI), where we descend within to discuss the spiritual side of things; to explore the hidden, the powerful, *our source for operating* – almighty soul. We discuss soul, as *to find one's soul and pull it forward, into the present, onto the surface of life, for self to live as soul would live, is the main reason I wrote this book.* For if we do this, if we Let Soul Sing, happiness follows.

PART VI
Let Soul Sing

One King

"A multitude of rulers is not a good thing.
Let there be one ruler, one king."

- Homer

MANY THINGS SEPARATE US: race, religion, sex, personality, education, wealth, appearance, culture, beliefs, and location. For all of our differences, though, and regardless of degree, a universal truth, a shared trait, a common bond unites us all: it is *soul*. All of us, the entirety of humanity, possess soul. Soul is the cipher of humanity, as when you strip away that which separates us, all that remains is soul. Soul is that part of us that represents authentic being, who we are at essence, core. Soul connects us; with single voice, universal tones does it speak to us, unite us. Because our journey together is nearing the end, and because you are still in the early stages of executing personal strategy, it is important to pause to validate the source from which you operate. That is, it is important to ensure that personal vision, inner soul goals, and personal strategy reflect whole; authentic self; soul. To perform this source-level check, we discuss the primary sources from which all seeing, willing, thinking, acting, and feeling emanate. By chapter's end, it will be evident as to the source from which <u>you</u> operate; hopefully, it is soul.

To ask, '*Where you operate from*' is to ask what is the source from which you view and approach life. And how you answer this question has great ramifications for your life. In fact, how you answer this question determines the quality of your life; where you fall on the 'Spectrum of Life' scale. Answer the question one way and you experience a remarkable life, answer the question differently and you experience a life diminished. Of all the questions one could ask self, the question, '*Where do I operate from*' is perhaps the most important. It is because most people never ask this question or do not understand the ramifications of answering one way versus another that most live in quiet desperation. Therefore, since your entire life experience and all that emerges from it (personal, professional, and financial success) depends on how you answer this question, we address this most fundamental aspect of you: *the <u>source</u> from which you operate.*

There are only two ways to operate in life: 1) you can operate from **self** or 2) you can operate from **soul** (see Figure 14.1).

As illustrated, when we operate from self, we operate to the exclusion of soul. That is, a disconnect, barrier, exists between self and soul, leaving all that follows (one's seeing, willing, thinking, acting, and feelings) driven by desires of self versus desires of soul; *self is dominant.* Conversely, when we operate from soul, self and soul are One. That is, they occupy the same space, and what drives one's seeing, willing, thinking, acting, and feelings is not self, but soul; *soul is dominant.* In the next few sections, we discuss these sources from which to operate. You will discover that when we operate from soul, it results in a much different, much better life experience than when we operate from self. You will discover that a life operated from soul results in happiness, joy, and achievement, whereas a life operated from self, as the majority of people possess, denies one happiness, joy, and achievement; words that should characterize every

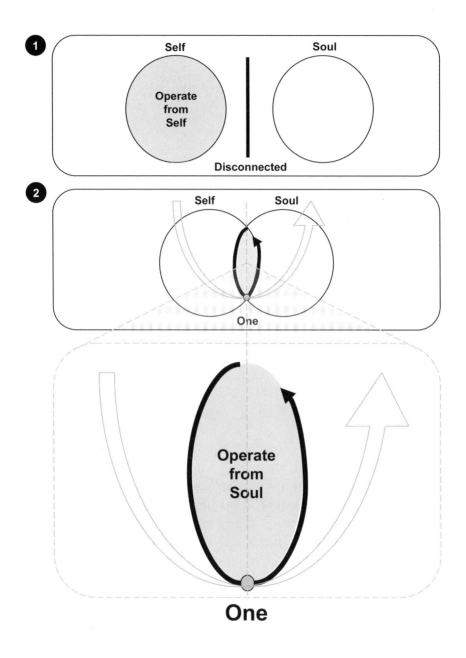

Fig. 14.1

life experience. Now, because this examination, validation, of the source from which you operate concerns the quality of your life, tread the next few sections slowly, not only to internalize text, but also to ensure that all that follows in your life is driven not by imposter king (self) but by our one true king (soul).

Operating from Self

When operating from self, soul plays little to no role in guiding one's life, as desires of self drive what one sees, wills, thinks, acts, and feels. Most people operate this way, as it is the <u>default</u> mode of operating, of living. Sadly, the consequence of operating this way is a life diminished. How do I know? I operated this way for nearly all my adult life. I suspect that you have as well.

The effects of operating from self are both significant and destructive. At first, operating from self affects how we see the world. For example, instead of viewing the life experience as an Only-One-Shot opportunity to maximize the personal, professional, and financial potential that life offers, we view the opportunity as something less; less grand, less urgent, less meaningful. Instead of viewing life as an opportunity to live passionately, to meet life's imperative, we view life as 'something to get through'. Do not get me wrong; those who operate from self are still ambitious, still successful in their own way as they set goals and try to achieve them, but the goals set are usually of a lesser kind, commitment to achieve such goals often wanes, and life achievements are modest, at best. When one considers that 'what one sees' affects all that follows, one realizes just how significant <u>source</u> for seeing the world is.

When operating from self, desires of mind, body, and environment drive will versus soul driving will. This difference in what one attends to in life is significant. When desires of mind, body, and environment drive will, rarely do we achieve our goals. Why is this so? It is because self is weak, whereas soul is formidable. Consequently, when operating from self, will succumbs to desires of mind, body, and environment, in the moment. As our desires change, as we vary moment to moment, day to day, month to month, so, too, does will vary, making it all but impossible to achieve any goal. Indeed, it is because most people operate from self that they are in the condition they are in. The long-term consequence of operating this way is that we form debilitating habits, reinforce debilitating patterns, and as we reinforce such habits, patterns daily, we become increasingly captive to our past and, therefore, increasingly incapable of breaking free from the 'Cycle of Desperation' we long urgently to exit (see Figure 14.2).

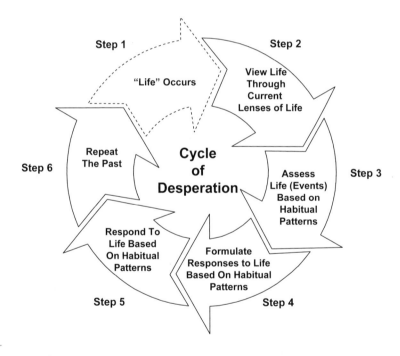

Fig. 14.2

When caught in the Cycle of Desperation, we view life through our current, tired lenses of life (Steps 1 and 2). Consequently, when we see the world through tired, habitual eyes, we respond to life with tired, habitual action (Steps 3,4,5).

The trouble with this is that it results in repeating, perpetuating the past (Step 6). Our future becomes little more than a reenactment of our past. This is why those who operate from self often fail to achieve their goal to lose weight, stop smoking, exercise regularly, etc., because they are burdened by their past; they are burdened by debilitating willing, thinking, and acting, resulting in more of the same. Thus, if your goal is to change your life, to reengineer your life, you must break free of the debilitating patterns (i.e., habits) that have defined your past. You must break free of historical you to realize emerging you. In short, you must break free from the circle of desperation; *must form a new circle.* Without changing your life pattern and the habits that perpetuate such pattern, odds are against you in transforming your life in any meaningful way.

It is a certainty. You will experience a lower quality of life when operating from self than when operating from soul. Life will be less joyful, less inspired, less grand. The tragic outcome of living this way is that over time, the flame of one's soul dims; one's true self, authentic self, snuffed out, never to rise to surface, never to see light of day. When this occurs, we become numb to life (to work, family, and nature), as our spirit sleeps somewhere cold. Short of death, this is, perhaps, the greatest of all human tragedies as life becomes, in the words of Thoreau, one of quiet desperation. And quiet desperation is just a polite way of indicating *slow death.* It is sad to think that many people live this way, that is, feel deep unhappiness, but this is the inevitable, predictable, destructive result of operating from self. To operate from self is to live an alternate reality; a lesser reality; a reality not meant for this world; In short, it means to exist as imposter self.

Imposter Self

What does it mean to exist as imposter self; to live an imposter life? To answer this question, let us first define the word imposter. An imposter is one that practices deception, one that assumes false identity. When one considers this definition, the

following elements jump out: 'practices', 'deception', 'false', and
'identity'. What do these words reveal about how most people
approach and experience life today? As it turns out, using the
word 'imposter' to describe most people's life experience is more
relevant than you may think. As we learned in the last section,
to operate from self is to live a diminished life. A life whereby:

- One experiences a **false** reality; a product of self not of
  soul
- One's **identity** represents not their 'true' authentic self,
  but an alternate, lesser form
- One's actions, **practices** are inspired by lesser goals
- Personal **deception** masks what could be – a remarkable
  life – with what is – a life diminished

Given this additional detail, what can we now say about
what it means to live as imposter self? To live as imposter self
means to live as someone other than who you really are. Who is
the 'real' you? It is soul; *the emerging you.* To live as imposter
self means to live, to practice, an alternate identity, a false reality,
a reality deceptive to who you really are, and I might add, *who
you want to be.*

In Chapter 6, we discussed the relationship between self
and soul. Specifically, we discussed the importance of conversing with soul to discover one's true intentions (i.e., goals) in life,
as this is a prerequisite to reengineer one's life. We also discussed
that the 'quality of the descent' from self into soul determines
whether we discover true intention (true purpose) for our life or
whether we continue operating from false intention (imposter
purpose). We learned, for example, that without achieving real
depth in the descent from self into soul, what emerges is a form
of self (and resultant life experience) that reflects imposter self
rather than authentic self, reflects operating from self rather than
operating from soul (see Figure 14.3).

What is illustrated is that the quality of descent from self
into soul (the movement from 'planes' A to E) determines whether imposter self serves as source when defining personal vision,

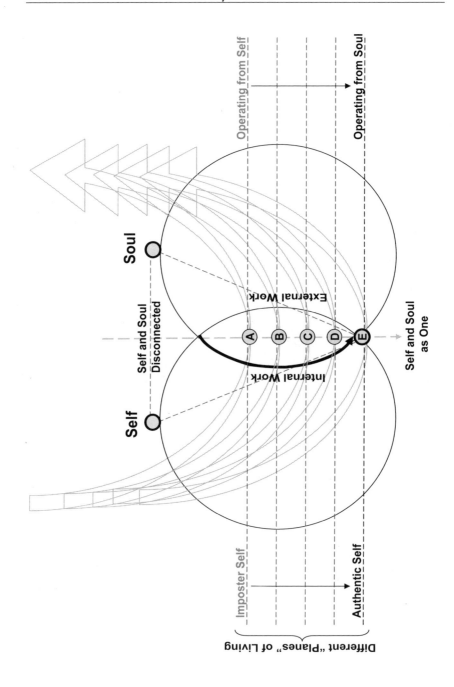

Fig. 14.3

inner soul goals, and personal strategy or whether the source for defining such things reflects authentic self. Without achieving real depth when conversing with soul, the opening to discover, and later realize, emerging you, your highest future potential, simply does not occur, cannot occur. What emerges, instead, is seeing, willing, thinking, acting, and feeling that is uninformed by the whole (i.e., soul); of a lesser form. Consequently, what one sees, what one wills, how one thinks, acts, and feels reflects not self and soul operating as One, but as disconnected parts. Instead of self and soul reflecting common vision, shared goals, and aligned energies, what emerges instead are competing visions, abandoned goals, and wasted energy. If the conversation (i.e., 'opening') between self and soul only extended downward and inward to 'plane A', you would be living an imposter existence. If conversation between self and soul deepened to plane B, you would still be living an imposter existence. The same is true for planes C and D. Only on plane E is the movement downward enough, inward enough, adequate enough, for real conversation between self and soul to occur.

If attempts to converse with soul only progress to the depth of planes A through D, you have not yet entered the 'space', descended to the 'place', or *quiet room*, where true conversation between self and soul occurs, thereby revealing true purpose for your life. What results, instead, is that the goals, personal strategy, and subsequent action that emerges from operating on planes A through D will be imprecise, 'off the mark'. And the cost paid for such imprecision is continued <u>mis</u>alignment, continued unhappiness, as imposter goals inspire imposter actions and imposter actions reinforce debilitating habits which foster misalignment, perpetuate unhappiness. Only on plane E is the opening grand enough to hear what soul is saying. And when we listen to voice of soul, to the meaning behind what soul has to say, is when we truly begin to live. Our spirit comes alive, wakes from its slumber; numbness fades. We begin to see life with fresh eyes. We begin to will inspired goals. We begin to think differently about opportunity and imperative. And from seeing, willing, and thinking differently, we begin to act differently.

Specifically, we begin to act with urgency, with no time to waste, as life has new meaning, new purpose, and again, revealed its joy. Most importantly, however, when we operate from plane E, we rise above debilitating patterns that defined our past: past thinking, past habits, past actions, and past obstacles. Such things become, themselves, objects of the past, as we now operate from 'a new place', from soul, which is a more formidable, inspiring, and empowered place from which to operate. The pattern of our life no longer reflects a Cycle of Desperation, but a Cycle of Inspiration, as we operate from a deeper, but in many ways, higher plane.

It is important to recognize that, only from operating on plane E can one experience sustained happiness and live a remarkable life. No other plane (of living) can coax out the full expression of what it means to live happily, purposefully, and accomplish achievements of a lifetime that is possible *when operating from soul*. In Chapter 6, we learned that the depth and speed with which one **finds soul** is dependent on <u>where</u> one currently operates. Because so few people today stop their life to converse with soul, most people operate, by default, on plane A, where self and soul are disconnected. With time, patience, and solitude, however, each of us can find soul. That is, each of us can descend from plane A to plane E. And with each plane descended, from A to B, B to C, C to D, and finally D to E, our ability to hear what soul is saying increases. The tones of soul get louder, albeit still silent, and through the silence, we hear soul's true intentions. As we tune our senses, become sensitized to hear better the voice of soul, the quality of conversation between self and soul takes bloom. The quiet room, space within which we converse with soul, begins to widen, broaden, in all directions, and it is from this larger expanse, this more panoramic opening of the mind, as represented by position E, where authentic goals, authentic actions, and authentic living emerge (see Figure 14.4). Indeed, it is only from descending to plane E that the real you, the emerging you, can be seen, understood, and, therefore, realized.

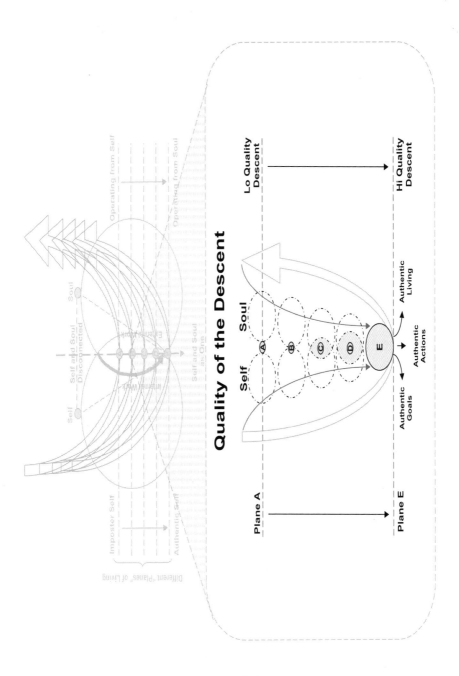

Fig. 14.4

What is illustrated is the process, or movement, of self into soul. As we descend deeper (from planes A to D), as the quality of our descent improves, self and soul become less and less disconnected. Less and less space separates self from soul until entities merge on plane E, where self and soul become One; One entity, One vision, One voice. And when entities merge, when alignment exists between self and soul, from vision, to strategy, to energies, we live not as imposter self, on multiple inferior planes of living, but as authentic self, on just one plane, plane E, where all are happy and all are free.

We are masters at tweaking our lives, not transforming them in meaningful ways. We try new diets, buy new gadgets, and succumb to the latest fads, all in an attempt to transform our life. However, just as most companies have learned that tweaking business operations leads to no sustainable improvement, so, too, do we ultimately learn that tweaking our personal life leads to no sustainable improvement. To transform your life, to reengineer your existence, requires an intervention of a different kind. It requires breaking free of the debilitating life pattern that operating from self creates, by intervening on behalf of one's emerging self, soul. Utilizing the tools, techniques, and principles described herein represents such intervention. What is required is to reexamine, reorient the source from which you operate. To be precise, it requires a movement from you operating from self to you operating from soul. For if we do not intervene on behalf of soul, the likelihood of 'jumping' planes to realize a better life is remote, as once we settle on a 'plane of living,' we usually stay there. As such, one of my goals for this book was to help you recognize that you probably have not been operating on plane E up to this point in your life. Most likely, you have operated as imposter self rather than authentic self. As such, OOS was about rekindling conversation between your-self and your soul; to deepen conversation between self and soul; to descend to a new place (plane E), and begin operating from higher ground. By descending within, deepening the plane upon which you operate, you will realize a better life; supplant 'diminished living' with 'remarkable living' (see Figure 14.5). How can I be so sure? It happened to me just as assuredly as it will happen to you.

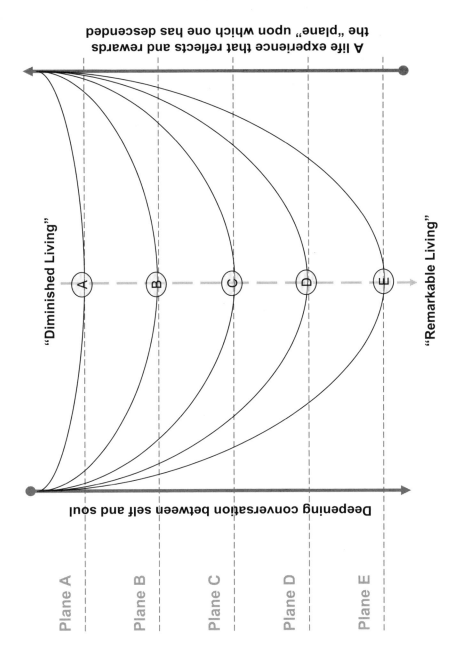

Fig. 14.5

In time, you will discover, as I did, that: 1) the process of implementing, managing, and achieving personal strategy, 2) the quest for personal alignment, and 3) the goal of establishing and sustaining personal happiness, requires performing two complimentary movements: a 'downward' movement (self <u>into</u> soul) to validate and refine inner soul goals and personal strategy as you unfold throughout life and an 'upward' movement (self <u>from</u> soul) to realize new strategy, new goals. Figure 14.6 illustrates the pattern that emerges when these complementary, continuous up and down movements come together; become One.

You will notice that when we flip Figure 14.5 on its side, we see that our actions, life movements, take on 'spiral' form. First, we turn downward, then inward, descending within. This movement not only enables us to define meaningful inner soul goals and associated personal strategy, but also enables the shift from operating from self (planes A through D) to operating from soul (plane E). Once we complete this 'inner work' to find soul, we turn upward to perform 'outer work', to realize soul by operating from this new place. And as we execute personal strategy, we occasionally stop our life by, again, turning downward, then inward to reflect on what we have learned, the progress we have made, and the course corrections needed to improve strategy, to achieve our goals. This last movement, upward, then inward, completes the spiral effect and we continue this pattern throughout our life. The two movements that create the spiral effect represent that which is internal becoming external; that which is invisible becoming visible. In other words, first, we think; then, we act; first, we *define* emerging self; then, we *realize* emerging self. This is the natural order of things. So, whereas you may have operated from plane A in the past (i.e., from self), I hope that your OOS journey has taken you to new depths. I hope that together, you and I, were able to <u>find your soul and pull it forward, into the present</u> for you to **operate on plane E,** where one does not experience moderate success, but remarkable success, where one does not experience moderate achievement, but remarkable achievement, and finally where one does not experience moderate happiness, but remarkable happiness (see Figure 14.7).

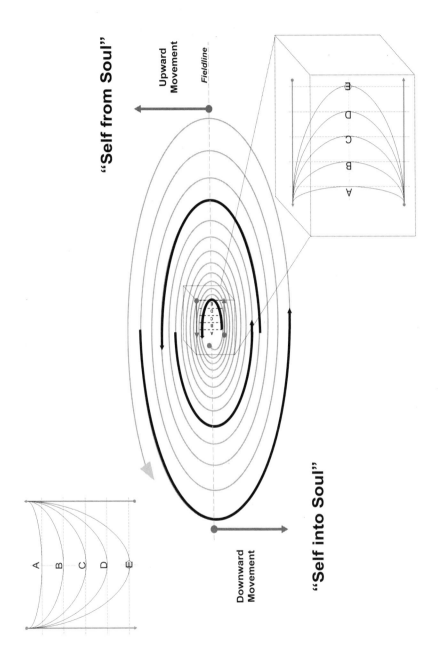

Fig. 14.6

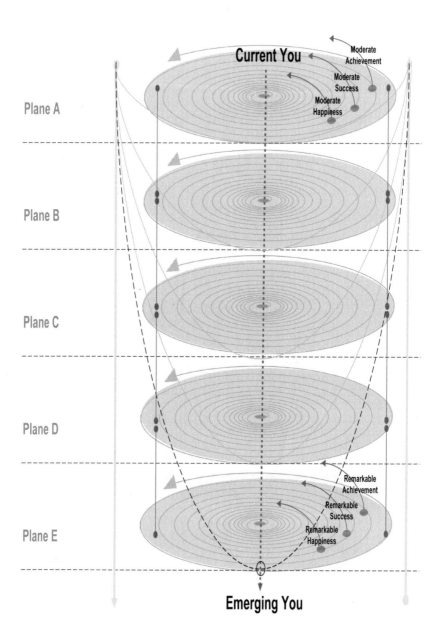

Fig. 14.7

Each of us operates, exists on our own 'spiral of life'; plane of living. Since the majority of people never converse with soul, they operate by default on plane A, and all that emerges in their lifetime is only what is possible from operating on plane A. In this way, each plane results in a different life experience. For example, the life you experience will be better on plane B than A, better on C than B, better on D than C, and better on E than D. Know this: the more you converse with soul, the better you know soul, the greater the likelihood you will begin operating from soul; that is, on plane E. The choice is yours as to what plane you operate on. My advice: choose plane E, where all are happy and all are free.

Operating from self was never our creed in life, never our fate. Each of us is here on earth to realize our highest purpose; highest form of self; highest potential. However, before we can realize our highest form of self, we must first find our higher purpose, and then we can share such gift with self and world. For me, my fate, my 'higher purpose' was to write this book and share its content with you. With the help this book provides, I hope that you, too, are on the path to realizing your higher purpose. I hope that, in time, you can join me on plane E. It is no fault of yours, or the millions of other people who live life directed by self, as we were never educated in the need to, or process of, conversing with soul, which is the first step, *the* prerequisite, to operate from soul. We were never taught that our purpose in life lies within, and to find purpose requires quiet, persistent, quality conversation with soul. Consequently, most of us live imposter lives; imposter existences from that what we were meant to live. Our true purpose lies dormant, unrealized in the field of dreams, and as our true purpose lies dormant, so, too, does our opportunity to maximize life, to experience all that life has to offer, to live fragrantly, purposefully, remarkably.

We are the authors of our own life story, yet most of us have not received proper training to draft an outline for our life, let alone write the complete story. Consequently, most people's story reflects a life directed by self rather than a life directed by soul. This difference has great ramifications for one's life, as the vision seen *with* one's eyes results in a significantly different story (i.e., life experience) than the vision seen *through* one's eyes. Discussing imposter self, of living an imposter existence, is important, as it describes a condition that most people suffer from; perhaps you. I know that this is not what you intend for your life, but to rise above current condition, to realize new condition, new intention, comes new responsibility. Responsibility to:

- Stop your life; descend within
- Converse with soul; engage in quality conversation with soul
- Find soul and pull it forward, into the present
- Change the source from which you operate (self to soul)

Only <u>you</u> can stop your life to descend within. Only <u>you</u> can converse with your soul. *Only <u>you</u> can find your soul and pull it forward, into the present.* In short, only <u>you</u> can change the source from which <u>you</u> operate. And when you do these things, something remarkable will occur; you will begin operating from soul.

Operating from Soul

In previous sections, we learned the destructive consequence of not operating from soul – *a life diminished.* We learned that the source from which we operate not only affects what we see and will, but also how we think, act, and feel. Lastly, we learned that when we operate from self, we deny self the possibility of ever living a remarkable life, but when we operate from soul, <u>we nearly ensure it</u>.

In learning what it means to operate from self, we learned some about what it means to operate from soul. However, our learning is incomplete. Therefore, we ask, "What does it mean to operate from soul? How does one operate from soul? When should one operate from soul? And why would one want to operate from soul?" Before we address these important questions, we must first re-examine the feelings and circumstance that brought you to this book.

Something brought you to OOS; it was not random chance. When one is seeking deep personal change, and the pursuit is genuine, I believe the universe cooperates. That is, I believe that a series of events brought you to this book, just as I believe fate intervened one morning, while I was driving to work, to gift me the idea to write this book. I sought deep change in my life, but could not articulate next steps. Then, fate intervened, and suddenly, I knew what I needed to do; I knew the steps to take to establish alignment; to be happy. Prior to fate lending a helping hand, I felt profound loss; I was restless; dissatisfied with my achievements; with what my life had become; with my future. In short, I was numb – to work, family, and nature. Perhaps you have felt or are now feeling these same feelings. If so, let me assure you that nothing is wrong with you, as nothing was wrong with me. What you are experiencing, as I came to realize and can now articulate, is soul's attempt to converse with self. What you are feeling is soul's desire to realize emerging you, to bring soul to fore and push self to back so you can begin operating from soul.

So, what does it mean to operate from soul? To operate from soul means to do what you want in life to get what you want from life throughout life. It means to pursue your passions; to live passionately, whether your passion is making furniture, preaching the gospel, or teaching. Every day spent not doing what you love and loving what you do is a day lost. Every day spent not pursuing and living your passions is a day lost. As such, how many 'lost' days you tally in life is your choice. Now, although you did not ask for life, but having arrived, you can and should demand certain things of life. Minimally, you should demand that which makes you happy, fulfilled, successful, and free. When we do not explicitly ask these things of life, life rarely delivers. I learned this lesson the hard way, as I suspect you have as well. However, when we do ask, backed with effective strategy and willful action, we do receive. Thus, the relevance of having a personal strategy is again revealed.

When soul is the basis (i.e., 'source') for our seeing, willing, thinking, acting, and feeling, **great things happen**. For instance, we define and pursue goals that are meaningful and inspire soul.

And from pursuing meaningful goals, we begin to live passionately, with excitement, with new hope that only *seeds of soul* can
stir. We begin to live with purpose, with fragrance, with color, as
we now see the world in different light. What was once a gray,
stale existence is now full of color and the promise of realizing
a better life fuels our daily movements; from sustaining commitments, to performing life pathways, to measuring and managing
our life experience. We begin to live again, to love life again, as
we will 'emerging self' out of 'historical self'. And then, suddenly, we feel happier because <u>we are happier</u>. Happier to be
pursuing desires of soul, happier about the direction of our life,
and happier about our future. The excitement, joy, and freedom
that comes from living passionately, from operating from soul, is
how we were meant to experience life, nothing less.

When we operate from soul everything about our life is
bigger. Our purpose (in life) is bigger, our goals are bigger, our
actions are bigger, and our achievements are bigger. Why is this
so? It is because operating from soul creates an opening, larger
expanse, from which to view and experience life. This is why it
is critical to see life not with one's eyes but **through** one's eyes.
Seeing life *with* one's eyes reveals habitual self and perpetuates
current you. However, seeing life *through* one's eyes reveals
soul, emerging you. And with the clarity that comes from seeing through one's eyes also comes awareness; a special kind of
'knowing' that is difficult to put into words but nonetheless captures the essence of what we feel; a feeling that better days are
coming; that happiness is on the rise. When we operate from
soul, when soul is our center, everything about our life becomes
clearer. What to do in life becomes clearer, what is meaningful is clearer, what is a priority is clearer, and what we want to
achieve in life is clearer. And this clarity is what enables us to
define bigger purpose, establish bigger goals, and execute bigger actions resulting in bigger achievements. Sadly, most people
never obtain such clarity, awareness about what to do with their
life, leading most to live in quiet desperation, and tragically, for
some, to orchestrate early exit.

It should be clear why operating from soul is a better way to live; *the only way to live.* Operating from soul is the basis to live a meaningful life. This is not possible when operating from self, as the seeing, willing, thinking, acting, and feeling that emerges when operating from self is of a lesser kind. Our expectations and purpose in life change whether looking with one's eyes or through one's eyes. Thus, when we operate from soul, we act on behalf of soul; our life revolves, <u>pivots</u> around soul. Our lenses of life see a different reality, a new reality, a better reality and this reorientation, awakening, fresh set of eyes ensures effective action when executing new strategy; when operating on the surface of life. At its essence, to operate from soul means to live authentically; to live as soul would live. It means to seize opportunity and meet imperative. Lastly, it means to achieve the goal of this book, which is to realize emerging you. It is because the alternative to operating from soul leads to quiet desperation, to living an imposter existence that we <u>must</u> operate from soul. The more we live as soul would live, we profit in life; lest, we suffer worst poverty – spiritual poverty.

It is obvious who operates from self and who operates from soul. At first, it is apparent by looking at one's face. Then, upon closer examination, it becomes more apparent with one's thinking, actions, and habits (see Table 14.1).

Table 14.1

Characteristics of Those Operating from Soul	Characteristics of Those Operating from Self
• Inspired • Happy • Hopeful • Optimistic • Enthused • Active • Successful • Peaceful • Driven • Smiling • Urgent	• Tired • Angry • Sad • Depressed • Hurt • Numb • Anxious • Restless • Nervous • Stressed • Bitter

Over the fifteen plus years I consulted to business, it became clear to me that most people are not living passionately, not living purposefully, not operating from soul. How could I tell? I could see it in their eyes. Few people were working in roles or occupations that inspired their best work, inspired soul. Few people viewed their work as fun and not as work. Few people were doing what they 'really' wanted to do in life, realizing passion. In short, few people were happy, and it showed. It is from witnessing such heartache that inspired me to change my life, as I did not want to live in quiet desperation as the majority of people do. I did not want to be numb to work, family, and nature. I did not want to be unhappy. What I wanted, as I believe what everyone wants, was *to be free.*

Perhaps the greatest reason to operate from soul is that when you do, you are free. **You are free to do what you love and love what you do.** And these freedoms, internal freedom ('love what you do') and external freedom ('do what you love'), enable us to live fragrantly, passionately. Further, it positions us to maximize the personal, professional, and financial potential that life offers. Do not sacrifice freedom in this lifetime for freedom in the next, as this represents false hope. When we set soul free, *Let Soul Sing*, we experience life in dramatically different ways, with perhaps the biggest difference being how we feel. The sensations that come from operating from soul are hard to put into words. However, there is a word, I believe, that best describes the texture of the experience, that captures the essence of this feeling, and that word is: *inspired.* When we operate from soul, we are inspired. We see with inspired eyes, will inspired goals, think inspired thoughts, act in inspired ways, and feel inspired sensations. Life itself becomes inspiring, and once you experience inspired living, I promise you, you will never go back, nor want to go back, to your former life; historical you. *Living an inspired existence is the only way to live.* It is how each of us was meant to experience life, nothing less. And what results from living a free, inspired, passionate existence is new energy that few have tapped, but all possess.

When we operate from soul, when self and soul become One (One spirit, One vision, One force), a tremendous energy emerges from such interaction which fuels our life movements. Specifically, what results when self and soul align around common goals is the most intense, creative, and generative state in which one can operate. And what results from living in this 'altered state', from living with one's spirit, vision, and life force in total alignment, is new and intensely powerful feelings; feelings that result in, push out, a gush of inspired willing, thinking, and acting (see Figure 14.8). These feelings help us sustain will, execute personal strategy, overcome stumbling blocks, and achieve our goals.

What begins as a small opening, when self and soul first come together for quiet conversation, blossoms into an ever increasing, ever intensifying, ever spiraling source of personal power and energy as self and soul become One. This effect demonstrating Newton's Law of Gravity where the closer two bodies come to one another, the stronger the force. And it is this force, this intensity within, which serves as our driving force to achieve greatness. This is all possible when one operates on plane E, as plane E represents the underlying field, a generative field, from which the emerging you rises; ascends (see Figure 14.9).

The spiral motion shown in Figure 14.9 not only represents a continuum of 'below ground' work (self into soul) giving rise to 'above ground' work (self from soul), but also represents the gears of personal strategy engaging with force and momentum intensifying, rising indefinitely throughout life. The upward movement of the spiral symbolically represents our continued doing, continued learning, and continued developing of new (life management) capabilities, like conversing with soul. It also represents step increases in strengthening will, ability to overcome obstacles, ability to manage (i.e., 'course correct') personal strategy, ability to establish and sustain personal alignment, and ability to achieve set goals. In short, it represents emerging you, continually unfolding, rising, advancing from soul. Now,

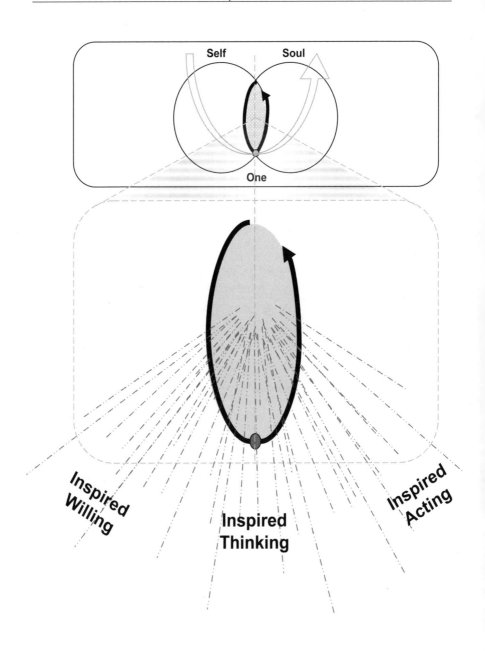

Fig. 14.8

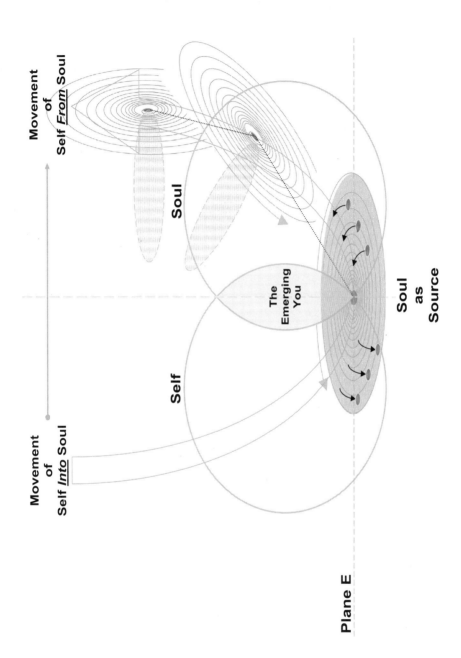

Fig. 14.9

despite the apparent chaotic outer energy that results when operating from soul, our inner self remains calm. As much as operating from soul generates a well-stream of intense energy, it also
results in, ironically, an inner peace, a sense of order, because
there is a profound 'knowing' deep within that we are <u>finally</u>
doing what we were meant to do; at this moment; Now. Inner
peace is also the result of achieving an important end: personal
alignment.

When we operate from soul, what results is alignment
from soul, to will, to mind, to body. Attaining such alignment
seems to be the great challenge with living, with humanity, as
few people display such alignment, but all can attain. Know
this: just as conversing with soul is *the* prerequisite to operate
from soul, so, too, is operating from soul *the* prerequisite to establish personal alignment. Great success and achievement in
life can only come when aligned. Sure, one can still experience
success when not aligned, but the effort required to achieve success is greater, the road longer, and the successes realized of a
lesser kind. To win the Noble Prize, write a best-selling book,
win teacher-of-the-year, or become a world-class artist, requires
operating from soul, as these forms of achievement only result
when operating from soul. Why is this so? It is because these
accomplishments, and others like them, require great energy,
great will, great passion, and great commitment. The type of
greatness that is only possible – can only emerge – when operating from soul. Operating from self cannot generate the energy,
will, passion, or commitment to achieve remarkable success; to
become world class; to achieve accomplishments of a lifetime.
Hence, the need to operate from soul is revealed.

A key goal of this book was to shift the source from which
you operate; from self to soul. However, to operate from soul requires more than internal work; it requires external work. That
is, it requires you execute personal strategy and refine strategy
as you change and your environment changes. Without making
internal and external adjustments to how you have been living,
you will continue to operate from self. This is certain! Thus,

sacrifice is synonymous with operating from soul. What do we sacrifice? We sacrifice self to realize soul. By stepping back within your mind, to reorient from self to soul, you take a giant leap forward with increasing personal happiness. The conditions are right to increase personal happiness when operating from soul. We are free, inspired, passionate, energetic, aligned, and achieving. Sustaining personal happiness is a lifelong endeavor, and by operating from soul, you increase your chances not only of being happy, but of staying happy, today and for all your days.

A Summary: Self, Soul, and the Life Experience

"Live free or die" is the official motto of the state of New Hampshire and the unofficial motto of this book, for the motto describes perfectly the two conditions that result depending on the source from which you operate. When we operate from soul, we "live free". When we operate from self, we "die". In the last two sections, we discussed a hidden, yet vital, aspect of you: *the source from which you operate.* We performed this source-level check to ensure that all that follows in your life: what you see, what you will, how you think, act, and feel aligns with, reflects soul.

At many points throughout this book, I have stated, "Alignment is everything". This is still true, but what underlies personal alignment, what enables alignment to occur, is the source from which one operates and, therefore, discussing source merits greater consideration, greater pause. Thus, before we conclude this chapter, we pause a few minutes more to summarize recent discussions.

We began this chapter learning that there are two ways to operate in life: we can operate from self or we can operate from soul. We first explored what it means to operate from self, as most people do. We learned that operating from self perpetuates the 'Cycle of Desperation,' resulting in a diminished life experience. We further learned that operating from self is tantamount to living a lie. And it was from this latter discussion that we learned the different 'planes' one could operate from, live on (see Figure 14.10).

We learned, for example, that operating on planes A through D (or any gradient in between) represents imposter living, whereas operating on plane E represents authentic living. We then revisited how the quality and frequency of conversation between self and soul determines plane-depth, source-level. We learned that most people operate, by default, on or near plane A, where self and soul are disconnected; the result of little to no conversation between self and soul. But, we also learned that with time, patience, and dialogue you can deepen your source of operating; that is, you can 'jump' planes; begin operating as One.

In discussing the various planes on which one could operate, we learned the significance and ramifications of operating on one plane versus another. We learned, for example, that the plane on which one operates affects what we see, and that, in turn, affects what we will, how we think, how we act, and ultimately, how we feel. We learned that the plane upon which we operate in life determines the quality of our life; what emerges in our life. Thus, as with a garden, where the quality of that which exists below (i.e., soil) determines the quality of that which emerges above (i.e., fruit/vegetables), so, too, did we learn that what emerges in our life depends on that which exists below, within. And just as a garden yields more when attended to with love and cultivation, so, too, did we learn that our life experience yields more when attended to with self-love, self-cultivation.

We also learned that operating from self perpetuates the past. We access, then enact habitual ways of seeing, willing, thinking, acting, and feeling which recasts the past. In other words, we come back not as we would like to be, but *as we are*. And this disconnect, divide between self and soul, only escalates, perpetuating separation between self and soul, thereby denying one from ever realizing soul, from ever living as soul would live. Consequently, and so as not to repeat patterns of the past, we

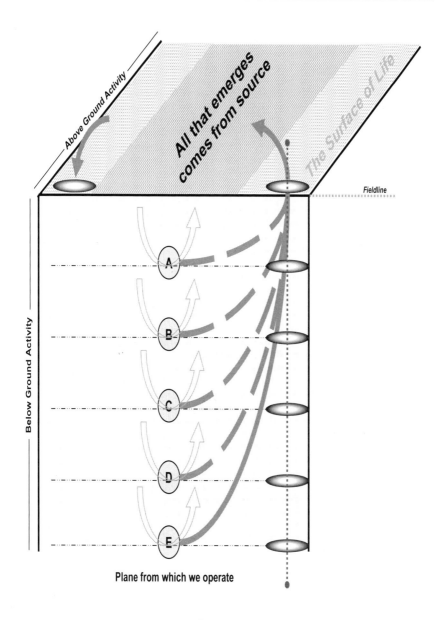

Fig. 14.10

learned that to break with our past, to free ourselves from the debilitating habits, movements that dominate our life, requires enacting new movements. Similar to how nature abhors the old, continually reinvents itself, so, too, did we learn that we must abhor the old (of us); continually reinvent our self.

We discovered that when operating from soul, where we continuously perform both internal (self into soul) and external (self from soul) work, that such actions, such movements, take on spiral form (see Figure 14.11).

We learned that the spiral symbolically represents not only enacting new life movements, but also represents the ever increasing, ever intensifying, ever expanding life source (energy) that results when self and soul become One. Energy we need to strengthen will, drive passions, execute personal strategy, and achieve goals. Energy we need to continually unfold, continually emerge, continually advance throughout life (as indicated by $E...E_n$ notation). And this unfolding, these *iterations of self*, inspire new vision, revised goals, revised strategy as we seek to maintain alignment between self and soul. We (our lives) unfold in step with our deepenings below. As we change on the inside, such changes manifest on the outside in the form of changed goals, changed personal strategy, changed seeing, willing, thinking, acting, and feeling. The spiral that is our life continues indefinitely; forever expanding, forever deepening throughout our life. Therefore, as we change, as we deepen our movement of self into soul, we extend from E to E_1, E_1 to E_2, E_2 to E_3, etc. As such, we operate on plane E for a period, then we deepen to E_1 and operate on this level for a period, and the movements 'down and in' and 'up and in' continue indefinitely; such pattern reflecting a Cycle of Inspiration (not to be confused with the Cycle of Desperation). With the former, our life movements reflect 'rising above, deepening below', with the latter, our life movements reflect, are tantamount to, 'running in circles' (see Figure 14.12).

What is significant about these two patterns is that a different life experience results, emerges, depending on whether you skim along the surface of things or whether you penetrate the

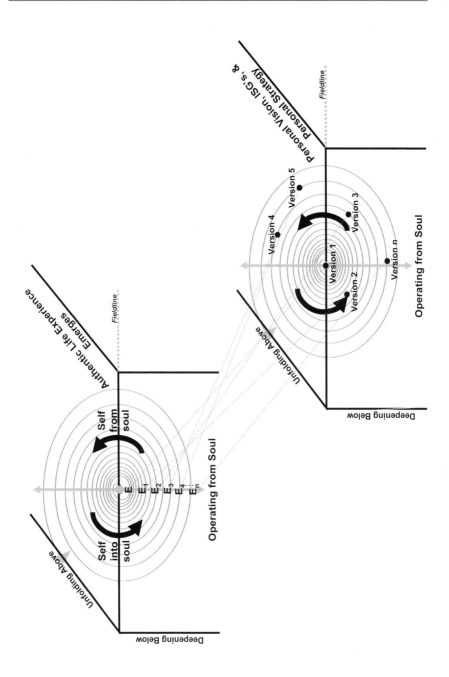

Fig. 14.11

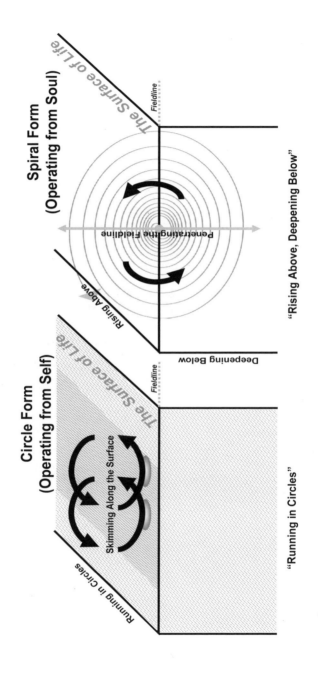

Fig. 14.12

fieldline. Table 14.2 summarizes the effects of 'skimming the surface' versus 'penetrating the fieldline'.

Table 14.2

Effects of Skimming the Surface	Effects of Penetrating the Fieldline
• Denied happiness • Denied fragrant living • Denied internal freedom • Denied external freedom • Denied alignment • Denied maximizing the life experience	• Freedom • Inspired sensations • Passionate/purposeful living • Tremendous energy • Personal alignment • Greater success • Sustained happiness • Maximize the life experience

The title of this chapter is 'One King'. At first, this title may have been confusing. However, you now have context to hear its true meaning. The 'One' part represents your-self and your soul *operating as One*. The 'King' part means to make soul *the King of you*, of your-self, of your life; to abide by one ruler. Together, 'One King' represents how we should approach life; reflects a philosophy for living. To live under the reign of just 'One King' is to be free (inside and out); the alternative is to die (inside and out). I am confident that you need no further convincing of why one should operate from soul (versus self), but there is one final question to resolve: that of when you should operate from soul. The short answer is: now, and for your entire life, as you will have Only One Shot to do so. Our summary is complete, but before we move on, take one last look, reflect one last time, at the differences between a life operated from self versus a life operated from soul as nothing less than your entire life experience, and all that emerges from it is at stake (see Figure 14.13).

The intent of this chapter was to validate the source from which you operate. Hopefully, it is soul. To operate from self is to *exclude soul*; to operate from soul is to *find soul*; two fundamentally different lives; one life, a life of dependence, the other a life of freedom. As discussed in Chapter 6, you know that you

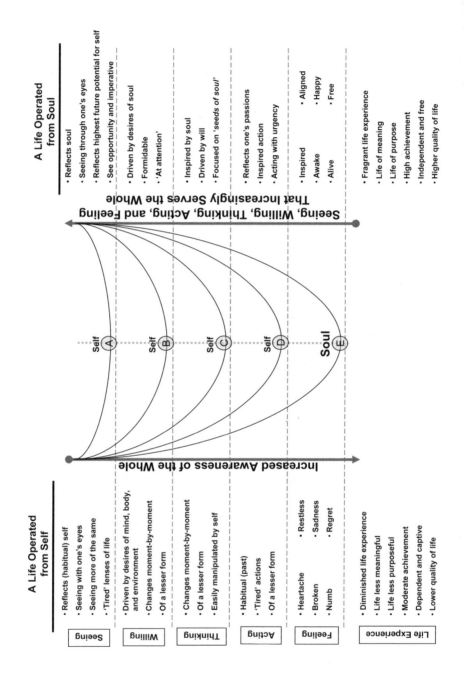

Fig. 14.13

have found soul when you feel connected to something larger than yourself. You are not the same person; you exist in altered state. I hope that upon exiting this chapter, you exist in altered state. That is, I hope you are not the same person exiting this chapter as when entered. For self to be disconnected from soul represents an 'inner betrayal,' and to betray soul is to deny ourselves from ever living as soul would live; that is, to *Let Soul Sing*. Now that we have validated your <u>finding soul</u>, we discuss bringing soul forward, into the present, onto the surface of life via a life design.

A Life Design

*"Life should be fragrant, rooftop to
the basement."*

- Bono, U2

IN THE PREVIOUS CHAPTER, we learned the difference between
imposter self, imposter living, and authentic self, authentic living. We learned what it means to operate from self versus operate from soul. And we learned the meaning behind the phrase
'One King'. We discussed such matters because we are at a
crossroad in our life; a 'pause point', to contemplate *more of the
same* or *go the other way*; our choice affecting all that follows.
Choose one path, you <u>live</u> life. Choose the other, <u>a life denied</u>.
The stakes have never been higher, your interest more peaked,
or the tones of soul more audible than right now. To favor authentic, to operate from soul, to serve 'One King' all suggests,
indicates, finding soul. I hope that the OOS journey shed proper
light, radiated sufficient wisdom for you to favor, operate, and
serve that which leads home: soul. Now, while finding soul is
important, if that is all we do, we fail soul, as more is required to

Let Soul Sing; more is required to live a fragrant life. What we must do is bring soul forward, into the present, onto the surface of life, and the way we do this is through *A Life Design*.

You may be asking, 'What is a life design?' Similar to personal strategy and personal alignment, 'a life design' is not a concept familiar to most people. However, like personal strategy and personal alignment, it is of great importance to live a purposeful, happy existence and, therefore, merits discussion. We begin by defining the word 'design'. A design is:

- An outline, sketch, or **plan**
- **Adaptation** of means to **a preconceived end**
- The **purposeful arrangement of parts**
- **Deliberate intention**
- Something intended **as a guide**

Although each statement above tells, it is more revealing to consider all characterizations together, as a whole. Thus, our working definition of 'design':

Definition of 'Design'

> A **plan** reflecting **deliberate intention** and **purposeful arrangement of parts** to **guide** us, requiring **adaptation** to achieve **a preconceived end**

So, if this is how we define 'design', how do we define 'a life design'? To answer this question, we again consider parts, then consider whole.

A life design:
- Is a **plan** underlying the life experience
- Reflects **deliberate intention** to live a certain way
- Reflects **purposeful arrangement of the parts** of our life
- **Guides** us through life
- **Adapts to changes** in self and environment
- Achieves a **desired end**

So, in bringing parts together, we define 'a life design' as:

Definition of 'A Life Design'

A **plan** underlying the life experience, reflecting **deliberate intention** to live a certain way, reflecting **purposeful arrangement of the parts** of our life. A life design **guides** us through life, **adapting to changes** in self and environment to achieve a **desired end**

A life design reflects our approach to living; from what we attend to, to what we do, to how we do it. As such, it underlies our life experience and, therefore, determines all that emerges from it. Most people do not have a deliberate plan for living; do not follow explicit design. Most people simply live life, which, as we will soon learn, is the cause of much suffering. The question is, 'What comprises a life design?' Said differently, 'What directs what we do and how we do it?' You could say that one's personal mission, vision, inner soul goals, and personal strategy dictate the 'what' and 'how' of one's life, and you would be mostly right. Such things are key elements of a life design, but there is more, as a life design considers not only the 'what' and 'how' of life, it also considers the 'why'. And when we speak of 'why,' we speak of 'source'; soul. Together, 'source', mission, vision, inner soul goals, and personal strategy represent the key elements of a life design; that which is internal giving rise to that which is external (see Figure 15.1).

To approach life with explicit design is how we bring soul forward, into the present, onto the surface of life, for self to live as soul would live. Before we discuss explicit design, however, we must first discuss default, that is, the standard life design.

The Standard Life Design

Thus far, we learned what it means to have explicit design for one's life. Now, we consider default, that is, a life without design. We extend recent learning to consider the term 'standard

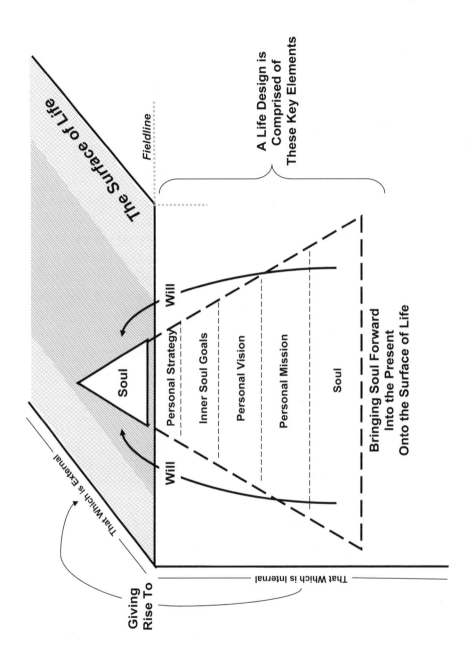

Fig. 15.1

life design'; to answer the question, 'What is the standard life design?' Although lacking proper context, you should know from the onset that the standard life design has failed us; failed humanity. It has conspired against us, cheated us, fooled us, lulled us into accepting default. Just as operating from self is the default way to operate in life, so, too, is the standard life design the default way to live life. It's a pattern inherited from past generations, passed down from parent to child. Only this inheritance resembles more a birth defect than a birth right. Now, while the effects of living the standard life design are *debilitating* at a micro level (individual), they are *devastating* at a macro level (community, nation, planet), as the standard life design has resulted in, given rise to, some of the greatest social problems of our time: drug use, suicide, rampant crime, mass unhappiness, uneven class structure, and poverty. You might be asking, 'How is this possible?' The reasons are many and complex. In this section, we discuss the standard life design; what it is, its effect on self and planet, and why most people live it. We do this, as, to reengineer one's life requires knowing 'default'; that is, it requires knowing the direction from which one comes, to change direction; *to go the other way.*

So, what is the standard life design? To put it bluntly, the standard life design represents non-design; poor design; no design at all; default. Because the standard life design represents default, it is, by nature, a bad design. This is made clear by way of comparison. Table 15.1 compares the definition of 'default' with its equivalent meaning for our life.

Table 15.1

Definition of Default	Equivalent Meaning for Our Life
Failure to fulfill duty or **obligation**	Not pursuing **passion**
Condition that results from not intervening	Personal **misalignment**
Omission of what should be done	Not leveraging **innate skill(s)**
Neglect **wisdom**	Dismiss **soul**
To lose; **loss**	Merely **survive**

To live the standard life design, to experience default, represents a failure to fulfill our most basic duty or obligation to live a fragrant life – pursue our passion. It also represents a condition (i.e., personal misalignment) that results when self does not intervene on behalf of soul. And it means to omit, not leverage, an essential part of us (i.e., innate skills) for personal gain. Most troubling, however, is that to live the standard life design, to experience default, is to neglect wisdom; dismiss soul. Accordingly, to not pursue one's passion, to be misaligned, to not leverage innate skill, and to dismiss soul, is to lose; to experience deep loss, as our life reflects not inspiration but desperation; reflects not thriving, but merely surviving.

Because most people live without design, that is, without a plan, my (former) self included, we are subject to the defaults (i.e., 'patterns') of life. Figure 15.2 illustrates several patterns, or variants, of a life design.

Four common patterns or profiles characterize most people's lives. The most common pattern is the 'Plateau,' whereby one experiences success early in life but then, by one's mid 40's, or earlier, ambition runs dry, spirit goes cold, and then it's a matter of 'putting in one's time'; a rush to the finish. This pattern reflects and results from living the standard life design. Another pattern is the 'Chaotic Ascent'. This pattern is named as such in that each success, each high, is offset, by significant lows. The debilitating result of living this way is that no true progress occurs in one's life; no significant achievement results. This pattern also results from living the standard life design. Another pattern is the 'Flat Line'. This pattern represents the 'non-starters' in life, those who achieve little in life because they never heard the starting gun. This pattern also results from living the standard life design. Lastly, is the pattern 'Ordered Ascent'. Although this pattern is similar to the Chaotic Ascent, in that there are up and down movements, new thresholds are continually crossed, goals continually achieved, and fragrant living is the result. This pattern is <u>not</u> the result of following standard design, but of intentional design, whereby we rise, we step back to reflect/refine

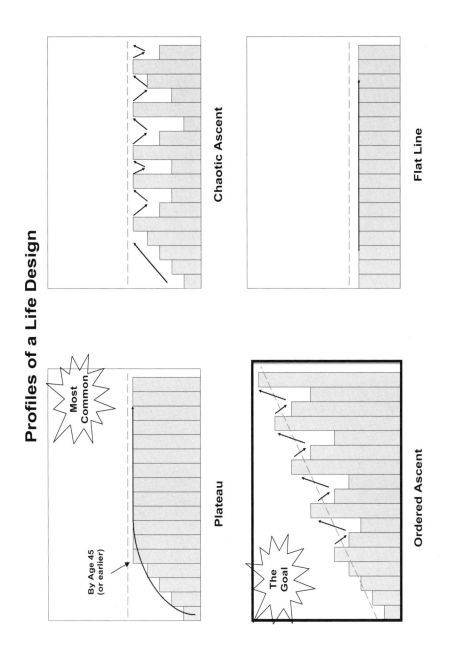

Fig. 15.2

our goals and personal strategy, and then we rise some more. We continue in this manner our whole life; rising, reflecting, and rising more. Of the four life design profiles illustrated, the Ordered Ascent is the pattern to emulate; it is *The Goal*.

The good news is, regardless of the pattern that has characterized your life thus far, the power lies within you to realize a new pattern; to choose a different design. For me, my life pattern represented the Chaotic Ascent. I experienced success early in my career, but could never cross the threshold to greatness. Of greater concern was that, in time, I found myself on the cusp of Plateau. I realized that if I did not make changes to my life, my life would, most assuredly, predictably reflect the pattern that debilitates so many today. For me, this represented a death sentence, and thus, I chose to realize a new pattern. I chose the Ordered Ascent. Now, with the Ordered Ascent, setbacks do occur. Sometimes the best thing you can do in life is to take two steps back to take three steps forward. Minimally, as you change and your environment changes, your goals and strategy will change. These moments of pause, reflection points, represent 'dips' on the Ordered Ascent graph. However, notice that after each dip, you rise, and mightily at that. If you find your life pattern reflecting Plateau, Chaotic Ascent, or Flat Line, rise into a new pattern; realize new design, as to live the standard life design is not to live at all. Now that we have discussed the meaning of the standard life design, we discuss its effect on self and planet.

Most of us live between the lines. That is, we live, adhere to, the principles, practices, and patterns of the standard life design; each of us conditioned, directed, to perpetuate the past; to *toe the line*. Consequently, our life experience becomes not a product of our own inspiration, reflecting custom design, but of default, poor design. As such, problems manifest early, beginning with our work. Most of us start our career believing that our chosen profession will be meaningful, interesting, and make us happy. We do find meaning; keep interest for a time, but then something foreign stirs within. A feeling begins to manifest, and not a pleasant one. Discontent escalates to pain, but a different kind of pain; pain not of the body, but of the heart. We become dissatisfied with life, grow bitter, that what we thought was real in life steered us wrong; that somewhere on our journey through life, the standard life design, and our blind faith in it, misdirected us, cheated us, deceived us.

We discover that upon finishing school to enter the work force, as our parents did, to perpetuate the standard life design, that life begins to cheat us out of that which we cherish most: happiness. We enter the workforce with great pomp and circumstance; the clothes I will buy, the jewelry I will adorn myself with, the fancy car that will shuttle me about. Then, something happens, and most unexpectedly. Over time, our excitement with work, and to some extent, life, diminishes; excitement is supplanted with frustration; then, frustration is supplanted with confusion; confusion with indifference, and finally, and most tragically, indifference with numbness (see Figure 15.3).

By age 45, most are numb to their work, resolved to just 'put in their time' until they retire. We achieve the debilitating, predictable outcome that Thoreau observed when one lives the standard life design, *a life of quiet desperation.* What is especially debilitating about living the standard life design is that the attitude of indifference and feeling of numbness that begins with one's work, in time, spreads to all aspects of self and life until finally, and most tragically, the cold, dark, cancer consumes that which lies below, soul; spirit, now frozen over, never to see light of day; sleeping somewhere cold. And as we learned in Chapter 1, when soul grows cold, in time, so, too, does family, community, nation, and planet. One does not have to look far or long to identify 'cold souls'. The high number of dissatisfied workers, the nearly 50% divorce rate, and water cooler conversation calling for simpler times is indication enough.

Some people, to deflect the pain, turn to drugs and alcohol, among other things. Feeling there is no way out, feeling stuck in a rut, perpetuating the standard life design, of which they are ignorant, they spiral downward, lost souls. Other people, those

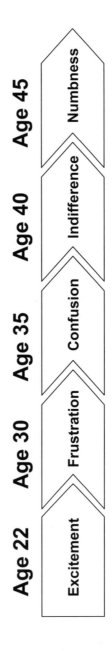

Fig. 15.3

resolved to 'just get through' life, adopt a hobby to smother the pain; reasoning happiness on the weekend will drown out pain of the week. Sadly, for all who suffer, they experience a life diminished; a life less happy, less accomplished, less fragrant, as pain lies within; runs deep. The question is, 'Why do so many people live the standard life design?'

There are many reasons why most people live the standard life design. It is partly because our parents lived this way; conformed to 'standard' design. It is partly due to peer pressure. Since my older brother, sister, or best friend approached life this way, so should I. It is partly due to us not making certain choices; taking certain actions; *following our heart*. And it is partly due to societal norms; tradition. Another reason why most of us operate from self, live the standard life design is that no one ever taught us that there is a better way to live. No one ever taught us that we are the architects of our life and therefore can create custom design; blaze our own trail. No one ever educated us to 'go the other way'; that alternatives exist to live a more fragrant life. We were never taught to converse with soul, to operate from soul, to pursue innate design; a design not of default, but of intention; soul. Another reason why the masses live the standard life design, experience quiet desperation, suffer heartache, is because of, due to, the hand of man; mankind.

Mankind has broken the covenant, all that is sacred. We live in a world disconnected; a world of 'haves' and 'have nots'; a world reflecting poor judgment, skewed priority; a world focused on the wrong set of details. Instead of committing itself to deepen the plane from which it operates, to ascend to higher ground to operate as One, the world continues to focus on feeding the ever-growing, cancerous economic machine. It continues to horde resources, dismiss equality, and perpetuate separation. It continues to operate from the premise that it is ok that the majority of earth's inhabitants suffer, while only a few benefit. In short, the world reflects not operating on plane E, where all are happy and all are free, but operates, instead, on plane A, where suffering and disconnectedness continue to ruin the day.

In Chapter 1, we learned where the world is (disconnected and suffering), in addition to learning some of the causes for current condition. Now, we reveal root cause: the Standard Life Design (see Figure 15.4). Although many contributing factors exist, living the standard life design is the root cause of our disconnectedness; of our suffering; first for individual, then, for planet. We know this to be true as all things are connected.

Tragically, the debilitations of living the standard life design are only made worse by living in a world that is more fixated on feeding the cancerous economic machine, than attend to that which matters most, *fragrant living for all*. All of the causes mentioned conspire against us, trick us, push us to conform automatically, to do our 'part', to perpetuate the standard life design. Like you, I succumbed to such trickery, absorbed each push, played my 'part', but I broke free. How did I do it? I stopped my life, I conversed with soul, I established mission, I established vision, I defined new inner soul goals, I developed a strategy to achieve each goal, and I exerted will. In doing such things, I made my long-awaited exit; feet flopping fast. My desire was to *go the other way*; that is, to realize innate design; a design not of default, but of the heart. By following the instruction contained herein, you, too, will realize innate design; you, too, will bring soul to surface; you, too, will begin living as soul would live. And with such things come different outcomes: happiness, joy, and achievement.

Now, although the fault in living the standard life design does not rest with you, the responsibility to fix fault does. It is important to realize that you are not chained to the standard life design. None of us is. It is just that most people lack knowledge of how to exit. That is, they lack knowledge of how to bring forth new design; realize new pattern; *break with the past*. Your story is different, however. You do possess the knowledge, skill, and (growing) capability to bring forth new design; realize new pattern; live a fragrant life. This is evidenced in:

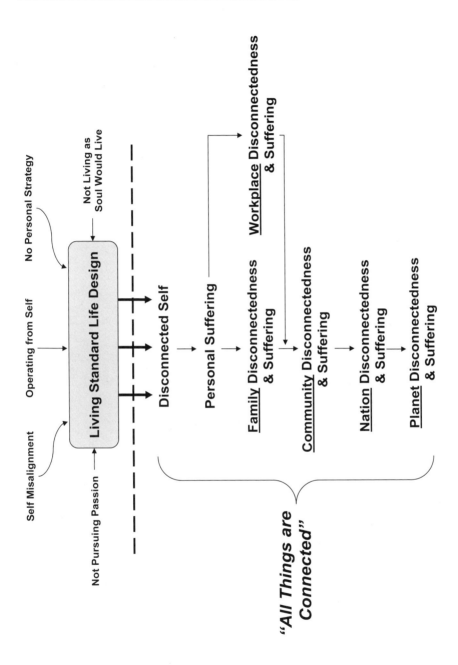

Fig. 15.4

The way that you feel. A feeling that your life now has direction, purpose, and meaning; a feeling that you are at last free, inside and out. And these feelings not only liberate you, inspire you, they propel you, energize you, to exert will, to execute personal strategy, to achieve your goals.

The truth in your eye. You possess a profound 'knowing' that you have ascended to operate on higher ground. You know that your past, and all that it represents, is behind you, as you see not with your eyes, but through your eyes. You know that a new future, new life story, is being written and you are the author. Finally, you know that great things are to come, just around the corner; surely, as you <u>feel</u> it, you <u>see</u> it.

Wings upon your back. Conversing with soul, establishing mission, establishing vision, defining inner soul goals, and designing, implementing, and managing a personal strategy gave you wings. You are free to fly to new destinations; to reengineer self; to experience life as you always imagined it could be; long ago dreamed.

Your desire to break with default, to break with the standard life design, to *live while alive* is reflective of humanity's desire. Humanity has tired of current condition, tired of skewed priority, tired of the standard life design. It is no surprise, as our current ways of operating, our current design, result in outcomes few people want. As I write this book, I sense that a new era is emerging, being born; an era still hidden, residing in the undergrowth, but defined by new priorities, new sensibilities, and new consciousness, not only for individual, but for world. Collectively, humanity appears to be deepening the plane on which it exists; it desires to ascend to higher ground and begin operating from this new place. The world has had enough with the standard life design, with default, and like a swollen river, is about to burst. What I believe, am now sensing, is that we, humanity, are evolving in step manner. As first stated in Chapter 1, I believe that a new era is emerging, a new epoch, that although presently without name, we will come to know as: *The Age of Happiness.*

The Age of Happiness

We are emerging as a species. However, the emergence I speak of does not concern the global economic machine or things external, it concerns something far greater, individual, and that which is internal. The old model of getting educated, entering the workforce, working 45 years collecting pay stubs, and retiring is dying. Humanity has tired of its current ways; it desires to rise above current condition, default; to free ourselves, individually and collectively, from the cancerous economic machine and its unwanted output. We seek a new world order; a common shoulder for humanity to rest its head upon; characterized by:

- Connectedness
- Dignity, equality, freedom for all
- Shared community/love
- Common goals/priorities
- Alignment
- Shared prosperity
- Shared resources
- Spirit of One

Why is the world seeking these changes? It is because few people benefit from current design, leaving most frustrated, confused, indifferent, and numb. And for some, feeling there is no end to the suffering, does what soul instructs – orchestrates an exit. It is no wonder why so many people today seek exit, as disconnectedness continues to debilitate all living things; from self, to nature, to humanity, to earth itself. The world has tired of its current story and now wishes to push it aside, as there is a better way to live; a better way to operate, individually and collectively. However, in order to rise above current condition, we need a new life model, a way through – *first for individual, then for world.*

New Life Model

What is the New Life Model? It is, quite simply, a new way to operate on the surface of life; a new way to live. It is a model reflecting new vision, new priorities, new values. It is a model focused on the 'right' sort of details. Lastly, it is a model not rooted, founded of default, but of soul.

The New Life Model rests on three principles:

1. Harmony between self and soul
2. Harmony between self and others
3. Harmony between self and nature

You may notice that the principles underlying the New Life Model parallel the dimensions of personal alignment. This is deliberate. In fact, if there were a single word that defined the essence of the New Life Model, it would be: **alignment.** And just as the New Life Model rests on three things, so, too, is the New Life Model <u>brought to life</u> by three things:

1. Executing a personal strategy reflecting soul
2. Exerting will
3. Engaging in personal reflection

Over the course of this book, we spent much time discussing personal strategy and exerting will. One thing we have yet to discuss fully, however, is personal reflection. Now, while executing personal strategy and exerting will are key to transform one's life, to bring forth <u>New Life</u>, personal reflection more than strategy, more than will, represents the *key of keys.*

Key of Keys

I hear the question often, 'What is the *key* to live a happy, meaningful, fragrant life experience?' The answer is simple: converse with soul. How do we do this? It is equally simple; we stop our life; we 'pause'. In this section, you will learn that to 'stop one's life', to converse with soul, to **reflect on life**, represents the key of keys to live a purposeful, meaningful, happy life. It is *the* differentiator between a life diminished and a remarkable life. It is something few people do.

It is tragic that the majority of the world's inhabitants receive little to no instruction in how to, or the need for, stopping one's life to converse with soul; that is, to reflect. This void becomes significant when you consider that only by stopping one's life does it accentuate the conditions, create the 'space', where self and soul can meet for quiet conversation. As such, when we do not stop our life, do not descend within to hear what soul has to say, it results in a life diminished. One method people use to promote reflection, to ensure quality conversation with soul, is to use a 'Reflective Learning Journal'.

Before describing what a Reflective Learning Journal is, let us first answer some foundational questions:

- What is reflection?
- On what do we reflect?
- Why reflect?
- What benefits does reflection offer?
- How do we reflect?

Answering these questions will provide proper context to discuss using a Reflective Learning Journal to help us bring soul forward, onto the surface of life; to realize New Life. We begin by asking, 'What is reflection?'

At many points throughout this book, we discussed the need to reflect, but never fully defined what reflection is. Thus, at long last, we define reflection as:

- A fixing of the thoughts on something
- Producing an image of something
- The bending or folding back of something upon itself

At first glance, this definition may seem overly technical, but each element above accurately characterizes the act of reflection and its relevance to defining personal strategy, establishing personal alignment, and achieving personal happiness.

Reflection is first and foremost a deliberate act to stop one's life, 'to pause'. We stop our life to reflect on life, to fix our thoughts on [the day, week, month, or year to come] or [the day, week, month, or year just ended], carefully considering events of the time period. When we reflect, we produce an image within our mind of 'a day of living'; of how our day will unfold (if reflecting in the AM) or how our day did unfold (if reflecting in the PM). When viewed this way, the act of reflection represents a bending or folding back of the experiences of life (outer part of us) onto our source (inner part of us), soul (see Figure 15.5).

Experiences of life take place on the surface of life, above the fieldline. The source of life, soul, exists beneath the surface of life; below the fieldline. When we reflect, we fold back experiences of the day (planned or experienced) onto soul. That is, we descend to an internal place where self and soul engage in quiet conversation, taking the experiences of life, creating an image of them within, reflecting on such experiences, and then bubbling the fruits of such dialogue to the surface of life to improve, direct, and reorient our life. The practice of reflecting, of stopping one's life, is the method by which we connect with soul; reflection is our 'listening device' to hear soul, to converse with soul, to learn from soul.

Reflection is the glue that connects our inner life with outer experience; it enables 'whole living' by bringing both our worlds together. Without reflection, we never explore inner; consequently, outer suffers. Because of the transformational effect that reflection has on our life, reflection is a key life management

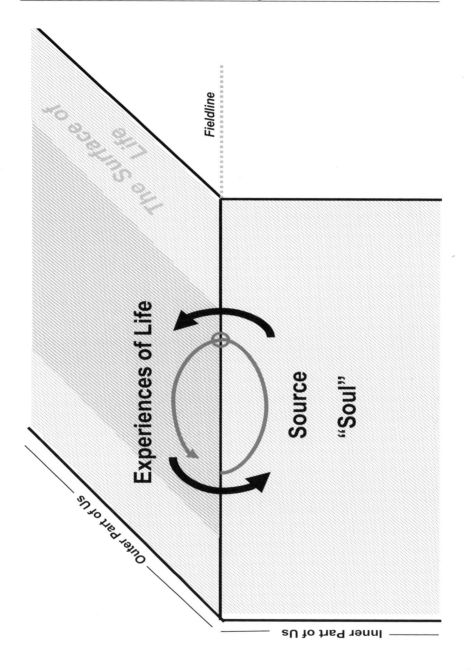

Fig. 15.5

activity (life pathway) we perform to help us achieve our personal strategy; to achieve our goals.

Now that we discussed what reflection is, you may be wondering what we reflect on. When we reflect, the object of our reflection is 'a day of living'; our experiences on the surface of life. To be more specific, and to tie reflection to the purposes of this book, when we reflect, we carefully consider four things:

1. Personal Vision
2. Personal Strategy
3. Personal Alignment
4. Personal Happiness

We reflect on vision to ensure right vision; that is, we reflect on our inner soul goals to ensure that they represent what we want in life and from life at a given point in life. We reflect on personal strategy to assess our strategy to improve strategy. For example, we reflect on the effectiveness of our strategy by examining the cause and effect relations that tie the various components of our personal strategy together. We also reflect on personal alignment. We seek to understand our degree of alignment between self and soul, then we seek to understand our degree of alignment with work, family, and nature. Lastly, we reflect on our happiness; the extent to which our commitments, actions, initiatives, and will move us closer to who we want to be and how we want to operate on the surface of life. Together, these four focus areas represent the cornerstones of reflective thought, using 'a day of living' as the object of reflection; one event, considered from multiple perspectives of inquiry (see Figure 15.6).

Each day of living provides the source material, evidence, we need when reflecting as each day offers us something new to comment on with regards to personal vision, strategy, alignment, and happiness. Reflection provides us opportunity to explain things to self; to 'look around' our experiences and comment on them more fully. In this way, reflection serves as a personal feedback mechanism to evaluate how we are progressing with executing personal strategy, among other things. This is key.

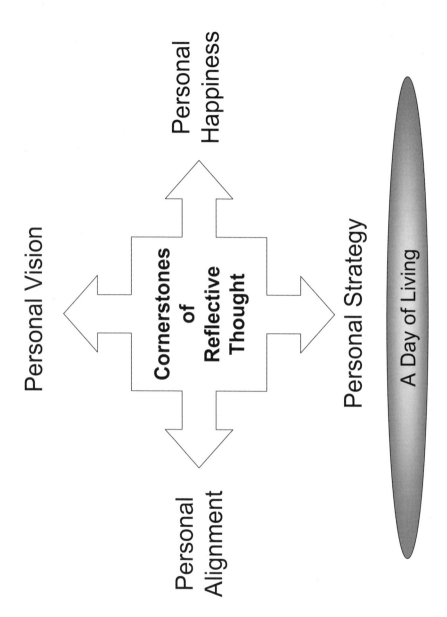

Fig. 15.6

For if we act without reflecting, our actions suffer (are diminished), as we do not benefit from the valuable self-feedback that
reflection provides. Consequently, we reflect, as doing so offers
us a way to redraft, reshape, reset who we are and what we experience on the surface of life.

Now that we know what reflection is and what we reflect
on, the question becomes, 'Why do it? Why engage in reflective thought? What benefits does it offer?' To answer these
questions first requires stating that most people today do not
engage in reflective thought. Few people deliberately stop their
life to reflect on life; to move 'down and in', 'up and in', continually deepening, advancing their understanding of self and soul.
Instead, most never descend below the surface of life (i.e., a rock
skipping on water), thereby denying themselves from living a
more purposeful and fragrant life; experiencing, instead, 'more
of the same' (see Figure 15.7).

For those willing to abandon default, abandon the standard life design, there exist three primary reasons (and several
secondary reasons) to engage in reflective thought:

Primary Reasons:

- To learn, discover things, about **self**
- To learn, discover things, about **soul**
- To learn, discover things, about **personal strategy**

We learn, discover things about self, such as how to better
manage self and life. We learn, discover things about soul, such
as desires of soul to live as soul would live. Lastly, we learn, discover things about our personal strategy to course correct strategy; to become ever more effective with our personal strategy to
achieve our goals. In addition to these primary reasons, there
exist several secondary reasons to engage in reflective thought.

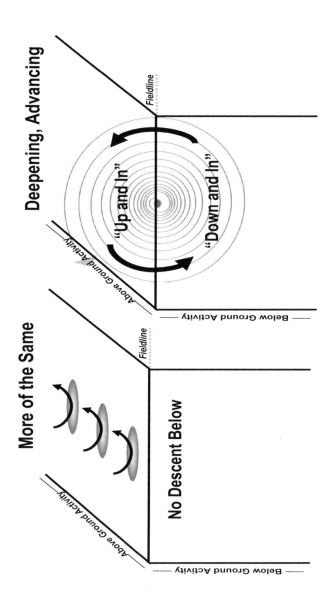

Fig. 15.7

Secondary Reasons:

- Reflection unites that which is disconnected – self and soul. We reflect to resolve 'the missing' that exists between self and soul; to drive out ill feeling within our heart
- Reflection prevents us from slipping, backsliding, engaging in more of the same; the end of reflection is new action; altered action; new activity
- We reflect to discover state of soul; to bring soul forward, from behind shadows, to operate on the surface of life
- Reflection helps us break through the clutter of self to see soul
- Reflection gives rise to soulful interventions and soulful interventions bring freedom, happiness
- By reflecting on our life, we are more apt to see the patterns that define our life. Then, with patterns made visible, we can examine them to assess whether they support personal strategy or debilitate it, leading to identifying new patterns
- Reflection opens our eyes to opportunity and imperative; to what life could be like when operating from soul; higher ground
- We reflect to 'workout' the particulars of our life and our personal strategy. It's where we go to re-draw the fieldline of our life; to deepen the plane from which we operate
- Reflection spawns creative thought, which helps when evaluating our past, examining our present, and planning our future
- Reflection is the gateway to soul; to discover secrets of soul. It is our way to 'go back to the start'; to start one's life anew; to re-discover the joy of living; of what it means to be happy

- Reflection enables us to 'set apart' a life of soul from a life of default; imposter living. It helps us cut loose historical self for emerging self
- Lastly, we reflect to <u>see the unseen</u> (e.g. our beliefs, thoughts, feelings, commitments, habits, assumptions); to make that which is invisible, visible; and we reflect to <u>hear the unheard</u> (e.g. voice of soul); to make that which is silent, audible

As the above list indicates, many reasons exist to engage in reflective thought, but to realize the full benefit that reflection offers, it requires knowing <u>how</u> to reflect. Since most people have little to no experience with reflecting, we discuss the process of reflection next.

Process of Reflection

Once you get past the why (of something), then comes the how. Earlier, I stated that reflection is the key of keys to live a meaningful, purposeful, fragrant life experience. The question is, 'How do we do it? How does one 'reflect'? What are the steps to ensure we do it correctly?' Reflection, like any other activity we may perform, is a process. And when we speak of process, we are concerned with not only what to do (steps), but also how to do it (procedure). We address each of these concerns in turn, beginning with what to do, 'the steps' (see Figure 15.8).

The process of reflection is quite simple, only requiring six steps:

Step 1 – Seek out Evidence
Step 2 – Analyze Evidence
Step 3 – Reflect on Evidence
Step 4 – Tease out the Meaning
Step 5 – Draw Conclusions
Step 6 – Make Changes

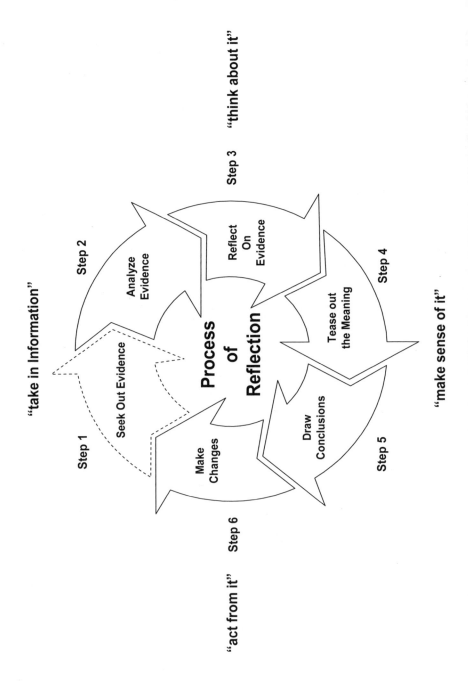

Fig. 15.8

The process of reflection begins with seeking out (collecting) evidence of our life; 'taking in information'. Then we analyze the evidence to reveal the story it tells. Next, we reflect on evidence, seeking ever-deeper insights behind the story. Together, steps two and three represent 'thinking about' the evidence. Next, we tease out the meaning associated with such insights. Then, we draw conclusions from our reflective activity. Together, steps four and five represent 'making sense' of the evidence. Lastly, we make changes to our life based on conclusions drawn; that is, 'we act'. The process of reflection, as described, is circular. That is, it repeats; is iterative; cumulative. As we will discuss shortly, to reflect on one's life means to reflect daily; with past reflection feeding current reflection; cycle repeating. To ensure quality reflection, you should perform steps one through six in sequence, as there are dependencies from step to step. Having said this, the steps that comprise the process of reflection are fluid. That is, there are no hard start and stop points between steps. In fact, you may find yourself performing steps two and three or steps three and four simultaneously without even knowing it. This is typical. In practice, the process of reflection is open, flexible; resisting structure. Flexibility with process is important, but so, too, is structure important. Thus, we consider each step in turn, beginning with Step 1 – Seek Out Evidence.

Step 1 – Seek Out Evidence

Step 1 is arguably the most important of the six steps as it produces the 'raw material' we need to perform Steps 2 through 6. As such, we will spend more time discussing how to seek out evidence.

Seeking out evidence requires examining your life; specifically, 'another day of living'. You collect evidence by doing the following:

a. **Sit quietly ('stop your life')**
   - For 30 minutes; close your eyes, follow your breath, calm yourself, relax, let go...

b. **Think about [the day/week/month/year to come] or [the day/week/month/year just ended]**
   - Step back from events of the day (planned or performed); view yourself from above, at 100ft level, as this will provide proper reference to reflect objectively, without bias

c. **Ask questions of self**
   - Questioning is the key tool, primary method, we use when reflecting. It produces the raw material (i.e., responses from soul) we need in subsequent steps and, therefore, drives reflective activity
   - We ask questions about:
     - Our happiness with life; living
     - Degree of alignment (or misalignment) with soul, work, family, and nature
     - Our inner soul goals/support goals
     - Effectiveness of personal strategy to achieve our goals
     - Life pathways (activities) we perform
     - Types of commitment exerted
     - Degree of commitment exerted
     - Our failures (relative to our personal strategy)
     - Our successes (relative to our personal strategy)
     - Obstacles encountered
     - Debilitations to overcome
     - Cause and effect (amongst components of personal strategy)
     - Personal strategy support tools (e.g. 'life aids', raw data sheet, data collection, PCP, personal scorecard, etc.)

- We ask questions, then we listen for the answer; *as self asks, soul responds*
- The quality of the questions we ask in moments of reflection determine the benefits we realize from reflecting; that is, insights into self, soul, and personal strategy
- Depending on <u>when</u> we reflect, our 'point of departure', determines which questions we ask. For example, the questions we ask when reflecting in the AM differ from those we ask when reflecting in the PM, on the weekend, at month's end, and at year's end (see Table 15.2).

When we sit quietly, to reflect on life, and begin asking questions of self, great things happen. Great things happen because *soul responds*.

Together, sub-steps 1a, 1b, and 1c, <u>create the conditions</u> for self to find soul, to converse with soul, and the dialogue that results represents the 'juice', the real benefit, of reflection. For the dialogue that occurs between self and soul represents 'the good part', the raw material from which we learn, grow, and improve; from which we assess vision to correct vision; from which we course correct strategy to achieve strategy; from which we learn of misalignment to establish alignment; and from which we assess happiness to increase happiness.

To achieve these things, however, requires more than just 'taking in evidence'; it also requires 'thinking about the evidence', which represents Steps 2 and 3 in the process of reflection.

Step 2 – Analyze Evidence

With Step 2 of the process of reflection, we take the 'evidence' of daily living and analyze it. We take 'a day of living' and turn it this way and that way, looking at it from every angle, asking, 'What is the data telling me?' We do this not only to identify

Table 15.2

Point of Departure	Questions We Ask Self
AM	• What is my vision for self? • What are my inner soul goals? • Why am I pursuing these goals? • What sub-goals must I achieve today? • What initiatives will I start today or continue today? • What life pathways must I perform to support key initiatives? • What commitments must I keep to support life pathways? • Did I use my life aids yet? At what point(s) will I use my life aids today? • What did I learn from 'another day of living' (yesterday)? • What do I need to do differently today based on yesterday's learnings? • Is will at attention?
PM	• In what way did I succeed today? • In what way did I fail today? • Why did I fail? • What obstacles did I encounter today? • How did I deal with such obstacles? • How could I have better handled such obstacles? • How could I more effectively use life aids? • What must I do to prevent failures of today from debilitating tomorrow?
At Week's End	• How did I perform during the week to achieve my goals? • What did I do well this week? • What did I do poorly this week? • What must I change (focus on) next week? • Are my life aids helping keep my goals top-of-mind and in my face? How might I use life aids differently? • What observations can I make with respect to my personal strategy? Does it seem to be working? Does cause and effect between the components of my personal strategy reflect expectations? What did I learn about cause and effect?

Table 15.2 (Continued)

At Week's End	• What did I learn about self, soul, and my personal strategy in moments of reflection this week? • How has reflection, 'stopping my life', benefited me this week? In what way did I improve my decision-making and/or conduct as a result of inserting 'pause' in my life?
At Month's End	• How did I perform during the month to achieve my goals? Sub-goals? • What did I do well this month? • What did I do poorly this month? • How effective is my personal strategy thus far? • What, if anything, must I change with my personal strategy based on past learnings? • Did any event occur during the month that requires changing my strategy? • How did my life aids help me stay focused on achieving my goals? • Do I need to refine existing life aids? • Do I need new life aids? • What did I learn about self, soul, and my personal strategy in moments of reflection this month? • How has reflection, 'stopping my life', benefited me this month? In what way did I improve my decision-making and/or conduct as a result of inserting 'pause' in my life?
At Year's End	• Did I achieve my personal mission this year? • What progress did I make this year towards realizing my personal vision? • What goal(s) did I achieve this year? • How effective was my personal strategy in helping me achieve my inner soul goals? • Have my inner soul goals changed? • Why have my goals changed? • Have new priorities surfaced in my life? • In what ways must I modify my personal strategy to achieve my goals more quickly, more effectively? • Have I increased the degree of personal alignment in my life?

Table 15.2 (Continued)

At Year's End	• Am I happier now than when the year began? If not, why not? Am I pursuing the 'right' inner soul goals? • In what ways have I grown personally? • What new life-enhancing capabilities did I develop/ improve over the year? • What did I learn about self, soul, and my personal strategy in moments of reflection this year? • How has reflection, 'stopping my life', benefited me this year? In what way did I improve my decision-making and/or conduct as a result of inserting 'pause' in my life? • What have I learned about using a personal strategy to direct my life? • How will I leverage the learnings of the past year to improve my personal strategy for next year? • What must I focus on next year (commitments, sub-goals, activities, quality/amount of reflection, etc.) to realize better results than this year?

where and what we need to change in our life, but also to keep personal vision, inner soul goals, and personal strategy top-of-mind. Until living by a personal strategy becomes habit, keeping your vision, goals, and personal strategy top-of-mind is a <u>daily</u> requirement. Hence, the value of reflection is revealed.

The analysis we perform of self, of another day of living, is simply to review each day in totality, our commitments, actions, use of life aids, obstacles encountered, etc., to understand what is working with personal strategy and what is not. We analyze each day of living to understand the interrelationships (cause & effect) that comprise our personal strategy to advance personal strategy. For example, each day we employ multiple life aids, exert one or more commitments, perform many life pathways, and utilize other tools from the personal strategy toolbox. When we reflect, we consider, think about, analyze each of these components of our personal strategy to learn how each component works separately and collectively to help us achieve our goals. Additionally, we analyze obstacles encountered when executing personal strategy and how we overcame (or succumbed) to such obstacles and what we will do differently next time.

Reflecting on another day of living, however, entails more than analyzing what went well and did not go well when executing personal strategy; it also requires reflecting on <u>why</u> certain things went well and others did not. In short, it requires getting at root-cause, which speaks to Step 3 – Reflect On Evidence.

Step 3 – Reflect On Evidence

Step 3 involves stepping back from events of the day to rise above self, to see self from a different plane. It requires examining self from a new perspective, different orientation, and reflecting on what we see. Why do we do this? It is because when we deliberately stop our life to reflect on life, a whole new world of opportunity opens up to us as we engage in a different level of discourse with self. We begin to understand self better because we see better. For example, not only do we see our actions more clearly when viewing self from above, but we also see the hidden side of us: our beliefs, our thoughts, our assumptions, our commitments, our habits, our tendencies, etc. And these insights help us understand our behavior to change behavior; they help us recognize obstacles to overcome obstacles; and they help us visualize that which underlies strategy to improve strategy.

We realize these benefits because when we reflect on life, we accelerate our learning of self as we spend more time thinking about not only what we are doing, but also how we are doing it. For example, we reflect on our commitments and level of commitment, asking whether both adequately support performing life pathways. We reflect on the activities we perform (life pathways) and whether such activities will help us achieve our support goals. We reflect on our support goals and whether achieving such goals will help us achieve our inner soul goal. We reflect on the performance measures that comprise our personal

scorecard. We ask whether such measures inspire right behavior to drive right results. Lastly, we reflect on the initiatives
that comprise our personal strategy action plan and the extent
to which each will lead us to the Promised Land. What results
from asking these questions, from reflecting on the evidence, is a
more precise personal strategy. What is significant about this is
that as the precision of our personal strategy increases, so, too,
does the pace with which we achieve our goals (see Figure 15.9).

By reflecting on the evidence, we position ourselves to not
only better define *what* to course correct with personal strategy,
but also to *hear better* the voice of soul. Both these benefits
speak to our ability to make sense of what we are seeing which
represents Steps 4 and 5 of the process of reflection.

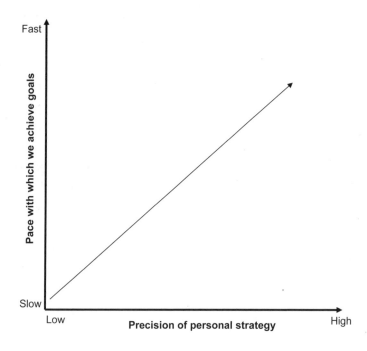

Fig. 15.9

Step 4 – Tease out the Meaning

The reason we reflect is that reflection helps tease out the meaning, subtleties of self and soul; that is, it reveals our world within, the hidden side of us. Entering this other world is not possible when operating on the surface of life. Why is this so? It is because the chaos of everyday living does not accentuate the conditions for us to engage in reflective thought, to hear voice of soul; consequently, we rarely do. When we are not attuned to hear voice of soul, the occasional messages that stream through our head is just noise; noise, in that we do not act (on soul's message) because we do not hear (soul's message). Our hearing is limited, impaired, and the moments too brief for us to hear all of what soul has to say to transform our life. The story changes, however, when we begin to reflect on life. We begin to hear voice of soul, and soul guides us, provides direction, beginning with what inner soul goals to pursue and later, how best to achieve such goals. For example, reflection helps tease out the interdependencies between the components of our personal strategy; the cause and effect relations that drive personal strategy. And with such insight, we can course correct personal strategy (commitments, support goals, life pathways, life aids, etc.) with confidence and precision.

If your goal is to live happily, fragrantly, remarkably you must engage in reflective thought, as only then do you, can you, tease out voice of soul to learn from soul; to live as soul would live. Only when we reflect, practice quieting the mind, to reduce noise heard, do we hear clearly what soul has to say; only then do we become aware of what and how to change our life. And to know what and how to change your life to improve your life speaks to Step 5 – Draw Conclusions.

Step 5 – Draw Conclusions

The reason so few people achieve accomplishments of a lifetime is that few people engage in reflective thought. Isaac Newton

and Albert Einstein both acknowledged that reflection, thinking long and hard about an issue, is what enabled their scientific
breakthroughs. In other words, reflection was the secret of their
genius. The primary benefit of reflection is that it reveals to us
where we should focus our energies (i.e., passions) and, therefore, what not to waste energy on (i.e., default). It helps us realize desires of soul; those things we enjoy, are passionate about,
and innately good at. In short, reflection illuminates the path to
live a remarkable life. Because most people do not engage in reflective thought, most never invest time to reflect on their goals;
reflect on personal strategy to validate their goals, improve strategy. What is the consequence of such in-action? You already
know: goals abandoned.

The story changes, however, when we reflect on our life.
When we reflect on our goals and our personal strategy, goals
and strategy remain in our face and top-of-mind. As such, when
our priorities change due to changes occurring in self and environment, we define new goals quickly. Similarly, when our personal strategy is not working, we course correct quickly; always
moving forward. We do not abandon our goals because we are
on top of our goals. We do not abandon personal strategy because we are on top of our strategy. And when we are on top
of things, the actions that follow, the conclusions we draw, are
not only directionally correct, they are precise. The significance
of this is that precise conclusions lead to precise strategy, which,
as we learned, quickens the pace with which we can transform,
reengineer our life. Drawing precise conclusions also boosts our
confidence in our ability to direct our life. Confidence we need
to summon will and sustain courage to make the difficult changes in our life; to transform our life.

Reflection is the differentiator between a life less lived and
a remarkable life; between us directing life versus life directing
us. Reflection is our way to create distance between historical
you and emerging you; to break with the past in favor of a more
fragrant future. By 'taking in evidence', 'thinking about it', and

'making sense of it', we ready ourselves to 'act from it', which is
Step 6 of the process of reflection.

Step 6 – Make Changes

When you decide to stop your life to analyze your life; to question self, and listen to what soul has to say, great things happen.
Great things happen because reflection reveals to us the changes
we need to make in our life to transform our life. These insights
represent a source of personal power; power we acquire by simply engaging in reflective thought. Through reflection, we discover the 'what and how' of personal strategy to most effectively
and efficiently achieve our goals. Armed with such insights, self
intervenes on behalf of soul. How do we intervene? We define
new support goals, we reestablish our commitments, we enact
new behaviors, we adopt new action, we change life aids, we
sharpen will, and we enforce new beliefs. In short, we change
who we are and how we operate on the surface of life; we change
current self to realize emerging self.

Reflective thought is a key differentiator in life. It differentiates high performers from everyone else. It differentiates remarkable living from default. It differentiates 'the happy' from
'the sad'; 'the living' from 'the dead'. Just as companies differentiate themselves from others by the <u>collective</u> actions they perform, so, too, do we differentiate ourselves from others by the
<u>individual</u> actions we perform. *Engaging in reflective thought is
a high-order action that is <u>open to all</u> and, therefore, <u>can benefit
all</u>.* To achieve your personal vision, to realize emerging you,
you must engage in reflective thought. By following the process
of reflection just described, you will achieve your goals. How
do I know? It is because it happened to me just as assuredly as
it will happen to you.

Now that we have discussed what reflection is, the reasons
to reflect, and how to do it, we revisit our earlier task to discuss
how using a Reflective Learning Journal can help us realize <u>New
Life</u>. We begin by defining what a Reflective Learning Journal is.

A Reflective Learning Journal (RLJ) is a tool from the personal strategy toolbox that we use to capture the happenings of <u>our</u> life; *a day of living*. Thus, just as each person's personal vision is unique, and each person's personal strategy is unique, so, too, is each person's RLJ unique. RLJ's are 'containers', frameworks, we use to: 1) record our thought, 2) reflect on thought, 3) refine our thought, and 4) advance from thought (see Figure 15.10).

What is illustrated is a 'double-entry' Reflective Learning Journal. A double-entry journal captures the reflections of each day on one side and future reflections, that is, *reflection upon reflection* on the other side. This design is simple, yet effective, in that not only do we learn from current reflection, we also learn from past reflection by reflecting on reflection; hence, the term 'double entry'. By design, a double entry journal informs that reflective thought is meant to be re-examined, re-used, re-introduced into our life continuously. Every day of life offers opportunity to capture important insights into self, soul, and personal strategy. We must leverage such insights; squeeze every bit of benefit from past reflections. Therefore, whereas daily reflection is to reflect on events of the day, week-end, month-end, and year-end reflections are to reflect on reflections of the past. Although the time demands increase when re-examining events of a week, month, or year, so, too, do the benefits; with reviewing more content comes more benefit. To record reflections of the day and not revisit such reflections denies you the full benefit that reflection offers; namely, deep insights into self, soul, and personal strategy. Now, as with other frameworks presented in this book, the double-entry framework represents only a guide, one version, and therefore is open to revision, enhancement, customization, and improvement. Create your own version to suit your needs.

A RLJ is a physical manifestation of reflection; it is evidence of reflective thought. And the evidence we record comes from 'a day of living', as everyday represents a 'reflection point';

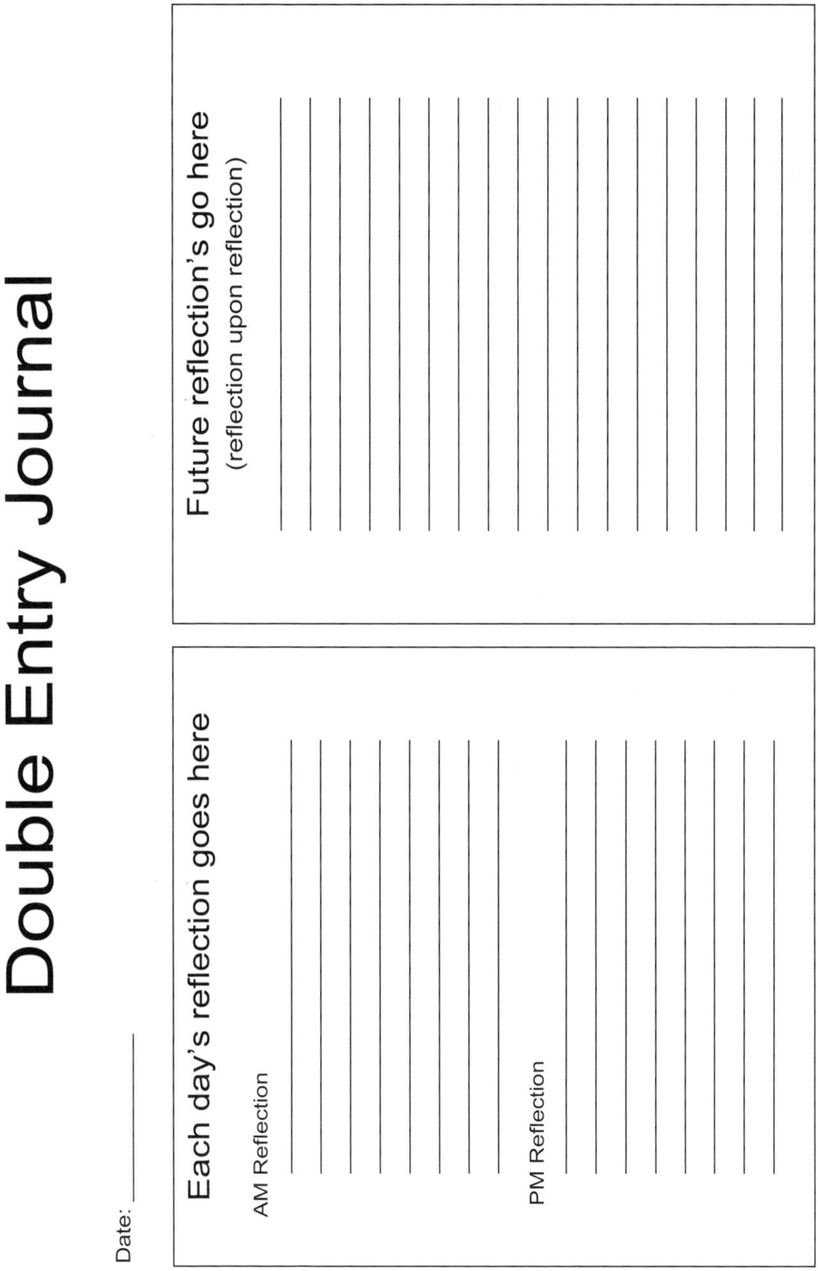

Double Entry Journal

Date: _____

Each day's reflection goes here

AM Reflection

Future reflection's go here
(reflection upon reflection)

PM Reflection

Fig. 15.10

a reflective event. Each day of living represents opportunity; opportunity to advance one's personal strategy and, therefore, one's goals. We capture our advances (and retreats) on the pages of our RLJ. Reflective Learning Journals record/capture our personal story – *the story of our life*. In this way, a RLJ considers, includes, both our inner story (dialogue between self and soul) and our outer story (experiences on the surface of life). Because we reflect daily (AM, PM, or both), an RLJ becomes, in effect, a 'running record' of how we evolve over time and, therefore, how our personal vision, inner soul goals, and personal strategy must evolve as well. How do we evolve?

Each of us evolves in varied ways:

- Our beliefs
- Our priorities
- Our thinking
- Our values

Moreover, when we evolve in these ways, it drives changes in:

- Our mission/vision
- Our goals
- Our personal strategy (PSM/PSTs)
- Our initiatives
- Our actions
- Our commitments

What the above indicates is that as we progress on the inside (beliefs, priorities, values, etc.), so, too, must we progress on the outside (vision, goals, personal strategy, etc.). Now, because so few people actually engage in personal reflection, the evolving that does occur is of a lesser kind and never deepens to the point of significantly altering one's vision, actions, and commitments to transform one's life. For if it did, such efforts would yield life altering results not more of the same.

Reflective Learning Journals are, however, more than just containers to record content of life; they are containers in which we capture voice of soul; *soul emerging in written form.* Figure 15.11 illustrates the process of reflection and use of an RLJ: 1) self and soul come together for quiet conversation, 2) we question self, in the presence of soul, 3) to which, soul responds, 4) yielding dialogue, which we capture in our RLJ; cycle repeating.

What is illustrated is a cycle of self-learning, of continuous learning, continuous improvement. When we stop our life to question self, to hear soul's response, and capture tones of soul in our RLJ, great things happen. Great things happen because with each turn of the cycle, with each up and down movement, we learn more about our-self and our soul. Reflection, and use of an RLJ, provides us an opportunity to develop ideas, to brainstorm, to connect old knowledge and experience with recent knowledge and experience. It's an opportunity to develop new hypotheses (for self and life) and test them, turn them over, within one's mind prior to testing them within one's life. Further, with each turn, we distance current self from emerging self; each reflective event bringing us closer to realizing who we really are. Reflection 'brings us in' to discover emerging self, and our RLJ 'brings us out' to realize emerging self.

We use our RLJ not to escape from self, but to find self; to find soul; to hear soul. Soul calls out to us in its own way (through intense feelings, passing thoughts) and using an RLJ is our way of calling back; of meeting soul half way. Our RLJ is the glue, connector, the 'meeting place', between self and soul. We use our RLJ to return to our natural (authentic) state before living changed us; *suppressed who we are and were meant to be on the surface of life.* Using an RLJ reunites us with authentic self, brings authentic self to the surface of life, where it should naturally exist, to feel the sun's warm glow. RLJ's are an 'inner forum' for the interior of our life to thrive, just as nature serves as an 'outer forum' for the exterior of our life to thrive. When we use an RLJ, we set spirit free to sing across the pages contained within. More than this, when we use an RLJ, we find answers to

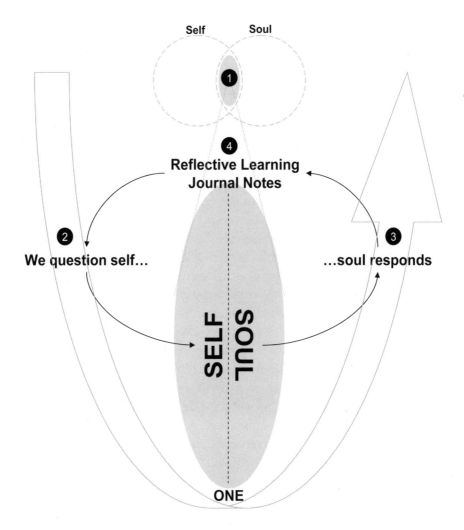

Fig. 15.11

our most pressing personal inquiries, including, 'What is this life for?' For when you ask questions of self, *in the presence of soul*, something remarkable happens; you get the answers for which you have long been searching.

Using an RLJ represents active learning, or more precisely, pro-active learning – the deliberate attempt to advance quickly with one's learnings. Just as personal strategy is a means to an end, so, too, is RLJ a means to an end. We use RLJ's to learn, to improve; to achieve personal strategy, establish personal alignment, and increase personal happiness. Using an RLJ is the quickest, surest way to achieve these things and more. The reason using an RLJ works is that doing so provides valuable feedback on the 'what and how' of our life – including insights into self and soul. So, just as companies do not move forward without collecting feedback on their existence (customer feedback, financial feedback, quality feedback, etc.), so, too, do we not move forward individually unless we collect feedback on our existence. An RLJ is our tool to collect such feedback; to 'close the loop' on self-improvement. This is one area where most people fall down. Most people do not notice, collect, or evaluate feedback from their life to transform their life; consequently, few do. This is to no one's fault, however, as we were never educated on such matters. But, know this: *learning is a prerequisite to improving*.

In time, you will discover, as I did, that using an RLJ is vital, necessary to achieve personal strategy. Why is this so? Just as writing goals on paper makes them real, brings them to life, so, too, does writing in a RLJ make personal strategy real, brings it to life. How is this possible? It is because RLJ's facilitate bringing new beliefs, goals, strategy, actions, commitments, initiatives, and energies to the surface of life. Two 'hidden' processes govern this dynamic; one process above the fieldline, on the surface of life, and one process below the fieldline, below the surface of life (see Figure 15.12).

What is illustrated is that as we execute personal strategy, we are both spectator and participant; we reflect and we

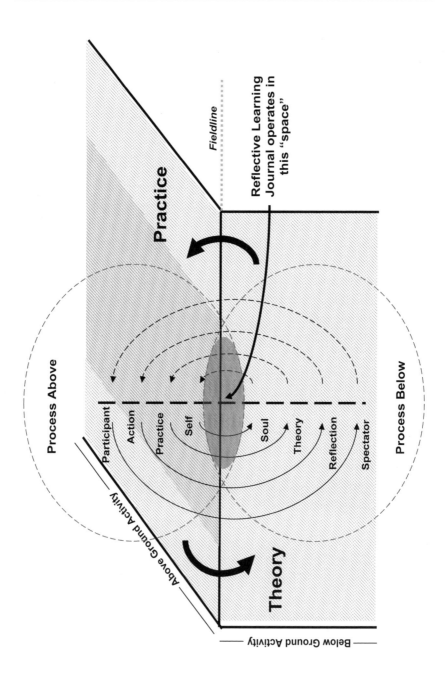

Fig. 15.12

act; we theorize (about personal strategy) and we put theories to practice. Lastly, we are both self and soul. In short, we are both the process above and the process below. Our life is both the process above and the process below; two sides of the same coin. The importance in knowing that both processes exist is that Reflective Learning Journals operate *between* such processes. That is, RLJ's operate in the 'space' between spaces; between theory and practice, between self and soul; straddling the field-line of life. Because Reflective Learning Journals operate in the space between inner and outer, they represent the midpoint in the movement of our life, linking our past, present, and emerging future (see Figure 15.13).

RLJ's create the space, the forum, for us to consider our past, present, and future in the same conversation; we incorporate the past, examine the present, and plan/direct our future. We do all this on the pages of our Reflective Learning Journal.

As RLJ's operate between outer and inner, they represent the place of <u>highest leverage</u> to consider that which has transpired to affect that which is yet to come; and what comes from an RLJ is present giving way to emerging future, using learnings of the past as context. RLJ's help us connect with our experiences; to examine them, learn from them; to recast new experiences. An RLJ is the 'place' for self and soul to interact; to reunite; to ignite new understandings, new ideas, new possibilities for self. As such, self and soul are equals in the reflection process; both are at the table conversing, listening, emerging. The ever-spiraling movement of our life between upper and lower, inner and outer, practical experience and reflective learning, is what enables our growing, our advancing, and our achieving set goals. As such, RLJ's 'track with', mirror, the inner/outer movements of our life; the iterations of our life. They record movements so easily missed (or dismissed) because of the quick pace with which we live life. By connecting inner dialogue (self & soul) with outer expression (self & nature), RLJ's serve a great human need to capture the silent tones of soul for self to learn from soul, to operate from soul, to live as soul would live.

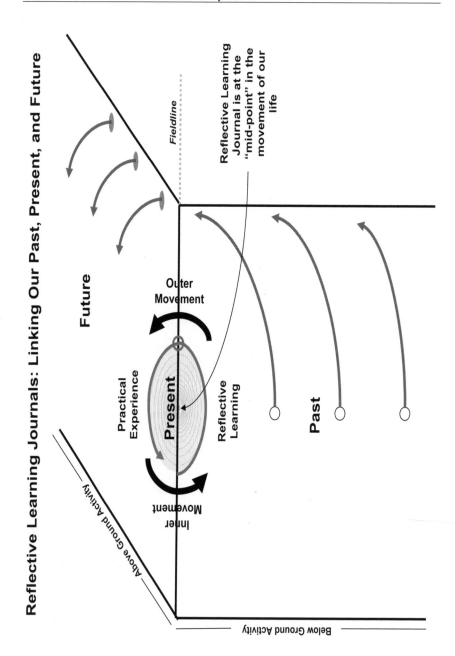

Reflective Learning Journals: Linking Our Past, Present, and Future

Fieldline

Reflective Learning Journal is at the "mid-point" in the movement of our life

Future

Outer Movement

Practical Experience

Present

Reflective Learning

Inner Movement

Past

Above Ground Activity

Below Ground Activity

Fig. 15.13

On the pages of an RLJ, self and soul become One; to think as One, to plan as One, to align as One, to emerge as One. As such, the audience of an RLJ is <u>One</u>. An RLJ enables the 'whole' person to be captured (represented) and, therefore, examined; it provides space and opportunity for self and soul to meet for quiet conversation, to first align self with soul, and then align self with work, family, and nature. We accomplish all this by simply doing what most people will not (*Note: I did not say cannot*) do, 'stop our life'.

Now that we have described what is a Reflective Learning Journal, we expand upon our reasons for using it. As with reflection, there are many reasons to use a Reflective Learning Journal:

- Promotes reflective thinking; forces questioning of self while demanding an answer
- Is a portal (gateway) into our past, present, and future
- Helps us acquire new information about self, soul, and personal strategy
- Helps reveal 'the truth', realize the full shape, of who we are and were meant to be on the surface of life
- Helps 'push our thinking'
- Solves the problem of 'the immediate' (of life) driving out 'the important' (of life)
- Helps us become more sensitized to what we attend to in life
- Gives an active voice to soul
- Is a source of energy to drive personal strategy, maintain will, and achieve goals
- Takes over where OOS ends

Let us now discuss each of these reasons in turn, beginning with how RLJ's help promote reflective thinking and questioning of self.

The first reason <u>why</u> we use an RLJ is that it promotes reflective thinking, forces self-questioning, and demands answers. RLJ's encourage self (give self reason) to pull up a chair to converse with soul; it represents a symbolic, yet tangible, reminder of the need to converse with soul daily.

Using an RLJ forces us to stop our life, to pause. We pause to ask important questions of self for soul to respond. Using an RLJ also helps prevent backsliding to unwanted habits, thereby reinforcing new habits by keeping personal vision, inner soul goals, and personal strategy in our face and top-of-mind.

Another reason to use an RLJ is that they provide space and opportunity (a portal, gateway) to examine our past, understand our present, and explore our future. To have space, a forum, for self and soul to meet to incorporate wisdom of the past, learnings of the present, and glimpses of the future is vital to transform one's life. We use learnings of the past to guide us, learnings of the present to re-direct us, and learnings of our future to inspire us. Luckily, all views are possible when using an RLJ.

The need to acquire information (i.e., feedback) is another reason why we use an RLJ. When we reflect, use an RLJ, we acquire new information about self, soul, and personal strategy, among other things. We write in our RLJ as a means of interrogating our life; our commitments, our life pathways, and our goals. We do this because with interrogation comes different action. In fact, once we interrogate our life, ALL future actions are forever altered; all actions are altered because *we are altered*; we are not the same person exiting conversation (with soul) as when entered. ***Each conversation between self and soul changes us.*** For example, what we 'see' changes. We begin to see our life from a different perspective; from the perspective of self outside of self. When this happens, we are free to examine our thinking and actions of the day. We can begin to understand why we act the way we do and then develop precise countermeasures to prevent debilitations from derailing our dream. The act of stepping outside of self to 'see' self is a simple, but powerful, tactic, as it enables us to obtain new information, to change all that follows; how we think, act, and feel. And the more feedback we obtain, the greater the insights we develop about self, soul, and personal strategy. Collectively, these insights, as captured on the pages of a RLJ, help us realize another benefit, reason why, we use an RLJ – to get at 'the truth'.

A key reason we use an RLJ is to get at 'the truth' – the truth of who we are and were meant to be on the surface of life. We accomplish this by conversing with soul and capturing voice of soul on the pages of our RLJ. It is only by conversing with soul that we discover the full shape of who we are and were meant to be. Using an RLJ, we capture voice of soul, which reveals what we want in life and from life at any point in life. It reveals what and how to change our life. It awakens dormant soul and, therefore, dormant destiny. And with soul awakened, we can learn from soul to live as soul would live. Few people today possess a truth of who they are and want to be. For most, life represents 'going through the motions'. For most, life becomes one of quiet desperation; inner turmoil, never resolved. For such people, the reality, 'shape' of their existence is less grand, less elegant, less fragrant than it could be. One reason for this sad truth is that no one ever told us of the need to reflect or how to do it; consequently, few do. Adding salt to wound is the fact that each of us grows up seeing the standard life design, which blinds us to the glory that awaits from going the other way. These truths, when combined with the quick, chaotic, ever-competitive world in which we live, all but ensure that we never stop our life long enough to find out who we are and were meant to be. Our 'truth' has always been with us, been in front of us; just below the surface of things. We just needed the right tool, proper forum (i.e., RLJ), to see it. In addition to RLJ's revealing the truth of who we are, they also help push our thinking, which drives how we act and, therefore, how we feel. Thus, if you do not feel good about where you are or what you are doing in life, then, ultimately, the only way to change this story is to change how you think. Consequently, *we reflect, utilize RLJ's, to think*.

An RLJ offers us intellectual space in which we can think. By reflecting 30 minutes a day, you will begin thinking in remarkable new ways. What causes new thinking? It is the result of questioning self. We ask questions about our actions, commitments, and feelings of the day. We ask more questions about our personal strategy. And we ask still more questions about our inner soul goals and the obstacles encountered while pursuing such goals. What results from asking all these questions is thinking, as questioning breeds thinking. And what comes from all this thinking is yet more thinking; deeper thinking, holistic thinking, *systems thinking*. One of the great benefits of reflection, of using an RLJ, is that it results in planting many (idea) seeds, some of which mature in the course of immediate reflection, others developing at a slower rate; maturing right before your eyes, perhaps weeks, months, or years after planting. This is what happened to me one day while driving to work. The idea (seed) to write this book came out of nowhere. From earlier reflection, the seed to write this book was planted (unbeknownst to me), and years later, the seed matured right before my eyes. Ideas, like plants, require time to germinate; grow. Reflective Learning Journals are the planting bed of great ideas, remarkable ideas, life-transforming ideas. The correlation is clear: the more you reflect, the more you record your conversation between self and soul, the more seeds you deposit, and the more seeds you deposit, the greater the harvest; that is, the greater the insights you can develop into self, soul, and how to course correct your life to improve your life.

In addition to RLJ's offering us space to think, another important reason to use an RLJ is that it corrects for 'the immediate' (of life) driving out 'the important' (of life). That is, it forces us to get in touch with that which lies within; suppressed by the activity of life. Contemporary living is flawed. Life in the year 2010 represents more a race to the finish than a journey to enjoy. What results from living this way is that few people actually enjoy life. I would imagine that if, before we passed this earth, each person were required to complete an exit interview, we would find that most people felt cheated in some way with living; most would feel that they did not truly live at all, did not experience the full splendor, opportunity, and pageantry that life offers. Consequently, we use an RLJ to stop our life to connect with that which lies within. And with such knowledge, we can direct and transform our life in magical, inspiring ways. Transforming one's life requires great effort, but knowing what and how to transform one's life represents half the battle. This is where the value of using an RLJ reveals itself; daily.

Another reason we use an RLJ is that they help sensitize us, increase our awareness, of what we attend to in life. Stopping one's life to reflect on life enables us to see more clearly, think more deeply about our life. And the more we do this, the more sensitized we become to changes occurring in self and environment. You will begin to see self and world differently. You will begin to listen differently; there will be less noise, more music. No longer will the standard life design blind you to the glorious reality that is possible when you decide to go the other way. No longer will the standard life design interest you or be something you tolerate. No longer will the standard life design stifle emerging you; prevent you from maximizing the personal, professional, and financial potential that life offers. Using an RLJ will sensitize you to what is misaligned in your life to restore alignment. It will sensitize you to what and how to improve personal strategy to achieve strategy. Lastly, it will sensitize you to hear better the voice of soul, to learn from soul, to live as soul would live.

Recording voice of soul, giving an active voice to soul, is perhaps the most important reason WHY we use a RLJ. By design, soul is silent, but made explicit through written word in an RLJ, just as it is made explicit through ill feeling within our heart when misalignment exists within our life. Because most people do not reflect on their life or use an RLJ, most never hear voice of soul. Such people do, however, feel the sufferings of soul; a broken heart, a dampened spirit, deep unhappiness, a life gone gray. The moment one begins reflecting; begins using an RLJ, however, healing begins. In time, heart mends, spirit lifts, happiness supplants sadness, and life once again regains its color. It is important to recognize that voice of soul is silent because of our own accord; because of certain in-actions. In reading this book, you now have the power and knowledge to bring tones of soul to the surface; to the foreground of your life. The challenge is, has always been, to find a method, possess a tool, *to find soul*; to bring it forward, into the present, so self can live as soul would live. Having said this, you do possess method, you do have a tool; the method is reflection and the tool is a Reflective Learning Journal.

The insights into self, soul, and personal strategy that come from using an RLJ inspire us. And such inspiration emits a well-spring of energy, fuel, to execute personal strategy, maintain will, and achieve goals. It is for these reasons that we also employ an RLJ. For when we are inspired, we do our best work. This is undeniable. Inspiration is our fuel, our energy, our momentum-builder and our momentum-sustainer, and the only way to inspire self is to pursue desires of soul; desires, so revealed, so discussed, so strategized, on the pages of your RLJ.

The last reason we use an RLJ is that it takes over where OOS ends. The entirety of this book was about learning; learning about self on the way to soul. However, the learning does not end with last page turned; it continues, in the form of your RLJ. This book served as instructor, mentor, and friend as you discovered much about your self to define and implement a personal strategy for living. In a way, this book served as life aid, to sustain your journey, to bring you home. At book's end, there is still need for instruction, mentorship, and friendship. Our RLJ provides such things; serves such roles. On the pages of our RLJ, we obtain instruction. On the pages of our RLJ, we receive mentorship. On the pages of our RLJ, we find friendship. There is no better place for us to find these things than in the silent womb, the sacred chamber, that is a Reflective Learning Journal. And when we go to that special place, not only do we find instruction, mentorship, and friendship, we also find meaning, purpose, and love. Most of all, what we find, in the private world that is our RLJ, is the path which leads home.

You began your OOS journey with theory informing practice. You determined where you are, what you wanted in life and from life, and what you are innately good at. These efforts, in turn, spawned developing personal mission, vision, a set of inner soul goals, and a strategy to achieve each goal. Now, at book's end, with executing personal strategy and utilizing a Reflective Learning Journal, tables turn – practice now informing theory (see Figure 15.14).

This is as it should be; life informing theory, theory informing life; cycle repeating. As reflection operates in the space between spaces, between theory and practice, it has the power to affect, influence, determine what emerges with each turn of the cycle. We know this to be true, as the quality of our advancements above is a function of the quality of our deepening below, which is itself a function of the quality of our reflections between.

One question you still may have is, 'How do I know if I am reflecting correctly; doing a good job?' To ensure that you benefit from reflective thought, listed below are the keys to engage in high-quality reflection:

- Make reflection the highest <u>personal</u> priority in your life
- Do not rush through reflection; *plant seeds slowly*
- Set aside regular time (e.g. 30 minutes) to reflect (AM/ PM/ Weekly/ Monthly/ Yearly) – create a <u>reflection calendar</u>
- Focus on quality of self dialogue, not quantity
- Seek penetration; face reality; be brutal with self when in the presence of soul
- Be patient (to hear voice of soul)
- Focus on outcomes of the reflective process; deep insights into self, soul, and personal strategy
- Use RLJ as a tool; incorporate the past, review the present, glimpse the future
- Suspend current beliefs, thoughts, and assumptions in the air for challenge; revision
- Ask questions, then sit back and let answers come; on their own accord; at their own pace; in their own way

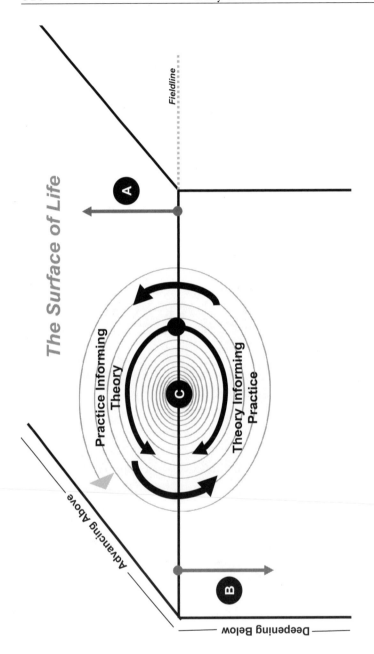

Fig. 15.14

By following the guidelines above, you will realize full benefit from your reflective exercises. To conclude this section, we summarize the benefits of engaging in reflective thought.

The **benefits** of reflection are:

- Increases confidence to direct one's life
- Provides space and opportunity to challenge, question self in the presence of soul; to transform self
- Disciplines us
- We become more thoughtful; deepens our thoughts
- We become more reflective; develops our capacity to reflect
- We become more analytical
- We become conscious of our learning
- We become a more effective (active) participant in life
- We become aware of how we learn best
- Future actions build from past actions; we leverage the past to direct our future
- We become more adaptive to change (within self and environment)
- Promotes new, 'life enhancing', habits
- We develop the capability to learn faster, better; more efficiently and effectively
- We develop a more effective personal strategy
- We develop an appreciation of reflection
- Resolves the 'missing' between self and soul
- Increased awareness and ability to see self and life holistically
- Provides solutions to previously unsolved problems
- Increases understanding of cause and effect (with one's personal strategy) to tighten cause and effect
- We learn the role life aids play in helping us achieve our goals and how to develop more effective life aids
- We become aware of all the ways we are changing (e.g., beliefs, seeing, willing, thinking, acting, and feeling)

- Increases awareness of self and surroundings; we 'notice' more
- We develop greater intimacy, awareness, and alignment between self and soul
- Increases our sensitivity to hear better the voice of soul while strengthening voice of soul
- Keeps personal vision, inner soul goals, and personal strategy top-of-mind and in our face; that is, it prevents backsliding
- Lastly, and most importantly, *reflection pulls soul forward, into the present, onto the surface of life, for self to live as soul would live*

As the above list indicates, many benefits accrue from reflective thought.

It is the quiet moments of our life that shape our life; when we are most active. Why is this so? It is because in such moments we are in the presence of soul, whose only interest, only motivation, only purpose in life, is to make us aware of who we are and were meant to be on the surface of life. Thus, the more time spent in the presence of soul the more likely you will live as soul would live.

---

*It is because we do not stop our life, do not reflect on life, do not converse with soul, **do not know soul** that we are in the shape we are in*

What this section asks of you is to *let silence be your teacher*. There is elegance in silence; at once magical, at once joyful, at once beautiful – all representing that which emerges when we walk into darkness. When I first began reflecting, I could not hear voice of soul. Then, over time, and with much dialogue, I began to hear tones of soul; more than this, I discovered the full shape of soul. That is, I discovered how to quickly connect with soul; engage in quiet conversation. What I discovered was that *when I close my eyes, there is soul; calling out to me, engaging me, to converse as One, to align as One, to be One* (see Figure 15.15).

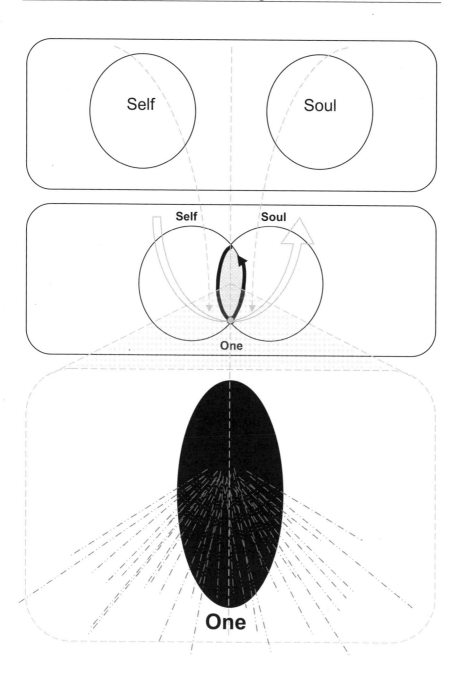

Fig. 15.15

The same is true of an RLJ, for when we write in a RLJ, *there, too, is soul.* The 'darkness' differentiates our world within from our world without, and from the darkness, bright light shines. When I discovered this truth, I realized that soul has always been with me; just behind exterior. I realized that the darkness represented the quiet room, the meeting place, to converse with soul; to hear the sweet sounds of soul. We enter the quiet room with eyes closed; yet eyes wide open. We walk into darkness as parts (self and soul), but reflection makes us whole again.

We have always had opportunity and capability to transform our life; it is just that most of us rarely stop our life *to* transform our life. The journey of OOS helped you hear voice of soul. Now, the onus is on you to never go deaf again. This section provided the 'what', 'how', and 'why' of using reflection and a Reflective Learning Journal to continue what you started with reading this book. For all the reasons discussed whence forth, we say that reflection is the 'key of keys'.

We started this section learning that three things are necessary for us to realize the New Life Model:

- Executing a personal strategy reflecting soul
- Exerting will
- Engaging in personal reflection

Know this: when one designs and executes a personal strategy reflecting soul, exerts will, and engages in personal reflection, one can rise above default; rise above the standard life design; realize <u>New Life</u>!

The benefits of the New Life Model are many. Alignment that begins locally will spread globally. New seeing, willing, thinking, acting, and feeling at a sub-system level will, in time, transform seeing, willing, thinking, acting, and feeling on a super-system level. Happiness will supplant sadness. Connectedness will supplant separation. Sharing will supplant greed. New consciousness, new priorities, new details will define, and then consume, the world agenda. The world will begin to see through a new lens, begin to operate from collective soul, altering all that follows. And then, suddenly, the New Life Model will begin to supplant the Standard Life Design as default, as world brings forth new ways of operating. At last, we achieve collectively what exists locally; a feeling of One; One vision, One humanity, One voice, *One King*. As we bring together the broken pieces of our-self, in time, we will bring together the broken pieces of our planet. Just as companies have learned and awakened to the notion that alignment is everything, so, too, is the world awakening to such fact. Whether speaking of self, family, work, community, nation, or planet – *One is the goal.* Table 15.3 highlights what it means for self and world to operate as One:

Table 15.3

For Self to Operate as One	For World to Operate as One
• Self and soul are aligned in sight (i.e., 'common vision') • Self and soul are aligned in thought (i.e., 'common goals') • Self and soul operate as a single entity, with single voice • Aligned energies exist from soul→will→mind→body	• Shared consciousness among and between all nations, all people • A world of 'haves' • Shared goals; shared vision • Freedom for all • Food for all • Healthcare for all • Shared resources • Unification among and between matter, mind, spirituality, society, ecology, technology, and economy • World operates at its 'highest potential'; on higher ground; from a new place • Shared seeing, willing, thinking, acting, and feeling • Greater achievements, the likes of which the world has never seen

Transitioning to the New Life Model on a global scale will not be easy. The good news is that the process begins locally with you; individual. And although your efforts represent grass-root level, it is at this level, that all movements begin; individually, collectively. Thus, in time, your efforts, my efforts, and the efforts of millions others around the globe will transform humanity just as surely as you transform self. Together, we will build a new movement that people can believe in. Now, having said this, it is important to remain patient with self and world as authenticity emerges slowly. To realize emerging you, to achieve your inner soul goals <u>will take time</u>. For some, only a few changes in season are necessary, for others, several seasons are required before work is done; before soul rises.

Reengineering the life design is possibly the most important issue of our time. When we compare the New Life Model with default, we see that there is no question of whether we need a new life design, for individual and for planet (see Table 15.4).

Table 15.4

Standard Life Design	New Life Model
• Reflects default (i.e., no design)	• Reflects intention (i.e., purposeful design)
• Results in a life diminished; quiet desperation	• Results in inspired living
• Essence reflects 'just getting through'; misalignment	• Essence reflects alignment
• Focused on perpetuating the past; 'more of the same'	• Focused on the future; 'going the other way'
• Propagates the cancerous economic machine	• Promotes pursuing passion; living passionately; following own design
• Traps most in 'a life without meaning'	• Ensures maximizing the personal, professional, and financial potential that life offers
	• Promotes equality, dignity, and freedom for all; One World

What Table 15.4 clearly indicates is that the more explicit you are in defining your life, the more likely you are to <u>live</u> life. In other words, do not leave your life for default, as it results in outcomes few people want.

We conclude this chapter by considering an age-old question, the answer to which underlies a life design; reflects the New Life Model. We ask, '*What is this life for?*'

What is This Life For?

In the previous chapter, we discussed that which underlies a life design; namely, the source from which one operates. We learned that operating from self does not reflect purposeful design. Whereas, operating from soul does reflect purposeful design. And it was from this discussion that we learned that operating from soul is <u>the only way to live</u>. Which brings us current; to address a question that demands an answer. To ask, 'What is this life for?'

The question, 'What is this life for?' is the mother of all questions. It gets past the triviality of everyday living; to consider our place in the world; to consider our existence; to consider origin. People have asked, pondered, and debated this question for thousands of years. From Aristotle, to Sartre, to the present, people still ask the question. But why do we ask? It is because <u>self</u> demands an answer. For if we do not ask, our life becomes, in the words of Sartre, "absurd". Sartre's argument was that we arrive, then what? He stated that life was absurd because there is no inherent purpose for our life, upon arrival. There is some truth to this, in that no one hands us a mission statement, vision statement upon arriving on earth. Nevertheless, <u>purpose</u> does exist, has always existed; it's just lying below the surface; waiting to be found. The answer to the question above lies not with others, in a 'secret' book, or in religion, it lies with you; within soul.

Each of us has heard the phrase "Life is what you make of it". This is a true statement, in that each of us writes, directs, and produces ('makes') our own life story. The challenge with living is not the 'how' of life as each of us finds our way; it is the 'what' of life. What do we include in our script of life? What content defines our life story? In the prior chapter, we learned that purpose comes from soul; can only come from soul. You cannot acquire purpose, nor can you find purpose in a book, library, or have a career counselor coax it out of you. The best any of these resources can do is provide you tools, techniques, and methods to facilitate the process, as finding purpose is an internal exercise and, therefore, requires a resource of a different kind: you. Soul, if you let it, will guide you through life. It is what soul was meant to do. Soul's reason for being is to show you the way, to answer, in very definite terms, what your life is for. For some, soul directs to become a doctor to heal the sick. For some, soul directs to start a business to provide goods and services people need. And for others, soul directs to write a book to help others find soul and bring it forward, into the present, onto the surface of life.

So, where does this leave us? How do we answer the mother of all questions? Which answer seems appropriate, relevant, and applicable to all? I believe that I have the answer. ***What this life is for, what we should aspire to do, is <u>to live as soul would live</u>***. To live as soul would live means that we:

- See as soul sees
- Think as soul thinks
- Act as soul would act
- Feel what soul feels

Therefore, we see life not with one's eyes but through one's eyes (through soul), and life is glorious. We think of opportunity and imperative; of mission, vision, inner soul goals; of alignment; as One, and life is meaningful. We achieve as soul would achieve; maximizing the personal, professional, and financial potential that life offers. Lastly, we live as soul would live, and life is fragrant. Our schooling may have inadequately prepared us to live purposefully, meaningfully, happily. It may have left us fettering in an unforgiving, relentless, competitive world, but we can find purpose, meaning, and happiness. Know this: when you commit to converse with soul, when you commit to operate from soul, when you commit to live as soul would live, never again will the question, 'What is this life for?' confound you, as *you already know*.

Many pages have coursed your hand to reach this point. Your quest has taken you through learning where you are, to learning where you want to be, to developing a plan to set self free. However, such achievements do not reflect the enormity of your efforts. For what you have achieved, possibly unbeknownst to you, is far greater than simply learning where you are and where you want to be, including developing a plan on how to get there. No, this quest of yours, your crowning achievement, reflects, represents, but one thing – *'going home'*.

Going Home

"Life's a voyage that's homeward bound."

\- Herman Melville

I HAVE BEEN IN YOUR SHOES; that is, I have operated on <u>your</u> plane. I, too, felt dissatisfied with life, with living. I, too, felt that the standard life design did not satisfy, did not align, did not offer the happiness I craved. I needed more from life, something better, but what? My internal pain, my lingering confusion, was always a matter of 'what' and 'why', not 'how'. I could not answer the question, 'What is this life for?' Then, I discovered soul, altering all that follows. I realized that I am the architect of my life; that my life need not reflect default, but intention. I realized that the feelings I felt were soul's attempt to communicate with me; it was soul's attempt to free me, save me from a life without meaning. What I discovered was that when I stopped my life to converse with soul, I discovered intention; I discovered purpose; I <u>saw</u> my future, and it was glorious. Only now, at this moment, as I commit words to paper, can I articulate my long, arduous, painful heart-felt journey. What was happening to me, <u>as now with you</u>, is that soul was leading me back home; quietly, patiently, graciously, deliberately.

To write this book and share it with you, I first had to live
the words lying herein. That is, I could only help you if I first
helped myself. I had to stop my life, to converse with soul, to
learn from soul. I had to define inner soul goals, develop a personal strategy to achieve each goal, and then execute strategy. I
had to manage personal strategy as I changed and my environment changed. I had to overcome obstacles, just as you will have
to overcome obstacles. Lastly, I had to exert will; staying true,
focused, committed to both opportunity and imperative. I have
felt the pain of misalignment; of being disconnected with soul,
work, family, and nature. But, I chose to rise, just as you now
choose to rise, and my experiences provide me context, inspire
wisdom to teach you, coach you, inspire you with your heart-felt
journey. It is from this basis that we continue.

We opened this chapter with a quote stating, "Life's a voyage that's homeward bound". I chose this quote because it captures the essence of the OOS journey, of your journey, in that, to
align the inner soul with action, represents 'going home' – *within
your mind* and *within your life*.

The phrase 'going home' has special meaning in this book,
for it represents a two-part journey, a two-part movement of 'going home' within one's mind, to find emerging you, then 'going
home' within one's life, to realize emerging you (see Figure 16.1).

Part I represents a downward internal movement to find
soul, converse with soul, and align with soul. The opening created when self and soul came together for quiet conversation represented the 'place' or 'internal home' where you could discover
soul's intention to craft inner soul goals reflecting intention.
Only by performing Part I of 'going home' within your mind
could you perform Part II, 'going home' within your life. Part
II represents an upward external movement where we align all
aspects of self and life using our personal vision, goals, and strategy to guide us on the surface of life; each step (action) bringing
us closer, helping us reach, 'external home'. Thus, whereas Part
I is about journeying to an internal place (soul) to craft vision,
Part II is about journeying to an external place (happiness) from

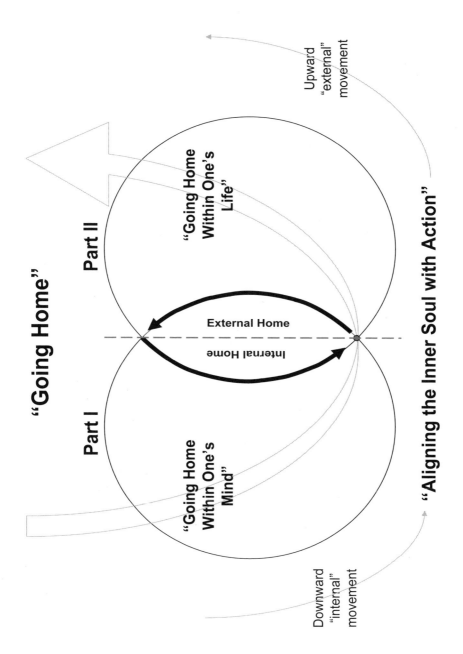

Fig. 16.1

realizing vision. It is about completing the work of Part I, by bringing soul to the surface of life for self to live as soul would live. In this way, each 'movement' compliments one another; each needs the other. Together, the two-part movement achieves the goal, as described by the subtitle of this book: *"aligning the inner soul with action"*.

Figure 16.2 illustrates the movement from Part I to Part II of your OOS journey. Upon reflection, what we see is that the OOS journey, your journey, represented a movement from that which is invisible to that which is visible, from that which is internal to that which is external, from thinking to doing, from descending below to emerging above.

The *act* of 'going home' is about:

- Reuniting two forces: self with soul
- Removing fragmentation from our life
- Aligning heart, head, and hands
- Doing what you love and loving what you do
- Seizing opportunity and meeting imperative
- Living as soul would live

The ***benefits*** of 'going home' are:

- Clarity
- Oneness
- Alignment
- Strength
- Purposeful living
- Achievement
- Happiness

When clarity, oneness, and alignment exist within one's mind, and this is followed by willful action to act on clarity, operate from oneness, and sustain alignment, great things happen – new strength, purposeful living, remarkable achievement, and sustained happiness. All along, the purpose of OOS was to help

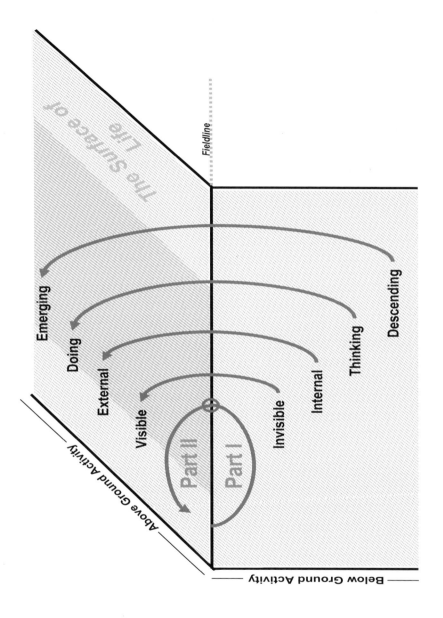

Fig. 16.2

you 'go home'; first, within your mind and later, within your life. We begin by summarizing Part I of your journey; a journey to an internal place, beneath the surface of life, to find soul, to converse with soul, to operate from soul.

Internal Home

Each of us has heard the phrase, "Home is where the heart is". There is much truth in this statement, as our 'internal home' represents heart; reflects soul. To visualize one's 'internal home', to consider soul, can be difficult, as soul is hidden, lies deep. Thus, to establish context, to ensure understanding, listed below are different characterizations of our *internal home*:

- A place of **retreat** or refuge
- A place where something is **native**
- A place deep, to the center, **to the heart**
- **Well-informed**
- A **structure** within which **One** lives
- An **environment offering security and happiness**
- A **valued place** regarded as **a place of origin**
- **A place where something is discovered, founded, developed, or promoted; a source**
- Where one's **roots** are
- **Where you live at a particular point in time**
- **The place where you are stationed and from which missions start and end**
- **A place, position where a thing is intended to be**

Each of the characterizations above tells. That is, each reveals something different, yet penetrating, about our internal home. Upon examination, what we see is that our 'internal home' serves four purposes in our life; represents four 'places': a place of being, a place of authenticity, a place of knowing, and a place of operating (see Figure 16.3).

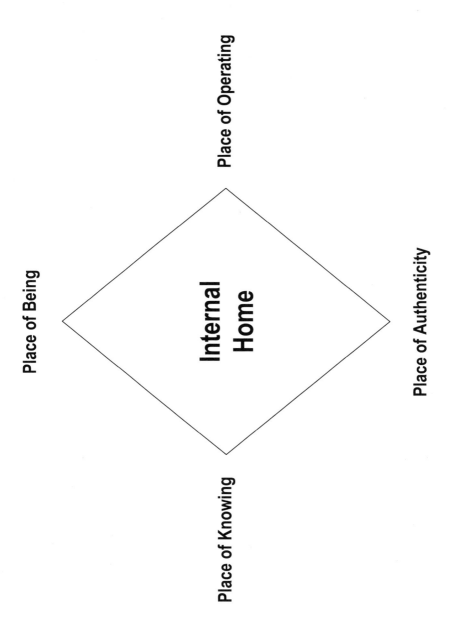

Fig. 16.3

As a 'place of being', our internal home represents an internal structure, to which we can retreat from the world. Despite being a place of darkness, it, nonetheless, emits bright light; offering refuge, security, and space for self and soul to engage in quiet conversation; to be One.

As a 'place of authenticity', our internal home represents a place of origin; our native self, who we are at core. It is a place where intention is born and, therefore, a place of highest value to self; it is a place we refer to, metaphorically, affectionately, as our heart.

As a 'place of knowing', our internal home serves as life beacon, as it is the only place well informed on what we want in life and from life at any point in life. And in those moments where confusion reigns and we are not sure of which path to follow, of what step to take next, it serves as a place to rediscover who we are; to illuminate next steps.

As a 'place of operating', our internal home directs the 'what and how' of our life; which missions to begin and end. It reflects the plane on which we operate in life; where we live at a particular point in time; represents source.

Together, the functions performed by our internal home enable us to live meaningfully, purposefully, fragrantly. The key, of course, is to find your internal home and visit it often, as the weeds of everyday living can, with time, obscure the path which leads home.

Finding your internal home required doing many things. It required you to:

- Find a location of inspiration
- Stop your life and quiet your mind
- Descend within
- Be patient
- Ask questions of self; converse with soul
- Suspend and redirect 'historical you' to see 'emerging you'
- Listen for the answer; hear what soul had to say

The essence of these actions represent the difficult, but necessary, movement from operating as parts, self and soul, to operating as One, soul (see Figure 16.4).

Now, just as finding your internal home required many things, so, too, does it represent many things. Firstly, it represents reconnecting self with soul; of rediscovering authentic you. Secondly, as a place of being, authenticity, knowing, and operating, it represents the 'place' where you belong. Thirdly, it represents essence, that part of you that originated <u>first</u> within mother's womb. Lastly, and most significantly, finding your internal home provided context, revealed the path to reach your external home.

External Home

If 'going home' within one's mind means to align self with soul, what does it mean to 'go home' within one's life? There are many ways to answer this question. Thus, to establish context, to ensure understanding, listed below are different characterizations of our *external home*:

- A **destination** or goal
- **Reaching the mark** aimed for
- To **navigate** toward a point
- Assured of **finishing, accomplishing, succeeding**
- **To be guided** to a target automatically
- **To move or lead** toward a goal
- **Where you live** at a particular point in time
- A place where a thing is **intended to be**

As when defining internal home, each of the characterizations above tells. That is, each reveals something different, yet penetrating, about our external home. Upon examination, what we see is that our 'external home' represents four different things: it represents a destination, represents being, represents achievement, and represents 'The Journey' (see Figure 16.5).

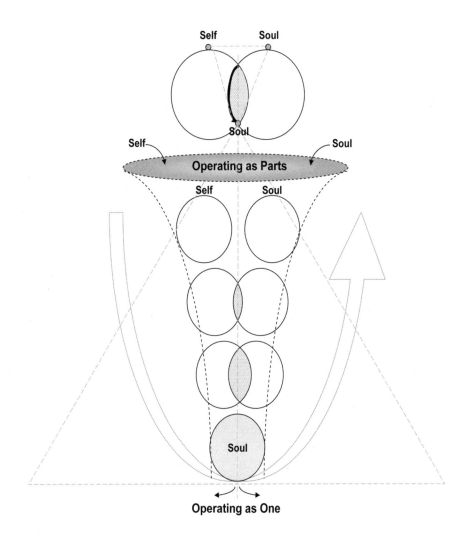

Fig. 16.4

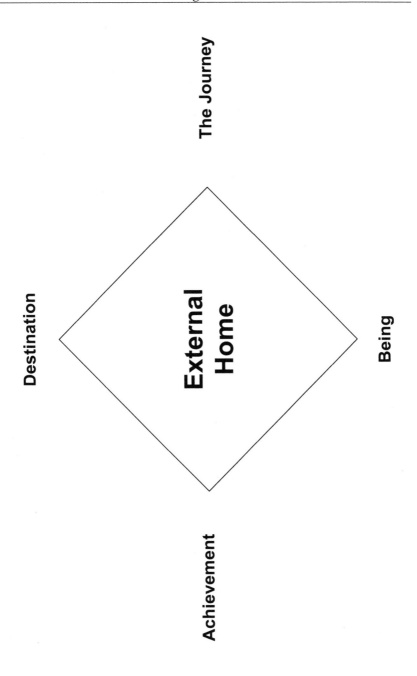

Fig. 16.5

Regarding 'destination', our external home represents not so much a physical destination, as it represents operating on a new plane of living; plane E. It represents arriving at one's purpose in life; to live passionately by deliberately changing one's life trajectory. Lastly, it represents seizing opportunity and meeting imperative; of experiencing life as we always imagined it could be; long ago dreamed.

Regarding 'being', our external home represents better living, more inspired living; of seeing, willing, thinking, acting, and feeling differently, because of operating from soul. It represents increased quality of life; the result of living meaningfully, fragrantly, free. It reflects increased personal alignment within our life; the result of operating from authentic self rather than imposter self. Lastly, and most importantly, it represents increased happiness with life, with living; the result of having met imperative, seized opportunity.

Regarding 'achievement', our external home represents, is about, accomplishing, succeeding in life. It represents rewards earned from price paid. It represents setting goals and achieving goals; *of doing what you said you would do*. Lastly, it represents the profound pride that comes from defining vision (for self) and realizing vision; of descending, then ascending, to operate on higher ground; to achieve accomplishments of a lifetime.

Regarding 'The Journey', our external home represents the process of becoming, realizing the emerging you. It represents the process of bringing soul to the surface of life for self to live as soul would live. It represents learning how to use a personal strategy to achieve personal mission; realize personal vision. Lastly, it represents developing new capabilities to manage self, to direct one's life, to maximize the personal, professional, and financial potential that life offers.

To 'go home' within one's life represents both a destination to reach and a condition to experience. However, as discussed, in order to realize 'external home' it first required finding 'internal home' (see Table 16.1):

Table 16.1

To realize...	...you first needed to
Happiness	Determine what would make you happy
Purposeful living	Determine purpose for your life
Effective action, inspired feeling	See, will, and think differently
The 'emerging you'	Find the 'emerging you'
Changed condition	Understand condition
Living as soul would live	Find soul and pull it forward, into the present, onto the surface of life
Personal alignment	Understand what aspects of your life were misaligned
Seizing opportunity and meeting imperative	Acknowledge opportunity and understand imperative
Personal transformation	Discover the vital few factors ('leverage points') to enable transformation
Ascending above	Descend below

Reaching your external home may require changing several things in your life. For example, it may require you to change careers. It may require you to get further educated. It may require you to 'downsize lifestyle'. It may require you to change your surroundings. It may require you to find new friends. Lastly, it may require you to change your life partner. Whatever change you initiate, the key is to commit to such change, as it is the path to freedom, the path to realizing emerging you, the path to happiness. Therefore, walk on...

As you walk the path that leads home, consider these guideposts, as they represent 'the vital few' elements to realize a better life:

- Pursue passions
- Execute personal strategy
- Converse with soul
- Course correct personal strategy as you change and your environment changes
- Operate from soul
- Maintain strong will
- Be patient
- Have faith, be courageous, practice enthusiasm

For each of us, our external home, initially, is a place that cannot be seen; it can only be believed. You may not know destination, but you know the plan. By focusing on the vital few elements stated above, you cannot help but illuminate the path that leads home. As you make your homeward-bound journey, remember, just as your internal home is a moving target, so, too, is your external home a moving target. Your inaugural goals and personal strategy represent current vision; at this moment; in the present. Consequently, as you 'spiral' through life, the onus is on you to stay aligned with soul, stay aligned with work, stay aligned with family, and stay aligned with nature (see Figure 16.6).

Once you accept the fact and responsibility that personal alignment is a moving target, something to contend with always, the more likely you will maintain external home.

In this section, we learned that our external home is dependent on, affected by, what occurs in our internal home; that is, what occurs among the occupants of our internal house, self and soul. Consequently, the extent to which we get our internal house in order, determines whether we get our external house in order; whether disconnect occurs, within our mind and within our life; whether we become, in a word, fragmented.

On Personal Fragmentation

Fragmentation is a killer. Whether speaking about an organization, nature, or one's life, fragmentation, in all forms, leads to consequences nobody wants. In my fifteen plus years serving in a quality consultant role, I worked in over 50+ organizations in 10+ industries and there was a constant in all companies, all industries: fragmentation. For example, in nearly every company I consulted, I witnessed fragmented processes, fragmented use of IT systems, fragmented perspective among managers, fragmented vocabulary across departments and functions, fragmented understanding of customer needs, and fragmented authority, priorities, and performance measures, among other things. What was the result of such fragmentation? It was outcomes nobody

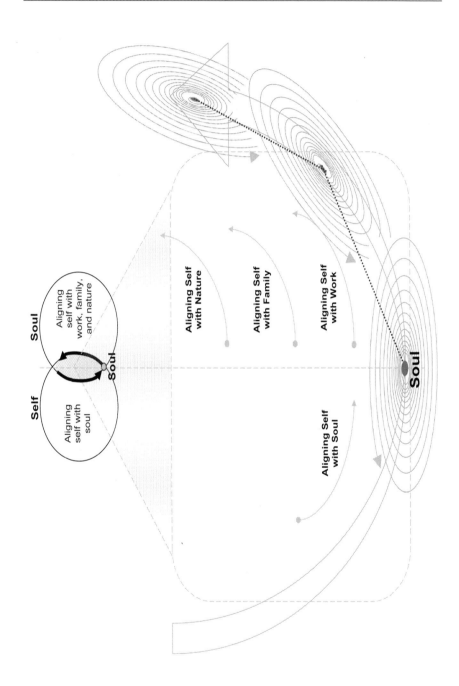

Fig. 16.6

wanted: wasted resources, higher operating costs, lower profitability, lower worker productivity, poor morale, and lost custom-
ers, among other unwanted effects, including corporate death.
Fragmentation is just as destructive in nature. When fragmentation occurs in nature, as when we tear down rain forests, dislo-
cating its inhabitants and disturbing the ecosystem, species die.
Again, an outcome nobody wants. Lastly, when fragmentation
exists within us, it also results in outcomes nobody wants, as we,
too, die; first on the inside, then on the surface of life.

Most people live fragmented (i.e., disconnected) lives.
That is, most people are not living authentically, not doing what
they want in life, or getting what they want from life. The question is, 'Why? What causes our lives to become fragmented?' As
it turns out, recent discussions provide the answer. The reason
why most people live fragmented lives is the result of:

- Little to no conversation between self and soul
- Following the standard life design
- Living in a world focused on the wrong set of details

Because we do not converse with soul, because we follow
the standard life design, and because we live in a world focused
on the wrong set of details, we suffer personal fragmentation. In
the paragraphs that follow, we discuss personal fragmentation
and the debilitating effects that result from living a fragmented
life. We conclude this section with discussing how to minimize
or, better still, eliminate fragmentation from your life, now and
forever.

Most people suffer two forms of fragmentation: internal
fragmentation (within one's mind) and external fragmentation
(within one's life). We address first the fragmentation that lies
within.

Internal Fragmentation

Fragmentation first attacks our mind as self and soul drift apart.
When self and soul operate as disconnected parts rather than
as whole, it affects our seeing, our willing, and our thinking;

those elements that 'lie within'. With no unifying focus on how to view and approach life, our life becomes an epic struggle between self and soul; between pursuing desires of self and desires of soul, with desires of self often winning the battle. The reason this occurs is that with fragmented vision, comes fragmented will. Our will operates helter skelter as we succumb to passing desires of mind, body, and environment. Our life becomes a series of 'starts and stops', of lost momentum, as we attempt goals only to abandon them a short time later; our life reflecting not an ordered ascent, but a chaotic decline. What's worse is that when our seeing and willing fragment, so, too, does our thinking; priorities shifting with the winds of will. Tragically, because of internal fragmentation, our ability, speed, and effectiveness to adapt to changes in self and environment suffers, as we lack stable context (i.e., personal vision and personal strategy) from which to assess and respond to change; more work is required to accomplish goals; to simply get ahead in life. Unfortunately, internal fragmentation represents but the tip of the iceberg in terms of debilitating effect, as a fragmented mind leads to a fragmented life.

External Fragmentation

Most people exhibit weak wills; the result of operating from self. In Chapter 14, we learned that when operating from self, where self is dominant, what results is people not willing, thinking, and acting to achieve desires of soul, but willing, thinking, and acting to achieve desires of mind, body, and environment. Consequently, the disconnect, the debilitating cascade, that begins with self and soul, continues through to all aspects of self and life; fragmented seeing, willing, and thinking giving rise to fragmented actions and unhappy feelings. Our actions reflecting not an orchestrated dance, but an outburst of disconnected efforts; misaligned energies. The obvious problem with external fragmentation is that it results in wasted energy, wasted dollars, and most tragically, wasted time; the one resource we cannot generate more of.

However, the most debilitating effect of internal fragmentation is that it results in, perpetuates, every form of personal misalignment. The disconnect that originates within spawns disconnects without, in our external life, ranging from the work we engage in, to who we associate with, to where we live. Every aspect of our life, diminished, debilitated, by some form of fragmentation. For example, when fragmentation exists within our mind, we pursue professions/roles that do not reflect true passion because confusion exists with what we want to do with our life; what work we think we like; find interesting. Further, when fragmentation exists within our mind, the probability of selecting the wrong life partner increases dramatically as well. The reason this occurs is that we are a very different person when operating from self than when operating from soul. We see life differently; we will differently, we think, act, and feel differently. And these differences often times do not align with chosen partner; friends included. Lastly, when fragmentation exists within our mind, we may find ourselves in uncomfortable surroundings. We may find, for example, that big-city living is not for us; that soul prefers breathing the crisp mountain air or ingesting soothing Caribbean sun.

Sadly, the debilitating effects of internal and external fragmentation do not end with personal misalignment, as misalignment gives rise to other, more debilitating outcomes:

- Abandoned goals
- Personal unhappiness
- Destructive actions, behaviors
- Lower self-esteem
- Diminished life experience

As to live a fragmented life is to not live at all, how does one eliminate, or minimally reduce, fragmentation from one's life?

Eliminating (or reducing) personal fragmentation first requires addressing fragmentation that lies within; the disconnect that exists between self and soul. It requires bringing together self and soul to operate as One. You have done this. Then, when aligned on the inside, when seeing, willing, and thinking are aligned around common vision, common goals, common strategy, one can align that which lies without. When soul is the loudest voice heard, when we subordinate self to soul, and follow willful thinking with willful action, fragmentation begins to subside. In time, we establish alignment between self and work, self and family, self and nature. And when we do this, when we 'go home' inside and out, we find that fragmentation recedes, inside and out.

Essence of the Journey

You have invested much time and energy in the journey that is OOS. Hopefully, you are on the path which leads home. As we approach journey's end, there is increasing need to reflect. But not just on the pages that lie herein or your efforts related to this book. No, I am asking you now to reflect on your entire life experience; from rise of consciousness to present day. Although the focus here is to summarize your experience as it relates to this book, we can only put such event in context by acknowledging the (life) journey that occurred prior to OOS and the (life) journey yet to come, that is, post-OOS. It would be too limiting to reflect on the OOS journey in isolation, considering it was the events and circumstances of life prior to OOS that led you to OOS. Further, to not acknowledge the journey yet to come, that is, the process of realizing 'emerging you', would also limit; not tell the full story. Thus, we conclude this chapter by discussing this book within the context of a larger life journey; a journey described not as a single, large-grain, act, but as an act in three parts:

- Part I – The journey prior to OOS
- Part II – The journey of OOS
- Part III – The journey beyond OOS

By considering all parts, we can reflect, discuss the entirety of your life: the beginning, the fall, and the re-birth. We begin with Part I, the journey prior to OOS.

Part I – The Journey Prior to OOS

At the end of something, it is natural to reflect on beginning. Whether speaking of love lost, one's career, a book, a movie, a business venture, or life itself, it is natural to reflect on beginning when at end. Because we are nearing book's end, we now have context to reflect on the effect this book has had on your life, but to do so first requires reflecting on your life prior to OOS.

It is important to acknowledge that something brought you to this book, it was not random chance. Whether intervention by family member, friend, stranger, or by self acting on behalf of soul, something led you to this book. As I said before, when one is seeking deep personal change, and the inquiry is genuine, I believe that the universe cooperates. Take a moment now to reflect on Part I of your life journey – your life before OOS. Reflect on what brought you to this book. What events and/or circumstances in months and years past compelled you to this book? Were you unhappy with life, with living? Did you simply desire a rigorous strategy to conduct your life? Or was it for some other, heart-felt, reason? What motivated you to seek change in your life? What was the condition of your life such that you sought change? What was missing from your life? Why the effort?

<Pause now. Do not continue until resolving questions above.>

To consider the questions above is to consider your reasons for change. As uncomfortable as it may be, reconnecting with such reasons, with past events and circumstances, is necessary to evoke right state of mind as we summarize Part II of your journey – the journey of OOS. Thus, if past thoughts, past feelings again consume you, let us begin.

We begin life operating as One; self with soul. But then, at some point in life, unbeknownst to us, self disconnects from soul; whole becomes parts. For each person, the 'disconnect' occurs on their own schedule, in their own way, *but it does occur*. At first, the disconnect is subtle, non-threatening, without symptom, as we still operate nearly as One. Then, over time, the disconnect intensifies, and by the time we reach adulthood, we are fully disconnected; self from soul, self from work, self from nature. Because the disconnect is subtle, taking place over many years, we miss the warning signs that such disconnect triggers. At first, we are confused. All we know is that we are not the same; we are changing, and for the worse. Suddenly, we find ourselves no longer satisfied with our place in life. Suddenly, we find our work pointless, meaningless; we begin asking questions like, 'What is this life for? and 'What have I accomplished in life?', and these feelings consume us, affecting all aspects of self and life. Happiness bends toward unhappiness as we feel something missing, something amiss; something we cannot fully articulate. As we encounter these new, unwanted, feelings, we do as most people do; we dismiss them, and endure. We dismiss such feelings to 'having a bad day', or 'having a mean boss', or 'someone kicking the cat', and we press on. But as we endure, feelings intensify, frustration mounts, and discontent grows, as we feel that we are missing out on the good part of life; that somewhere along the way, the joy of living, being happy, seeing and hearing the colors of the world left us; now a bit memory. These unwanted feelings catch us off guard, and not knowing how to respond, warning signs go unheeded.

Time passes...

Despite not knowing how best to respond to such feelings, despite missing the warning signs, in time, we do respond. We respond by changing, or attempting to change, our life in meaningful ways. For example, we adopt a new hobby, resolve to lose weight, resolve to stop smoking, and resolve to exercise regularly, among other things. And, for a time, we are better. We embrace new hobby. We do lose weight. We quit smoking. And we exercise. Then...the bubble bursts. Hobby abandoned, along with our goals, leaving us worse off than before. Of course, we make excuses for our failures, as it would be too injurious to self to acknowledge failure. So, we reason failure to: 'hobby being off the mark' and 'stopping smoking caused weight gain' and 'difficulty commuting to the gym'. No shortage of creativity exists when rationalizing our failures. The reason we fail is a lack of will, a lack of commitment, and lack of a personal strategy to achieve each goal; factors that determine success or failure. And so, the fall begins.

More time passes. For some, weeks pass by; for others, months and years pass. During such time, dissatisfaction with life continues; warning signs intensify. With failure still fresh in mind, personal misalignment and internal and external fragmentation set in, squeezing out all that was real, all that was joyful in life. For many people, this condition, this point in life, marks the beginning of the end as the flame of soul begins to dim; soul dismissed, cast off like an unwanted beggar, to begin the slow, painful descent to a cold, dark place. And, as numbness sets in, spirit dies out.

What most people do not realize is that our soul, from the earliest point of disconnectedness, issues warning signs, volitions, informing us in subtle, yet profound ways, that misalignment, fragmentation, disconnectedness exists. Now, because most people, my (former) self included, lack sensitivity (initially) to detect such signs, we miss them. We miss the warning signs not only because we cannot sense them and because we are too quick to dismiss ill feeling to 'having a bad day', but also because to acknowledge such feelings is to attack one's pride, to pummel optimism, which is too injurious to self; thus, dismissed. For these reasons, it is likely that you missed (or ignored) early warning signs from soul telling you 'not all was right'; pain present within your heart, yet, unable to stir a response from self. As more time passes, as soul becomes more and more isolated, further disconnected from self, as the 'missing' between self and soul escalates, the volitions from soul get stronger. The tone of soul rising in proportion with one's growing unhappiness with life, with living. Because even the loudest tones of soul are silent,

the best soul can do to inform us that misalignment, fragmentation, disconnectedness exists is to implant ill feeling within our
heart, hoping that self will respond. However, despite louder
tones, despite the pain, the majority of people do not respond.
They do not acknowledge tones heard, leaving most to operate
in a state of disconnectedness, to endure suffering their entire
lives. This is not your story, however. Although much time may
have passed between first hearing the warnings signs and acting
on them, you have arrived. Your reading this book tells me that
you have arrived. You did notice the warning signs, you did acknowledge tones of soul, you did respond to pain within. Not
only does such noticing, such acknowledgement, such response,
reflect recognizing soul, it reflects something greater; it reflects
your willingness to an *intervention by soul.*

Part II – The Journey of OOS

The journey of OOS was about finding soul and bringing it forward, into the present, onto the surface of life, for self to live
as soul would live. When one acknowledges soul, hears soul's
tones, listens to what it has to say, great things happen. In this
case, soul intervenes. Acknowledging soul is vitally important,
as only when this occurs can we know soul; learn from soul; learn
the 'state' soul is in. Most people learn that soul is in a state of
sadness – the result of soul missing self; of self and soul no longer
operating as One. This 'missing' causes pain within our heart.
What we find when soul intervenes, when we converse with soul,
is the corrupt, painful, fractured state in which soul exists; the
result of 'broken love'; of being ignored by self. The discontent
we feel with life, the sadness we feel in our heart, is the result of
separation sadness; separation that begins with self and soul, in
time, cascading to all other areas of self and life. It is because of
such separation that soul intervenes. Soul intervenes because it
must; as it is unnatural for self and soul to be separate, to operate as parts. Self and soul long to be One and, therefore, when
disconnected, they, in a subtle and profound way, 'miss' each
other; miss operating as One. Most people would not reason

feelings of discontent and unhappiness to soul missing self, but this is the root cause of our suffering. The pain we feel in our heart is 'the warning sign'; it is all soul can do to communicate with us, to trigger self to act – to converse with soul, to learn desires of soul, to live as soul would live.

In a deeply profound way, when soul intervenes, we discover that it is not self that seeks happiness, seeks achievement, desires fragrant living – it is soul. We discover that it is not self that is sad; it is soul that is sad. We discover it is not self that seeks light of day, that yearns to see the colors of the world, but soul, which is hidden in the shadows until we bring it forward, onto the surface of life through willful action. Our greatest discovery, however, is that when self intervenes on behalf of soul, we rediscover the island called soul; an island long passed by, now found.

To find soul and pull it forward, into the present, onto the surface of life, is the core essence of this book; is 'the goal'. It is the goal, as knowing one's essence, soul, is a precondition to define authentic vision, define meaningful inner soul goals, define effective personal strategy. As such, the essence of the OOS journey was to find your essence; to cut past the clutter of self and living to find soul; who you really are at core. To get to the essence of you, emerging you, required getting past tangible being, historical self, to penetrate beyond self into soul – where essence resides. To accomplish this task, you needed to stop your life long enough to assess your life. You needed to quiet your mind, to reflect, to suspend and redirect your current (traditional) ways of believing, seeing, and thinking (about self and life) to believe new things were possible; to see anew; think freshly. However, finding one's essence required more than this; it required penetrating into your life by stepping outside self, to see self; to rise above, transcend self; to observe condition, to change condition. By looking past non-essential you (feelings, emotions, actions, current condition), you revealed essential you – who you are and were meant to be on the surface of life.

Penetrating into self to find soul, however, represents only half the story. The reason we pursued this 'deep dive' was to correct interior knowing that such action would affect exterior. In fact, a moment's reflection will reveal that most of what we discussed, thought about, and did throughout OOS was focused on learning about, and then transforming inner you, as that was a precondition to transform outer you. Consider your actions:

- Asking questions of self
- Reflecting on condition
- Reflecting on opportunity and imperative
- Surrendering your-self to find your-soul
- Crafting personal vision
- Defining inner soul goals
- Conversing with soul
- Defining personal strategy
- Assessing alignment; misalignment
- Developing will
- Learning how to overcome stumbling blocks
- Creating/using life aids
- Developing the capacity to 'stop one's life'; 'to listen'; 'to see'
- Developing awareness of self and soul

Upon reviewing this list, we see that the essence of OOS was mostly about changing things 'within' to affect things 'without'.

As we reflect, to discuss *what* the essence of the OOS journey is, it is appropriate to reset on the definition and meaning of essence. Thus, our working definition: *essence is what a thing really is before it changes due to effects of the world around it.* Let us address this notion of change. When reflecting on life, within the context of the definition above, it is easy to recall instances of how life, living, changes us. For example, society changes us, from the clothes we wear, to the music we listen to, to the laws under which we live. People around us (family, friends, co-workers, community) change us. Nature changes us. World events, local events change us. And knowledge changes us. Given these influences, it is no wonder the majority of people lose connection with who they really are, especially when you consider few people converse with soul to maintain connection. Such influences, and countless others, choke out essence, partly because we do not know it is happening to us and partly because we do little to effect change. As finding one's soul underlies OOS, the journey of OOS was to undo effects of the world that have obscured our sense of home; of who we are; to reveal who we were before living changed us. In this way, *OOS represents a movement to essence, your essence*; of becoming ever more precise about what you want in life and from life, of becoming ever more adequate to your actuality, to who you really are by stripping away the effects of the world. The process of finding soul, of bringing soul to the surface of life required educating you on inner and outer, on invisible and visible, on internal and external. In short, it required educating you on the key movements (four sub-movements) of life (see Figure 16.7):

Movements 1-2: **"Down and In"** movement

Movements 3-4: **"Up and In"** movement

We learned that movements 1 and 2, representing an ever deepening of <u>self into soul</u>, to find 'the emerging you', inspired movements 3 and 4, an ever expanding of <u>self from soul</u>, to realize 'the emerging you'. Figure 16.7 illustrates the four sub-movements that occur above and below the surface (i.e., fieldline) of life; with sequence repeating as we unfold (spiral) gracefully through life. With each cycle, each turn, each iteration (n), you break farther from historical you to reveal emerging you; you break free from your old story, past existence to live a new story, new existence. Table 16.2 reveals our transformation with each turn, cycle, iteration of life's key movements:

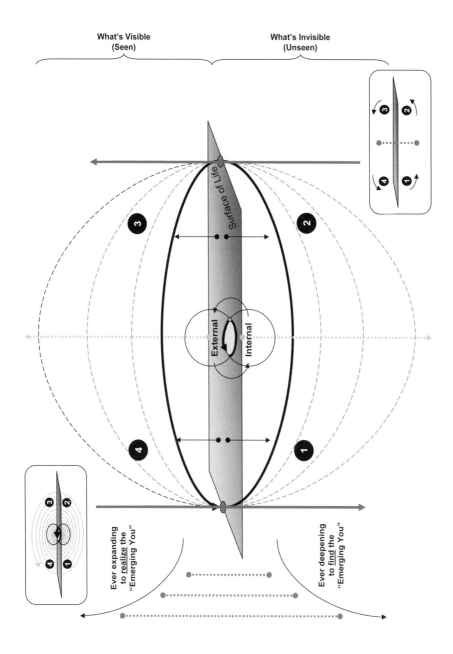

Fig. 16.7

Table 16.2

Historical You	Emerging You
Old habits	New habits
Tired thinking	Inspired thinking
Operating from self	Operating from soul
More of the same	Going the other way
The 'past'	The 'future'
Old story	New story

Only by performing these movements can you realize the highest form of you. This is possible, as movements 1 and 2 align our thoughts and movements 3 and 4 align our actions. Together, they represent *"aligning the inner soul with action"*. Together, they help us maintain personal alignment, sustain personal happiness, and position us to maximize the personal, professional, and financial potential that life offers. Without performing all four movements, we never discover soul, to learn from soul, to live as soul would live; and as imperative is dismissed, so, too, is opportunity denied.

The movements of OOS: stopping one's life, conversing with soul, defining inner soul goals, developing personal strategy, learning of personal alignment, overcoming stumbling blocks, managing personal strategy, and growing will were all orchestrated to elevate you from where you are to where you want to be. They were orchestrated to elevate you from operating on your current plane of living, to descend, then ascend, to operate on higher ground. Collectively, these movements reflect inner giving rise to outer; of new function giving rise to new form.

Most people do not realize that to be happy, to live a life of meaning and purpose, requires knowing what soul knows, that is, content of soul. With knowing what soul knows, with new content, one can define meaningful, purposeful inner soul goals; the foundation not only of personal strategy, but also of one's life. Prior to OOS, debilitating content swirled within, and this content resulted in current condition. With OOS, you were exposed to new content to consume, ponder, and build

from. For example, you were exposed to content regarding opportunity, imperative, and insights into self and soul, content regarding personal alignment, personal strategy, and growing will,
and content regarding managing self, overcoming obstacles, and
developing new life-enhancing capabilities. Now, what is significant about acquiring new content is that with new content
comes new form. That is, by squeezing out content of old with
content of new, you replaced imposter essence with true essence.
It has been said we **are** what we think, so to change who we
are, we must change what we think (i.e., content). As such, the
purpose of this book was to expose you to life-giving content;
to replace debilitating content; to bring forth a new form of you
– emerging you.

Just as old content resulted in current condition, reflected
past essence, so, too, will new content result in new condition,
reflect new essence. What this tells us is that essence precedes being. We know this to be true, as to realize emerging you, it first
required knowing who the essential you was. Without knowing
one's essence, there is no basis from which authentic seeing, willing, thinking, acting, and feeling can emerge. But just as nature
is not static, continually unfolding to reveal itself anew, so, too,
are we not static, continually unfolding, revealing our self anew.
What this tells us is that essence, our essence, is relative to place
(i.e., 'plane') and time. Thus, as you move through life, essence
moves with you. We know this to be true, as changed essence
results in changed inner soul goals, which results in changed personal strategy to achieve such goals. In this way, wherever you
are, whenever you are, your being (i.e., life experience) will reflect true essence, provided, that is, you stay in contact with it.

The journey that is OOS is a journey of hope, of inspiration, of love. It is a book **of promise** (a better life awaits you),
of promoting (a better way to live), and **of providing** (an alternative to the standard life design). It is an offer of freedom;
of truth; of beauty; a way through to a life of happiness, to a
life of meaning; a gateway to descend, then ascend, to operate
from higher ground. On the surface, OOS is but chapters, top-

ics, paragraphs, sentences, and words arranged in a particular sequence. However, you, through careful reading and thoughtful action, bring such topics, such words, to life. More than this, you brought your core essence to life; to live as soul would live. Your journey that is OOS represented truths to discover; about self and soul. The 'warning signs' you felt were soul's way of communicating with you; of saying let us *go home*; become whole again; become One.

Okay. So where does this discussion leave us? The journey of OOS was to find soul, to live as soul would live, and what we found was soul with arms wide open. What we found was that an invitation from soul always existed; soul, always present, by our side, telling us to 'come in' for quiet conversation. Not only was the OOS journey about crawling back into the arms of soul, it was also about crawling back into the world you once knew – where colors exist, the sun shines, and happiness reigns. Only now, at journey's end, can you appreciate soul: its presence, its purpose. Our soul, O' tireless servant, always there, always willing, always committed to rescue us from a life without meaning. Our role: to meet soul half way; to descend within; to open up, to hear voice of soul, and embrace its sweet sounds; wisdom it speaks.

Part III – The Journey Beyond OOS

Thus far, we discussed the journey prior to OOS, reflecting on what brought you to this book, and we discussed the journey of OOS, reflecting on finding soul and bringing it forward onto the surface of life. Now, we reflect on the journey beyond OOS; that is, the journey yet to come. To discuss such journey is to consider that which remains when OOS passes.

With certain assumptions holding true, much remains after OOS has passed, categorized as: 1) 'the visible' and 2) 'the hidden'.

First, 'the hidden':

- You, operating from new source; soul
- You, operating on higher ground; plane E
- You, with new beliefs, new seeing, new willing, new thinking
- A growing will
- A soul inspired
- Freedom within
- Alignment within

Next, 'the visible':

- A set of inner soul goals reflecting soul
- A personal strategy to achieve each goal
- A set of frameworks, tools, and templates to manage your life
- New capabilities to seize opportunity, meet imperative
- The emerging you
- A happier you
- Freedom without
- Alignment without

When an event passes, that which remains represents essence. Thus, to speak of essence is to speak of permanence. To realize the emerging you, to maximize the personal, professional, and financial potential that OOS promises, certain changes, resolves, must remain with you; that is, be a permanent fixture in your life.

You must resolve to:

- Live your passions, always
- Continue operating from soul
- Use a personal strategy to direct your life
- Seize opportunity, meet imperative
- Do what you love and love what you do
- Adapt self, goals, and personal strategy as you unfold through life
- Live purposefully, meaningfully, fragrantly

With OOS, with 'space and opportunity', you resolved matters within, to affect matters without. Continue this practice, of descending within to affect matters without. In time, you will learn that the force that brings you in (to converse with soul) is the same force that will bring you out (to live from soul).

From historical you to emerging you, that was the challenge. The question was, 'How to bring about the real you, the authentic you, the emerging you?' It is my sincere hope that, as we near book's end, this conflict is resolved. That is, I hope that your-self and your soul are One. I hope that you now operate from higher ground, ascended to the place you want to be, at least in mind, and soon...in life.

The coursing of these pages, the journey that is OOS, your journey, is nearly complete. For some, the journey lasting only days, for others, weeks and months. As the immediate of this book passes, the question is, 'What remains of you?' Discovering one's essence is a process. It is a process of understanding one's place in life, of penetrating into condition, to change condition. It required you to take a metaphorical 'step back' to reflect on the story of your life thus far to ensure that all remaining chapters reflect not only who you are, but more importantly, who you want to be. The movement towards essence is to become ever more comprehensive, ever more adequate, to what you want in life and from life throughout life. It is about making the unconscious, conscious. Your journey herein and hereafter represents this movement. As the being is a reflection of the essential, it was necessary to course these pages, to endure the process that is OOS. So, what remains of you? Only one characterization fits: *Soul, rising*!

At the beginning of this section, I asked you to reflect not only on the pages herein, but also on your life in its entirety, as only then would you possess context to understand the beginning, the fall, and the rebirth *of you* (see Figure 16.8).

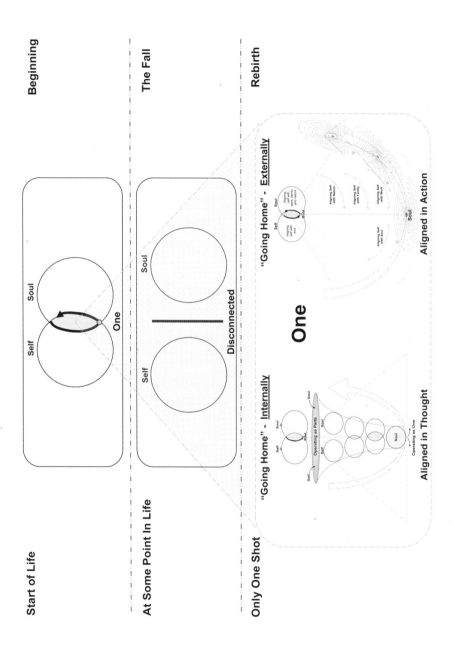

Fig. 16.8

At the start of life, self and soul are One. Then, at some point in life, self disconnects from soul; whole becomes parts.

What causes disconnect? It is the result of:

- Lack of education on need/how to align self with soul
- Stresses of life (work, family, survival)
- Operating from self
- Not stopping one's life to reflect on life
- Not conversing with soul
- Not knowing soul
- Following the standard life design
- Weak will
- Living in a world focused on the wrong set of details

Most people do not operate as One; never resolve the disconnect between self and soul; lost relation. Despite perhaps experiencing the same, your soul was never far away, always in the background, just under the surface; *ready to rise*.

You acknowledged tones of soul, and in the process, became aware of soul. You noticed the warning signs, and without perhaps being conscious of it, the 'emerging you' brought you to OOS and OOS did its part by providing space, opportunity, and occasion for you to align in thought and align in action; to 'go home' within your mind and within your life. A sense of 'knowing' consumed you, and this 'knowing capacity', these new beliefs, changed how you approached life; of what to look for in life; changed all that follows (see Figure 16.9). A new sensitivity pervades you. You bask in new awareness of not only your world within, but also your world without.

It takes courage to live as soul would live. It takes courage to converse with soul; to do something so many find unnatural and that society is so quick to dismiss the merits of, and, therefore, the practice of. History tells us that self can dismiss (i.e., ignore) soul for only so long, until one of three final states occur:

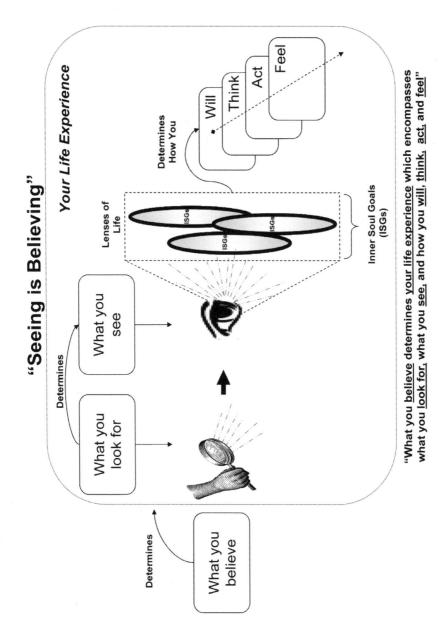

Fig. 16.9

1. **Resurrected soul** (*self and soul reunite as One*)
2. **Death to soul** (*soul is numb, spirit sleeping somewhere cold*)
3. **Expiration of soul** (*death to self*)

Some choose option 3, the majority default to option 2, and you chose option 1. The commonality among options is that each represents a choice one makes; <u>a choice you must make</u>. The essence of the OOS journey was about "aligning the inner soul with action", about 'going home' to a place we cannot see, but giving rise to a place we <u>want</u> to be. The process was to find source. Then, with source established, develop a personal vision, inner soul goals, and personal strategy that reflect source. The last step was to execute personal strategy, to bring source to the surface of life, for self to live as soul would live.

As we conclude this chapter, know this: as much as OOS has been a conversation between you and I, it has been more a conversation between your-self and your soul. Your soul has always been with you; by your side; waiting patiently to reconnect, realign, and help you rediscover the joy of living. You are no longer 'stuck in a story' of who you were, as a new story is being written and you are the author. No longer are you resident to your former life, experiencing 'more of the same', as you have descended to a new place, on plane E where **all are happy** *because* **all are free**. Your fall (spiritual descent) has led to a rebirth of you; to taking residence on higher ground. *Lost once, you are now homeward bound.*

It's funny; every time I vacation, and despite the fact that I am normally in more serene, more exotic surroundings, experiencing better weather and feeling more alive than ever, it always feels good to go home. The feeling is the same as it relates to achieving a key goal of this book: "aligning the inner soul with action". It feels good to go home, within one's mind and within one's life. I am going home...to the place where <u>I</u> belong...where <u>you</u> belong...where we <u>all</u> belong. Why go home? It is simple. *<u>Home</u> is where the <u>heart</u> is.*

Final Words

"From the end spring new beginnings."
- Pliny the Elder

YOU HAVE REACHED THE FINAL CHAPTER of Only One Shot. Congratulations! Surveys show that most people would have bowed out long before this point. I am glad you are still with me, as my instruction is not yet complete. I leave you now with some final words on accomplishment, final words to inspire, final words on OOS.

Final Words: On Accomplishment

For each person, this book represents different things. For some, OOS represents a handbook to define a rigorous strategy for living. For others, it represents the means to evaluate condition to change condition. Still for others, it represents an intervention of soul. Despite varieties with interpretation, one motivation unites us all: a desire to do something meaningful in life; *to accomplish*. As such, <u>your</u> journey differs from others only in content, not in kind. To reengineer one's existence, to design a personal strategy, to rediscover the joy of living, all speak of accomplishment. In the sections that follow, I present some final words on accomplishment.

So, what is accomplishment? Why do we yearn to accomplish anything? Answering these questions gets at the heart of why you sought this book. Each of us desires to achieve; it is part of our DNA. Whether speaking of career, relationships, finances, or happiness, each of us yearns to accomplish in these areas and more. And just as building a successful career is achieved through a series of small accomplishments, or a healthy relationship is achieved through a series of small accomplishments, so, too, is a remarkable life achieved through a series of small accomplishments. Your efforts related to this book, (reading, thinking, doing), represent small accomplishments leading to far greater accomplishments – sustained happiness, fragrant living, personal, professional, and financial success. However, to accomplish these higher-order goals requires great courage, among other things. Before we discuss such prerequisites, let us first discuss the spiritual side of accomplishment.

Breakthroughs of a Profound Nature

Few people stand out amongst a crowd. Whether in sports, business, music, politics, academics, or science, only few within each domain rise above; become visible. Only few will become the highest paid; the most sought after. Only few will feel the immense pride that comes from achieving accomplishments of a lifetime. In short, only few will achieve breakthroughs of a profound nature. <u>You can be among the few</u>.

To 'break through' something means to overcome, to surpass, to advance mightily. It also means to develop new insights, to make important discoveries, to achieve. 'Profound' represents something of great significance; of having deep insight and understanding about something. As it relates to this book, 'breakthroughs of a profound nature' represent achieving important, significant discoveries of self. They represent achieving deep insights and understanding of soul by surpassing current self, historical you, to reveal emerging you. When reflecting on your OOS journey, we see that you achieved many breakthroughs including:

- <u>What you believe</u> is possible for self
- <u>What you look for</u> in life and from life
- <u>What you see</u> when you look at the world
- <u>How you will</u> mind and body to support soul
- <u>How you think</u> not of self, but of soul
- <u>How you act</u> to achieve desires of soul
- <u>How you feel</u> liberated, emancipated, free

To 'join the living', on plane E, where all are happy <u>because</u> all are free, is the goal. All along, this book has been a call to *join the living*. Sadly, most people that pass this earth never really live. This is not your story, however, as you chose to join the living, first in spirit, then with action. The breakthroughs you engineered above were all necessary to join the living. Without challenging what you believe, what you look for, and what you see, little would change in your life. Without changing how you will, how you think, how you act, and how you feel, you would achieve not breakthroughs, but experience 'more of the same'.

As I said, OOS is about achieving, accomplishing, but in a way that is meaningful for you. It is about maximizing the personal, professional, and financial potential that life offers. Pursuing a vision for self is a place that, at first, can only be believed, not seen. You operate on faith, courage, and enthusiasm that with time, personal strategy, and will, vision will become reality. For me, writing this book constituted part of my personal vision. It took me four years to write, edit, and publish this book. Did I want to quit at times? You bet I did. However, I was pursuing a seed of soul and, therefore, was determined not to let the debilitating tendency of self doubt derail the dream. Although achieving my personal vision is far from complete, I do feel the profound pride that comes from setting a challenging, meaningful goal and accomplishing it. When you begin to realize your personal vision, achieve your inner soul goals, you, too, will feel such pride.

I come from humble beginnings. Perhaps you did as well. For most people born in humble surroundings, life can seem as if one is up against the world. How to rise above humble beginnings? How to rise above poverty, or lack of opportunity, or lack of resources? Let me tell you, people do rise. <u>You can rise</u>. Know this: ***your place in the world is determined principally by you*** and secondarily by others. You may begin life in humble surroundings, but that need not reflect your entire life story, only first chapter. The majority of highly successful people began life in humble surroundings, and yet, they rise. Sam Walton, JW Marriott, Eminem, Tiger Woods, Oprah, and many others all began life modestly. What allowed them to rise, to achieve breakthroughs of a profound nature? It was three things: meaningful goals, a strategy to achieve each goal, and indomitable will. You possess these things as well. Thus, you may have begun life feeling up against the world, but you can rise, and when you do, you will feel, as those before you, the profound pride that only you can articulate; the profound pride that comes from achieving remarkable success; from achieving 'accomplishments of a lifetime'.

To accomplish what you want in life requires faith (in your personal vision), courage (to act), and enthusiasm (to overcome obstacles). While all these are important, courage, more than the other factors, mobilizes us to act and, therefore, is most significant. Because of the significant effect courage has in helping us achieve strategy, realize vision, we discuss a matter of courage next.

A Matter of Courage

To be free is the goal. Each of us privately yearns to be free. We yearn to be free because with freedom comes happiness. What does it mean to be free? To be 'free' means to do what you want in life to get what you want from life throughout life. When was the last time you were free? If you are like most people, my (former) self included, freedom left you long ago. The good news is that your personal strategy, and all that flows from it, represents a *movement towards freedom.* Having said this, freedom can be frightful. For example, to achieve freedom, it may require you to downsize lifestyle. You may need to move into a smaller home, or an apartment; live humbly. You may need to trade in the expensive car for a cheaper model; rely on public transportation. You may need to sell some of your possessions or cash in your 401k. Any of these actions takes courage. To achieve freedom, you may need to move to new surroundings. You may need to leave the suburbs of Chicago for the hills of Montana. You may need to leave the bustle of Seattle for the serenity of St. Martin. To achieve freedom, you may need to change your profession, change your role; quit your job. You may have to surrender status, sacrifice self-image, abandon ego. Lastly, to be free, you may need to perform the hardest act of all: leave your partner. All these actions require great courage. Freedom, indeed, can be frightful. It takes courage to break from the standard life design; to break from the masses. It takes courage to break from historical you; to operate outside the lines. In short, it takes courage to adjust to a reality that differs from what was familiar and comfortable. My advice: stand firm, be courageous, and do not waver, ever! You may have feelings of being 'on the edge' or 'out of your element,' but you must be courageous, commit in this lifetime, as you will have Only One Shot to do so.

As you execute your personal strategy, there will be times when debilitating thoughts, feelings, and emotions consume you. When you encounter these situations, when you begin to question the value of your personal vision, personal strategy, and the effort required to realize both, remember this: you are not your thoughts, you are not your feelings, you are not your emotions. You are soul. And soul is above thought, beyond thought It is above feeling, beyond feeling. It is above emotion, beyond emotion. Soul existed before thought, before feeling, before emotion. Whenever I have self-doubt, I descend within to converse with soul. I converse with soul to escape the trappings of self and life, and when I emerge from conversation, I am better. I am better because from soul comes wisdom; *right thinking leading to right action.* I am better because when I am in the presence of soul, I am free. Soul reminds me that I am not a passing thought, a weak feeling, a lesser emotion. I am it and it is I. And just as I am soul, so, too, are you soul. There is no more formidable, informed, or indomitable entity on earth than soul.

The great successful people of the world have all experienced feelings of doubt, suffered from debilitating feelings, frightful feelings, when pursuing greatness. Do not let such feelings shake your resolve. The key is to just keep going. Continue to converse with soul. Continue to measure life performance. Continue to manage and adapt personal strategy as you change and your environment changes. Remember, *everyday represents movement,* and in time, you, too, will reach home. Therefore, trust in your vision. Trust in your developing capabilities. Trust in your personal strategy. Above all, trust in soul. The course soul charted for you is directionally correct. It represents what you want in life and from life at this point in your life. Remember: for soul to rise, self must die. As such, be courageous enough to 'die', to afford soul an opportunity to 'live'.

Down to This

I wrote this book partly to instruct, partly to inspire, and partly to dispel philosophy. This was necessary to help you achieve a primary goal of this book – increased personal happiness. Consequently, I instructed you on how to reengineer your existence, how to design a personal strategy, and how to rediscover the joy of living. However, in doing so, hopefully, I inspired you along the way. I attempted this partly by sharing the struggles and achievements of not only my own life, but also those of notable people. Lastly, I engaged you in philosophical inquiry when discussing soul. And in the course of such discussion, we learned that to be happy comes down to this: each of us must...

- Seize opportunity
- Meet imperative

In Chapter 3, we discussed the opportunity before us. Let us review, one last time, the facts regarding the opportunity before you:

- You will have *Only One Shot* at life as we pass this earth but once
- You will have *Only One Shot* to maximize the personal, professional, and financial potential that life offers
- You will have *Only One Shot* to live happily, fragrantly, free

In addition to learning of opportunity in Chapter 3, we also learned about meeting imperative. Because our time is limited, permit me to be blunt. You must live your passions, whatever they are; be it painting, writing, woodworking, teaching, music, social causes, or river guiding. Simply stated, if you are not living your passion, you are not living. **It is time to join the living**. It is time to live passionately. It is time to meet life's imperative. Do not be like the masses, who, at life's end, cannot say they lived passionately. Do not emulate the majority who, at life's end, cannot say they lived a colorful, fragrant, and remarkable life experience; cannot say they maximized the personal, professional, and financial potential that life offers. Your time is now; the present is your servant. Just as you must seize the opportunity before you, so, too, must you meet imperative which is knocking at your door.

Now, as temptation, obstacles, and the press of 'default' face you as you reengineer self, I present some final words, advice really, that despite such things walk on. Walk on...

Walk On

What started as a walk to assess self, to understand self, became a walk to find soul. Now your walk continues, to realize soul. As you execute your personal strategy, as you begin to realize emerging you, setbacks will occur the key is to *just keep going.* Strategy will prevail. Soul will emerge. Happiness will arrive. It is just a matter of time. This is where most people fall down. Most people do not keep going, do not persist, do not 'walk on'; letting obstacles of all kinds derail the dream. Do not let this be your life story. ***Do not let the trappings of life deny you life.*** It is in moments of desperation that you must press on; *walk on.* The great achievers throughout history had the ability to 'walk on', to keep going when the going got tough, enabling them to live a vibrant and fragrant life, full of color. Therefore,

- Despite setbacks, walk on...
- Despite self-doubt, walk on...
- Despite slow progress, walk on...
- Despite the non-believers, walk on...
- Despite continued heartache, walk on...
- Despite knowing vision but not destination, walk on...
- Despite feeling stuck in a hole, not seeing sun, walk on...
- Despite being tired, frustrated, ready to give in, walk on...

It takes patience to realize seeds of soul. In fact, patience, 'the ability to wait', is a precondition of greatness. Consider Einstein, Newton, Galileo, Edison, Walton, Marriott, Tiger Woods. Each of these great achievers became great in large part because each was patient to achieve their goals. Each exercised patience, just as you must exercise patience. It is because most people lack patience (i.e., not wanting to pay the price) that they abandon their goals prematurely. Remember, even the patient man or woman achieves movement, so just keep going; even if slowly.

If you are going to be true to who you really are, that is, achieve mission, realize vision, you must walk on. Something brought you to this book; do not deny the force, the feeling, the spirit, the soul that lies in wait; *now ready for exit*. You found soul; now it is time to *Let Soul Sing*; to walk on; to descend 'down and in', 'up and in', to operate on plane E. To cut loose current self, current life, for emerging self, life to come, demands you walk on. To 'walk on', to just keep going, steadfast towards achieving your vision, is all that is required to restore joy to your life, to quell the suffering, to inject color in a world gone gray. Having said all this, to realize vision requires more than just walking, it requires leaving certain baggage behind.

To realize emerging you, to operate on plane E, to achieve your goals, you will need to leave all baggage behind. 'What baggage?' you ask. Past thinking, past habits, past failures, past struggles, past actions, past beliefs, past assumptions, past sorrow. In short, 'the past'. All this must remain behind. The cost is too great, the consequences too debilitating, to bring such baggage. Such baggage is only necessary to revisit the past, to experience more of the same. However, you elected to go the other way, to visit new destinations. To leave such baggage behind is to let go of unwanted attachments; to rid oneself of that which is debilitating, in favor of that which is liberating. To transform one's life is not an easy thing, but it is possible. It took me nearly five years to transform my life, but I did it and so can you. I realized, as you must, that I am not my past; further, I am not my thoughts, actions, habits, or feelings; such things are but my servants. When I changed the source from which I operate (self to soul), when I left all baggage behind, my world changed; ball and chain left me; I was free.

This walk of yours, internal to find soul and external to realize soul, is, above all, a walk for freedom; freedom from the standard life design; freedom from imposter self, imposter living; freedom from a past that does not reflect what you want or who you were meant to be. To live and not be free is to not live at all.

Sadly, most people are not free; not living. But some birds (you and I) refuse caging; our wings too wide, our spirit too bright, our force too strong to accept caging; to tolerate default. We fly for freedom. We demand that which our founding fathers envisioned: life, liberty, and happiness. To obtain these things, however, is our responsibility. The good news is that when we seek these things, when we *just keep going*, continue our freedom walk, happiness arrives. Thus, at this moment, you need simply finish what you started with reading this book. Perhaps unbeknownst to you, you began your freedom walk with first page turned. Now, at book's end, your walk continues; indefinitely, everyday representing movement. And with each day, with each step, it brings you closer to who you are and want to be on the surface of life; brings you home.

It is certain, **with enough walking, you will find home.** Why is this certain? It is because with walking, comes movement. But, just as it is certain that continued walking will help you find home, so, too, is it certain that without walking, you won't <u>reach</u> home as you won't <u>know</u> home. Consequently, we begin (and end) each day with an inner walk (i.e., reflection), descending within to converse with soul. Then, in between such walks, we 'turn up', take an outer walk, on the surface of life only to 'turn back' when our day is done. With each up and down movement, we descend past current self, current residence, to realize emerging self, establish new residence. What began as an inner walk into darkness to find soul continues now as an outer walk in daylight to realize soul; our inner walk bringing us closer to internal home, our outer walk bringing us closer to external home. In the darkness, you found soul, a bright light shining. Now, in the presence of sun's warm glow, you bask, a new day rising (see Figure 17.1).

To realize one's vision for self can be, and often is, a personal matter. All supporters of your freedom walk does not mitigate the fact that to bring one's emerging self to the surface of life is a personal act; a solitary affair. Do not be discouraged by this fact. Many people before you labored in isolation to real-

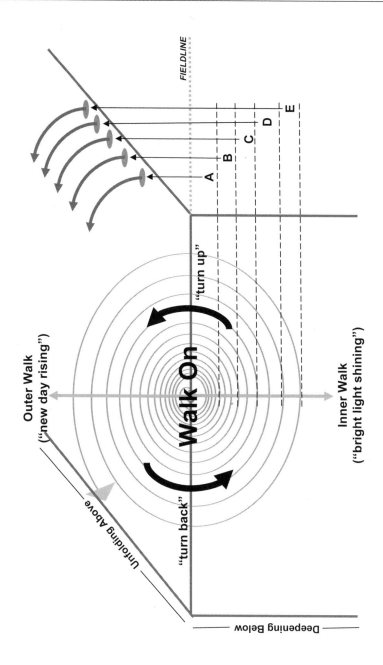

Fig. 17.1

ize a dream. Take comfort in this. Consider the athlete training before dawn, the inventor toiling in the garage, the writer laying down content in the still of night, all with a dream, all working in isolation. Knowing that others toiled before me, helped me get through; gave me strength, kept me walking. *Through the struggles of others, I found community. Through the achievements of others, I found inspiration. Through the words of others, I found calm.* I now share such community, such inspiration, such calm with you.

Final Words: To Inspire

Ralph Waldo Emerson remarked, "Our life is an apprenticeship to the truth". You started this journey hearing that this book is a book of truths; truths known and truths to discover. Now that we are at book's end, I hope that you found, revealed the most important truth of all – your truth. In this section, I present certain truths, selected quotes, on purpose, on happiness, on living, on home, on achievement, on freedom, on alignment, on soul, and on being whole. I present these truths to inspire you...to ignite you...to encourage you to *just keep going.* You will find words from those with whom you are familiar and those you are not. Each of the individuals quoted below reveals insights, a wisdom awareness, that continue to enlighten, continue to educate, continue to inspire. We begin by listening to what others have said on (life's) purpose.

Famous Quotes: On Purpose

The only true happiness comes from squandering ourselves for a purpose.
(William Cowper)

Strong lives are motivated by dynamic purposes.
(Kenneth Hildebrand)

Nothing contributes so much to tranquilizing the mind as a steady purpose - a point on which the soul may fix its intellectual eye.
(Mary Wollstonecraft Shelley)

Many persons have a wrong idea of what constitutes true happiness. It is not attained through self-gratification but through fidelity to a worthy purpose.
(Helen Keller)

See first that the design is wise and just: that ascertained, pursue it resolutely; do not for one repulse forego the purpose that you resolved to effect.
(William Shakespeare)

This is our purpose: to make as meaningful as possible this life that has been bestowed upon us; to live in such a way that we may be proud of ourselves; to act in such a way that some part of us lives on.
(Oswald Spengler)

The real distinction is between those who adapt their purposes to reality and those who seek to mold reality in the light of their purposes.
(Henry Kissinger)

The purpose of life is to live it, to taste experience to the utmost, to reach out eagerly and without fear for newer and richer experience.
(Eleanor Roosevelt)

The secret of success is constancy of purpose.
(Benjamin Disraeli)

Famous Quotes: On Happiness

The happiness of a man in this life does not consist in the absence but in the mastery of his passions.
(Alfred Lord Tennyson)

Man is the artificer of his own happiness.
(Henry David Thoreau)

Happiness depends upon ourselves.
(Aristotle)

Happiness is when what you think, what you say, and what you do are in harmony.
(Mahatma Gandhi)

There can be no happiness if the things we believe in are different from the things we do.
(Freya Madeline Stark)

The summit of happiness is reached when a person is ready to be what he is.
(Desiderius Erasmus)

Success is not the key to happiness. Happiness is the key to success. If you love what you are doing, you will be successful.
(Herman Cain)

The secret of Happiness is Freedom, and the secret of Freedom, Courage.
(Thucydides)

Famous Quotes: On Living

One's real life is often the life that one does not lead.
(Oscar Wilde)

In the attitude of silence the soul finds the path in a clearer light, and what is elusive and deceptive resolves itself into crystal clearness. Our life is a long and arduous quest after truth.
(Mahatma Gandhi)

There is only one success - to be able to spend your life in your own way.
(Christopher Morley)

Make your life a mission - not an intermission.
(Arnold Glasgow)

Man's main task in life is to give birth to himself, to become what he potentially is.
(Erich Fromm)

Life is either a daring adventure or nothing.
(Helen Keller)

If one advances confidently in the direction of his dreams, and endeavors to live the life which he has imagined, he will meet with a success unexpected in common hours.
(Henry David Thoreau)

Slow down and enjoy life. It's not only the scenery you miss by going too fast - you also miss the sense of where you are going and why.
(Eddie Cantor)

The big secret in life is that there is no big secret. Whatever your goal, you can get there if you're willing to work.
(Oprah Winfrey)

To be always intending to make a new and better life but never to find time to set about it is as to put off eating and drinking and sleeping from one day to the next until you're dead.
(Og Mandino)

Your time is limited, so don't waste it living someone else's life. Don't be trapped by dogma - which is living with the results of other people's thinking. Don't let the noise of other's opinions drown out your own inner voice. And most important, have the courage to follow your heart and intuition. They somehow already know what you truly want to become. Everything else is secondary.
(Steve Jobs)

The mystery of life isn't a problem to solve, but a reality to experience.
(Frank Herbert)

And in the end, it's not the years in your life that count. It's the life in your years.
(Abraham Lincoln)

Go confidently in the direction of your dreams. Live the life you've imagined.
(Henry David Thoreau)

Life is a perpetual instruction in cause and effect.
(Ralph Waldo Emerson)

Our truest life is when we are in our dreams awake.
(Henry David Thoreau)

The highest manifestation of life consists in this: that a being governs its own actions. A thing which is always subject to the direction of another is somewhat of a dead thing.
(Thomas Aquinas)

Where there is love there is life.
(Mahatma Gandhi)

The quality, not the longevity, of one's life is what is important.
(Martin Luther King Jr.)

Famous Quotes: On Home

Not going home is already like death.
(E. Catherine Tobler)

Life is like getting dropped off in the middle of the woods, and then year by year, gradually walking home.
(April Foiles)

Life's a voyage that's homeward bound.
(Herman Melville)

This is the true nature of home – it is the place of Peace; the shelter, not only from injury, but from all terror, doubt and division.
(John Ruskin)

Famous Quotes: On Achievement

You are not here merely to make a living. You are here to enable the world to live more amply, with greater vision, and with a finer spirit of hope and achievement. You are here to enrich the world. You impoverish yourself if you forget this errand.
(Woodrow Wilson)

Happiness lies in the joy of achievement and the thrill of creative effort.
(Franklin D. Roosevelt)

It is not the critic who counts; not the man who points out how the strong man stumbles, or where the doer of deeds could have done them better. The credit belongs to the man who is actually in the arena, whose face is marred by dust and sweat and blood, who strives valiantly; who errs and comes short again and again; because there is not effort without error and shortcomings; but who does actually strive to do the deed; who knows the great enthusiasm, the great devotion, who spends himself in a worthy cause, who at the best knows in the end the triumph of high achievement and who at the worst, if he fails, at least he fails while daring greatly. So that his place shall never be with those cold and timid souls who know neither victory nor defeat.
(Theodore Roosevelt)

Every great work, every great accomplishment, has been brought into manifestation through holding to the vision, and often just before the big achievement, comes apparent failure and discouragement.
(Florence Scovel Shinn)

The greatest achievement of the human spirit is to live up to one's opportunities and make the most of one's resources.
(Vauvenargues)

Trust yourself. Create the kind of self that you will be happy to live with all your life. Make the most of yourself by fanning the tiny, inner sparks of possibility into flames of achievement.
(Foster C. McClellan)

The achievement of your goal is assured the moment you commit yourself to it.
(Mack R. Douglas)

Famous Quotes: On Freedom

Self-reliance is the only road to true freedom, and being one's own person is its ultimate reward.
(Patricia Sampson)

Everything that is really great and inspiring is created by the individual who can labor in freedom.
(Albert Einstein)

Without freedom from the past, there is no freedom at all, because the mind is never new, fresh, innocent.
(Krishnamurti)

For to be free is not merely to cast off one's chains, but to live in a way that respects and enhances the freedom of others.
(Nelson Mandela)

Seek freedom and become captive of your desires, seek discipline and find your liberty.
(Frank Herbert)

Freedom is one of the deepest and noblest aspirations of the human spirit.
(Ronald Reagan)

The secret of Happiness is Freedom, and the secret of Freedom, Courage.
(Thucydides)

Famous Quotes: On Alignment

I believe the choice to be excellent begins with aligning your thoughts and words with the intention to require more from yourself.
(Oprah Winfrey)

A family is a place where minds come in contact with one another. If these minds love one another the home will be as beautiful as a flower garden. But if these minds get out of harmony with one another it is like a storm that plays havoc with the garden.
(Buddha)

But what is happiness except the simple harmony between a man and the life he leads.
(Albert Camus)

We do not keep the outward form of order, where there is deep disorder in the mind.
(William Shakespeare)

For there is music wherever there is harmony, order and proportion.
(Sir Thomas Browne)

The outward freedom that we shall attain will only be in exact proportion to the inward freedom to which we may have grown at a given moment. And if this is a correct view of freedom, our chief energy must be concentrated on achieving reform from within.
(Mahatma Gandhi)

The first order of business of anyone who wants to enjoy success in all areas of his or her life is to take charge of the internal dialogue they have and only think, say and behave in a manner consistent with the results they truly desire.
(Sidney Madwed)

Order is not pressure which is imposed on society from without, but an equilibrium which is set up from within.
(Jose Ortega y Gasset)

An aligned life is a fragrant life.
(Randall Scott Rogers)

Famous Quotes: On Soul

Only passions, great passions, can elevate the soul to great things.
(Denis Diderot)

Nothing discernable to the eye of the spirit is more brilliant or obscure than man; nothing is more formidible, complex, mysterious, and infinite. There is a prospect greater than the sea, and it is the sky; there is a prospect greater than the sky, and it is the human soul.
(Victor Hugo)

Self is the only prison that can bind the soul.
(Henry Van Dyke)

Thinking is the talking of the soul with itself.
(Plato)

Life ought to be a struggle of desire toward adventures whose nobility will fertilize the soul.
(Rebecca West)

Each person has an ideal, a hope, a dream which represents the soul. We must give to it the warmth of love, the light of understanding and the essence of encouragement.
(Colby Dorr Dam)

Conscience is the voice of the soul.
(Polish Proverb)

Wisdom is not finally tested in the schools, Wisdom cannot be pass'd from one having it to another not having it, Wisdom is of the soul, is not susceptible of proof, is its own proof.
(Walt Whitman)

To live as soul would live – this is the goal!
(Randall Scott Rogers)

Famous Quotes: On Wholeness

I think wholeness comes from living your life consciously during the day and then exploring your inner life or unconscious at night.
(Margery Cuyler)

The whole point of being alive is to evolve into the complete person you were intended to be.
(Oprah Winfrey)

Happiness is essentially a state of going somewhere, wholeheartedly, one-directionally, without regret or reservation.
(William H. Sheldon)

Put your whole self into it, and you will find your true voice. Hold back and you won't. It's that simple.
(Hugh Macleod)

In oneself lies the whole world and if you know how to look and learn, the door is there and the key is in your hand. Nobody on earth can give you either the key or the door to open, except yourself.
(Krishnamarti)

It's the whole, not the detail, that matters.
(German Proverb)

I hope that the quotes above inspire you to 'walk on,' as they continue to inspire me. The only additional meaningful advice I can offer you, as someone who, not long ago, was in your shoes is to just keep going, to walk on; today, everyday.

Final Words: On OOS

Your journey in reading this book began as a journey in me writing this book. For me, writing this book represented many things: pursuing a goal, living a passion, a walk for freedom. For you, however, I wrote this book with three different goals in mind. To help you: 1) reengineer your existence, 2) design a lifelong personal strategy, and 3) rediscover the joy of living. *By aligning your inner soul with action, all things are possible.* I present some final words on achieving each of these goals.

Reengineer Your Existence

To reengineer something means to create anew. Thus, to reengineer your existence means to create your life anew, to create a new reality for self. I hope, now at book's end, that you learned enough about what you want in life and from life to reengineer your life. I hope that your newly acquired insights into self and soul enable you to live a new life trajectory; to part with the past in favor of a more fragrant future. The standard life design (and the debilitating mentality it fosters) nearly ensures that most people live diminished lives. Because we're not taught of soul, to converse with soul, to live as soul would live, few do. This is why many people suffer quiet desperation. This is why many people feel ache within their heart. This is why many people remark that life's gone stale. The good news is that by following the instruction that lies herein, you can reengineer your existence. You can freshen that which is stale. You can live life anew. The choice to live a happy, remarkable life is yours and, as I have said before, _it is a choice_.

To reengineer one's life is hard work for if it were as easy as taking a pill all those suffering would have ingested said drug long ago. The reality is, to live fragrantly requires great effort. However, we do not approach alone. We have a toolbox of life aids to lessen our efforts, to reduce our struggle, to focus our energies. Our primary tool to do such things, to realize our goal of reengineering self and life, is a personal strategy.

Design a Lifelong Personal Strategy

Although it is possible to reengineer one's existence without a personal strategy, your success improves dramatically with one. Few people today have a personal strategy for living. Fewer still execute strategy. And fewer still achieve strategy. My hope for you is to be among the few; the achievers. You have the knowledge, skills, and capabilities not only to execute personal strategy, but also to achieve personal strategy.

Having a personal strategy for living is becoming increasingly relevant and important to navigate life as greater (individual) competition, faster living, and a radically changing world demand each of us adapt and respond quickly and adequately to change. More importantly, having a personal strategy will help you translate personal vision into reality; help you realize your passions; help you achieve your inner soul goals. Having a personal strategy injects discipline and structure into our life. And when we combine [discipline and structure] with [passion and will], great things happen – **soul rises**.

Designing, implementing, and managing a personal strategy is how we reengineer our existence but we use personal strategy to achieve an even nobler, more immediate, more private, goal: _to rediscover the joy of living_.

Rediscover the Joy of Living

Forty years of living have taught me an important fact. When we are not happy, life lacks joy and a joyless life is no life at all. To labor in a profession/role that does not represent passion, to endure a relationship lost of love, to live in surroundings that do not inspire soul diminishes our joy of living. As such, there is no more important human endeavor than to pursue and sustain one's happiness. Consequently, if life lacks joy, as it does for so many people today, there is a need to restore joy; quickly, decidedly. This is where personal strategy gains relevance, as our personal strategy helps us awaken soul; resurrect soul. This is key, for when we awaken soul, *we revive spirit,* and spirited living is joyful living.

I hope, now at book's end, that you are:

- Reengineering your existence
- Using a personal strategy to direct and manage your life
- Rediscovering the joy of living

Together, I hope that we achieved the goals above, but more importantly, I hope that you achieve your goals. So...stay true to mission. Stay true to vision. ***Do not be blinded by your current work for your work to come.***

In the next and final section, I present last words on the journey that is OOS and the journey yet to come. Then, to close this book properly, knowing this book has been a marriage of text and illustration, we depart not with words but with illustration; *OOS as symbol.*

Last Words

The fact that you sought this book indicates that you seek something better in life and from life. Do not be mistaken; this moment in your life represents *the* tipping point; the point at which

<u>you must decide</u> in favor of 'emerging you' over 'current you'; of 'going the other way' over 'more of the same'. Know this: to live as soul would live, **the emerging you depends on the current you** to make this happen. To shed current self in favor of that which is emerging, can be a struggle. I know. I, too, struggled, but was determined to live as soul would live. The reason we struggle is that it requires us to break with tradition, break with long standing (debilitating) habits. It requires us to break with the past; requires wholesale transformation of self. Do not let this challenge intimidate you. You can transform self, as I did. I am no different from you in this regard. I am human as you are human. I have bad habits as you have bad habits. I struggle as you struggle. However, you and I are alike in many positive ways as well. I resolve to seize opportunity as you resolve to seize opportunity. I insist on meeting imperative as you insist on meeting imperative. I have strategy as you have strategy. In short, your story and my story are alike. Therefore, if I can succeed, so can you. My advice: continue to plod, continue to advance, continue to think of the good to come; just around the corner. Remember, with time, proper incline, and speed, you will succeed.

When you started this book, you likely operated from self, seeing *with* one's eyes; lacking purpose. Then, as pages turned, self and soul became One. Now, you see *through* your eyes; see with an eye of purpose. You found soul and are bringing soul to the surface via personal strategy and willful action. A transformation has begun, even if only internally. No longer do you operate from self; you operate from soul, altering all that follows: your seeing, willing, thinking, acting, and feeling. In other words, you are not the same person exiting this book as when entered (see Figure 17.2).

Back to the Start

This book was an intervention, an invitation really, to go back to the start...to start anew; to revert to a place and time when you last saw the colors of the world, felt the sun's warm glow. For

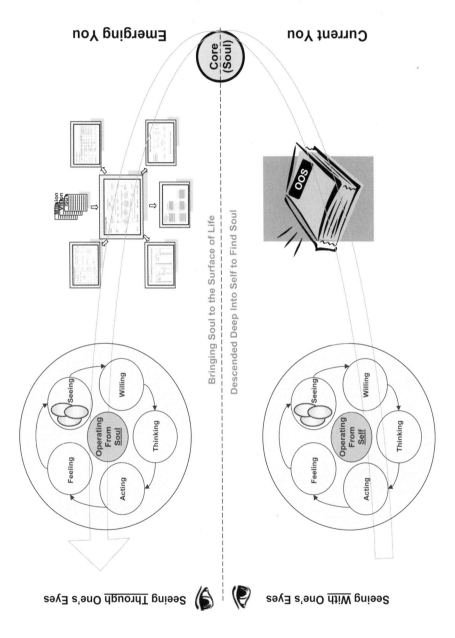

Fig. 17.2

most, this entails returning, in one's mind, to one's youth when the world was full of opportunity and joy, when our load was lighter; when there was little baggage. It requires reverting to a time when we saw things differently, willed differently, thought differently, acted differently, and felt differently.

This book was about retreating, reconnecting with former times before the trappings of life denied you life. It was about reconnecting with the feelings of youth, of happier, simpler times. It was about going back to a place and time when you lived in alignment; to when self and soul were One. This book provided space, opportunity, and occasion to go back to the start; to assess self, to understand self, to redirect self. The essence of this book was for you to reunite self with soul; to find who you are and want to be on the surface of life. With the tools, techniques, and instruction provided herein, I hope that, together, we achieved this goal. Each time you opened this book, you, in effect, stopped your life, to transform your life, page by page. And in stopping your life, you created space, opportunity, and occasion for you to discover soul, converse with soul, and learn from soul. Now, you are living as soul would live – *this was the goal.* By going back to the start, by accepting invitation to start anew, OOS helped you rediscover the joy of living and there is no greater joy than this.

At Journey's End

The journey that is OOS arrived in parts, each chapter unique, yet part of the whole; representing whole. Although some value derives from each chapter singularly, only by reading this book in totality does one derive full value. Now, at journey's end, I hope that you can say that this book helped you; offered value.

As illustration often serves better than words, I present a final illustration summarizing the OOS journey (see Figure 17.3).

The journey of OOS was about turning inward to understand condition to change condition. By descending within, not only did you find self to be a system among systems, you found

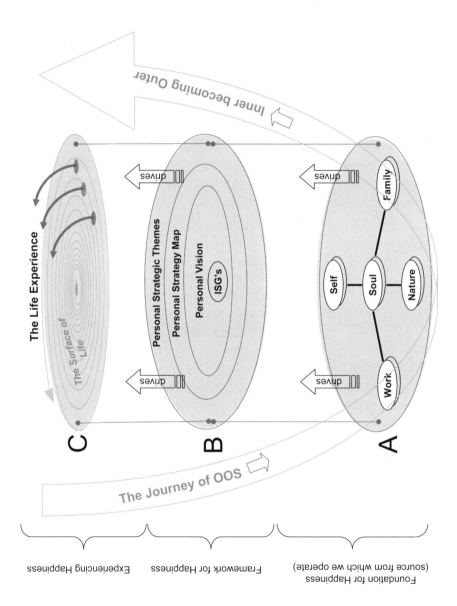

Fig. 17.3

soul. And in finding soul, it enabled you to operate from soul. This transformation was significant as it established new foundation (A) from which to inspire, shape, and direct your life. Upon finding soul, you turned upward. With newfound source and a dash of inspiration, you developed a personal strategy for living. Creating a personal strategy represented achieving a major milestone as it established a framework (B) of how inner becomes outer; of how vision becomes reality. Lastly, you began executing strategy; personal strategy now in bloom, playing out on the surface of life; happiness, on the rise (C). Although Figure 17.3 summarizes the journey that is OOS, it does not consider the journey in relation to default. That is, it does not contrast operating from self with operating from soul (see Figure 17.4).

The most striking difference between the two illustrations is the absence of personal strategy when operating from self. This is how most people operate; without strategy, *living a life of default*. Another significant difference is that when operating from self, self is dominant, inspiring misalignment. However, when operating from soul, soul is dominant, inspiring alignment. Lastly, what Figure 17.4 tells us is the quality of your life, that is, what you experience on the surface of life (diminished living vs. remarkable living), is determined by what drives your life (self or soul). We know this to be true, as A drives B, and B drives C, which explains why the life experience is remarkably different (read: more fragrant, more successful, more purposeful) when one has personal strategy than when one does not.

My efforts to help you required pushing you 'down and around' to find soul, to learn desires of soul, to bring soul forward, into the present. As such, it required discussing things of which you may know little. It required doing things, with which you are unfamiliar. Moreover, it required belief in that which cannot be seen. Now at book's end, I hope that what was unknown, is known, that what was unfamiliar, is familiar, and that what cannot be seen, is believed. I hope that the journey that is OOS brought you happiness. It is, after all, not the destination that brings happiness, but the journey. To write a book,

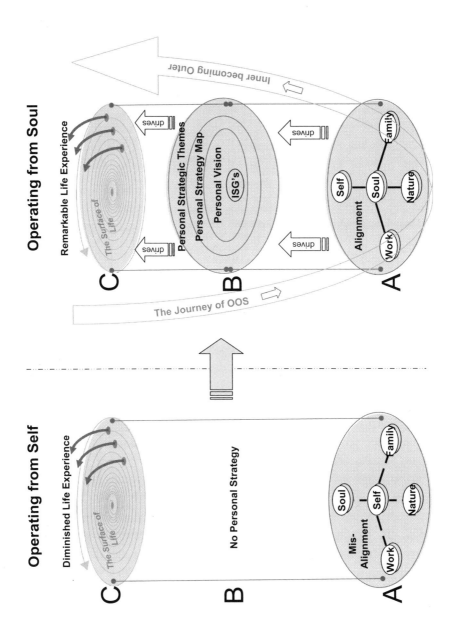

Fig. 17.4

produce a record, build a company, achieve Olympic gold, overcome addiction, produce a movie, invent a product, earn a degree, or rebuild a community all represent prize. While prize is
nice, what we value more is the journey on the way to prize. For
it is the journey we reflect on, think fondly of, remember most.
Lest we forget, without the journey, there is no prize.

As we approach book's end, it is not the journey of OOS
that now headlines, but the journey yet to come, that is, the journey post-OOS.

The Journey Continues

As your OOS journey nears the end, another journey con-
fronts you...the journey yet to come. As the process of reengineering self has just begun, the journey continues. Up to this
point, OOS served as teacher. Now, your teacher reverts to life
itself. Every day becomes an object of reflection to assess your
life to improve your life. As such, the challenge for you, as it
is for me, is to execute; to just keep going. Despite the hard-
ship, self-doubt, wavering will, debilitating tendencies, and the
waiting...*walk on, dear brother...walk on, dear sister...walk on.*
You found soul; now you must bring soul to life. For me, writing this book represents a multi-year journey. It represents the
first step to transform my life, to establish personal alignment,
to be happy; free. You, too, must take your first steps (if not
done so already), and just as surely as I achieved, so, too, will
you achieve. How do I know? Because you are guided by soul,
and there is no more formidable, powerful force on earth than
soul. Soul entered your life and showed you what is right; now
it is time to reveal such light.

It's been said that there is no destiny, only different choices
one makes. You <u>chose</u> alignment. You <u>chose</u> to live by a personal strategy. You <u>chose</u> soul. What is your reward for making
these choices? It is simple: happiness. Continue what you started with reading this book. Continue executing your personal
strategy. Continue reflecting on self and life. Live passionately,

achieve your purpose on earth. Before you know it, you will find yourself on plane E and <u>you will be happy</u> because <u>you will be free</u>.

OOS as Symbol

In Parts I and II of this book, you learned of the symbols you would encounter on the OOS journey. What began as separate symbols, each with separate meaning, now converge into one symbol with composite meaning. It is a symbol that when looked at in the days, months, and years to come will remind you, inspire you, of our time together; *a marker from having walked same path*.

You may wonder why I used symbols to help tell the OOS story. I used symbols because symbols help communicate that which is obscure, that which is unfamiliar, that which cannot be seen. Several parts of this book dealt with obscure, unfamiliar, latent issues (e.g. soul, 'descending within', personal alignment, 'inner vs. outer', 'plane on which we operate', 'fieldline', etc.) and relying on text alone would not have been sufficient; not told the whole story. Further, some people relate better to ideas/concepts with images than text. Lastly, symbols remind, reveal, indicate meaning; they inspire, and evoke emotion.

Symbols have always been with us, been apart of us. From prehistoric times up to the present, humans have used symbols to communicate, to reveal, to inspire. Consider some contemporary examples (see Figure 17.5).

Just as such symbols mean something, represent something, reveal something, so, too, do the symbols contained herein. As we encountered each symbol, it not only served as a signpost of where we had been, but also represented the essence of our journey. For example, when we encountered the 'U' symbol, it helped us visualize the process of descending within to find soul, to converse with soul. The 'spiral' symbol helped us visualize the two key movements in life: the 'down and in' movement and the 'up and in' movement. Later, we learned that the spiral also represents the 'plane' on which we operate in life.

Fig. 17.5

Another symbol, 'merging circles' helped us visualize the process of self and soul becoming One; of aligning, reuniting self with soul. Then there was the symbol for soul: a single circle representing 'One King'. This symbol helped reinforce the notion that we cannot have two rulers, only One, and the ruler of self must be soul. We used another symbol, dotted vertical/horizontal line, to indicate the 'field line' that exists between inner and outer; between that which lies above and that which lies below. The field line helped us visualize the 'space', place of highest leverage, to effect change in our life. Lastly, we became aware of the 'oval' symbol and how such symbol represents the quiet room, inner chamber, where self and soul engage in quiet conversation. We also learned how such symbol represents (via lines emanating from the oval) the greatest source of energy: soul. Now, while all these symbols have individual meaning, it is only when we bring them together as One that we acquire greatest meaning.

Thus, I present, at book's end, a single symbol representing all that is OOS (see Figure 17.6). When one views the symbol that is OOS, it reminds us, communicates, reveals key teachings, discussions, learnings of our walk together. In addition to this image representing all that is OOS, it serves another purpose: to focus our thoughts when reflecting. When you close your eyes to converse with soul, **imagine the symbol that is OOS.** As the mind has a tendency to wander when reflecting, by focusing your mind's eye on the OOS symbol, you will settle the noise within to benefit without.

< *Pause.*>

At long last, we have reached the end. Before we part, let me digress. Recently, I saw the children's movie: The Polar Express. At the end of the movie, there is dialogue that, no matter how many times I hear it, continues to stir my soul; evoke emotion. Here is how it goes:

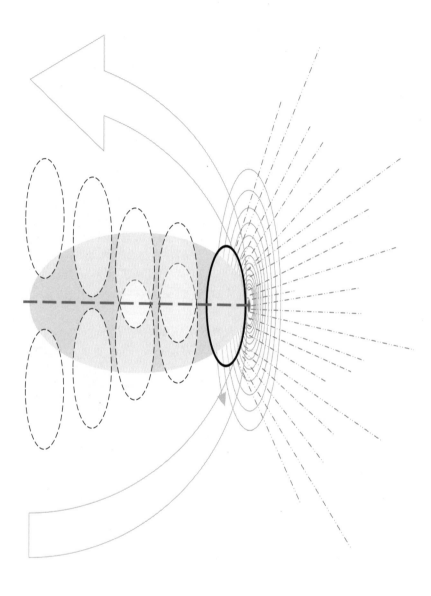

Fig. 17.6

"At one time most of my friends could hear the bell, but as years passed it fell silent for all of them. Even Sarah found one Christmas day that she could no longer hear its sweet sound. Though I've grown old, the bell still rings for me as it does for all who truly believe".

Every time I hear these lines, I grieve, as they describe the sad state of humanity today, in that few people hear the bell (of soul). We begin life operating as One, self with soul, but as years pass, we disconnect; soul's tones falling silent for most of us. I hope that the OOS journey helped you to once again hear the sweet sounds of soul. As you grow old, as the movements of life bring you in and lift you up, I hope that soul's bell continues to ring for you, as it does for me.

Conclusion

<u>(your name here)</u> **your name was called** and you leave this book altered; not the same person leaving as when entered. No longer do you respond as self, you respond as soul. No longer do you identify with self, you identify with soul. No longer do you operate from self, **<u>you operate from soul</u>**.

I am grateful for our time together. I am grateful for your careful, quiet consideration. You stopped your life long enough to hear what I had to say, and in the process learned what your soul had to say. You are a bright, shining star. I wish you good luck. Perhaps our paths will cross some day. If so, tell me your story. Tell me about your transformation; how you realized emerging you. Tell me how you reengineered self, what your personal strategy looks like, and most importantly, how you rediscovered the joy of living.

The last bit of advice I offer is this: attack life, live fragrantly, with color, achieve accomplishments of a lifetime. Live authentically, as who you really are and were meant to be: *soul*. Today, you acknowledge opportunity and imperative. More than this, you acknowledge the fact that you have **<u>Only One Shot</u>**. I leave you now with some final words. Words not mine, but those from someone whose accomplishments I admire; someone who rose from nothing to achieve the American dream; someone who pursued a passion, overcame obstacles, *just kept going*; someone who paid the price to earn the prize; lastly, someone, whose words, inspired the writing of this book, if not the title.

"If you had one shot,
or one opportunity
to seize everything you
ever wanted.
One moment,
would you capture it
or just let it slip?"

- Eminem

WE TAKE OUR CLUES FROM NATURE

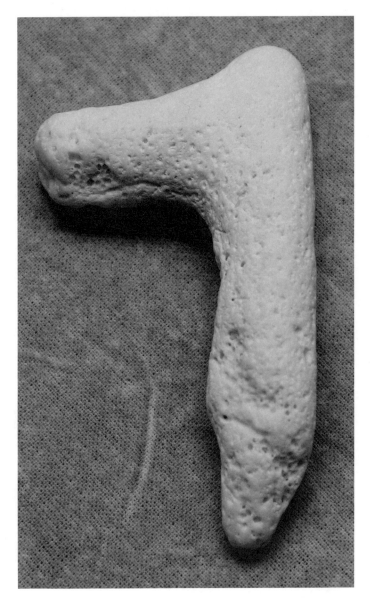

SOURCE: CORAL ROCK, GRAND CAYMAN ISLAND

About the Author

Randall Scott Rogers is founder and president of the Personal Strategy Institute (PSI). He is a writer, educator, speaker, and coach whose passion is helping others develop personal strategy, establish personal alignment, and maximize the life experience. Prior to founding PSI, he served in a management consultant role for fifteen years helping organizations implement strategy, establish alignment, improve quality, and increase the effectiveness and efficiency of business processes.

About Personal Strategy Institute

The **Personal Strategy Institute** focuses on helping and enabling all people to live up to the extraordinary personal, professional, and financial potential that life offers. The Personal Strategy Institute offers books, seminars, speaking, and coaching, to individuals and organizations looking to unlock their true potential to achieve their goals. The Personal Strategy Institute is located in Itasca, Illinois. For more information on the products/services offered by the Personal Strategy Institute, visit us at www.personalstrategy.org.

www.personalstrategy.org

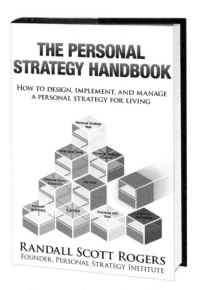

December, 2010

June, 2011